1992

WHY BE MORAL?

Books by the author

WHAT MAKES ACTS RIGHT?

ETHICS AS A BEHAVIORAL SCIENCE

ETHICS: THE SCIENCE OF OUGHTNESS

AXIOLOGY: THE SCIENCE OF VALUES

PHILOSOPHY: AN INTRODICTION

METAPHYSICS: AN INTRODUCTION

THE WORLD'S LIVING RELIGIONS

COMPARATIVE PHILOSOPHY

THE PHILOSOPHER'S WORLD MODEL

WHY
BE
MORAL?

SECOND EDITION

by Archie J. Bahm

WORLD BOOKS

Albuquerque

International Standard Book Number: 0-911714-19-7

Library of Congress Catalogue Card Number: 92-90090

Printed in the United States of America

Chapter   Page

CONTENTS

Preface   ix

INTRODUCTION

I. What is Ethics   3

PART I. SELF		PART II. SOCIETY	
II. Individual Ethics	17	XVII. Social Ethics	245
III. Self as Physical	21	XVIII. Society as Dependent Upon Individuals	254
IV. Self as Social	27	XIX. Society as Interdependence of Groups	260
V. Self-Interest	36	XX. Social Policy	269
VI. Self as Value	54	XXI. Social Values	285
VII. Self-Improvement	91	XXII. Social Improvement	295
VIII. Self-Obligation	101	XXIII. Social Obligation	303
IX. Self as Agent	136	XXIV. Social Action	328
X. Self as Free	158	XXV. Social Freedom	337
XI. Self as Soverign	186	XXVI. Social Sovereignty	343
XII. Self as Owner	189	XXVII. Social Ownership	355
XIII. Self as Just	196	XXVIII. Social Justice	363
XIV. Self as Conscientious	216	XXIX. Social Conscience	372
XV. Self as Intelligent	225	XXX. Social Intelligence	374
XVI. Self as Organic	232	XXXI. Society as Organic	382

PART III. SATISFACTION

XXXII. Final Ethics   393

XXXIII. Satisfaction as Aesthetic   396

XXXIV. Satisfaction as Cosmic   408

XXXV. Satisfaction as Organic   423

Index   429

To

Charlie

PREFACE

Ethics? What's that?

Crime rates are increasing, with no end to such increases in sight. The power of traditional religions to inspire moral conduct continues to decline, with nothing visible to stop such decline. Wars, i.e., little wars, persist even when there is no world war; and military budgets grow despite capacities for overkill. Politicians, legislators, administrators, police and judges seem ever tempted by bribery, and exposés of corruption in "the highest places" create doubts about whether honesty in government is possible.

Industrial pollution, planned obsolescence, misleading advertising, deceptive labeling, crooked insurance adjusting, unfair wages, crime syndicates, illegal gambling, forced prostitution, hijacking, tax loopholes for the wealthy and faked claims by welfare clients all exemplify prevailing trends. Distrust extends from government and the military to news media, clergy, authors, teachers, parents ("anyone over thirty"), other races, men ("male chauvinist pigs"), and now women (as I write, a report has reached me that several local women have beaten up a man). Few areas in life remain untouched by growing demoralization. Are we being sucked into a moral vacuum? Is this our way to the end of ethics?

If we look to scientists for help, we find many of them claiming helplessness and innocence. Some say that "Science is, or ought to be, completely value-free. So it cannot, and ought not, deal with values or ethics. Pure scientists are responsible for theories, but not for their applications, whether constructive or destructive." Some scientists, namely anthropologists, have reached, and teach, a conclusion: cultural relativism, including moral relativism. "Rights and wrongs are relative to cultures; there are no universal rights or wrongs."

Recent philosophies, such as Existentialism, advocate relativism of the moment. Idealizing *authenticity* as not permitting one's *existenz* or momentary act of will, to be imposed upon by anything, not by laws of government, not by laws of logic or reasoning, not by mores, not by other wills ("Hell is other people"), and not even by one's own previous promises. To admit submission to any ethical principle would be "to be inauthentic." Is ethics ending in the name of "authenticity?"

Rights and duties are correlative; that is, if one person has a right, then other persons have duties to respect that right. But after World War II, some rebellious youths proclaimed "a new freedom," namely, "freedom from responsibility." This means freedom from duties. What then happens to the correlative rights? Is this another way of ending ethics?

But both those who despair at demoralization and those who gloat over destroying a moral trap do not understand ethics. Misunderstanding of ethics is widespread, and much of it is culturally induced. Confusions abound at many levels. A major purpose of this volume is to help clear up some of these confusions.

What is ethics?

The end, the goal, or the purpose of ethics is to attain what is best. Acts are right because they are intended to produce the best results for oneself in the long run. A self is naturally and essentially social, something which selfish people often overlook. Any adequate self-interest theory must show how self-interests are sometimes best served through social interests.

Why be moral? Because this is what you most want to be. That is, you want what is best for yourself. This is what you want most. Ethical principles are discovered, and moral practices are designed, in the first place, as ways of behaving which are most conducive to attaining what is best. This is the end, the proper end, of ethics.

Why, then, do we develop dislikes for moral rules, standards, laws and institutions? First, we do not know the reasons for, i.e., the goods anticipated from, establishing them. If we knew the benefits expected for all, including ourselves, we would have less cause for dissent.

Secondly, institutions develop cultural lag. Laws designed to solve one problem often remain on the books long after the problem itself has disappeared. When formalism sets in and then disorganization, people suffer compulsions without receiving benefits. Then institutions, designed to make life better, actually make it worse. Failure to keep our institutions efficient is an evil, and to consent to such inefficiency is itself immoral. We ought to dislike deficient mores and institutions. Why? Because they function as immoralities. Moral rules, standards, laws and institutions themselves ought to be accepted or rejected depending upon whether or not they serve the end of ethics.

At stake in the foregoing are two views of ethics. The first claims that ethics consists of undesirable duties imposed upon us by others. The second holds that ethics consists of internal interests which naturally seek fulfillment and the wise choices and prudent actions which aim at maximizing such fulfillment. In this view, ethics is concerned with what is good and how to get it, or with what one ought to do in order to get the most out of life.

The first view originates, unfortunately, in early childhood, when loving parents protect their children from harm by restrictions, the reasons for which the children do not understand. They learn that ethics means "Don't do this." "Stop doing that." "Do as I tell you." "Go to bed now." Children who advance to Sunday School sometimes find religious ethics also stated in negative terms: "Thou shalt not...." Schools with regulations, empty streets with stop signs, police who apprehend us for violating laws we did not know existed, add to our education that ethics consists of "don'ts," of laws, of commands, and of demands made upon us by other people, often by people we do not know, such as ancient religious writers, distant legislators, administrators, specialists.

When negativity of commands combined with a negative conscience seems to demand duties and responsibilities without benefit of rights and privileges, "ethics" is a word for something evil, and something to be avoided or evaded when we cannot rid ourselves of it altogether. But what we ought to eradicate is this mistaken conception of oughtness.

The second view can be stated as a description of the way people behave relative to values and obligations when they behave naturally. I do not wish to convey the idea that the first view is not also acquired naturally, because we naturally try to protect our children from harm and they naturally resent restrictions when they do not understand the intended benefits. But even when freed from all social restrictions people still act ethically naturally in the sense that they naturally seek what they believe to be good, better or best for themselves. So, when faced with a choice between two alternatives, one of which appears better than the other, what ought one to do? Choose the better. Why? Just because it is better.

Oughtness consists in the power which an apparently greater good has over an apparently lesser good in compelling our choices. It is this apparently greater good which is the source of oughtness. There is no other source. There may be other explanations of this source, but however the explanation is conceived, inherent in it in some way is the view that what one ought to do is what is best for oneself in the long run. Social and religious ethics are extensions of personal ethics. How one is naturally, even essentially, social will be explained in the text, as will how altruism, concern for the welfare of others, often results in what is best for oneself and thus is an important part of the way one most wants to be. One ought to want to know the difference between wise and foolish self-interest. So long as wise self-interest is recognized as the end of ethics, ethics will never end.

INTRODUCTION

Chapter I

WHAT IS "ETHICS?"

Beginning definition. Simply stated, "ethics" pertains to what is good and how to get it. By "good" we mean either "good things" or "goodness," or both, for goodness is something which all good things have in common. By "how to get it" we mean either, or both, "how, in fact, do we attain goodness" and "what ought we to do in order to obtain it."

To ask "How in fact are goods achieved?" involves inquiring into the nature of things. That is, things (i.e., everything, including human beings and their experiences) have natures such that when influenced in one way they yield one result and when influenced in other ways produce different results. If understanding of the natures of things and how they work may be called "science" and "technology," then the more we know about each science and technology, the greater our understanding of them. Hence, our knowledge of all sciences, such as physics, biology, psychology, epistemology, logic and sociology, should provide a foundation, supplementing our own practical experiences, for knowing "how to get what is good."

To ask, "What ought I to do in order to obtain what is good?' is to become involved in two kinds of "oughts": "conditional" and "actual." A "conditional ought" is a feeling of obligation to do something if I want to produce a certain result. Conditional oughts may be deduced directly from one's scientific knowledge, assuming this knowledge to be accurate and adequate. For example, if I know that water boils at 100 degrees Celsius, and if I want to boil some water, then I ought to heat that water to 100 degrees Celsius. In this example, two different kinds of "ifs," or conditions, appear. One has to do with my knowledge of the fact, i.e., how water boils; the other with my wants or needs. As long as no actual necessity occurs, neither condition makes any actual demand upon me. Merely conditional oughts involve no actual obligation. They do not compel us to act. An "actual ought," on the other hand, is a genuine must. It occurs as a recognition of an actual need expressing itself as a feeling of compulsion. If an urgent need for sterilized water occurs in a medical lab, then I develop feelings of obligation to obtain such water. Such feelings constitute an actual ought which involves at least two conditional oughts: I ought to know when water boils and I ought to act in such a way as to boil the water. The same conditional oughts which produce in us no feeling of compulsion in the absence of need become transformed into parts of an actual ought when need actually arises.

Failure to realize that the word "ought" has both of these meanings is a source of much misunderstanding about ethics.

Ethics has a negative side also. That is, it pertains to bads and how to avoid them, and thus to "ought nots." Unfortunately, a child's first acquaintance with oughts and ethics tends to be negative. Those interested in children's welfare try to prevent them from harming themselves and consequently advise, or compel, them restrictively: "Don't do that." "Thou shalt not...." "It's against the law." Moral codes appear more often as sets of tabus than as guides to positive achievement. When a child does not understand why they are restricted, they often interpret moral commands not only as external authority but also as quite arbitrary. Many never outgrow their childish notions of ethics and obligations as entirely social and entirely negative. Yet actually, good is primary; evil acts are those that destroy or endanger goods. One who seeks what is good automatically desires to avoid what is evil or that which endangers achievement of that good. A negative side of ethics exists only when and because a positive side is presupposed.

In sum then, "ethics," according to our beginning definition, pertains to what is good and how to get it, and what is bad and how to avoid it, or to oughtness, i.e., what ought to be done to achieve what is good and what ought not be done to avoid what is evil, both actual and potential. Furthermore, I propose that every interest in what is good and how to get it, and in what is bad and how to avoid it, is thereby automatically "ethical."

"Codes" versus "Principles." Much confusion about ethics inheres in the distinction between codes and principles. Many believe that ethics consists mainly, if not entirely, of codes. Reasons for such a belief are many. Children learn duties of etiquette, the "Ten Commandments," school and community regulations, and traffic laws. The more groups that persons join the more codes they become acquainted with: laws of school, church, clubs, community, county, state, nation, banking, commerce, profession, labor union, and military, including building codes, sanitation codes, traffic codes, criminal codes, etc. When we believe that "ethics" consists primarily of codes which restrict one, we are inclined to withdraw from, resent, and even reject, ethics. Thus, unfortunately, ethics, which deals primarily with what is good and how to get it, comes to be misinterpreted as a set of evils, necessary evils perhaps, but evils which should be avoided if possible. A basic thesis of this essay is that

principles, not codes, constitute the foundations of both ethical theory and practice.

Ethical principles also are assertions about oughts. But they state "Why ought?" rather than "ought" merely. Ethical principles explain rather than command. Like all principles, they should be soundly based in experience. Yet confusion regarding codes and principles exists, in part, because both occur in varying levels of generality. For example, "one should obey this stop sign" is an item in a more general code item, "one should obey all stop signs," which is an item in a more general code item, "One should obey all public ordinances." When a code item, "One should obey all stop signs," is explained by the principle, "Because this is the best way to prevent accidents," he may find this principle explained by the more general principle, "So that one will not endanger one's own life," which may be explained still further by the more general principle, "So that one will live longer," which may be explained further by the more ultimate principle, "Because life is good and a longer life is better." Confusion occurs because principles can easily be restated as codes: e.g., when one explains the code item, "One should obey all 'Stop' signs," by the principle, "Because this is the best way to prevent accidents," he may, impatiently, simply assert the code item: "Prevent accidents." Without minimizing the practical need for codes, we here emphasize that the distinction between them, between what one ought to do and why one ought to do it, needs to be kept in mind if one is to understand the nature of ethics. The purpose of ethical inquiry is, first of all, to discover, as far as possible, the most ultimate principles of explanation or the most ultimate reasons why one ought to do anything.

"Theory" versus "Practice." Another issue facing anyone wishing to define "ethics" is whether it consists entirely, or primarily, in theories or practices. Many studies in ethics have been devoted entirely to a history of ethical theories or to types of ethical theory. On the other hand, some studies in ethics, anthropology, sociology and history treat ethics as if it consisted entirely in the customs, conventions, mores and folkways of various peoples. Surely neither of these emphases adequately represents the whole picture. The view presented here claims that "ethics" properly extends over both of these areas. But, granting such extension, one then faces the problem of how theory and practice are related in ethics. Does one depend upon the other? Which came, or should come, first? Which is more fundamental?

Advocates of the view that practice is primary point out that, historically or prehistorically, centuries of practice preceded the first theory. The development of theory as such, including ethical theory, came very late in human history. Furthermore we need merely recall that the biological and physiological nature, which all persons share, involve certain needs which have to be fulfilled. We should expect that these common needs tend to beget common behavior patterns. We can even observe some similarities between persons and animals in these respects. If we note, additionally, that human beings are somewhat alike psychologically and sociologically, we realize that we can expect as a consequence still other common behavior patterns. Also, children learn how to behave before they become able to discover why, and certainly before they can theorize about why. Many people participate in some mores for a whole lifetime without ever finding out, or even inquiring into, why these mores exist. Ethical theories, according to this viewpoint, appear as attempts to generalize about existing ways of behaving or to rationalize, i.e., to think up reasons for justifying, them. Practice comes first; a person does not discover theory about action until his action gets him into trouble. Thus, that ethical practices exist before, and thus without depending upon, ethical theory should be obvious.

Advocates of the view that theory is primary, however, cite other evidence. They contend, first of all, that we should be concerned with what the theory is about, not with the time and place or language in which it is formulated. Ethical theory was implicit in humanity's first actions, even though not explicitly formulated; it had to be, if the action was ethical. Just as, in physics, the recently-formulated law of gravity has always operated, so also, in ethics, the not-so-recently-formulated principle of reciprocity has always operated. And, even though our currently accepted formulae may be relatively recent, primitive people tried, in their own primitive ways, to formulate theories -- many of which have come down to us in the form of myths. Just as children, in learning not to fall, must develop some, no matter how crude and imprecise, conception or theory about what causes them to be drawn toward the ground, so children, in learning that they cannot slap without expecting to be slapped back, formulate at last a crude idea about why they cannot do so. Granted that primitive and childish theories are primitive and childish, they do not therefore, cease to be theories.

However, some advocates of the view that theory is primary will say that the foregoing discussion has been misdirected. Ethical theory pertains not so much to how we do act as to how we should act. Even if it were granted that common behavior patterns develop prehistorically without anyone formulating a theory about them, such practices did not become "ethical" until someone formulated ideals as to how one ought to act. And theory is implicit in the formation of the first ideal. What is an "ideal?" Ideals are unreached goals which, if and when reached, become actual, actualized, or realized. Ideals involve ideas, but not ideas merely. Ideals are ideas of goods we have not yet attained and which we believe that, because they are goods, or betters or bests, they ought to be achieved. If we have an idea but do not believe that it represents a good which we ought to seek, then that idea is not an ideal for us. When we acquire more ideals than can be achieved, then we become "unrealistic." One believes one ought to do more than one can do, and then, if one thinks about the matter, tends either to dream about becoming able to do more than one can do or to idealize not having more ideals than can be fulfilled. In any case, ideals do not arise when one is satisfied. Ideals involve dissatisfaction, or awareness of incomplete satisfaction, with things as they are. Theory about human nature does not become "ethical," according to this view, until such behavior involves ideals, with accompanying feelings of obligation to achieve them, and it is the "theory" -- the conceptions implicit in what one believes is required to achieve them -- which makes an act being "ethical." If one conceives ideals as "norms" or "standards" of achievement which ought to be aimed at, "ethical theory" comes to be thought of as consisting in description of such norms. The goal of ethical theory is, then, a clear statement of such norms, standards, ideals, or oughts. Primarily, "ethics" consists in concern for what persons ought to do, not merely with what persons do regardless of such oughts.

We turn now to a third view, one which advocates that "ethics," adequately conceived, involves devotion to both practice and theory. It partly agrees with each of the foregoing views because each has asserted something fundamental. But it also condemns both as mistaken to the extent that each holds that its own emphasis upon what is primary implies denial of what the other view contends is primary. Theory and practice interact and depend upon each other, for theory is nothing if it fails to be theory about practice, and practice, whenever it involves recurrences, can be generalized or theorized about. Also, ideals and practices interact and depend upon each other. For ideals not only arise out of our practical frustrations but have their goals in, or can be realized only in, other actualized practices. All practice motivated by endeavor to improve is, thereby, a product of ideals. Ideals themselves, especially to the extent that they prove unworkable, tend to become modified through attempts at practice; and to the extent that we successfully realize our ideals, practice becomes modified by them. The truest perspective, according to this third view, sees theory and practice as organically related, and believes that understanding both and thus, more generally, "ethics," can be adequate only to the extent that their mutual interdependence and cyclical succession in playing a predominant or primary role is recognized.

"Individual" versus "Social." Another oft-debated issue needs to be settled before our comprehension of the scope of "ethics" is clear. Distinction has been made between "individual ethics" and "social ethics." Some contend that the term "ethics" applies properly only to the social. Others claim that "ethics" is primarily individual. Still others maintain that the term extends over both areas of life, and some of these believe that its primary problems should be located in the interaction between them.

Those who contend that "ethics" is social only point to the fact that the English word "ethics" evolved from the Latin (ethicus) or Greek (ethikos) terms meaning "custom." "Ethics" refers to customs, mores (whence "morality"), conventions, institutions, laws. "Ethics" deals with how people treat each other, not with how they act when they are alone. Terms denoting the major problems of ethics, such as norms, standards, codes, justice, rights, duties, obligations and responsibilities, all have to do with relationships between persons. Duties consist in what we owe others; rights consist in what others owe us. The terms "rightness" and "wrongness" apply to our conduct when it has consequences for others; what we do in our own private lives is our own business and may be spoken of as "non-moral" or "non-ethical" or outside the realm of ethics proper.

Those who claim that "ethics" is primarily "individual" cite as evidence other terms and other problems which seem more, or most, basically crucial to the nature of ethics. "Ethics" centers about the problem of choice, and choice is decidedly personal. Only intentional or voluntary acts are ethical; and intention is personal, not social. Freedom of choice involves freedom of will, and will is individual, not social. The statement of Jesus, "As a man thinketh in his heart, so is he," has been quoted to emphasize the personal and inner nature of genuine rightness (as against external or "social" and even showy "righteousness"). No term stands closer to the core of ethics than "conscience," and surely conscience is individual, not social. One's conscience may compel him to go against the mores, to revolt against social tyrannies, whether they appear in the form of kings, institutions, laws or moral codes. Whereas those who believe that morality resides in the mores must judge all rejection of the mores as "immoral," the conscientious rebel revolts because he believes that his first duty is to be "true to himself." Many ethical philosophies which differ regarding the ultimate nature and locus of oughtness nevertheless agree that it is individual, not social: for example, Rationalism, as represented by Descartes, advocates following "the inner light of reason" present in all of us, not the unreasoning crowd; Romanticism, including Existentialism, insists that one should follow one's own vital impulses, resisting mechanization of life by submitting to dead customs; Yoga and most of Buddhism, including Zen, see the achievement of life's goal, and hence fundamental oughtness, as entirely a self-help affair, and all social concerns as undesirable distractions which ought not to be permitted; and the Taoism of Lao Tzu idealizes shunning everything social as man's chief ought. Finally, such terms as "virtue" "character" and "wisdom" refer to individual rather than to social traits.

We come now to the third view, i.e., that of those maintaining that "ethics" extends over both "individual" and "social" areas of life. It holds that those who claim ethics to be primarily individual are fundamentally correct, since without individuals and their interests no ethics could exist. Yet they are mistaken to the extent that they believe that ethics can be exclusively individual, since it conceives individuals as inherently social by nature. It believes that those who contend that ethics is social only are correct in recognizing the social nature of ethics but mistaken to the extent that they deny or minimize the individual foundation of all ethical endeavor. This third view does not conceive ethics as merely a collection of two relatively independent areas, called "individual ethics" and "social ethics." Rather it conceives the two as organically related because the interdependence and interaction between individual and social aspects of life continues to be a constant condition of life and, consequently, of ethics. Although it may continue to employ the term "individual ethics," it does so only because it conceives "self" to be essentially social. As we shall show later, many sources and goals of each human being seem to be inherently social. Also, when the term "social ethics" is employed, it takes on an additional meaning by referring to the interests of, and oughtness relative to, groups as groups and institutions as institutions. Some groups and institutions have both rights and duties relative to other groups and institutions, as well as to individuals; and a person acting as an agent for them has duties as an officer to pursue their welfare.

This third view does not ignore or deny the existence of simpler ethical oughts as envisaged by each of the first two views. It presupposes them and builds upon them. But it also believes that we not only do, but ought to, see as a primary locus of ethical decisions those areas in life where individual and social interests interact. That is, not only should a person be aware of mores and follow them when appropriate, and be aware that one's intentions, choices and conscience are one's own, but also a person should understand that the kind of person that one is depends on how sensitively and wisely one acts in those areas where one must decide between one's more personal interests and one's interests in the groups or institutions in which one serves as a member or officer. As life becomes more civilized and more complexly interdependent, each person spends more time functioning as a member of more, and of more specialized, groups through each of which one's welfare may be promoted or retarded and in which one must constantly decide how much effort one will devote to it. It is in these areas of decision, where the individual and social aspects of lives interact, that our moral vitality may be strengthened or dissipated. Yet if we fail to be spontaneously aware of both our actual interdependence and of the complex and ever-shifting responsibilities required to maintain a pliable and efficient individual-social organism, then our individual and our social, as well as our individual-social, values may be expected to suffer.

This third view obviously arises out of, and grows as a response to, the cosmopolitan conditions of our own time. Cosmopolitanism is not new in human history, but the accelerating tempo of increasing complexities of our interdependence is a peculiarity of our own century. The simpler ethical perspectives represented by the first two views, which may seem complex enough in themselves, should not be despised, for they still work and are best suited to certain social conditions. In being superseded, they become incorporated into, rather than nullified by, the insights believed required by this third view.

We shall not explore here the future issues as to the extent that either "social" or "individual-social" ethics extend beyond the human, to animals (as with vegetarians), to plants, to other planets and to the gods or God. Nor need we inquire here how far our responsibilities extend into the future of mankind or, for that matter, into its past. Yet surely any adequate definition of the scope of "ethics" will remain open to dealing with questions of this sort.

Why Be Moral? The answer to the foregoing question, although involving many aspects, may be stated very simply. Even though the full significance of the answer may not be apparent at first glance, the answer may be stated clearly. Why be moral? Because this is what you most want to be.

The typical reader will tend to resist, if not entirely reject, this assertion, because the term "moral" popularly connotes external morality, as illustrated by codes which function as commands by others preventing one from doing what one wants to do. To the extent that morality seems to be imposed on us from the outside, it not only seems unwanted but appears, consciously or unconsciously, as an evil. As long as morality consists in something that frustrates one's desires, then it is not what one wants, and certainly not what one wants most. In fact, the less one has to do with it the better.

On the other hand, if one discovers that the sources and foundation and goal of morality are all inner first, and outer only secondarily, and thus that the popular conception of morality as external is superficial, then one may be ready to reconsider one's typical attitude. As indicated above in our beginning definition, ethics has to do with what is good and how to get it. Now getting what is good is what one wants. And getting what is good is what one most wants. So ethics is concerned not merely with what is good but also with what is better and, especially, with what is best. Its ultimate goal is to achieve the most good or "the highest good" (summum bonum). If so, then we can deduce that "being moral" is the same as "doing what you most want to do." Or, to say the same thing in other words, "Morality is simply the best way of living." (Durant Drake, Problems of Conduct, revised, p.5, Houghton Mifflin Co., Boston, 1914, 1921, 1935.)

However, even though one may want what is best, one may not know what is best. Whoever asks, "What is best?" is faced with several questions. Best for whom? Myself? Others? God? Best for how long? Now? For a lifetime? Forever? Best of what kinds? Physical health? Wealth? Spiritual values? Does "best" mean dealing with each of the foregoing questions separately, or with all of them at once, or with them both somewhat independently, somewhat as all alike, and somewhat interdependent? Suppose that a person decides that "best" means "best for oneself." Does one then know what is best for oneself? Only if he understands himself and his interests. He may know what he wants at a particular moment. He may have a strong desire which seems to demand satisfaction. It may seem at the moment to be his only desire or certainly his strongest desire and thus as what he most wants. Yet if he endures his passion for only a few minutes he tends to become aware that he has other desires also, some of which support and some of which conflict with his passionate desire. If and when he becomes able to stop and reflect about the conflicts among his own desires, he raises within himself the question: "What do I really want?"

When doubts about his real nature and genuine wants get the better of him, he will ask others (unless they have already told him). If he receives but a single answer which satisfies him, he can go on in quest of what is best for himself. If however, as seems more common, he receives conflicting replies, his problem deepens. Today, each of the sciences has its contributions to make, telling him that his nature and interests consist primarily in the physical and chemical, or in the biological, or in the physiological, or in the psychological, or in the economic, or political, or material, or recreational, or linguistic aspects of his life. Furthermore, in each of the fields many different schools of thought prevail which compete for his attention and conversion. As fields divide and subdivide into specialties and subspecialties, those answers which will require the services of the subspecialist increasingly try to attract, and succeed in attracting, attention.

If he happens to be wise enough to look above specifics to some overall view, he may hear the appeals of "religious" sectarians advocating ancient nostrums, but these become both less satisfactory as they fail to incorporate consistently the more recent discoveries and less convincing as he becomes aware of the multiplicities of different "religions" each of which authoritatively provides its own, somewhat different, solution. If he turns to philosophy, he finds its history too long and complex to digest with ease and his contemporaries hopelessly divided into warring factions and progressively devoted to specialized sections. The conflicts he discovers among the sciences and "religions" and philosophies become conflicts within himself and tend to confuse rather than to clarify for him what he really is and what he actually most wants. He may realize that, the further he searches, the more "lost" he becomes. Yet he cannot give up, unless the problem grows too big for him and he just stops thinking.

Finally, one's struggle with the problem of the nature of oneself is a part of one's effort to discover what is best for oneself. If one cannot get what is best for oneself without knowing what is best, then one ought to seek to find out. When one accepts this to be a fact, one realizes that a study of ethics not only is itself an ethical obligation but that it may be one's most important obligation. In fact, if one believes that a study of ethics can assist one in knowing what one really is and what is best for one and what one has to do in order to attain it, then such a study tends to be a part of what one most wants to do.

PART I

SELF

Chapter II

INDIVIDUAL ETHICS

The division of this volume into three parts, entitled "Self," "Society" and "Satisfaction," represents three emphases which need differentiation even though they remain interdependent and mutually supplementary. Each part begins with an introductory chapter, "Individual Ethics," "Social Ethics" and "Final Ethics," summarizing and surveying the problems being faced. "Individual Ethics" pertains to what is good for the individual self. "Social Ethics" deals with what is good for society. "Final Ethics" aims at comprehending and achieving final, full or complete satisfactions which, as we shall discover, involve two aspects, the one being concerned with what is good for all (all that exists), here termed "cosmic," and the other with the allness or completeness of the good experienced, here termed "aesthetic," both of which may be experienced as aspects of "what one most wants." Some ethicists focus so exclusively upon one or the other of these three areas that they leave the impression, sometimes intentionally, that ethics consists only of one and excludes the others. Failure to distinguish and interrelate all of the most general phases of ethics leaves the false impression that ethics is a confused subject. One virtue of the present approach consists of its endeavor to include and interrelate all three of these aspects of "what's good and how to get it."

Part I focuses attention persistently upon what is good for the individual self. The natural and normal, as well as the ideal and obligatory, aim of each person is to seek what is good, or best, for oneself. Hence, for purposes of "Individual Ethics," we may say that "acts are right because they are intended to produce the best results for oneself in the long run." (See my Philosophy: An Introduction, p. 312, John Wiley & Sons, New York, 1953, and "Rightness Defined," Philosophy and Phenomenological Research, December, 1947, p. 266). Or, alternatively we may say that "acts are right because they are intended to lead to self-realization." Although either or both of these statements may seem clear immediately, their full meaning can be understood only after such terms as "best results," "self-realization," "intentions," "long run," and especially "self" have been examined.

The term "self" is at once the most obvious and the most obscure of the terms involved. Everyone knows what "self" is, until one stops to think about it, inquire about it, or define it. On the one hand, nothing is more central to a person's thinking and acting. It is the one who thinks and acts. It is that which does whatever one does. It is both agent or actor and the receiver of the acts of others -- both subject and object --

at all times. It is that which desires, wants, wishes, intends, decides, chooses, accepts, rejects, commits. It is that which is aware that it is wanted or rejected, used or discarded, appreciated or despised. It is that which seeks to preserve itself, defend itself, improve itself, and which may or may not become "selfish." The existence and nature of one's own self is so obvious that it seems foolish to raise questions about it. In fact, the existence of self is presupposed even in raising questions about it, for a self must exist if it is to raise questions about itself.

On the other hand, once one stops to think about oneself, many paradoxes arise almost immediately. For example, should I say that "I have a self" or that "I am a self?" Is the "I" in "I have a self" and in "I am a self" the same or different? By analogy, when I say "I have a desire" do I mean that "I" and desire are different or that "I" and my "desire" are the same? When I say "I desire," do I mean that "I am desire" or that "My desire is a part of me?" Or, if I say that "I am reasonable" (or, for that matter, "unreasonable"), do I mean that "reason" (or "unreason") is a part of me or merely that I possess reason (or "unreason") and that the "I" which has these things is different from them? If they are parts of me, then is everything which I call "mine" really a part of me? Are my clothes, as "mine," part of me? Or are some things which are "mine" part of me while other things which are "mine" not part of me? Where, then, do I draw the line between "me" and "not me" or between "I" and "not I" or between "self" and "not self?"

Is my "self" simple or complex? "The soul is simple," many say. Is one's "self" the same as one's "soul?" If we distinguish between "soul" and "body," or between "soul" and "mind," or between "mind" and "body," is the "self" the same as one or all of these, or different from some or all? If I say, "I have a soul," do I mean that "I am a soul?" If I say, "I have a body," do I mean that "I am a body?" If I say, "I have a mind," do I mean that "I am a mind?" If I make two or three of these statements, is the "I" the same "I" in all; i.e., is the "self" complex in having and being both soul and body, or mind and body, or soul and mind, or soul and body and mind? Or is it different from each of these because each of these is different from the other? How can a "self" be both simple and complex at the same time? And if one seeks what is best for oneself in the long run, does one aim at what is best for one's soul, or one's body, or one's mind, or oneself as being all three of these, or of oneself as different from one or all of them?

Even if we can settle the question of whether the self is simple or complex "at the same time," what about the self at different times? If I say, "I have grown," does this mean that I have changed? If I have changed, am I the same "self" before and after the change? If so, is such a change genuine? If not, then are all my beliefs about myself as changing false? If I cannot change, then how can I realize myself, or how can I do what is best for myself in the long run? If I cannot change, then I cannot improve, or, for that matter, become worse, or even cease to be. If I can and do change, then what happens to my "self" when it changes? Does it become different? If so, is it a "different self?" Do I have only one "self" or many "selves?" If many, then when I seek what is best for myself, which of my selves do I have in mind?

If my "self" is complex, does it really consist of many different selves, or is it "organic," i.e., both one and many, both simple and complex, both a unity and at the same time a whole with genuinely different parts? May my many "selves" or the many parts of my "self" be in conflict with each other, or must they necessarily be consistent, compatible, harmonious? If they conflict, ought I seek to eliminate some parts so as to retain harmony, or should I seek to grow and expand myself by acquiring additional parts even at the cost of further disharmony? Is there some limit to the size and complexity of a self which is best for itself, or is a self essentially unlimited, and should it aim to ever expand itself endlessly? If one desires what is best for oneself in the long run, should one endeavor to simplify and harmonize oneself or to grow and extend oneself in new directions as much as one can?

Thus, although the answer to the question, "What am I?" at first seems so obvious as not to need asking, once the question has been raised and an answer attempted, the "self" seems to become an increasingly complex puzzle -- paradoxical, mysterious, multi-faceted, and marvelous. Yet, if one cannot intelligently intend to do what is best for oneself when one does not understand oneself, one must grapple with the problems of self-understanding.

The purpose of Part I is to explore many different aspects of self, each significant and obvious from a common sense viewpoint, and to raise questions and to suggest answers regarding ways in which each involves, and is involved in, what is best for self. In this process, most of the traditional problems of individual ethics will be introduced and examined. Although each chapter in Part I will emphasize a different aspect of self and its value, endeavor will be made, in a concluding chapter, to observe how all may, and do, participate organically or interdependently in the vital unity of one's self and how settlement of questions regarding their interdependence constitutes a fundamental part of what is best for oneself.

Chapter III

SELF AS PHYSICAL

Do you have a body? Or are you a body? Is your body a part, or all, of you, or different from you? If your body is part of you, and if you desire what is best for yourself, must you not seek what is best for your body?

Now your body is not simple but itself has many parts. If your body is part of you, is each of the parts of your body also a part of you? Some parts seem rather obvious, such as your arms and legs and head and hands and feet and nose. But other parts, especially those hidden inside, may not be so obvious. The science of human physiology describes the parts of your body and how they grow, develop and function. Do all parts of your body described by physiologists constitute your self, even those which you have not yet learned about, such as, perhaps, your pineal gland, your metatarsals or your ventricles? If some parts of your body remain unknown to you, must not some of your self be unknown to you? If so, how can you intend to do what is best for yourself relative to those parts which you do not know about?

Your body is composed of cells -- tissue cells, nerve cells, blood cells (red and white corpuscles), gametes, etc. -- all of which may be essential to the existence of your body. Your cells have parts, such as nucleus, protoplasm, chromosomes, which consist of complex molecules. Your molecules consist of atoms and atoms of electrons, protons and various other particles. Are your molecules, atoms and electrons also parts of you? If not, where do you draw the line between which parts are and which are not you? Biochemistry analyzes the chemical constituents of your body and can aid in maintaining your health by making possible the manufacture of medicines, vitamins, hormones, and other dietary supplements. Pursuit of physical health may be facilitated by greater knowledge of physiology and physiological chemistry which explain what is needed to keep the parts, and the whole, of your body functioning properly. Since the principles discovered by these sciences operate in your body, do these very principles themselves constitute a part of your self?

Turning from chemistry to physics, we may note that all of the general laws of physics hold for our physical bodies. Our bodies have weight, mass and size, and involve principles of mechanics, optics and electronics, for example. Are your mass and weight and size, as yours, parts of you? Some women seem to be especially concerned about their size and weight. If you want what is best for your self, ought you to seek your best weight and size, or what is best for your weight and size?

Biology, by giving us insight into heredity and evolution, reveals other questions about the nature of our selves. As biological beings, we have been produced by amazingly complex processes of evolution, which involve "struggle for existence" and "survival of the fit." We enjoy a precarious existence, both as individuals, in danger of death, and members of a species, which may become extinct. We bear hereditary characteristics, which make us humans rather than horses, mammals rather than oviparians, vertebrates rather than crustaceans, multi-celled rather than single-celled beings. To say, "I am human" signifies, biologically speaking, that I differ from members of more than a million other species in intricate complexes of ways. Hence, I am inescapably limited by, but also magnificently endowed by, my hereditary potentialities. When one aims at what is best for oneself, surely one's conception of such best should be conditioned by an understanding of both one's capacities and limitations as a biological being. Does, or should, what is best for oneself as a member of the human species include an interest in survival of the species, even over and above one's survival as an individual?

If you happen to be a prospective mother, expecting childbirth soon, do you regard your fetus as a part of you? Do you feel your self identified with it? Or did it become, immediately after conception, a separate being? If you identify yourself with your child before birth, will you continue to do so after birth? For how long? Forever? Or until it becomes antagonistic to you? If you seek what is best for your self, to what extent must you also seek what is best for your child?

Biologists explain that the biological traits of a child tend to be determined equally (i.e., approximately, with chance variations due to relative dominance and recessiveness of traits) by both parents. If you have a child, to what extent do these traits, as yours, constitute parts of you? As they become transmitted to your child, do parts of you live on in your child? If you should die, would some parts of you still exist as long as your child lives? If you have more children, will more of you continue to exist in them? If you have grandchildren and great grandchildren, etc., will some of you continue through them? Does your self multiply its parts as you have more children?

Or, since each additional generation which joins your genes with those from other sources diminishes the percentage of your own genes in your grandchildren and great grandchildren, do you gradually diminish, become less significant, and eventually perish through such dilution? (If inbreeding prevents such dilution, ought you to promote or prevent inbreeding?) Although we have focused our attention upon biological aspects of self, we may note that our children are also, in a fundamental sense, social, and thus our expansion and perpetuation through them requires them, as other persons, to be means to our own ends. To the extent that we remain identified with our children we owe it to ourselves to take care of them for thereby we are caring for ourselves also.

Reversing the direction of our attention from our children to our parents, to what extent did we preexist in them? If our parents have other children, our siblings, do we, consequently, have a partial, if somewhat indirect, identity with them? What about our preexistence in our grandparents, and great grandparents, and more distant ancestors? When did I begin? How far back in biological history did I already partly exist? Does any reverence which I may have for my ancestors serve in part as a kind of reverence for my own previous self? When I desire what is best for myself, how much of my efforts should be devoted to that part of me which is located in my relatives, whether ancestors, siblings or descendants?

Not only do I say, "I am human," but also, "I am an animal" and, "I am a living being," thereby indicating awareness of sharing certain traits with all animals and still other traits with all living beings. The great Hindu ethical doctrine, "Ahimsa," shared by many vegetarians in other cultures, considers all killing, especially of animals but even of plants, a form of violence to fellow living beings. The more closely one feels oneself identified with other forms of life, the more one seems to be eating oneself (being, in effect, a cannibal) when one consumes them. Where, really, does one's self stop? To what extent ought one who is interested in oneself look after other living beings?

Sometimes we seem to identify ourselves with physical things outside our bodies. For example, when a person tries on a new suit or dress, one inquires, "How do I look?" About new clothes one may have some doubts, but one's old clothes, those one is accustomed to wearing, one accepts as a part of one's own normal appearance. Sometimes we oppose ourselves to our clothes, as when they itch or bind. When playing checkers, one automatically says, "I jumped you," thus indicating a feeling of identification of oneself with one's checkers. When the game is over, a person forgets, and may even deny, ever feeling identified with a checker. Thus it seems obvious that our conceptions of self change, quite rapidly at times. While playing checkers, one says, "I ought to have moved there first." Is this an ethical "ought"? Yes. Although playing this particular game of checkers my not have deep significance for one's long-range interests, to the extent that a person now feels identified with his side in the game he is faced with doing the best that one can for oneself as a player of this game where the object is, of course, to win.

With how many other physical things, such as my home, my land, my car, my tools, my functions, at times, are parts of me? Certainly when one develops facility as a skater, typist, carpenter or driver, one's mechanical instruments, responding sensitively and automatically to one's wishes, come to seem as parts of oneself, sometimes as much so as one's fingers or limbs. When one puts them aside, of course, one thinks of them as separate from oneself; but while one uses them, and satisfies one's desires through them, one seems to find oneself extended through them. For example, when one reaches for a stick, it seems to be something separate. But after he has grasped it and starts poking about among other things, he may feel himself, i.e., his own power, effectiveness and interests, functioning through and right up to the end of the stick. A person tends to be proud of his tools because he is proud of himself, and the more closely he identifies himself and his welfare with them, the better care he takes of them.

A farmer once described the extent of his land as follows: "I go two miles south and one mile west." Feelings of identity with property may be very strong, especially if it has been "in the family for generations," and if one has lived upon it for most of one's life, and more especially if it has been carefully fenced in response to disputes with neighbors, or, if one has purchased property over a long period with hard-earned money and finally has obtained a clear title to it. Do you feel that you extend yourself every time you become an owner of something new, something additional which is now "your own"? Does your self extend geographically to your neighborhood, your city, your state, your nation, your continent, as when you say, "I am a Harlemite," "I am a Detroiter," "I am a Texan" or "I am an American?" How much of your time do you devote to thinking about the welfare of your community, city, state or national territory because you consider them as yours and thus your own interests as bound up with them?

If you have ever seriously discussed astronomy, you can recall that in thinking about "all those planets and stars out there," you automatically began to think of "our earth" and of what would happen if "one of those bodies should collide with us." If you kept at the subject very long, your thoughts about, and identification with, "our earth" shifted eventually to "our solar system" and perhaps finally to "our galaxy," but, by contrast with it, your interest in your earth and dangers to its existence seemed, during such a discussion, quite close to your own personal interests. Your welfare obviously depends upon its continuance, and you may even have thought about what we ought to do in order to try to keep it on its course if it should tend gradually to move too far from or too close to, the sun.

Now, although we may be carrying geographical and astronomical extensions of self-concepts too far, awareness of how we feel about ourselves under such circumstances can be very instructive regarding how our self-ideas expand and contract rapidly. If you can recall, also, that your expanded interests were felt as involving goods for yourself, or of yourself and as involving a grandeur from which those who fail to appreciate astronomical interests are excluded, you may discover how increased value of, and for, yourself can come into being. Persons unable to appreciate their own cosmic nature and interests lack something of the richness of which life is capable. Anyone who, in aiming at what is best for oneself, wants to live life to its fullest, shortchanges oneself to the extent that one misses enjoyment of such astronomical values. Not only an astronomer, but also an ethicist, may be expected to say that, unless one is too busy with other, more important values, one ought to pursue and enjoy, so far as one can, those values available only through understanding and appreciating one's cosmic situation.

Another, perhaps more intimate, portion of self as physical is that investigated by physiological psychology. Your brain, nervous system, sensory end-organs, conditioned reflexes, memory, imagination, emotions, feelings and sensations may be thought of as constituting parts of your self. The more fully you identify yourself with your feelings, emotions or vision, the more their values seem bound up with your self. Regarding each, then, you may have oughts, such as, for example, you ought to be careful not to puncture your eyeball, or to read too long in a dim light, or to fail to correct your vision with glasses when needed. If long-range goods can be derived from developing habits of solving problems automatically, interest in the nature of, and techniques for, learning becomes a significant ought. If conscience can be acquired as conditioned reflexes, training your nervous system, and conscience, may be a most useful kind of asset.

In the foregoing survey of aspects of self as physical, we have stressed the numerous kinds and the vastness of the extent of things with which you may feel identified. But with regard to each you may have noticed also that, at times, you feel opposed to each of these kinds. You may separate soul and body and regard your body as a carnal carcass imprisoning your soul; if you conceive yourself as a soul which may be freed from its body, you may believe yourself opposed to your body. You may doubt whether your molecules, atoms or electrons are really parts of you. They may come and go, as we eat and excrete, for presumably our chemical contents undergo a complete change once every seven years. How can you identify your enduring self with these passing elements which remain invisible anyway? Even your blood cells, which you wash down the drain after bleeding, may seem to make no real difference in your self. You may regard excess fat, which contributes to your weight, not really part of your self. Long and bitter conflict with a parent, sibling or child may create irreconcilable feelings of enmity. Animals and plants more often seem like different species. A car that will not start, a hammer that strikes your finger, a neighborhood that fatigues your nerves, a territory too vast for you to see, travel through or even comprehend, can hardly always be thought of as part of you. Your sun seems very far away, so hot that it burns your skin, and your own earth may seem to batter you with intolerable heat or snow or wind. Even your own intimate emotions may overwhelm you, as when you are crippled or shaken with fear.

Hence, your self seems not only complex but variable. Even merely as physical, you exist as a complex variable. When seeking what is best for yourself in the long run, how should you decide in regard to the extent that you should feel identified with, or opposed to, each and all of the foregoing factors? Is it better to expand whenever you can? Is it better to contract as often as possible? Is it better to remain stable than to fluctuate? Is it better to adapt yourself pliably to changing circumstances as they arise and to opportunities for greater values as they come and go? That is, in addition to specific oughts pertaining to the many parts of your self as physical, are there some general oughts regarding keeping your self-ideas stable or flexible? Too rapid fluctuation of self-feelings may create confusion. Too rigid conceptions may make you unadaptable. The more complex and variable you find yourself to be, the more you will welcome discovery of reliable general principles for guiding your judgment. If so, then to attain assurance regarding what is best for you is a fundamental part of what you most want to do.

Chapter IV

SELF AS SOCIAL

Even though "ethics" pertains not merely to "society" but also to "the individual," nevertheless the social aspects of each individual self are central to "individual ethics." Many different ways in which each self is inherently social may be explored with benefit. Some of these will be examined in the present chapter, and divided, somewhat arbitrarily, into three groups entitled "Self-Ideals," "Sources of Self" and "Cultural Riches."

Self-Ideals. You commonly think of yourself, and describe yourself, in terms of your group memberships and social roles. For example, when you give your name, saying "I'm John Jones," you automatically identify yourself with the Jones family, at least with your parents and possibly with a whole host of Joneses. If the name "Jones" happens to meet with approval, i.e., "The great Jones family," you may feel yourself thereby honored. Or, if it has gained an unsavory reputation, you may feel yourself chagrined. Consequently, to the extent that you feel identified with the Joneses you will try to elevate their reputation by defending them against slander or by helping them improve their actual conditions so as to warrant a better rating. You may feel yourself compelled to act discreetly so that their collective reputation, in which you share, may be enhanced.

Recall what happens to you whenever you join a group. After joining you describe yourself in a way which you could not properly do before: "I'm a Boy Scout." "I'm a seventh grader." "I'm an alumnus of Washington high School." "I'm a student at State University." When you travel away from your school, city, state or nation, you become known as a representative of that group and, especially when visitors from such a group are rare, you acquire significance as a representative of the whole group and find yourself expected to play your role fittingly. When in a foreign land, you tend to forget your family difficulties, your interschool rivalries, your interstate conflicts, your interdenominational differences, and find your "I-am-an-American" feelings pervading your whole nature. You discover yourself to be a "Yanqui" or "Gringo" in Latin America, an "Imperialist" or "Capitalist" in Communist countries, and "Occidental" in the Orient and a "White" in Africa. How you feel that you ought to act flows from your acceptance, willingly or unwillingly, of the role you find yourself playing, or forced to play. Fear of foreigners, which is a common experience, may overwhelm you. But the discovery that you are feared or hated or admired because you stand out as representative of your national group can help to make you aware of how much your citizenship means to you as a self.

When you attain status in a business or profession, you acquire recognition, and recognize yourself, as functioning in the ways required. You become, and you are, a carpenter or an accountant or a nurse. Your developed skill is embodied in you and thus determines you as substantially a being with such status. The very tools involved in your skill, be it a hammer, a slide rule or a hypodermic needle, become both symbolic and actual extensions of your nature. You may leave one profession or corporation and join another. But while you actually function in it, such functioning entails a substantiality which constitutes a living part of you. As long as it does, you have a natural interest both in the welfare of your profession and in your own excellence, efficiency and rating in it, and this interest constitutes a part of your personalty and your desire relative to it determines part of what you regard as best for yourself in the long run. One faces, here as elsewhere, the question as to what extent one should permit one's professional interests to dominate one's personality. Some do this, some have to do this, more than others. But the question of how much one should devote to one's professional, as against one's familial, community, religious, recreational and other interests, itself persists as a recurring ethical question.

Turning from the foregoing samples of kinds of group memberships which tend to modify conceptions of self, we may observe how specific roles within groups affect one's personality. Whenever one who is elected to, or selected for, an office (such as clerk, sergeant, receptionist, manager, secretary, president, judge, dean, administrative assistant, director, custodian) accepts his appointment, he naturally assents in trying to fulfill the duties of his office. In doing so, he discovers, even when he does not undergo a training program, certain ideals of achievement which grow naturally out of the functions of his office. When, as a responsible functionary, he strives to accomplish these, he finds himself not only making the judgments, decisions and demands required by his office, but also that he accepts them as his own judgments, decisions and demands, at least to the extent that he feels himself identified with his office. The more fully one devotes himself to his job, the more deeply he feels that what is good for the office is good for himself. Its oughts become his oughts, his fears of harm to the office are felt as his own fears, and his success for his office becomes experienced as his own success. Although one ought not to permit his interest in any office to crowd out other interests essential to his life, such as those in his family and community and physical health, one who has failed to respond to the thrill of realizing himself as a responsible officer lacks one of the greatest of human values.

A person appreciates his social role as more significant when it carries with it a rank or rating, especially one in which he is recognized as a bit superior to his fellows in some important respect. In fact, the closer his office is to the core of his welfare, the more important to him does such a rating seem. Regardless of whether one is, for example, an employee, a manager, a technician or a mother, the more one realizes that one's efficiency as a functionary pays psychic as well as cash dividends, the more one will strive for excellence.

One can more truly recognize the importance of his position when he knows, and knows that others know, that they are dependent upon him. Although one ought not to accept more responsibility for the welfare of others than he can bear, the more responsible he becomes, the more both he and others have to recognize his actual importance. A raise in rank which does not carry with it increase in actual responsibilities has a hollow character about it, which does not long escape notice and evaluation. One who wins a prize which he does not deserve may enjoy a surface happiness, but he must, when honest with himself, despise himself at least a bit for any false pretence which accepting it or displaying it entails. Delinquency in children and habitual thievery by adults results naturally from their having been denuded of self-respect, of being dispossessed or any social stature which they feel is so worth defending that they cannot risk losing it. When one discovers how essential to his welfare is the attainment of a responsible office and of excellence in performing its functions, the more fully does he realize that this is part of what he most wants to do.

Sources of Self. Distinguishing between having complex and variable ideas of self as social and the social origins of our ideas and ideals of self, we turn now to explore the latter. We are not born human, except as members of a biological species, but we become human after birth through the socializing influences of others upon us. Human beings are essentially social animals, and socialization, and thus humanization, occurs after one is born. Not only must a helpless infant be cared for by others, if it is to live at all, but its early conditionings, its pattern of responses, and the kinds of things it is permitted or encouraged to do all result from it's interaction with others. A person learns to speak and how to act and even what to want by observing and imitating others, for "one can no

more organize his personality than he can be born without a mother."
(Ellsworth Farris, <u>The Nature of Human Nature</u>, p. 279, McGraw-Hill
Book Co., New York, 1937).

Social psychologist L.L. Bernard presents, in Part III of his
<u>Introduction to Social Psychology</u> (pp. 342-343. Henry Holt and Co., N.Y.,
1926), an excellent account of how personality normally develops through
imitation. "The first model which the young child copies in his personality
integrating process is ordinarily his mother. . . . He copies her acts of
affection, such as caressing with his hands, kissing, pressing his cheeks
against the mother's cheeks, cooing in response to her cooing, smiling,
and even a little later responding to signs of fear and anxiety. . . . He
adopts her tone of voice, forms of expression, gestures, even carriage, and
attitudes of sincerity and insincerity, her benevolence, devices of lying
evasion. . . . The child by his third or fourth year is a simplified miniature
of the mother. If the child is a daughter, she has the same taste in
clothes, the same company manners, the same social prejudices,
judgments, techniques, virtues and absurdities."

After stressing the importance of the mother model, because it lays a
foundation for all the rest, Bernard compares typical mother and father
models and advantages and disadvantages of each, and notes "the
necessity of turning from the mother to the father as a model," the
"incompleteness of the father model," and the availability of other outside
models, such as the postman, the delivery man, the fireman, the
policeman, the bus driver, nurses and teachers. Older brothers and sisters
and gang leaders exercise a tremendous molding influence, but these too
give way eventually, as do all actual models, to ideals. Ideal models may
appear quite early in life, in fairy tales and fables, stories of heroic
figures, or accounts of the lives of Jesus and the saints. History,
biography and fiction provide additional examples for admiration and
emulation. But despite the great value of live or ready-made characters
for vicarious integration of personality, a person gradually outgrows all of
them and imaginatively constructs one's own ideal, whether vague or
clear, including parts selected from many earlier heroes. Yet even when
one has broken away from, and grown beyond, all models provided by
others, one's own ideal has been constructed out of them. It is one's own,
but it is none the less fundamentally social in its origin.

Another important aspect of the social origins of your self has been
discovered and described in detail by philosopher George Herbert Mead.
(<u>Mind, Self, and Society</u>. University of Chicago Press, Chicago, 1934.)
Distinguishing, as we all do, between "I" and "me," he notes that

consciousness of "me" arises as a consequence of the attitudes and actions which other persons take toward us. A child, like an animal, at first acts without being aware of himself as a self. He just acts, waving his hand, looking, babbling. He looks at other things without being aware that he is looking or that there is a "he" which looks. But when someone acts toward him, looks at him, tickles him, waves at him, chucks his chin, the child then discovers himself as something which is acted upon, or looked at, tickled, waved at and chucked. Only by becoming aware of his reaction to the actions of others does his own self-awareness emerge into being.

Furthermore, the kind of self-conception which arises from self-awareness is a product of those ways in which others act toward us. Thus, we depend upon others for their actions upon us in order to develop not only self-awareness but each detail of our self-conception. The kind of self we become is thus itself a product of the attitudes which others take toward us. We find ourselves not merely growing to fit ourselves to the demands of an adult office, as previously mentioned, but always, and from the very beginning of our lives, we constantly react to, and in the light of, the attitudes and expectations which others have about us. A person "enters his own experience as a self or individual, not directly or immediately ... but only in so far as he first becomes an object to himself only by taking the attitudes of other individuals toward himself...." (Ibid, pp. 140, 142, 143).

Thus far, we have considered only the "me" or object in the "I"-"me" or subject-object situation. "I" am the agent, or the actor, but "I" come into my awareness first not as an actor but as a reactor, as that which responds to the actions of others upon "me." Thus "me" arises first into awareness, and "I" emerges afterwards as that which reacts to the treatment of "me." "The 'I' is the response of the organism to the attitudes of the others; the 'me' is the organized set of attitudes of others which one himself assumes. The attitudes of others constitute the organized 'me,' and then one reacts toward that as an 'I.'" (Ibid, p. 175.) Afterwards, both "I" and "me" grow and evolve as we discover how others react to our reactions to them, and as we try out all sorts of ventures regarding how we would like to have others think of us and discover, accidentally or pragmatically, what kind of selves we have by how much we can "get away with" in dealing with others.

Although we cannot here follow Mead further into the detailed evidence which he assembles for his view, and we may not be able to accept his view as the whole story, nevertheless after examining his evidence we can hardly avoid the conclusion that self-concepts, both concepts of self as object and of self as subject, depend upon others for their origin and development and, indeed, for their maintenance -- for as we grow up, mature and age, and as we change our groups and social roles, our self-concepts also change somewhat. Now if all this is true, then when we try to get what is best for ourselves in the long run, we do so in light of the selves we believe we have -- beliefs which we owe to others. Of course, once we discover that our self-concepts are due to others, then we may conclude that a most fundamental ought is to locate ourselves, in so far as we can, in those environments in which our potentialities for growth will receive a most favorable stimulus through the opinions and attitudes and actions of others toward us.

Cultural Riches. Self-ideas originate in and become molded by not merely interaction between persons in groups but also by "culture" or from socially inherited traits resulting from living together. "Culture" consists of all ideas about how to do things, the language required to convey those ideas, and the tools and techniques involved in doing them. Such ideas include beliefs about the nature of self and its goals as well as about the universe and all other things in it. They include ideas of how to do and how to be and how to think and feel, as well as how not to do or be or think or feel. Culture includes all tools, not only hand tools, but also houses, factories, cities, and whatever material objects, ideas and techniques for producing and using them, which still exist. It embraces all of the sciences and the humanities, histories, philosophies and religions, the arts such as literature, painting, poetry, drama, dance and music, and games. It consists of everything supervening upon our biological inheritance, and even the effects upon such inheritance of controlling and modifying ideals.

Anyone acquainted with cultural variations knows they produce differences in the behavior patterns, the ideals and the viewpoints of people. The more broadly one travels the more obvious becomes the truism that every person is a product of his culture. The more widely divergent cultural ideals make greater differences in conceptions of the nature of self, its worth, its potentialities and its goals. Most people still have little choice in the matter, but when one does discover that some cultural ideals seem more useful, fruitful or satisfying than others, one acquires an obligation to oneself to try to adopt the superior traits. Most of the cultural traits that one acquires from others embody results of centuries of effort and ingenuity. No person, merely as a biological animal, has the ability to produce, or reproduce, the whole, or even very little, of human cultural history by himself. We accept our cultural heritage as ours so naturally that we can hardly imagine the myriads of independent discoveries, and the toil, sweat, anxiety, and toll of life and death, required by the trial-and-error processes involved in producing it. Each cultural trait is a value graciously (i.e., without our deserving it) provided for us. We accept our endowment of cultural riches so unquestioningly that we cannot imagine what it would be like to be without them (for the very structure of our imagining "what it would be like without them" is itself culturally conditioned).

Acquisition of most other cultural traits depends upon the cluster of traits called "language" -- which itself is one of the miracles constituting human nature. A person is not merely an anthropoid mammalian, not only a social animal; a person is a linguistic animal or a symbolizing animal. (See Ernst Cassirer's Essay on Man, Yale University Press, New Haven, 1944.) The symbols required for communicating and cooperating in groups, for inheriting our culture and for thinking abstractly become primary constituents structuring our minds. Not only our self, but also our mind (not to be confused with brain) "arises in the social process;" and "the language process is essential for the development of self" (Mead, op. cit., pp. 134, 135) and its mind. The difference between a child and an adult is more than physiological, even more than sociological; it is linguistic. By structuring your mind and shaping your self-concepts, language participates in making you what you are. If so, then, of course, if you desire what is best for your self, you naturally develop interest in your language -- not merely efficiency in the use of your "mother tongue" but, if you care to expand yourself so you can enjoy the inherited riches of other cultures conveyed best only through other languages, also in "foreign" languages. (High school and college requirements in "English" and "languages" are no arbitrary whims of educators but represent minimums needed for becoming "human" in our multi-lingual world.)

Our linguistically-shaped conceptions of our selves depend not merely upon words and sentences and grammatical syntax but upon the small and great systems of thought, such as the sciences and the humanities. Not only do we become scientists and humanists, but each of the sciences and of the humanities contributes its own share to the infinitely complex shapings of our minds. Nothing can be more revealing of the nature of yourself than a review of the cultural history of mankind.

Each contemporary Western person has been produced by several intricate series of long developments. The main trunk of Western

civilization has two major taproots in the Hebraic and classical Greek
traditions, which in turn fed upon earlier Egyptian, Babylonian and other
more primitive cultures.   The birth and growth and synthesizing of
Christian thought, especially by Augustine, provided an enduring pattern
for organizing great portions of our minds. After Arab contributions, the
Medieval synthesis expanded and stabilized Christian mentality most
effectively, yet too rigidly, because the Renaissance and Reformation,
followed by the Enlightenment (with its Rationalistic, Empiricistic and
Mechanistic phases), and Romanticism, German Idealism, Marxism,
Evolutionism and Pragmatism, may be seen as successive steps away from
that established framework. Each new step has added its own values to
enrich our cultural outlooks. Each new national language had the virtue
of stretching the human mind in its own unique ways.   Every new
philosophy and new religious sect developed its own variation of Western
idealism. Although some of these may be incompatible with others, each
has suggestions to offer which one can, like the aforementioned child who
transcends actual models to construct one of its own, use to construct
one's own system of the universe, one's own intellectual home for
mankind. If you cannot find a ready-made system that answers your
needs, then you have an obligation to yourself to construct from the
better parts of each of your cultural sources one best suited to yourself.
     Of course, Western civilization is only one of the three major
civilizations through which the human mind has evolved. The others, the
Hindu and the Chinese, have proved to be as rich and varied and as
useful and satisfactory in their own ways as the European heritage is in
its way. Fortunately, in addition to those traits found to be common to
mankind everywhere, some aspects of human nature have been exploited
and refined more fully in some cultures than in others. The more deeply
we penetrate into the unique ideals of each culture the more we realize
the profundity of the saying that "A person who knows only one culture
knows none." People whose training is limited to one culture can hardly
begin to realize the significance of some of their own self-concepts until
they have contrasted them with those which have emerged in a different
culture. Not only, as Mead has said, does a self not discover itself until
it becomes aware of itself as reacting to the actions of others, but also a
culturally-conceived self does not begin to discover the culture-produced
aspects of its self-conception until it becomes aware of alternatives to
such conception. Once we realize that we may enrich ourselves, both our
conceptions of ourselves and others and of kinds of values available to us
as human beings, by drawing upon Hindu and Chinese cultures, then,

assuming we are able, we have developed an obligation to ourselves to pursue these riches. If our children inherit a world culture enriched by all three major civilizations, we will seem to them as poverty-stricken minds to the extent that we have failed to attain at least a glimpse of these other traditional treasures.

Enough has been said in this chapter on "Self As Social" to illustrate the multifarious ways in which a self has its origin, its nature and its riches in the social and cultural aspects of life. Although socialization and acculturation involve evils also, something which will be discussed later, one who enjoys the needed capacity and opportunity can find what is best for oneself in the long run somewhat in proportion to embracing and embodying additional social responsibilities and wider cultural perspectives. And when persons advance far enough, they can first guide themselves into opportunities and capacities of their own choosing and then become producers of, not merely products of, culture.

Chapter V

SELF-INTEREST

When beginning another chapter on ways in which a self is social, we turn to some ways in which one can deliberately use others to one's own advantage. Some of these ways seem obvious, but others hide from us much of the time. In doing so, we adopt, for convenience, a four-fold classification of desires (originated by William I. Thomas and Florian Znaniecki, The Polish Peasant in Europe and America, Vol. I, p. 73, Knopf, New York, 1927, developed by Joseph K. Folsom, Social Psychology, Chapter IV., Harper and Brothers, New York, 1931) and observe how principles, apparently inherent in human nature, operate effectively in all of the four areas.

These four classes of wishes will be spoken of as "the desire for recognition," "the desire for companionship," "the desire for adventure" and "the desire for security."

Desire for Recognition. Each person is "somebody" and wants to be recognized as such. Each normally desires to be admired by others for what he is. Each wishes to be appreciated, approved, accepted. Each rates, high or low, in the estimation of others. Whenever two people meet, for long enough to pass judgment upon each other, recognition is involved. When they remain together for long periods, and especially when they come into frequent and close contact, the factor of recognition becomes very important. Examples of situations in which you have ratings, if such are needed, may be observed in your relations with your colleagues, wife, neighbors, friends, and even passersby. You can be rated in as many ways as there are traits with respect to which you can be liked or disliked, such as your clothes, good looks, strength, poise, manner of expression, vivacity, generosity, self-confidence, reliability, adaptability, tolerance, popularity, ability to influence others, achievements in work, professional success, hobby and money to spend.

Ten principles related to ways in which you can satisfy your desire for recognition (or companionship, adventure and security) may be distinguished with profit.

1. Recognition is necessarily social. For to be recognized, one must be recognized by others. To be esteemed, one must be esteemed by others. To be rated, one must be rated by others. Here is a very simple and obvious fact about human nature which may be taken as a condition, or principle, basic to ethics.

2. To satisfy one's desire to rate highly, one must somehow do, or be, what others admire. If one does not, one will be disliked, disesteemed, despised or, at worst, ignored. Here is another obvious condition, or principle, upon which ethical decisions should be grounded.

3. One naturally likes to be admired, esteemed, recognized. One enjoys being appreciated. One feels proud when approved, accepted, praised. One likes rating high. Now when this happens, one tends to want this admiration to continue and to increase. So one naturally tries to do or be what will bring more such admiration. Here we may note an additional tendency in human nature foundational to ethics.

4. Desire for more approval, as it grows stronger, tends to shade imperceptibly into desire for more approval than one can get. Although, if one stops to think about the matter, one has no insistent desire to be overrated, nevertheless the intensity of one's desire, and the confidence that one would enjoy being rated more highly, often leads one to believe that one ought to be esteemed by others more highly than one actually is esteemed. That is, one easily tends to overestimate one's worth in the eyes of others. Here is another, not so obvious, and yet easily observable, tendency normally present in human beings.

5. Desire for more approval than one gets has certain unfortunate consequences. One's belief that one deserves more than one gets implies distrust of the opinions of others. Then, the others, when they discover that their opinions, honestly given, are distrusted, find themselves thereby rated low, and below what is actually the case. Thus, by distrusting the opinion of others, one causes others to believe themselves underrated. Then these others do just what one would do under the same circumstances. They resent the fact that they have been underrated, and try to do something to correct the mistake. They naturally retaliate. They distrust one's distrust. They depreciate, they disesteem, disapprove one's distrust. Hence one is distrusted. One is disesteemed. Thus the desire for more approval than one gets tends to result in less approval than one already has. Hence, excessive desire for recognition is self-defeating. Here, apparently, is another extremely important tendency in human nature which permeates most social situations.

6. A principle of reciprocity seems inherent in human nature, if not, indeed, in the whole world. We can easily see how it operates. People tend to treat others as they are treated by others. the principle works both positively and negatively. (a) Negatively: Slap me and I will want to slap you. Condemn me, and I will condemn you. Despise me and I will despise you, at least for despising me. (b) Positively: Admire me and I

will admire you, at least for admiring me. Help me, and I will want to help you. The principle of reciprocity is well-known, has been held for a long time, and has found expression in many different ways. If one has any doubts about the pervasiveness of this principle, one need merely recall one's past experiences, observe the behavior of others, or, if doubts persist, one may deliberately experiment by appreciating or depreciating others and observing persistently the consequences resulting for oneself.

7. One who is interested in one's own esteem and who knows that the principle of reciprocity works, will need to do what, in order to satisfy his interest? (a) Not despise others. Withhold initiating a process which will bring negative results. (b) Appreciate others. Initiate processes which will produce positive results. Since the power of initiation rests with oneself, the wisely self-interested person will freely choose to initiate appreciation of others. Self-interestedness, or desiring what is best for oneself, should not be mistaken for selfishness, which consists in intending to get more than one deserves at the expense of others. Wise self-interestedness may promote itself through unselfishness. So, the more you desire to increase your esteem, the more unselfish you should be in esteeming others. Here is indeed a most important principle of prudence.

8. The principle of reciprocity usually reflects sincerity and insincerity. If one evaluates genuinely, what one receives in return tends to be genuine. If one evaluates others insincerely, one's insincerity tends to be reflected. When one gives, freely and without demanding, or even expecting, return, one is more likely to get an unexpected return. But when one gives, and then stands awaiting returns, one obviously gives in order to get, and one's gift is not genuine. When a receiver realizes that a gift is not genuine, will one not despise the giver rather than appreciate him? Only when you praise sincerely can you expect, according to the principle of reciprocity, sincere praise. Wise self-interestedness requires some genuine altruism, some genuine unselfishness, some genuine gifts to others. Wise self-interestedness is altruism's strongest ally. Genuine altruism pays the surest dividends to wisely self-interested persons.

9. The principle of reciprocity does not work with mathematical precision. One does not always give exactly as one gets or get exactly as one gives. Sometimes we give less than we receive; sometimes we give more. Two important factors condition such impreciseness. (a) Delay should be expected in receiving rewards. Our appreciation of others does not always make its full effect felt by others until later. But if we give with confidence, giving honor where honor is due, without requiring return, probably we have established in others an attitude which will

express itself on future occasions. When you give genuinely, you can be trusted; others will tend to express their appreciation of that trust whenever proper occasions arise. (b) When returns come later, they often appear as surprises. If your gift was genuine, you expect no return. When results arrive unexpectedly, they appear as undeserved or as more than deserved. Then, psychologically, the amount and quality of the reward may seem greatly out of proportion to the little that has been given. Furthermore, richness of variety may be added in your reward, for when others express their appreciation of you, they do so in terms of their own experiences which may be somewhat different from your own. Their different ways of seeing you as good may, in effect, lead you to accept yourself as possessing new values, additional worths, of which you were unaware before. In sum, returns may come (1) unexpectedly, (2) in unexpected ways, and (3) with unexpectedly new and different values.

Of course, on the other hand, others may forget our appreciation of them, even as we forget their appreciation of us. How does one fare, on the average and in the long run, in these matters? All this can, surely, be tested experimentally, if evidence is not already at hand. One may, over a long period of time, record the ratio of gifts to rewards, and calculate the effect of one's various kinds of actions and attitudes toward others, if one has any doubts about the matter. The principle that one may profit, i.e., get more than one gives, if one acts with sufficient unselfishness, is an old one. Jesus stated it thus: "Cast thy bread upon the waters, and after many days, it will return manyfold."

10. Although limits exist relative to what one can do or be, and to the number and kinds of people by whom one can be appreciated, the amount of opportunity for use of the foregoing principles surely is sufficient for all who wish to take the trouble to use them. Once we know about the principles and have sufficient faith in them to try them out enough to experience their workability for ourselves, then we must put the blame for our own unhappiness due to disesteem primarily upon ourselves. That is, to the extent that you have power of free choice regarding whether and how much you initiate appreciation of others, you can, in a very large measure, influence the way you are esteemed by others. Thus whoever is interested in what is best in the way of esteem for himself in the long run ought to employ the principle of reciprocity to his own advantage by initiating positively, and by refraining from initiating or perpetuating negatively, appreciation of others.

Desire for Companionship. A second group of human needs may be spoken of, alternatively, as the desire for companionship, the desire for friendship, or the desire for love. Each person normally desires to be loved, to be appreciated as an intrinsic value, to be treated as so basically worthwhile that even numerous faults will not be considered as detracting essentially from such appreciation. Companions feel free to share their innermost feelings, ideals, attitudes, without fear that their shortcomings will interrupt or destroy a persisting prejudice in favor of one's enduring worth. Although the distinction between esteem and love may be hard to draw at times, since esteem includes esteem through love, esteem may be directed toward some superficial attributes or qualities, whereas love involves esteem of one's very substance.

One may be admired, esteemed, praised, as an instrument, or as a means to an end, e.g., as a good warrior, good worker, good entertainer or good craftsperson, but one is loved as an intrinsic value, as an end-in-oneself, even regardless of one's instrumental value. (It is true that when both kinds of value, instrumental and intrinsic, are present, one is more valued than when only one or the other is present. But the difference in quality of the esteem with which one is appreciated as an instrument and with which one is appreciated as an end-in-oneself is tremendous.) Love has an enduring quality about it; even when permanent attachment is known to be impossible, one's attitude, when one loves, is such that one wishes it could be permanent. The distinction may be clarified somewhat by noting the opposites of esteem and love. The opposite of love is loneliness. The opposite of esteem is being despised, depreciated, humiliated. One may be in he midst of many people who admire him and yet be very lonely. Companionship, love or response is not essentially comparative or competitive, whereas esteem, recognition, or rating, involves comparison or competition with others.

Companionship can be of many kinds and degrees, varying primarily in degree of intimacy. (a) "Primary groups," those in which persons participate in relatively constant face-to-face association, as whole persons, usually seem the most intimate. Relations with parents, siblings, pals, playmates, pets, neighbors and relatives may be the commonest types of companionship. (b) Club, fraternity, society, church, lodge and school friends appear next most intimate, with visitors, guests, more distant relatives and travelling companions sometimes included. (c) Some secondary-group associates, such as those in one's profession, or community, state, nation, race or religion, may be adjudged intrinsically worthwhile because of their membership in one's valued group. (d) Some persons, perhaps all persons at times, especially in times of religious inspiration, may feel humanitarian, i.e., believe that every person, just by being a person, is intrinsically valuable. This may require a willingness to love without experiencing more than an imaginary, or token, return of such love. W.H. Roberts, in discussing Christian love, says: "By such a conversion the individual passes from a spiritual economy of scarcity to a spiritual economy of abundance. The old law of restraints and prohibitions is superseded by a vision of opportunities. Love refuses to be confined within the ordinary, or conventional, limitations. It leaps over the barriers of distance, or race, or of class. From very exuberance it goes out to the unworthy, to the wicked, even to enemies. It refuses to consider dangers, and sings in the midst of suffering. Love sums up and fulfills all obligations, whether to man or to God. It seeks expression in every possible form of service, in every enrichment of life." (The Problem of Choice, p. 172. Ginn and Co., Boston, 1941.) (e) Some love God and feel themselves loved by God, conceived as a cosmic companion. Others may keep company with many gods or other imaginary companions.

1. Love is essentially social. For to be loved, you must be loved by others. To have friends, you must have others for friends. You cannot have companions unless you have others for companions. Without others, love is impossible.

2. Hence, to satisfy your self-interest in companionship, you must do or be what it takes in order to have others as companions. If you do not do what is required in order to love or be loved, then you cannot have your desire for companionship satisfied.

3. When one enjoys being loved, one normally desires to be loved more. When you enjoy friendliness and intimacy, you usually desire more such friendship and intimacy. When you find yourself regarded as an intrinsic good, you naturally desire more such treatment. "More," here, may take the form of more friends, more time with friends, more value (being more highly valued by your friends).

4. Love is wonderful. So wonderful, indeed, that we naturally want more of it. How much more? The amount which we get, and are going to get, is limited. When we want more, we often, even usually, want more than we will receive. But if we can be loved only by others, then if we want to be loved more than others actually love us, or are going to love us, then we want more love than we are going to get. Such desire may properly be called "excessive."

5. When you express your desire for more friendly appreciation than you received from your friends, you make them feel that you depreciate either the genuineness or the adequacy of their appreciation of you. To say, for example, "You don't love me enough," involves negative, and hence derogatory, criticism. Such a statement implies some lack of appreciation of the fact that the other gives you as much love as he wishes and as much, thus, as you have coming from him. Whenever you depreciate your friends by such statements, you thereby in some measure withhold your appreciation of them as intrinsic goods. If you are truly friendly, you will accept them as they are as ends-in-themselves and trust their attitude as at least just, even if not generous. Friends who regard each other as intrinsic goods can take, and appreciate, each other's criticism and disesteem regarding superficial items of evaluation, as long as these criticisms do not endanger that deeper evaluation called "love." But the more you feel, and express your feelings, that your friends shortchange you regarding friendliness, the more you make them resent your attitude and withdraw some of their feelings of friendliness from you. Hence, excessive desire for love, companionship, friendship is self-defeating.

6. The principle of reciprocity, inherent in human nature, works regarding love and friendship just as it does relative to esteem. We tend to be intimate with those who are intimate with us and to withdraw, and remain reserved, from those who withdraw, or reserve themselves, from us. The principle works both negatively and positively. We cannot have companions without being companionate. We can hardly expect to be regarded as intrinsic goods without reciprocally considering our regarders as also intrinsic goods. Freedom from loneliness can be guaranteed only if one is willing to love others at least as much as one desires to be loved by them.

7. Initiative brings rewards. Although one may be loved if one merely awaits being approached by someone who happens to consider him lovable, one can be more sure of results if, by employing the principle of reciprocity, one initiates action. When we love others, are friendly with others, and try to be companions in the sense that we treat others as intrinsic goods, others tend to reciprocate.

8. Sincerity is necessary if we desire our sincerity to be reciprocated. Whoever cannot be sincere in love of others cannot have genuine friends. No matter how much superficial effort a person puts forth to "win friends," one remains lonely if, in praising others, one cannot "do it sincerely."

9. Love can hardly be rewarded with mathematical precision. Genuine love has an infinite quality about it: one who loves will forgive endlessly, or at least "seventy times seven." The principle of reciprocity has proven to be a general, but not a universally precise, principle. Yet one can expect unlimited forgiveness only if one is willing to forgive endlessly. If you have this willingness, you will even forgive when you are not forgiven; but the moment you are not willing to forgive when you are not forgiven, your love, your regard for the other as an intrinsic good, has diminished; and your own diminution deserves to reap its reward.

10. The power to achieve friends, or the ability to be loved, is under one's own control. The principle of reciprocity, although imprecise, is an unfailing tool for promoting love of oneself. The choice as to whether the effort involved in regarding others as intrinsic goods and then acting in accordance with such regard is worth your while rests with yourself. It may not be easy to love others; but then it may not be easy for others to love you. But you have the power to achieve such love if you desire it, if you recognize the social nature of love and the workability of the principle of reciprocity. If the desire for love is one of your most fundamental desires, then to love others unselfishly or genuinely is a part of what you most want to do, and hence a part of what you most ought to want to do.

Desire for Adventure. Although the desire for new experience may be a less obvious interest in the sense that one is more likely to attend to one's interests in security, esteem and friendship first, when these become endangered, nevertheless it appears to be common to all person who have any time or energy to spare. The opposite of adventure or novelty is boredom, and the desire for adventure, as interpreted here, is at the same time a desire for relief from boredom. Although special varieties of adventure have special names, such as "play," "fun" and "recreation," adventure may be an aspect of every kind of activity.

Whatever classification of human activities, such as physical or mental, individual or social, emotional or intellectual, may be preferred, they can also be used to classify areas for pursuit of the desire for adventure. Some persons prefer adventure through reading, others through watching or listening, others through travelling, still others through making new friends or exploring new ideas. Or, persons differ in regard to what most easily bores them: work, dress, food, location, friends, ideas, attitudes. Smoking a cigarette, for example, although it may also serve one's interest in esteem, friendship or security, is often intended or employed to relieve ennui. For some, the desire for novelty can be easily satisfied; merely a shift of attention suffices ("A change is as good as a rest"). Some persons have habitual desires which may be satisfied by habitual variations, such as smoking. For others, only what appears to be entirely new or strikingly new will suffice; the merest repetition becomes boring.

People vary not only regarding what constitutes adventure but regarding the relative importance which they attach to their desire for adventure as compared with their desires for security, esteem and friendship. Whereas some, perhaps most, seek adventure only when they already feel secure, and in those areas where they feel secure, others place desire for adventure above desire for security. Some persons appear willing to seek adventure only within certain limited, even specialized, areas, whereas others seem to have an ever-ready sense of humor, a willingness to enjoy every aspect of life. Whatever can be included under the term "aesthetic" may serve the desire for adventure, provided it is sought for its novelty. The merely-repeated aesthetic experience may serve the desire for security, for we feel more at home with the familiar. Some persons satisfy their desires for security, esteem, love and adventure through separate activities: security through work on the job, esteem through office in a club, love at home, and adventure at the movies or fishing. Others, however, achieve the ability to integrate them into a single activity, for example, as in a family grocery business. The issue of whether one achieves satisfaction more efficiently through separating the areas of activity through which one satisfies one's four kinds of desires or through uniting them is an important one.

1. Although you may satisfy your desire for adventure alone, by tinkering with tools, hiking or day-dreaming, the amount of adventure alone, even for one with an exceedingly fertile imagination, is likely to be less than what results from social interstimulation. In order to enjoy those kinds of fun, novelty, excitement, which can come only through groups, you depend upon the others in those groups for your satisfaction of desire for such enjoyment. Dancing, tennis, group singing and competitive sports, for example, obviously require cooperation. But even seemingly solitary participation in spectator activities, such as television, radio, reading newspapers, magazines and books, requires costly social cooperation for production of the means.

Many more ways of enjoying fun exist when people have their fun together. (a) First of all, more varieties of fun occur because more imaginations can be at work originating suggestions which stimulate each other, because more techniques and greater use of equipment becomes possible through a pooling of resources, and because more areas of fun, those arising out of interactions between persons, become possible only socially. (b) Then fun is enlivened by more enthusiasm, more excitement, more "spirit," because enthusiasm is catching and can be stimulated by social challenge. (c) Also, one may have more fun more often when more persons are available to play with. A child unwillingly shut away from his playmates believes himself to be the most unhappy of all creatures. (d) Finally, higher quality fun becomes possible through the increased complexity, endurance, scope, scale, as well as variety and interestingness, where mass production and mass consumption methods make possible benefits from highly professional skills and huge financial investments for more people, as in the United States National Park Services, golf courses, theaters, movies, television stations, country clubs, travel bureaus, etc. Purely private adventure appears best only to those whose social efforts have led to serious frustration and to introversion.

2. Of course, in order to satisfy your interest in adventure through groups, you must do or be what is required for participation in such groups. Sometimes one's qualifications come naturally and without effort. At other times training, adjustment, modification of one's nature or habits may be required. For example, tremendous effort must be put forth in order to enjoy being a concert artist.

3. If you enjoy any kind of fun, usually you would like to experience more of it. When adventure proves exciting, you desire more. When novelty arouses your curiosity, you seek more of it. Naturally whenever you enjoy what is good you want more such good.

4. The desire for more fun often turns into a desire for more fun than you can have. Enthusiasm has no built-in meter which automatically checks it when the limit of realization has been reached. The tendency toward excess seems to be ever-present.

5. Then, when you want more than you can get, you become disappointed. If you desire more fun to be provided by others than they provide, you become disappointed with them. When you express such disappointment, you, in turn, create disappointment in those others who had aimed to please and satisfy you. Disappointment can be as catching as enthusiasm, or perhaps more so. When the fun desired fails to come up to expectation, or to desire, you become bored, and when you are bored, you tend to become a bore. Each kind of fun has its own kind of excess. Teasing is fun, but one may easily tease too much. Exercise is fun, but you may easily become exhausted from too much. You may repeat an interesting act, yet too much repetition becomes tedious.

Novelty interests us, but too much novelty may turn into the absurd and ridiculous.

Furthermore, excessive pursuit of adventure may endanger satisfaction of your own interests. Guns may be fun, but they endanger life. Speed is exciting, but it involves risk of injury or death. Flirtation can be interesting, but it often destroys more enduring values. One may enjoy playing the role of a fool, but at the cost of ruining one's reputation. Some enjoy teasing so much that they finally lose their companions. Whenever you deeply frustrate others, either relative to their desires for fun or their desires for security, esteem, or love, they will tend to eliminate you from group participation with them.

6. The principle of reciprocity works regarding fun also. The more interesting you are to others, the more you will find others willing to cooperate with you in providing what interests you. The more interesting others appear to you, the more interested you become in them. Some, in fact most, games involve the principle of reciprocity. For example, ping-pong, badminton and tennis (and earlier in life, pat-a-cake) obviously demand give and take. Checkers, chess and cards require each taking his turn. Group sports, such as baseball, football, volleyball, etc., depend on cooperative competition. The principle of reciprocity occurs so significantly that unevenness in matching of teams tends to be discouraged, for when a game seems too uneven, or one-sided, fun becomes diminished. Dancing requires sensitive reciprocity, as does teasing, flirtation and interesting conversation.

7. Initiation gets results here also. Tease me and I'll try to tease you. Please me and I'll try to please you. Stimulate me and I'll want to stimulate you. If you imagine something new, I'll try to imagine something newer. Since desires for adventure commonly intermingle with desires for esteem, when you have been stimulated you tend to desire to rate as a superior stimulator and to respond with increased effort to stimulate. Hence, the principle of reciprocity proves profitable for having more fun.

8. But sincerity is required. Nothing seems more boring than the repetition of stale jokes. You find it difficult to fake enthusiasm. If you try to use others as means to your own ends, without first endeavoring to be a means to their enjoyment, you may expect to be rejected. When someone expresses the feeling, "I'm bored; come and entertain me," you tend to be disinterested, especially if your previous attempts to entertain this person failed to result in his appreciation of your efforts. A person who cannot initiate interesting experiences in others hardly deserves

interesting rewards from the principle of reciprocity. When anyone continues to be bored, one should recognize that one's boredom reflects one's incapacity to initiate interestingness sincerely.

9. Reciprocation of interestingness cannot be mathematically precise. At times one must entertain others more than one is entertained by them. Sometimes we are more entertained than entertaining. We cannot expect all of those whom we invite to our parties to return our invitation. Interests vary, and our capacity for enjoying particular kinds of novelties differ. What constitutes adventure for one often does not for another. Our health, strength, vitality, money and competing responsibilities and interests differ from time to time. Yet, in general, those who prove to be more interesting to others tend to have others respond to them in additionally interesting ways. When each tries to out-do the others, some surprises, some unusually novel novelties, often result.

10. The power to have fun, and to have more fun, through cooperating with others resides, then, in one's own self. The sufficient workability of the principle of reciprocity, combined with one's own willingness to initiate effort to help others enjoy themselves, puts under one's control opportunity to have genuine fun whenever others are present and have time for it. Although few can play the particular game which they want to play at the precise time when they want to play it with exactly the people they prefer as partners, nevertheless enough opportunity exists for most of us that we need blame only ourselves if and when we become bored. One who associates acceptably with very many others soon learns to develop a sense of humor, so one can even enjoy those situations in which one is frustrated. At the very worst, one can try to discover the number of different ways of becoming bored. The person who is most willing to stimulate others, e.g., to become a recreation leader, is most likely to have opportunity for enjoyment of such recreation. But anyone who desires to have the most fun for oneself in the long run ought to develop habits conducive to initiating fun for others.

Desire for Security. An individual's "desire for security" consists in whatever interests he has in achieving and maintaining what is best for himself in the long run. What he believes to be best for himself will depend upon how he conceives himself, and what he needs to attain and protect or conserve his values. Since feelings of security have their opposites in fear, a list of a person's fears should throw considerable light upon what he considers valuable.

We have, in the two preceding chapters, surveyed examples of ways in which persons conceive themselves. If all the parts of "self as physical," such as the parts of one's body, one's progeny and ancestors, one's clothes, tools and land, one's earth, solar system and galaxy, and one's brain, emotions and imagination, are values, then one's desire for security includes concern for all of these kinds of values. If all the parts of "self as social," such as membership in family, citizenship, professional and marital groups, and one's social roles and ratings as an officer, are values, then one's desire for security pertains to these also. Although we have yet to explore other important aspects of self in the following chapters, such as "self as value," "self as organic," "self as the source and end of social ethics," "self as cosmic" and "self as aesthetic," we may here generalize that the "desire for security" encompasses all such values.

Regardless of how complex or simple your self turns out, after examination, to be, you aim to secure, i.e., first to achieve, attain, acquire or realize its values and then to save, protect, conserve or preserve its values, as much as possible. If you feel unsure, you seek assurance that you can attain and maintain those values. So the desire for security then shapes itself partly into a "quest for certainty." Some kinds of aspects of your values may have to be secured by yourself alone. But many others can be secured only by, and still others more efficiently by, social cooperation. We propose, in the present section, to illustrate how, in those areas where one's values can be secured more efficiently through social cooperation, the principle of reciprocity may be used to advantage.

One kind of example will have to suffice. We might have chosen examples regarding health, physical or mental, such as those pertaining to contagious diseases, or regarding enemies, human or animal, which may threaten to attack us bodily, or regarding spiritual security from harm by "the flesh," "the Devil," or "God," or regarding physical catastrophe, such as earthquakes, floods or explosions. Somewhat arbitrarily, we choose a few illustrations relative to wealth. How can I best get and keep enough wealth, expressed in terms of money income and property ownership, to keep me alive and happy?

1. Although a few hermits and isolated nomads or farmers may be able to survive independently of others, most of us find our own welfare intricately, even when not intimately, bound up with that of others. Those who live in isolation can continue to do so only if others continue to leave them alone. A nomadic shepherd must constantly fear raiding robbers who may succeed more easily if they first kill him while he is asleep.

A merely cursory study of the long history of political and economic evolution should convince us, not only of the fact that, but also of the varieties of ways in which, people depend upon each other for survival and welfare. Current kinds of interdependence have become so complex that we cannot begin to imagine their intricacies without some introduction to the omnipervasiveness of factors dealt with by the social, economic and political sciences. Consequently, if you seek what is best for yourself and cannot do so wisely until you first comprehend your social, economic and political nature, then you owe it to yourself to put forth some effort to investigate those essentials of your nature which these sciences endeavor to explain. Increasingly, personal incomes depend upon the availability of employment in industrialized cities which can exist and prosper only if a relatively stable and powerful government can maintain "law and order" (including national or world-wide security, police protection, and workable and enforced legal and court systems which insure opportunity for, and protection of, ownership of property or other rights essential to economic welfare).

One can become an employee only through being employed by others, or an employer only by employing others. One can sell only if others buy and buy only if others sell. One is able to have ownership rights only if others agree to, or are forced to, respect such rights.

2. In order to satisfy your interest in security through groups, you must do or be what is needed for participation in such groups. You will be employed or maintain employment only if you have both the skill and willingness needed to do the job. You can be a successful employer only if you treat your employees fairly. You can expect to be trusted in business transactions only if you have earned the confidence of others by demonstrating habits of trustworthiness. You can hardly expect your property to be safe from theft by others if you yourself have become a thief.

3. We naturally desire to be rid of feelings of fear and insecurity. Or, conversely, our desire for security persists or intensifies itself as a desire for more security. Not only is this principle true in general, but as you expand yourself through identifying yourself with additional economic assets, you desire security for these additions also. The more you have, the more you have to lose. So, the more you own, the more fears of insecurity you tend to have and, consequently, the greater your desire for security. An employee desires a permanent job. An employer needs trustworthy, both skillful and responsible, employees. A banker wants a more rock-solid reputation and a trader hopes for sounder credit. An

owner desires stronger fences or walls or locks or safes, or more effective guns, police or armies, or more reliable friends. Whenever we become aware of additional ways in which we can become secure, we tend to wish for such greater security. We almost instinctively respond when an advertising person appeals to our fears: "Don't be half-safe."

4. The desire for security also tends to become excessive. When you serve an employer whose business depends upon an uncertain market, you may want him to guarantee your job even when he has no market. If you employ a skilled person and then expect him to exhibit more skills in protecting your business than he has, you desire more than you are going to get. When you overdraw your bank account or fail to honor debt obligations and still expect to be regarded as a sound credit risk, you want more than you deserve. If you lock your valuables, as for example in a hotel room to which others may have keys, you may be expecting more than reasonable security. All life, and all ownership, involves some risk; so desire for freedom from all insecurity is more than anyone has a right to expect.

5. Excessive desire for security tends to endanger security. For when others provide as much security as they can, or as seems suited to the risk involved, then any expression of doubt by you regarding their trustworthiness in making such provision may give rise to doubts in them. Security cannot be just a matter of locks or walls, for those who constructed them can also destroy them; security is basically a matter of personal and social integrity. Unwarranted distrust of a person's integrity gives that person less reason for maintaining that integrity. If, when a person has done all that can properly be expected of him, you still feel insecure relative to him, he becomes afraid that he cannot please you. Your fear of him creates in him a fear of you. Hence your effort to obtain more security than you have coming tends to reduce some of the security which you already have.

6. The principle of reciprocity works regarding security also. We tend to trust and support those who trust and support us, and to distrust and not support those who distrust and do not support us. The principle works negatively within business, political and military groups as well as between competitors, enemies and opposing armies. When an employer discovers that an employee has been careless with his property, he is not thereby motivated to assure permanent employment. An employee who fears imminent dismissal can hardly be expected to show as much interest in his employer's welfare as one who stands to profit from his employer's long-range security. When someone cheats you in trading, you will not

trust him with further business. If someone has disregarded your property rights, you will tend to be less concerned when his property rights become jeopardized.

But the principle works positively perhaps more significantly than negatively. We may be unaware of such significance since we tend to accept unquestioningly those areas where our security seems unchallenged and to focus attention upon those areas in which we have fears. But the areas in which we automatically trust each other are so vast that they are almost beyond our comprehension. Consider an analogy. Someone has said, "I was without shoes, and complained, until I met a man without feet." Most of us not only own shoes but shoes which do not even pinch. Consequently our attention is focused upon our fear that the shine on our shoes may suffer from a streak of dust. When the weather or way becomes more dusty, we may become terribly wrought up about our insecurity from dust, all the time forgetting our unquestioned trust in our shoes, and our feet, and the fact that we could live even without feet. So with our security generally. We have so much of it that we can hardly imagine, except perhaps in our nightmares, what is meant by being afraid. A visit to foreign slums could provide a more wholesome insight into the huge measures of security which we enjoy. When someone whom we distrust nevertheless knowingly and genuinely trusts us, we tend to feel ashamed of our own attitudes. Although prudent limits exist relative to whom and how much one should trust, prudent limits exist also regarding whom and how much we should distrust.

7. Initiative brings rewards. When our trust of others is obvious to them they tend to reciprocate. For, if they do not reciprocate with trust, but express distrust, then we tend to retaliate against their distrust by our distrust. The value of positive initiative in trusting others was stated long ago (Sixth Century B.C.) by Lao Tzu: "He who bares his flesh will appear to have no need for carrying weapons. He who does not flourish weapons, appears to have nothing to defend. He who does not prepare to defend himself appears to have no enemies. No one will attack a person unless he appears to be an enemy, for to attack one who is not an enemy is to lose a friend." (Tao Teh King by Lao Tzu, A.J. Bahm, ed., p. 100, Frederick Ungar publishing Co., N.Y., 1958.)

8. The security you provide for others must be genuine; otherwise the most that the principle of reciprocity can assure is ungenuine security. When you discover someone who "bares his flesh" nevertheless hiding a weapon, you fear him as doubly dangerous or respond to him with multiplied mistrust. False pretense deserves deep and abiding suspicion.

Your genuine trust of those who have proved themselves genuinely trustworthy (and genuine distrust of those who have proved themselves genuinely untrustworthy) is part of what is best for yourself in the long run and thus is something which you ought to want to achieve.

9. Security can never be perfect. Reciprocity of trust or suspicion can never be one hundred percent. Yet since we automatically become either trusted or distrusted in social situations, and thus automatically increase or decrease fear of us in others by our attitudes toward them, we have little choice but to evaluate as best we can how much trust each situation calls for. Certainly some kinds of efforts to attain security through groups bring much greater security than is possible by individual efforts merely. The main reason for popular support of effective government is to promote security. And, generally speaking, the greater the number of kinds of security for individuals which can be assured through political methods the better. So far as security is concerned, government becomes evil only at the point where it makes individuals less secure. The more complex the government, the greater the distance between the contributions of individuals, through voting or taxes, and the rewards they receive. Yet, so long as the general atmosphere of security is maintained so that one can enjoy, for example, the "Four Freedoms," in a way which he could not merely as an individual without the protection and provisions of such government, surely one will judge it to be worthwhile. Even despite the waste, graft and distributive injustice which may exist in complex agencies, the money one pays in income taxes, for example, is probably the most rewarding investment one makes with one's money, if one could but discern the magnitude and variety of general and largely unnoticed measures of security which it provides.

Turning from maintenance of security through government (and without mentioning any of the multitudes of types of social security thus provided or providable) to business, we may note some examples. Some employees serve their employers better than others for the same pay; yet whenever the employer is able to judge clearly, selective advances tend to go to those who do the most. Some employers pay less than others for the same amount of work. Workers will try to offer themselves first to those who pay more. One may, through deceit, make a first sale at a huge profit; but those who serve their customers with the smallest profit per item often find themselves rewarded with the largest volume of sales.

10. The power to achieve certain kinds of security through groups is at least partly, even very substantially, within your own control, for the extent to which you serve to promote the security of others, the more

these others become dependent upon you for that security; and the more others tend to become aware of their dependence upon you for their security, the more interested they become in making you secure also.

If, as seems highly probable, the ten principles reiterated in this chapter together constitute a generally reliable basis for pursuing one's interests through social interaction, one who seeks what is best for oneself in the long run ought to make the best use one can of them. Awareness of them reveals additional evidence to the extent to which each self is essentially social and of the importance of social factors in "individual ethics."

Chapter VI

SELF AS VALUE

Is a self good? The answer to this question is at once both obvious and dubious. An affirmative reply seems so obviously presupposed, subconsciously at least, in all our thinking and acting that we can only be annoyed with the folly of asking it. The very way in which we express ourselves through every act reveals an implicit faith in our own values. Yet, once the question has been raised and an explicit answer attempted, it soon becomes surrounded by a plethora of doubts. Without suggesting any standard way in which such doubts arise, we will indicate some of the kinds of doubts that may arise.

One can recall that he has judged others to be bad, that others have judged him to be bad and that he has condemned himself, on may occasions. So one is aware of himself as evil also. One can recall explanations of the nature of evil in human beings. Every culture has them. Living in Western Civilization, which has been dominated largely by Christian traditions, a person may remember the doctrine of "original sin" and one of its various interpretations by Christian philosophers. If a person yields to an impulse to treat the opposites, good and bad, as contradictories, he may be led momentarily to think of himself as completely evil ("total depravity") or, like a Christian Scientist, of evil as illusory and nonexistent. But more probably he will try to reconcile the existence within himself of both good and evil, either by having two independent parts ("spirit" and "flesh"), one good and the other evil, which oppose and compete with each other, or by accepting some intermingling mixture of good and evil tendencies, traits or aspects, as natural.

Evidence that you presuppose your own goodness may be noted in the response you feel you must give to the question: Does it make any difference to you whether you live or die, exist or not? If it makes no difference, then you should remain indifferent to any threat endangering your life. You should have no fear of any sort, for fear involves faith in the existence of some good which is being jeopardized. The very fact that you think and act, automatically and spontaneously, as if it does make a significant difference whether you live or die, implies your presupposing that your existence is worthwhile. Your interest in acting in such a way as to produce the best results for yourself, now or in the long run, entails a presumption that those results can make a difference to yourself as a being whose existence is itself good. If the existence of yourself were not good (i.e., were neither good nor bad), then any concern about what is good or bad for yourself would be foolish or unreasonable.

Evidence that you presuppose your existence to be good may be observed not merely in unreflective, spontaneous actions, but also in consciously considered, deliberately concluded, judgments. Your estimation regarding which of several paths of action would be most dangerous implies an assumption of value inherent in yourself as the basis for your reasoning about such action. All your calculations regarding how much effort you should put forth in order to realize your desires, hopes, dreams, ideals, have your own goodness, and continued goodness ("welfare"), as their ultimate "reason." Even when your judgments seem to refer entirely to the welfare of others, your reasoning is based upon the analogy that they are like you; and thus your judgments regarding what is good in, and for, others reflect the presupposition that you are good.

If more details are needed, we may recall how subconscious belief in goodness is required by each of the four kinds of wishes (for esteem, love, adventure, and security) surveyed in the previous chapter. Your desire for esteem by others involves a desire that others not only consider you as good but as more good or most good. Regardless of whether you are "egocentric," believing yourself to be better than others think you are, or "objective," accepting the valuations by others for what they are, belief in your own goodness is automatically assumed.

Your desire for companionship and love, or for treatment of yourself as good just as you are regardless of various deficiencies, involves belief in your goodness as a necessary precondition. Your love of another, whereby you regard him as an end-in-himself, not only implies your judging him to be good but also by analogy that you, to the extent that you are like him, are also as good. When two people "fall in love," their reciprocation presupposes prior belief that both are good, for one can hardly expect another to regard him as good unless he _is_ good.

Your desire for adventure, illustrative of all desire, consists in your self expressing itself as such desire. Satisfaction of your desire is, in a very fundamental sense, satisfaction of your self. For enjoyment, whether feeling of pleasure, enthusiasm, satisfaction, or contentment, is not merely "good for" you, but constitutes a part of your self as good through existing as an enjoying being.

Your desire for security, perhaps most obviously, assumes that you should seek to save yourself from harm because the self which you thereby save is good. If it were not good, there would be no sense in putting forth so much effort to secure and conserve its goodness.

Furthermore, our sense of duty, obligation, or oughtness can have significance only if our "oughts" presuppose values at stake in our actions.

If oughtness consists in the power that a greater good has over a lesser good in compelling our choices, surely such oughtness can be ours only if the values at issue are ours or if our own value is involved. We need not review the long history of political, religious or philosophical literature and doctrines proclaiming the ultimacy of individual value. Although they detail in many profound and picturesque ways how each self is both actually and uniquely good, all of them rest ultimately upon personal insights, of the kind we have just reviewed, in which a self intuitively apprehends its own existence as good.

Ends and Means. Before proceeding further, we must discriminate clearly between "means" and "ends," or "means values" and "ends values," or, more technically, between "instrumental values" and "intrinsic values." Even though you know, whether intuitively or demonstrably, that you are good or bad, you may still not be clear about the ways or senses in which you are good and bad. Except for the distinction between "good" and "bad" itself, no more fundamental distinction exists in value theory than that between "means" and "ends." And, although the distinction seems simple, exploration of complexes of factors occurring in the interdependence of these two kinds of values in their actual setting causes great confusion in many minds. Since clarity regarding it is needed by anyone grasping adequately the nature of ethics and achieving full satisfaction regarding ones's own ethical life, effort put forth here should prove worthwhile.

"Means" and "ends" are correlative terms. Their meanings depend upon each other. Each must be defined in terms of the other. A "means" is always a "means-to-an-end" whereas an "end" is always a product of the means to it. However, as far as they differ, an "end" is best thought of as an "end-in-itself" or as something complete in itself, without requiring anything further to complete it. For example, when you desire to enjoy your favorite food, the pleasure to be experienced while eating it is the end or goal at which you aim. In order to achieve this end, all of the things, efforts and activities needed to produce and prepare the food and convey it to your mouth constitute parts of the means to this end. The experience of enjoyment, the end sought, depends for its achievement upon all of the means required to produce it. So, on the one hand, an end results from a process and cannot exist without that process. But, on the other hand, you seek the enjoyment for its own sake regardless of whether it is a means to still other ends. You seek it and experience it as an end-in-itself. It does not require any other end in order to be worthwhile. Now, of course, you may also seek to enjoy your favorite food so much that such enjoyment will produce a favorable mood for dealing with a difficult task. When this happens, the enjoyed experience serves both ns an end-in-itself and as a means to another end. But these two aspects of one experience are distinguishable, and the distinction must be kept clear, and kept in mind, if we are to understand the nature of value, the nature of self as value, and the nature of ethics.

The reader should already be acquainted with the meanings of the common terms, "means" and "ends." But you may be unfamiliar with their technical synonyms, "instrumental values" and "intrinsic values," which convenience dictates that we shall use. They have proved, and will prove, to be needed aids to clarity. The problems confronting us have many subtle facets clearly discriminable only with the sharpest of intellectual tools.

These terms, "instrumental value" and "intrinsic value," depend upon each other for their meaning, because the existing values to which they refer depend upon each other for their existence. Anything is or has instrumental value when it serves as an instrument for bringing about or maintaining an intrinsic value. Anything is or has intrinsic value when it is or has such value regardless of whether or not it also serves as an instrument. The fact that most, if not all, experienced things may appear to possess both intrinsic and instrumental value makes it difficult for us to discriminate between the instrumental and intrinsic aspects of the value of such things. But, fortunately, certain linguistic clues may be relied upon if we will only bother to take notice of them. If one thing is said to be "good for" another, its goodness is instrumental. Intrinsic value is not, merely as intrinsic, good for anything else; it is "just good" or "good in itself." So, whenever the word "for" appears, we can be sure that the value referred to is instrumental.

A hypothetical test of whether or not a value is regarded as intrinsic may be suggested: If nothing except this value existed in the whole universe, would it still be good? If we answer yes, then the value must be intrinsic, for intrinsic value has a nature such that, even if it did exist in isolation from everything else, it would still be good. Instrumental value, on the other hand, cannot exist apart from some other value which it helps to bring about, or maintain, and from which it derives its own value as instrumental.

This distinction between being "good for something else" and being "good in itself" is very simple. But difficulties occur when we consider how these two kinds or aspects of value exist in the same thing. We must now make clear how they can both exist in one thing, and be both different and yet interdependent and, furthermore, how they are interdependent in at least two different ways.

1. Anything having intrinsic value depends for its existence upon whatever is instrumental in causing or maintaining it. For example, an experience in which you enjoy eating your favorite food illustrates such a thing "having intrinsic value." The experience is "the thing" and the enjoyment is "an intrinsic value." All of the causes and conditions needed to produce this experience are instrumental to its existence, and thus may be said to have instrumental value. Since this experience with its intrinsic value could not have existed without these causes and conditions, it depends upon them. Thus, in this way, intrinsic value depends causally upon instrumental value.

2. Anything having instrumental value depends for such value upon its service in bringing about or maintaining something else. This "something else" must have intrinsic value or must serve, directly or indirectly, some still other thing having intrinsic value. For one thing can hardly be "good for" another if the other can have no good done for it. And a thing can have no good done for it if it is not, or cannot become, good, or better. If one thing does not serve another, the one does not have value as a servant to that other. If the other did not exist, or come into existence, it could not be served by the one, and thus the one could have no value as instrumental to it. Hence, in this way, instrumental value depends upon intrinsic value.

Recalling our illustration of enjoying eating your favorite food, if the food is not eaten or if the eating is not enjoyed, then, no matter how much effort has gone into preparing the food, it cannot be, and cannot have been, instrumental in producing a nonexistent enjoyment. The value of the food, and of the work involved in producing it, acquires its instrumental value actually from actual enjoyment. If no enjoyment (intrinsic value), then no instrumental value relative to it. Nothing can be actually instrumental to the existence of something which never exists.

Now another problem suggests itself. A dish of food, a cherry tart, for example, could have been instrumental to someone's enjoyment if it had been eaten, though it never was. Did the tart have instrumental value? Actually, no. Potentially, yes. Most things, including persons, have abilities which they never use, capacities which they never activate, powers which they never exercise, potentialities which they never realize. These are genuine in the sense that they could have been used if conditions had been different. They were potential instruments and they had potential instrumental value. But their potentiality was never realized, and their potential instrumental value never became actual instrumental value.

Although we must forego further discussion of the intricacies of problems inherent in the nature of "potential values and actual values (both instrumental and intrinsic)," attention is directed here to the fact that these distinctions pervade the problem of understanding the nature of value, and of your self as value, and of ethics generally. You are good. But further, you are both intrinsically good and instrumentally good. You are, or have intrinsic value; and you are, or have, instrumental value. In fact, you are, or have, many values, both intrinsic and instrumental. Just how this is so I have yet to demonstrate. But first let me add that some of your intrinsic value is actual, or present, while some of your intrinsic value (or values) is yet to come, if there is more of you yet to be, which is now potential. And some of your instrumental value has become actual, for you have already produced some good results for yourself and others. Some of your instrumental value is potential, for you are able to produce still more good for yourself and others. Some of this potential instrumental value will never be actualized, for you have more such ability than you will ever use. And some of your potential instrumental value will become actual instrumental value as you actually help yourself or others. Hence, not only are you good, but you are good in these several different ways.

Self as Instrumental Value. Illustrating first ways in which a self may be instrumentally good, we differentiate between ways in which you are good for yourself and good for others, though interdependence between yourself and others may diminish somewhat the significance of the distinction.

You are good for yourself, or a means to your own ends, when you do anything needed to help you become, or to continue to be, healthy and happy. A long and enjoyable life needs proper food, exercise, fresh air, rest and sleep, and freedom from disease and danger. Fortunately we have been endowed with physical natures which so function as to take care of themselves, despite considerable misuse. If your body is part of you, then whatever your body does to continue your own well being illustrates how you are instrumentally valuable to your own self. How you answer the question of the size and extent of your self (see Chapter III, "Self as physical") will make a difference in how much, or in how many ways, you can be instrumentally valuable to yourself. But in addition to those ways in which one's physical nature serves itself automatically, any ideas which you have about yourself and any decisions and intentional actions which result in improving your lot exemplify yourself as instrumentally valuable. Your self-instrumentality may be relatively direct, as in deciding to eat when hungry or not to overeat when overweight, or it may be indirect, through effects you have on others who in turn influence you. Although the size and extent of your self as social may vary with many factors (see Chapters IV and V), your ability to influence others for good or ill constitutes potentiality for being instrumentally good or bad for your self.

You are good for others when you do something that helps them become or continue to be healthy and happy. You serve as a means to their ends. The more you help others the greater your instrumental value. Sometimes you benefit others automatically or without intending to do so, as when another enjoys your natural beauty or when your body protects him from a flying projectile. Sometimes you aid others intentionally, either for their own sakes alone or because your services to them may produce good results for you also. You may direct your efforts toward a specific person, a group, or even to mankind generally. You may serve those now living or those yet to come into existence, soon or in the distant future. Just as we today still benefit from the cultural achievements of our remote ancestors who invented workable mores, languages, ideas and tools, so you too may be instrumentally valuable not only temporarily but enduringly through culture. Your aid may be momentary and immediate, as when lifting someone from the floor, or indirect and prolonged, through providing them with instruments or teaching them skills to be used later when you are absent.

You are _actually_ good for self and others whenever you are actually using your abilities to produce results which will be enjoyed (by self or others) or whenever the results of your actions are actually being enjoyed (by self or others) even though you are no longer actively engaged in producing them. Hence, not only does your having more abilities constitute you a greater potential instrumental value, but the more you are actually using them or the more results which are actually being enjoyed, the greater your actual instrumental value. Anything that increases or decreases using your abilities or the enjoying of their effects increases or decreases your actual instrumental value.

You are _potentially_ good for self and others to the extent that you have abilities which can or could be used if all the other necessary conditions for actualization cooperate. For convenience, we shall distinguish between two kinds of abilities and arbitrarily name those which function as internal to you as your "capacities" and those functioning as external to you as your "opportunities." Since you are <u>able</u> to do only what you have a capacity to do and you are <u>able</u> to do only what you have opportunity to do, your capacities and opportunities together constitute your "abilities."

To the extent that your <u>capacities</u> are limited, your potential instrumental values are limited. Your biological and physiological limitations, for example, make it impossible for you to become a dog, live nine hundred years, fly like a bird or crawl through a keyhole. But to the extent that your capacities can be increased by your becoming able to do things which you cannot now do, you have a capacity to increase your capacity, or a potentiality for increasing your potentiality, and thus for improving yourself as potential instrumental value.

To the extent that your <u>opportunities</u> are limited, your potential instrumental value is limited. You cannot help yourself or others unless you have sufficient time, place and needed instruments, and unless you or others have a capacity for being influenced by and aided by you. A mother has no opportunity to serve a second child which she does not have, quite apart from her capacity to bear another child. You cannot help people who never exist or yourself after you are dead. Unchangeable limitations upon your opportunities constitute fixed limits to your potential instrumental value. But to the extent that your opportunities can be increased, you may have opportunity for increasing your opportunities, or potentiality for increasing your potentialities of this sort also, and thus for improving your potential instrumental value.

However, since neither capacity without opportunity nor opportunity without capacity constitutes genuine ability, to the extent to which these are not fitted to each other, they function as limitations upon your genuine potential instrumental value. If you happen to be skilled in the use of any instrument, a violin, for example, then, despite your capacity to perform, you still remain unable to do so without a violin. And if you happen to own any instrument, such as a violin, then, in spite of your opportunity to perform, you still remain unable to do so for lack of skill. Thus, although increase in capacity to use opportunity increases your potential instrumental value, increase in the fitness of capacity and opportunity to each other increases your ability in a way which the other increases do not. Of course, loss of potential instrumental value may also occur. A skilled violinist who loses his violin becomes unable to play, and a violin owner who loses his skill becomes unable to play, though one who loses both loses two kinds of potentiality and thus becomes doubly unable to play.

If your capacity can be increased, do you also have a capacity for increasing your capacity? If you develop a capacity for playing a violin, does such capacity provide you capacity for learning to play dance music, dinner music, symphonic music or, further, particular compositions by this or that composer? If your opportunity can be increased, do you also have opportunity for increasing your opportunities? If your opportunity can be increased through acquiring a machine useful for building other useful machines, does this not constitute an opportunity for increasing your opportunities? If increase in your capacity for increasing your capacities can be more closely fitted to increase in your opportunity for increasing your opportunities, what implications seem to be involved for your decisions? If you have ability to improve your ability, or potentiality (instrumental value) for increasing your potentialities (instrumental values), what bearing does awareness of this fact have upon your self-obligation, conscientiousness, intelligence, and upon ethics generally? As far as increase or decrease in potential instrumental value is concerned, what is it that you most want to do?

Self as Intrinsic Value. You are good in yourself as well as good for yourself. You can hardly be good for yourself unless somewhere, somehow, you are also good in yourself. Means to ends cannot exist without ends. We must now face the problem of clarifying the ways in which you are, or can be, an intrinsic value, and how you can know that you are an end-in-yourself. Without arguing or appealing to authority, we shall try to guide your thoughts into such a perspective as will reveal as obvious how you intuitively apprehend your own existence as good in itself. This problem presents us with a difficulty typical of basic philosophical problems, and regarding it we may be tempted to say what Augustine said about time: "If no one asks me, I know; if I wish to explain it to one who asks, I know not." But also, as with most typical philosophical problems, we can achieve a measure of success in providing ourselves with a satisfactory answer.

For convenience we shall at first limit consideration to the following four theories of the nature of intrinsic value, namely, that intrinsic value consists in (1) pleasant feeling, (2) satisfaction of desire, (3) enthusiasm and (4) contentment.

1. Pleasant Feeling. As everyone knows, immediately or intuitively, pleasant feeling is enjoyable. Pleasant feeling needs no description, no

explanation, no argumentation to convince us of its intrinsic value. And no amount of argument can refute the self-evident enjoyment of an enjoyed experience -- of the intrinsic value of a pleasant feeling while we are having it. At some other time we might be persuaded that a particular experience was not as pleasant as we had thought it to be, but during a pleasant experience its intrinsic value is self-evident, no matter what else it may also involve or lead to. Its opposite, pain or unpleasant feeling, likewise is experienced self-evidently as intrinsic evil.

The fact that pleasant feeling is experienced as good in itself serves as the basis for a theory stating this fact and proceeding to draw certain inferences from it. Since the time of ancient Greece, the theory has been called "Hedonism" (after the Greek Hedone, meaning "pleasure"). Very simply, Hedonism asserts that intrinsic goodness consists in pleasant feeling and intrinsic evil consists in pain or unpleasant feelings. Then it draws an inference: Since we naturally want what is good, we naturally seek pleasure. Human beings are, by nature, pleasure seekers.

We have now stated a theory of human motivation. This theory, although almost as obvious as the theory that pleasant feeling is good in itself, typically generates certain problems. If we seek pleasure, then pleasure seems to be the object which we seek. But, critics point out, we do not in fact aim at pleasant feelings as such but rather at activities that yield them as accompaniments. If we observe our own motives, when we set out to "have fun," for example, we can notice that we do not think of the particular feelings which we expect to experience but rather imagine some kind of activity. We plan to sing or dance or eat or play. These are activities, not feelings. Pleasant feelings may occur during such activities. We hope and expect that they will. But the object which we have in mind as the goal at which we aim is not pleasant feeling as such but some kind of activity that may yield it.

In response to the criticism that we do not naturally look for pleasure directly, defenders of Hedonism admit that we must recognize "the Hedonistic Paradox," as it is called, namely, that we obtain pleasure not by aiming at it directly, but by doing things that yield it as an accompaniment. The wise Hedonist accepts this paradox as inherent in human nature. Such admission slightly modifies, but does not basically change, his theory. Persons still remain pleasure seekers, but persons who search for pleasure, because they must, indirectly, rather than directly.

Hedonism became more than a theory of values, of what is good, and more than a theory of human motivation, of what people do in fact seek. It developed also into an ethical theory, a theory of what one ought to do or try to do. Since pleasure is good, and since we ought to aim at what is good, we ought to seek pleasure and to avoid pain and, where alternatives exist, we ought always aim at more pleasure, or, indeed, the most pleasure. As an ethical theory, Hedonism still remains fairly simple. However, complexities appear as soon as certain questions are asked.

Which is more pleasant, a more intense or a more enduring pleasure? The problem of judging what one ought to do offers little difficulty where pleasures remain the same in quality or intensity. If faced with the alternative such that, during a given period, such as ten minutes, one in which you will enjoy a pleasure for two minutes and one in which you will enjoy the same pleasure for four minutes, you ought to choose the latter. This is simple "moral arithmetic," as Jeremy Bentham (1748-1832) called it. You should take two rather than only one of your favorite chocolates, if no other consequences are involved. but, of course, if you have to pay for the chocolates, then you must balance the amounts of pain required to earn money to buy the chocolates against the pleasures produced by eating them. If some unit of pain of work is required to earn the price of one chocolate whose unit of pleasure equally balances it, then no significant difference exists whether you eat the chocolates or not. Of course, units of pain and pleasure do not correspond exactly with units or instruments such as chocolates, for the last minutes of a fatiguing day's work may be experienced as much more painful than the first, and the twentieth chocolate eaten in a series may be less pleasant than the first, or even very unpleasant due to fatigued taste buds. So it may be that you ought to eat one chocolate, because the pleasure produced is greater than the pain required for earning, but ought not to eat the second or twentieth because the pleasure enjoyed is less than the pain suffered in earning it. All this is still simple "moral arithmetic."

When we recognize that pleasures and pains differ not only in number, quantity or duration, but also occur in units of unequal intensity, we face the question of how to evaluate these intensities. Some experiences excite, enliven, elate us much more than others. "More pleasant" means "more thrilling." According to Ethical Hedonism, one ought to aim at the most delightful, not just the most enduring, pleasures. If a more intense pleasure has greater intrinsic goodness than a subdued pleasure, then, it appears, the most intense pleasures are best. One ought, then, seek thrill after thrill after thrill, whenever one has opportunity to do so. However, if we must pay for excitement, either in more money or in greater fatigue, the need for balancing intense pleasures against intense or enduring pains must be reckoned with. Consequently prudence dictates restraint upon abandonment to excitement in all but those whose youthful vigor seems to provide superabundant vitality. A psychological law of diminishing returns operates regarding thrills as well as more modest pleasures. One tires of tasting his favorite candy as well as the proverbial all-day sucker. One becomes bored with night clubs as well as with long novels. Stimulating music fatigues more quickly than a quiet serenade. So, even though one ought to seek the most intense pleasures, he should do so with prudence relative to the total amount of pleasure attainable, balancing pains against pleasures and intensities against durations.

Jeremy Bentham (Principles of Morals and Legislation, p. 29, Clarendon Press, Oxford, 1907) not only stated a "calculus of pleasures" but proposed six principles for use in it. "To a person considered by himself, the value of a pleasure or a pain considered by itself, will be greater or less according to the four following circumstances: (1) Its intensity. (2) Its duration. (3) Its certainty or uncertainty. (4) Its propinquity or remoteness." To these he added two more: "(5) Its fecundity" or chance of being followed by other pleasures, and "(6) Its purity" or prospects of not being followed by pains. The wise pleasure seeker calculates his returns not only now but in the long run. Both the "bird in the hand is worth two in the bush" and the "save some for a rainy day" principles enter into his computations. Uncertainties regarding actual prospects complicate decisions. Hence what at first seemed simple "moral arithmetic" turns into an uncomfortably intricate calculus whose pain of calculating motivates many to abandon it. Yet, whether consciously or subconsciously, we automatically "guesstimate" the pleasure-pain prospects of proposed actions.

Another important problem facing Hedonism as an ethical theory pertains to "quality" as distinguished from both the intensity and duration of pleasures. After upholders of "high ideals" criticized Hedonism as "the pig philosophy" because sensuous pleasures, enjoyable by pigs and persons alike, were equated in intrinsic goodness to "pleasures of the intellect," efforts were made to recognize and advocate that "higher quality" pleasures were better (i.e., "more pleasant") than "lower quality" pleasures even though the latter might be more intense or enduring. John Stuart Mill (1806-1873) defended Bentham's Hedonism by revising it to include "higher quality pleasures" in one's calculations. Poetry is better than pushpin (or chess than tic-tac-toe). It is better to be a Socrates dissatisfied than a fool or pig satisfied. The pleasure in knowing that one comprehends subtle nuances of intricate symphonies, the pleasures experienced when correctly and facilely deducing complicated mathematical implications, and the pleasures taken in enjoying self-respect accompanying a persisting ability to resist all temptations to be dishonest, are indeed pleasures. And their "quality" is higher than that experienced in tasting sugar. Mill asserted that "It may be questioned whether anyone who has remained equally susceptible to both classes of pleasures, ever knowingly and calmly preferred the lower." (Utilitarianism, Chapter II.) Although people differ in their capacities for experiencing higher-quality pleasures, we naturally take quality into account whenever we become aware of its presence. The "amount" of pleasure we ought to seek entails not only number, duration and intensity but also quality among the variables inherent in our "calculus of pleasures."

Thus far we have examined only Egoistic Hedonism, the view that one should aim at the most pleasure -- for himself. In response to critics who asserted that Hedonism is "a selfish theory," some Hedonists have affirmed Altruistic Hedonism, the view that one ought to aim at bringing about the most pleasure for others, even the most others. Discussion of "Utilitarianism," concern for "the greatest good (pleasure) for the greatest number" as social policy must await Part II, chs. XX ff, especially Chapter XXIII and as a religious policy must await Part III, ch. XXXIV. Here we may note that whether or not the charge is true will depend upon how self is conceived. If self and its intrinsic value are independent of other selves and their intrinsic values, then "Egoistic Hedonism" does not provide a sufficient basis for establishing "Altruistic Hedonism." Altruistic Hedonism must depend upon some additional premise, such as a theory of innate moral sentiments which itself needs further foundation, or as a theology in which God is pictured as demanding that his children treat each other with love or justice, or as a prudent "Compact" in which persons, suffering from mutual self-destruction in a "state of Nature" (Hobbes, Leviathan) agree to submit to a political government whose power to punish supposedly assures prevention of failure to permit minimums of personal pleasure-achievement. Despite ingenious efforts, most arguments for Altruistic Hedonism have remained weak. We propose to supplement or modify these arguments, in the following chapters, by examining implications of conceptions surveyed in the chapters on "Self and Social" and "Self-Interest" for further self-interest in support of Altruistic Hedonism. If and to the extent that a self expands its conception of itself, and of that in which it takes pleasure (including "higher-quality pleasures"), Altruistic Hedonism may be found to be more fully justified by an expanded Egoistic Hedonism.

But we have now gone far beyond the primary purpose of the present chapter which is to observe how far, and in what ways, a self is or has intrinsic value. It has seemed wise to indicate here that "Hedonism" is much more than a theory of value and to provide an anticipatory sketch of ways in which its supporters have attempted to promote it as a completely adequate theory of values and ethics. We contend that pleasant feeling is, in some sense, a necessary ingredient in intrinsic good, and that, therefore, Hedonistic theories offer considerable insight into the nature of value and obligation. But we also contend that Hedonism is insufficient, both as a theory of values and as a theory of obligation, and that, therefore, it needs supplementation.

The positive contribution of Hedonism as a theory of values emphasized here is that pleasant feeling as intrinsic good exists and that you as a being enjoying pleasant feeling embody such intrinsic good in you. You are good, intrinsically good, when and to the extent that such intrinsically good pleasant feelings exist in you or as part of you. The more such pleasant feelings that you embody, the more intrinsic value of this sort you have or are. Since both instrumental value and obligation depend upon intrinsic value, the existence of, and the possibility of increasing or decreasing, such pleasant feelings constitute a foundation upon which ethics rests.

2. *Satisfaction of Desire.* Everyone knows, immediately or intuitively, what it is to experience desire, satisfaction and frustration. In fact, when awake, we almost constantly experience desiring and satisfaction or frustration in mild, even if not intense, forms. In moments of quiescence, tranquility, rest, or of drowsiness and approaching sleep, we may seem relatively free from desire. But as long as we are aroused, alert, energetic or anxious, desire and its consequences pervade our consciousness, even though we may be aware only of the objects of our interest and not of our interests in such objects.

Desires range from minute and temporary, even subconscious, interests to intense, overwhelming and enduring demands, and from vague longings, experienced merely as restlessness, to clearly formulated schemes of attainment, often stated in written codes or contracts of self-commitment. You need merely observe, in yourself or others, how often and in how many ways expressions of desire occur: "I wish," "I want," "I shall," "I will," "I need," "I insist," "I propose." Yearning, longing, hoping, dreaming, hankering, craving, hungering, thirsting, coveting, aspiring, aiming, intending -- all express desire. Appetite, greed, passion, zeal, devotion, eagerness, avidity, ardor, impatience and anxiety -- all describe desirousness. Life and literature are replete with more complex modes of revealing desire, to say nothing of unverbalized groans, postures and gestures portraying our feelings of interest and urgency. Desire is almost omnipresent, and unless we have tricked ourselves into believing that we have none, we can observe our own experiences of desiring if we take the time to do so.

Once desire has been aroused, surely it must be quieted in one of three ways. Either it is satisfied, frustrated or forgotten. Fortunately, or perhaps unfortunately, nature provides us with a superabundance of desires -- so many, in fact, that some must subside of themselves if we are to be saved from constant inflammation beyond our energy to endure. Most of our desires, I suspect, are forgotten.

But many are frustrated. And frustration, like desire itself, may range from mild and momentary to unbearable and unending. Some frustrations occur in such a subdued and peripheral fashion, in experiences where attention focuses upon some object of overwhelming interest, as to appear as a negligible irritation. A baseball player ignores the annoyance of binding clothes while making a home run before a cheering crowd. But other frustrations, such as that experienced in failure to strike at an easy ball ending a game and a season in defeat, may grip one's whole being with exasperation. Frustrations vary also from vague foreboding fears to specific rebuffs, as when one learns that a badly-needed library book has just been withdrawn by another. Some frustrations persist for a moment, as when one's desire for a last puff from a cigarette which then accidentally slips into the water becomes replaced by desire for and satisfaction in a freshly-lighted one.

Frustration occurs in experience as intrinsic evil, intuitively apprehended as such. Feelings of satisfaction exist in experience as intrinsic good, immediately grasped as such. Whenever anyone experiences feelings of satisfaction or frustration, he thereby enjoys good in itself or suffers evil in itself. Whether or not you doubt what appears as thus given, as thus obvious and self-evident, you can find a long tradition of theories stating, clearly or by implication, not only that satisfaction and frustration exemplify intrinsic good and evil but also that intrinsic good consists exclusively in satisfaction and intrinsic evil entirely in frustration. These theories, sometimes grouped together under the general name, "Voluntarism," because they all interpret "will" or "desire," here considered synonyms, as the source of good and evil, have proliferated into many varieties.

Western civilization originated partly in early Hebrew ideals of a god (Yahweh) who wants what is good for his people who in turn will serve him because, implicitly, such reciprocal efforts bring increased satisfaction for both God and man. For Jesus: "God is love" (love which involves desire); "blessed (i.e., having prospects of enjoying intrinsic good) are those who love others" and they would be loved (thereby satisfying their desires to be loved as they desire to have their own desires satisfied by others); and "care not (desire not) for the morrow," since sufficient unto each day is the (intrinsic) good and evil thereof; "the Kingdom of Heaven (a condition in which satisfaction is enjoyed) is at hand," if one will but have faith (or the "will to believe") that it is. Christianity and Islam inherited and developed the ideal that God (deus or Allah) wants what is good and has power to attain what he wants for both persons and himself. A person can be saved from "sin" (willing to go against the will of God) only by surrendering will completely to the will of God. Only by willing (desiring) what is going to happen anyway (for whatever an all-powerful God wills is going to happen anyway), which is necessarily good if God wills what is good (which he must as omnibenevolent), can one attain complete satisfaction of desire ("heaven"). "Hell," whether a place or a state, consists in perpetual torment, i.e., having desires that can never be fulfilled or desires for being in some other place, time or condition.

Western philosophies have disagreed about whether desire is the cause or effect of good. Aristotle (348-322 B.C.), and later Thomas Aquinas (1225 or 1227-1274), defined good as "that at which all things aim." (The Works of Aristotle Translated Into English Vol. 9, 1094a, Nichomachean Ethics, I, Ed. W.D. Ross, Clarendon Press, Oxford, 1925.) We like things because they are good, and it is their goodness which causes us to desire them. Ralph Barton Perry defined good as "any object of any interest." (General Theory of Value, Chapter V., Longman's Green, New York, 1926.) Things are good because we like them, and it is our being interested in them which causes them to be good. Henri Bergson, Sigmund Freud, William James and John Dewey all relate value to desire, if in different ways. The history of Western philosophies of value has produced an interesting profusion of intricate distinctions and technical vocabularies which must be omitted here. Enough has been said to indicate that "satisfaction of desire" as the locus of intrinsic value has played a central role, even if so often as a target for attack.

Turning to Asian philosophies, Hindu schools (such as Buddhism, Jainism, Yoga, and Vedanta) typically conceive as the source of evil or at least of more evil than good. Frustration, an obvious evil, has its source in desire; therefore, "No desire, no frustration." The way to a free life that is idealized as a perfectly desireless state which, because completely freed from frustration, is called anda (bliss). And the ideal way of life progressively eliminates desire as much as possible by the study and practice of "yoga." (See my Yoga: Union with the Ultimate, Patanjali's Yoga Sutras, Fredrick Unger, New York, 1961.) A more modest and , it seems to me, wiser evaluation of life's situation portrays the evils of frustration arising not from all desire but only from desirousness or excessive desire. Gotama, the Buddha, announced a principle that should be intuitively clear to everyone: "Desire for what will not be attained ends in frustration; therefore, to avoid frustration, avoid desiring what will not be attained." (See my Philosophy of the Buddha, p. 15, Harper and Brothers, New York, 1958.) Gotama applied this principle, to the amazement of his hearers, to all phases of life and became, historically, probably the most influential single teacher of practical wisdom, rivalling, if not surpassing, in popularity, Jesus who lived about five centuries later. Despite historical proliferation of varieties of Buddhist doctrine (e.g., Theravada, Madhyamika, Shin and Zen), all have kept desirousness central to the problem of evil.

Chinese philosophies (Taoism and Confucianism) regard desire and its satisfaction as perfectly natural and good. But excessive desire, especially desire to meddle unnecessarily in the lives of others, naturally begets trouble. "Those too eager for activity soon become fatigued." "Going to extremes is never best." "Whoever gives up his desire to improve upon nature will find nature satisfying all his needs." (See my Tao Teh King by Lao Tzu, pp. 87, 89, 90, Fredric Unger, New York, 1958.)

DeWitt H. Parker (1885-1949), one of the ablest recent defenders of Voluntarism, says that "Every value depends upon the existence of something variously called appetite, wish, desire, interest...." "Desire is the only basis of value; value itself does not exist until desire is being satisfied." "We could not define value...as 'any object of interest,' but...as the satisfaction of any interest in any object. " "As satisfaction of desire is the only good, so frustration of desire is the only evil." (Human Values, pp. 22, 24, 21, 28, Harper and Brothers, New York, 1931.) "When value is defined as the objective of desire, we should mean the satisfying activity that realizes the goal idea or objective." (The Philosophy of Value, p. 10, University of Michigan Press, Ann Arbor, 1957.) Parker replies to typical criticisms of Voluntarism as selfish by citing evidence for the natural necessity of a self desiring satisfactions by others (required in "love"); also to the criticism that desires are temporary and trivial by expounding his theory of a hierarchy of desires in which the more profound and enduring, because their satisfaction embodies greater intrinsic good, take precedence over the trivial and temporary. Thereby he provides us with a basis for ethics.

Again we must resist going beyond the primary purpose of the present chapter. Enough has been said in the foregoing sketch of historical samples, surely, to illustrate clearly the type of view holding that intrinsic good consists in satisfaction of desire. As a self, you have desires, or you are a desiring being. You have feelings of satisfaction within yourself. Insofar as intrinsic good consists in satisfaction of desire, your embodiment of such satisfaction in yourself thereby incorporates intrinsic good into your being. If you live a more satisfying life, then you have, or are, greater intrinsic good. We contend that satisfaction of desire does, in some sense, constitute intrinsic good and thus that Voluntaristic theories can provide considerable insight into the nature of value and obligation. Implications for ethics, which will be drawn out in following chapters, include a need for awareness that you ought, as a moral obligation, to seek to satisfy your desires -- your greatest, deepest, or most, desires -- and that this is a part, at least, of what you most want to do.

3. *Enthusiasm.* Desire is the source of good according to another theory also. We do not have to wait until the desire has been satisfied, or is being satisfied, to enjoy desiring. The experience of desiring itself is felt as good. It is desire itself which enlivens us, makes us forward-looking, gives us feelings of anticipation, hope and visions of a good to be achieved. Some desires were immensely and enduringly enjoyed even though they were eventually frustrated. "It is better to travel hopefully than to arrive." (Robert Louis Stevenson, El Dorado.) "It is better to have loved and lost than never to have loved at all."

No single term, except perhaps "desireousness," quite captures the full meaning of experiences in which we enjoy desiring itself as intrinsic good. Part of the problem is due to the fact that desires are of different kinds and each kind is referred to by its own cluster of peculiar terms. "Yearning," "longing," "hoping" illustrate milder forms. "Ardor," "avidity," "fervor," "urgency," "anxiety," "impatience" exemplify more intense forms. "Eagerness," "passion," "desireousness," "gusto," "zest," and "zeal" might all serve as general terms for this kind of intrinsic good, but we have chosen "enthusiasm." This was chosen because its ordinary meaning more clearly gives us a clue to what is central in this value-experience. But, as we use the term, it represents symbolically the whole range of meanings of enjoying desiring as an end-in-itself, including any enjoyment of anger or rage.

This range includes at least three varieties of distinctions: (1) The enjoyment of desiring may be prolonged or momentary. Prolonged desiring may be illustrated by the longing of a child for growing up, of a maiden for marriage, of a scholar for success, of an employee for retirement, or of any devotee for his cause. Such desiring may be enjoyed more when it is felt as overwhelming or all-consuming devotion. Momentary desires illustrate such enjoyment when they are impulsive, spontaneous, exciting, exhilarating, or violent. Since enjoyment will be greater when more desirings are experienced, not only frequent recurrence but rapid succession of intense thrills becomes idealized.

(3) Desiring may be viewed either as self battling against the world or as self expressive of the world. (a) Desiring is most easily intensified in anger, so when your are convinced that the world, or major forces in it, are against you, you find great delight in damning it and fighting against it. Bitterness, hatred, antagonism and vehemence all give an impassioned person a sense of power and enjoyed self-righteousness to the extent that they intensify emotions and strengthen tensions. Some people enjoy struggle and strife, whether alone against great odds ("My unconquerable soul") or with like-minded companions. When the striver feels he battles against some overwhelming evil, he easily develops and enjoys sympathy for "the underdog." When he masterfully preserves some elite virtue from unworthy rebels, self-righteously he stamps out the "vermin." Bitter animosity justifies brutality, and brutality reenforces passions for revenge. War creates heroes and heroism; a soldier thrills as he surges forward against the enemy. War makes men enjoy their virility. (b) Others feel themselves embodying cosmic vitality, either as semi-detached portions of an external superior will or as living embodiments of a pervasive general will particularizing itself through their particular will. This cosmic vitality may manifest itself as God, the State, the Race or as some superior virtuosity. Those who see God as primarily an Other Power, who partly inspires us with his holy spirit, experience their desiring as a hungering or thirsting after righteousness, as a piteous yearning for salvation of the whole world, or as an unquenchable devotion to an infinite will. Christian evangelists "get on fire for the Lord." Patriots thrill with the ideal that their nation is destined to be invincible. Racists live their view, aiming to perpetuate their super-race. Devotees

of virtuosity believe in perpetual triumph of their elite cause. Some see God as the vital impulse within, which constitutes our lives and desires and prospers through us as we become more alive, more desirous, more vigorous and more violent. Mystical identity of self with God whose will particularizes itself as our wills justifies our appreciation of our own impetuosity as an end in itself because it is divinity manifesting itself in us. Henri Bergson speaks of elan vital. Freud thinks of God as a Cosmic Libido becoming recurrently alive through our own love, even sexual, impulses. Sufi mystics enjoy their appreciative moods as expressions of the "will of Allah." Fascists regard themselves as deriving their being, their rights and their wills from the State; what the State wills, they will, and they enjoy experiencing their desires for state superiority as bits of embodiment of the National Spirit. Racists "think with the blood," feeling procreation of children as a sacred duty, and thrill when feeling within themselves the urge toward perpetual dominance of the super race. (See Frederick Nietzsche, Thus Spake Zarathustra.) Those who voice the virtuosity of poetry or song feel themselves inspired by genius; God would be dumb if he did not come to life through my own creative imagination; I make the world of value by my will, shape its richness and give it vibrancy through my own efforts.

(3) Desiring may be enjoyed in simple heartiness or through perpetual reentanglement in "the dialectics of the romantic soul." (a) A person makes life worthwhile by appreciating its present impetuosities, its "Oh-ings" and "Ah-ings," screams of delight, its chuckles and grins, its sighing and wishing, all inherent in a will to experience good in the present. Whole-hearted enjoyment of simple, naive optimism is captured in "Pippa Passes." Profounder and subtler enjoyment appears in the writings of Ralph Waldo Emerson ("Give me health and a day, and I will make the pomp of emperors ridiculous." Nature.) and the British Romantic poets. Persons desire the world to be good, and so it is good, and the good appears in, and is experienced in, the desiring -- even if a person objectifies his desires in images or projects his image as desirabilities in things, persons or activities. Romanticism, which is the chief philosophy advocating enthusiasm as the sole or primary locus or intrinsic good, entails a paradox. Like the Hedonistic paradox, wherein pleasure seekers find pleasure not by seeking pleasure directly but by seeking those activities which yield pleasure as an accompaniment, the Romanticistic paradox consists in enjoying desiring itself most when desires are objectified in the sense that one desires objects or objectives (satisfaction). To desire is to seek satisfaction and satisfaction must be

conceived in terms of goals or objectives to be achieved; but, paradoxically, the intrinsic good exists, not in or as the goal or objective, but in the desiring itself. The Voluntarist says "We like things because they are good; they satisfy our desires." The Romanticist says, "Things are good because we like them; our desiring them is what makes them good."

(b) Enjoyment of desiring as an end-in-itself is greater when the desire is more intense, urgent, and all-consuming. Easily satisfied desires cease with their satisfaction. Hence, satisfaction kills the joy of desiring. If satisfaction destroys desire, how can we prolong and intensify desires? By having them frustrated. Frustration is not an evil for Romanticism as it is for Voluntarism. Rather it is a good to be deliberately sought. Since frustration intensifies desire, one ought to seek frustrating predicaments. That is, one ought to have desires which cannot be satisfied. Or, if this is impossible, at least one should be daring, risk insecurity, seek uncertainty, affirm the absurd, demand the impossible, hate what is lovely and love what is hateful, deny what is true. That is, seek conflict which will jeopardize all possibilities for satisfaction: be mean to your friends, be ruthless with society's standards, be brutal of enemies and animals. Fortunately, most people, although somewhat Romantic in nature, can be only partially so. The Romantic temperament, present implicitly in all, has been suppressed and supervened upon by Hedonistic, Voluntaristic and Anandistic temperaments, also present, at least implicitly, in all.

But the spirit of extreme Romanticism is clear. Want what you cannot have so that your wanting will continue unabated. Romanticists yearn for infinity. They long for endless longing. But they also want intensity, which emerges most strongly in violent anxieties, in bitter hatreds, in insistent cravings, in all-out thrusts, in embarrassing frustrations. Both intensity and prolongation occur when we risk our greatest values: life and love. I do not believe that persons have a "death-instinct," but apologists for Romanticistic daring seem to think they thereby account for it naturalistically. Most violent Romanticists want others to be violent too. They want others to be frustrated also, not because they really hate, but because they love others; they want others to enjoy hatred, anger, fear and frustration, and thus to experience life's summum bonum. Hence one should induce others to risk their lives and their loves. If stolen love is more impetuous, then steal. If love for another's wife induces greater passion, then love her; and then if betraying her to her husband intensifies embarrassment and conflict, do so -- not because you hate her or her husband but because you want them also to enjoy the heightened vitality experienced through violent, profound, and intricate frustration. As more people become involved in trouble, emotions become more complicated and anxieties become compounded. If the animosity becomes unbearable, so much the better; one has reached a pinnacle of intensity. Weak spirits exhaust themselves quickly, but the strongest souls endure endless self-torture, joyfully.

Romantic enjoyment of frustration is dialectical in several ways. We mention two. The first we may classify as "psychological," the second "historical." (a) A romanticist wants not merely desire but intensity. But even as awareness without desire is boring, so, after a while, the presence of ordinary desiring is boring. Enthusiasm is experienced only in excitement. Since desire is intensified by frustration, he seeks frustration. But recurrent frustration of ordinary desires also soon become annoying, so he seeks frustration of his most intense desires. This too, if it continues, becomes commonplace to him. Then he must desire to frustrate his desire for frustrating desire. This means he must desire the very boredom which he sought to avoid because only therein can he now find a new level of intensity of hatred for such boredom. He must seek the mundane so that he can sneer at it, rail at it, arouse resentment in others through his ruthless castigation of it. But this, too, eventually bores him; so he must desire to frustrate the desire for frustration of desire, and so on ad infinitum. The gyrating course of violent tantrums does not consciously follow such a logically simple pattern; but the apparent dialectical necessity of seeking to reject eventually whatever one has affirmed (frustrate whatever one has so intensely desired) is required as soon as one comes to feel habituated to it. The yearning for infinity, including infinity of intensity, necessitates repudiation as insufficient at any level of intensity that has been reached.

(b) Historically, Romanticism flowered during the first half of the Nineteenth Century in Europe, especially in France and Germany, preceded by Rousseau, the French Revolution, and Napoleon. Chateaubriand, Becquer, Novalis, Leopardi, Victor Hugo, Fichte, Schelling, Schlegel, Schleiermacher, Nietzsche, Goethe, Herder, Heine, Holderlein, all are names to be reckoned with. Since each impulse is unique and the ways in which each Romanticist expresses himself idealizes uniqueness, generalizations about the movement must meet with criticism, especially by Romanticists. Variegated richness remains characteristic. In an attempt to summarize, I use ideas from Mark Temmer. Thrills occur now, so enjoyment is experienced, and must be sought, in the present. But preoccupation with the present itself eventually becomes boring, so then one pictures his desires as realized in the future, and he becomes utopian, and also finds his agony primordially enacted in the past (see Lessing, Laocoon), which he mythologizes to fit his passionate sentimentalities. But dreams about the future and myths about the past wear out or become transformed as one discovers that creative imagination itself is the instrument of Romantic desire; so one then devotes himself to the arts, especially the novel, in which imagined frustrating entanglements can be dialectically intertwined, kaleidoscopically and endlessly. The British Romantic poets, Blake, Keats, Shelley, etc., and the American Transcendentalists carry on in a subdued fashion. Kierkegaard struggles Romanticistically with his angry love of God, a creature of man's own needs, and contemporary Existentialism continues, in its own variegated ways, to extol "authenticity" as self-willed appreciation of temporary (death-facing) will to live significantly in an otherwise meaningless, valueless, world.

In all of the foregoing views, if my brief comments have left unclear their complexities, desire itself is enjoyed as the end-in-itself, whether as enthusiasm, gusto, eagerness, zeal, yearning, anxiety, zest or tantrum. Intrinsic evil consists in apathy, experienced subsidence or disappearance of desire.

4. *Contentment.* The nature of intrinsic value as conceived in our fourth theory is more difficult to describe, though once understood, its end-in-itself character is obvious. Hindus call it anda, "bliss," and we adopt the term "Anandism" to name this theory. It is enjoyed quiescence. It is experienced as tranquility. It is felt as fullness of being, undisturbed by any awareness of lack. It has a timeless quality about it, or at least contains no element of fear, uncertainty, disappointment or deprivation. It consists in enjoyment of just being. No single English word captures its full meaning. With some misgivings, I choose the term "contentment" as approximating its meaning. But it will serve only if we can distinguish it from "satisfaction" with which it is popularly identified.

Anandism emphasizes awareness of lack of contentment rather than unpleasant feeling, frustration of desire, or apathy, as the locus of intuited intrinsic evil. Evil is experienced as deprivation of good, imperfection, or incompleteness. Since intrinsic good is conceived in terms of contentment, or enjoyment of being without awareness of lack, intrinsic evil is conceived in terms of discontentment, disturbance of serenity, awareness of lack of tranquility, or consciousness that peace remains defective. This occurs in all degrees, ranging from the barest doubt that perfection exists to violent rage or endless turmoil. I choose the word "anxiety" to represent this broad range of degrees of restlessness. But any awareness of lack of perfect quiescence is experienced as intrinsic evil.

But what about satisfaction? How does it differ from contentment? If satisfaction were felt as complete absence of desire, then it would equal contentment. But the key of Voluntarists locates value as a goal not yet attained and as that which will, or would, satisfy desire when attained. Even when attained, satisfaction is felt as being the culmination of a process, which process as well as its overcoming remains present in the experience. Contentment, in the sense in which we are discussing it, consists in enjoying being without awareness that one has had to struggle for it or that any desire for it or process of attainment was involved in bringing it about. Hence, from the viewpoint of desiring, satisfaction and contentment may appear to be the same. But from the viewpoint of contentment, satisfaction which retains remembrance of the desire which has been satisfied is infected with that desire and hence remains inherently disturbed and imperfect. Perfect contentment cannot exist as long as one retains any trace of ever having been discontented. Intellectually, one realizes that life is by nature an affair of struggle and desire; hence perfect contentment can be realized, if at all, only after death. But perhaps, Lao Tzu, Chuang Tzu, Confucius (in his doctrine of Chih), Mencius, Gotama, and Zen advocate acceptance of what is experienced as exactly what one desires so habitually that desire itself, as experience of lack, never troubles one. You are perfectly contented as long as you retain a disposition to accept whatever you get as if it were precisely what you wanted. This amounts to an attitude of enjoyment of being as experienced without any desire to have it different, which, from the viewpoint of Romanticists and Voluntarists seems to be advocating extreme desirelessness. Intrinsic value, for Anandists, consists in contentment so conceived.

If you cannot conclude from your own intuitive experience that contentment is a distinct kind of way of enjoying intrinsic good, may have to eliminate this aspect of "self as value" from your calculations. Such elimination does not refute the general thesis that self is or has intrinsic good but narrows the scope of consideration to "pleasant feelings," "enthusiasm" and/or "satisfaction of desire." Your interest in, and obligations regarding, your present and future existence will pertain to it as an instrumental value in so far as such existence is needed for enjoyment of pleasures, enthusiasms and satisfactions. But when you do intuit your being as intrinsic good, you will automatically feel obligated to try to continue it, even in the absence of other anticipated specific experiences of pleasure, enthusiasm or satisfaction. For you, to enjoy being and to continue to do so constitutes a fundamental part of "what you most want to do."

Ethical implications of the view that intrinsic value consists in contentment as enjoyment of being are many. The ought-not-ness of suicide, the ought-not-ness of killing others unless they threaten your own being, the oughtness of efforts to expand your own being and the beings of others, are all involved. If enjoyment of being is intrinsic good, as I think it is, then I ought both to be and to enjoy such being and ought to continue to be and to continue to enjoy such being, and ought to expand such being and to increase my enjoyment of such expanded being insofar as I can.

5. *Organic Enjoyment.* In the foregoing we have presented four aspects of "self as intrinsic good" and four varieties of theories, each emphasizing one of the aspects. A fuller, more adequate, and thus more wholesome, view will observe how all four function as aspects of an integral situation, and will express itself as a theory inclusive of the virtues of the four foregoing types of theories without their shortcomings. This view will be called, for want of a better name, "the organic view" or "Organicism." Warning must be given that we are using the term "organic" in its historically earlier and continuingly broader meaning than those found in various specific usages such as "organic chemistry," biological organism" and "organ of the body." More generally, "organic" means "interdependence of parts in a whole" or, better, "interdependence of a whole and its parts." Two things are "interdependent" when they are both "partly independent of" and "partly dependent upon" each other. Thus atoms, galaxies, societies, experiences, systems and the universe exist as "organic" insofar as they consist of interdependencies. Further reference to being as organic, and to "Organicism," will be made later. (Chapters XVI, XXXI and XXXV.) But here the term "organic" refers specifically to the interdependence of the four aspects of intrinsic value, "pleasant feelings," "satisfaction of desire," "enthusiasm" and "contentment," which we have just discussed.

Let us first consider their differences, then notice ways in which all are alike, and finally indicate how they supplement each other.

1. Differences between them are many. "Pleasant feeling" and "satisfaction of desire" differ, or seem to differ, in that some pleasures occur without our having desired them. Fragrant odors, vivid colors,

dulcet tones, sweet or tart flavors, warm blankets, smooth surfaces and tickling sensations all may appear in experience as pleasant surprises. When we did not expect them, we could hardly have desired them -- at least so the argument goes. Satisfaction, on the other hand, requires a desire. We cannot feel that a desire has been, or is being, satisfied unless we have, or have had, a desire. Furthermore, sensory pleasures, at least, can be localized, for if you close your eyes, color experience stops; if you withdraw you fingers, smoothness ceases; if you drop the feather, tickling ends. But feelings of satisfaction often pervade experience and may not stop with the closing of eyes or withdrawing of fingers. Also, sensory pleasures may have a more obviously temporal quality about them, not only starting and stopping with beginning and ending of sensory stimulation, but sensory end organs become fatigued with continued use so that pleasure not only ceases but may turn into displeasure or even pain. But feelings of satisfaction may persist long after a desired sensation has occurred. Not only do we experience "enduring satisfactions" but the feelings of satisfaction, though they may terminate, do not easily become fatigued. Finally, we may desire objects or events which, in themselves, neither have nor are expected to have pleasant feelings; yet we may experience satisfaction upon having attained the desired, but unpleasant, goal.

"Pleasant feelings" and "enthusiasm" differ not only in that some pleasures appear to be thrust into experience without our having desired them but also in that they may come against our will. I may wish to stop the tickling in my throat, the bright red light before my eyes, odor of musk in my nostrils, or the warm glow in my skin. I may even enjoy the vigor with which I want them to stop. Again, pleasant sensations are localized, involving specific sensory end organs, whereas enthusiasm is a general feeling of willfulness having no specific location, although we may localize sensations while pursuing our will by the kinaesthetic pressures in our muscles as we strain to assert ourselves, vocal muscles as we yell with glee, and our auditory sensations as we hear the intense reverberations from the resulting sounds. Enthusiasm may continue while particular sensations appear and disappear; though also one may continue to experience certain colors, sounds, flavors, odors or pressures as pleasant even before, during and after experiencing enthusiastic impulses. Pleasant feeling and enthusiasm, like pleasant feeling and satisfaction, may be interpreted as independent variables in the sense that a person may experience one without the other, or longer than the other.

"Pleasant feeling" and "contentment" differ in the sense that sensory pleasures have a more definite location, duration, and observable variation in intensity, whereas contentment seems more suffused, overarching, pervasive and indefinite. Although contentment, in its popular notion, may include multitudes of pleasant feelings, the Anandist ideal of contentment as experiencing perfect quiescence of being regards each specific pleasure as a disturbance of placidity and hence a form of intrinsic evil. Stimulating pleasures arouse desires for more of the same, hence create a sense of restlessness, anxiety, anticipation, desire. Contentment ceases as soon as desire becomes aroused. Hence pleasures and contentment are antipathetical.

"Satisfaction of desire" differs from "enthusiasm" in that satisfaction terminates desire whereas enthusiasm magnifies it. Satisfaction is enjoying the terminating of desire. Enthusiasm is enjoying desiring itself; such desiring is felt as continuing or unterminating and as best when it appears interminable. The greater the satisfaction, the more fully the desire is felt as terminating; the greater the enthusiasm, the more interminable it appears.

"Satisfaction of desire" differs from "contentment" in several ways. First, "satisfaction" normally involves more specific desires whereas "contentment" is more general. You usually know what desire is being satisfied, and you may feel that you are satisfying one desire while suffering frustration of another. But contentment is a feeling in which all desires have disappeared. Secondly, "satisfaction" is felt while the terminating process is occurring; "contentment" is felt after the terminating process has been completed. Thirdly, "satisfaction" involves retaining some awareness of the desire being satisfied, whereas "contentment" requires no such retention and is complete only when such desires have been forgotten. Fourthly, there is nothing in the nature of "satisfaction" which excludes recurrence of the desire (though specific desires for non-repeatable satisfactions may do so), whereas "contentment" exists fully only when all tendency for a desire to recur has been eliminated. In fact, some satisfactions are regarded as more satisfactory when they leave a residual tendency to desire recurrence. (Is candy which, when eaten, makes you want more, better than candy which, when eaten, makes you feel that you have had enough? The former may be "satisfying"; the latter is "contenting.")

"Enthusiasm" and "contentment" seem most different. "Enthusiasm" is enjoyment of desire aroused intensely and endlessly. "Contentment" is enjoyment of absence of desire. "Contentment" also may be experienced as if endless, but it consists in unending desirelessness rather than in endless desiring. "Enthusiasm" seems best when throbbing or pulsating with variegated turmoil. "Contentment" is best when all trace of desire, even of having ever desired, is gone.

Thus far, in stating four theories of intrinsic good, we have neglected to give due emphasis to their theories of intrinsic evil. Intrinsic evil consists, for Hedonism, in unpleasant feeling, especially in pain, for Voluntarism, in feelings of frustration, for Romanticism, in feelings of exhaustion of desire or of apathy, and for Anandism, in any felt disturbance of quiescent bliss, which we will speak of as "anxiety." Hedonism's bitter tastes, foul odors, toothaches tend to have a specific locus and may occur quite independently of desire, whereas feelings of satisfaction, enthusiasm, and contentment may appear to suffuse one's whole self and depend intimately upon desire or its subsidence. Voluntarism's frustrations range from minor irritations to violent rage, and from momentary inhibitions to a pervasive grouchy mood. Continuing restraints may produce a sullen, peevish, morose mood, felt as antipathy toward others or even repulsiveness toward life itself. Romanticism's apathy consists in felt exhaustion of desire. Desireousness itself takes two forms: wanting something positive, such as acquiring a new friend, and wanting something negative, such as killing an enemy. Intrinsic evil consists not in angry intolerance but in indifference, not in feelings of hatred but in lack of interest, not in ennui but in lethargy. Anandism's anxiety is likewise twofold: wanting something to be and wanting something not to be are equally forms of wantings; feelings of greed disturb a mind's quiescence just as much as feelings of fear or hatred. All desiring is wanting; all wanting is lacking; all feelings of lack disturb contentment. Each of the four theories has emphasized a particular correlative kind of intrinsic evil as opposing its particular kind of intrinsic good. Pain, frustration, apathy and anxiety are both clearly distinguishable from each other and quite clearly apposite opposites to feelings of pleasure, satisfaction, enthusiasm and contentment, respectively. (See Diagram I.)

2. Despite their difference, "pleasure," "satisfaction," "enthusiasm" and "contentment" (and their opposites) are alike in several respects. (a) All involve awareness, whether vague or clear, or whether conceptualized or unconceptualizable. Instrumental values may exist without awareness. Potentialities for experiencing intrinsic value may exist without awareness.

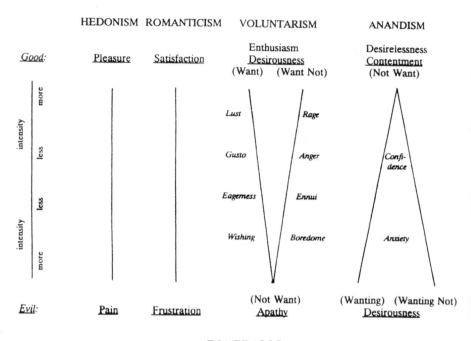

DIAGRAM I
Four theories (kinds) of intrinsic value (good and evil).

But intrinsic value itself, as all four theories agree, must be experienced in order to be. (b) All are thus intuited directly. None needs any proof of its existence because each is self-evident, and self-evidently good (or bad), while it is being experienced. (c) All vary. That is, sensations are more or less pleasant, more or less enduring, more or less intense, or have higher or lower quality. Satisfactions are felt as more or less satisfying, or desires seem more or less completely satisfied. Enthusiasm, zeal and eagerness effuse more or less intensely. Despite idealization by Anandists, one who experiences contentment may feel more or less contented; one feels perfectly contented only as an exceptional temporary extreme of contentment. (d) All may be spoken of as "felt" or "enjoyed." (e) All appear to have evolved out of and to continue to depend upon biological and physiological natures. Those beings which were able to achieve satisfaction of specific desires, and to enjoy such satisfactions as intrinsic good, and to enjoy resting from energy-consuming activities, were more likely to survive, other things being equal. Specific kinds of desires with supporting satisfactions, such as those of eating, drinking and reproducing, contributed to survival. And feelings of pleasantness connected with elation, emotion and particular kinds of sensory end organs, appear to have aided in survival.

3. These four kinds of value also supplement each other interdependently. Even though each may occupy a present experience with relatively complete dominance for a short time, all may also be present together as aspects of a whole value experience.

When sensation occurs, normally a tendency exists for our bodily organism to become aroused, especially when the sensation becomes intense, when one possesses sufficient energy with which to respond, when other factors such as competing sensations do not distract attention from it, and when one has not been conditioned negatively to resist arousal of desire. Sensation and desire interdepend in that sensation is required for arousal of some desires and that full functioning, continuation and recurrence of some sensations may depend upon arousing desire to attend to, continue and repeat them. Establishment of a habit of enjoying certain kinds of sensations serves to create or activate desires which will lead to further recurrences of those sensations. Such further occurrences depend for their existence in experience upon such desires. Some sensations cause desires and some desires cause sensations.

Desire, including desirousness, may be experienced without significant awareness of sensation. Desire is related to and dependent on the presence of sufficient energy. Sometimes energy production becomes superabundant and manifests itself spontaneously as desire for activity. One may not be able to act without involving some sensation, but awareness may be so fully occupied with the burgeoning of desire as to exclude attention to sensation. One may experience the surging of desire without having formulated conceptually anything that is desired. One may thus experience having a desire without knowing what one desires or what it would take to satisfy one's desire. In a developed person, ideas about what one wants may stimulate desires; but genetically the feeling of desire is prior to ideation about specific goals which will satisfy desire. Even adults sometimes become restless and want to do something without being sure what they want to do. Such restlessness may be felt as discomforting, but expansive bursts of energy may be enjoyed for themselves alone. If you do not enjoy desiring, you might never go on to seek satisfaction, especially when the course leading to some satisfactions is very arduous. Even though desire and satisfaction are linked together biologically, not only desire but even exuberance or desirousness are in a fundamental sense prior to satisfaction.

Nevertheless, perpetual exuberance results in exhaustion. Desire, even when not aroused by specific sensory stimuli or appearance of some problem needing solution, tends to formulate itself in terms of an objective or goal that will satisfy it. Without such goal, desire remains vague, inchoate, directionless. With such goal, desire aims at it, and satisfaction is conceived in terms of attaining it. When the satisfaction settles what was aroused, a feeling of completion results. The feeling of satisfaction lasts as long as there remains any awareness of this settling of what was aroused. That is, the feeling continues to be experienced while the desire is being satisfied.

Sometimes energy continues to produce desirousness, so that numerous feelings of satisfaction do not wholly quiet desire. But when you feel that all of your desires have been satisfied, so that desire itself ceases to demand further attention, then you feel contented. Contentment is full culmination of desire and, since satisfaction is felt as intrinsically good, feeling of contentment, or complete satisfaction, is felt as perfectly good or as the supreme intrinsic value.

In sum, sensation, arousal of desire, subsidence of a desire, and forgetting a desire succeed each other naturally, and pleasure, enthusiasm, satisfaction, and contentment, as four distinguishable kinds of intrinsic good, participate in a value-continuum in which each contributes more or less to the continuous whole. It is due to the fact that conditions of experience produce variations in the relative dominance of one or the other that we speak of experiences as being of one kind rather than another. The almost constantly varying role of desire in being satisfied or frustrated makes it difficult to assess precisely either the specific or general significance of any one of the four kinds of good. Such fluctuation in the occurrence of intrinsic good makes ascertainment of what one ought to do, when oughtness rests ultimately upon intrinsic good, very difficult. Yet, since all are in fact intrinsic goods, all have a role to play in ethics. One ought to neglect none of them. Yet, if greater attention to one rather than another results in experiencing more such good, then this is basic to obligation. But which of the four does tend to yield the greatest enjoyment may vary with numerous factors which themselves change, some of them with successive stages in the life cycle.

Infants and children seem more preoccupied with sensuous pleasures; and, though they often manifest violent exuberance, they seem more easily pacified by sensuous means. Youth is a period of energy, enthusiasm and eagerness; youth is forward-looking, desirous, not easily satisfied with anything. Adulthood tends to be more occupied with attaining the goals of life and with recognizing that they are being attained; its concerns emphasize feelings of satisfaction. Old age, when both energy declines and the goals of life have been largely achieved, devotes itself more to feelings of contentment. Exceptions to this generalization are easy to find; but throughout the history of mankind literature has recorded observations about such stages and value-variations relative to them.

The Organicist theory of intrinsic value is that all four kinds of value emerge from biological conditions which produce all four as parts of a natural succession. All participate in the experiencing of value. Sometimes one stands out with greater clarity. But most of the time they flow imperceptibly into each other, making analysis difficult. Yet, for example, their successive predominance may be observed in experiencing orgasm. Although abundance of energy may propel sexual impulses without initial sensory excitation, normally stimulation of erogenous zones, accompanied by pleasant feelings, tends to burgeon into passionately compulsive desire, enjoyed increasingly as desireousness intensifies, reaches a peak of intensity and subsides with an intense feeling of satisfaction, and is followed by relaxation, quiescence, and an all-pervading feeling of peaceful rest (i.e., contentment). Orgasms experienced without distractions often terminate in complete oblivion, so much so that the end-in-itself qualities of the experience leave little or no trace in memory. Yet, while being experienced, the enjoyment of orgasm tends to be intuited as the supreme intrinsic good; and when such enjoyment intermingles with thoughts signifying the experience as culminating a wedding, as anticipating wanted offspring, as achievement of social maturity, etc., it may be experienced and enjoyed as a concrete joint embodiment of many goods of one's life as a whole. One's self and companion and the whole world may be felt as if immersed together in an undifferentiated sea of intrinsic goodness.

We choose to speak of this variable enjoyment of the four kinds of intrinsic value, both with occasional independence and usual interdependence, as "organic enjoyment." "Organic enjoyment," then, includes feelings of pleasantness, of enthusiasm, of satisfaction, and of contentment, and their fluctuating occurrence and varying predominance in experience. Organicism depends upon the contributions of each of the four theories for its understanding of the four kinds of values; but it also condemns each as inadequate to the extent that each denies or neglects the positive contributions of the other four theories. Organicism asserts not merely that there are four kinds of intrinsic good but that they exist interdependently in experience. We cannot say that there is only one kind of intrinsic good, namely, "organic enjoyment," for "organic enjoyment"connotes both unity and plurality; all are alike in being intrinsic good and in supplementing each other in any whole value experience, yet each has its distinctive nature which cannot be reduced to any of the others.

Objectification of Values. Ordinary experience seldom consists in feelings of pure pleasure, enthusiasm, satisfaction or contentment alone. The flavor of a sweet grape in a combination salad eaten at a community banquet is almost submerged in a plethora of variegated sensory and socially stimulated emotionalized ideas and attitudes, for example. Hence, when trying reflectively to locate intrinsic good, a person can only with difficulty abstract particular kinds of good, such as a sweet flavor, from the dynamic whole of an intricate, conglomerate, kaleidoscopic experience. If asked whether one enjoys eating the grape, one's saying yes usually involves one in regarding the grape as an object or, rather, as a real thing which exists in a salad on a plate. Until they learn otherwise, persons are habitually naive realists about perceived values as well as about perceived things. But the intricate and technical analyses of epistemologists and aestheticians reveal certain fundamentals which every axiologist should take fully into account.

An experience is "aesthetic" when it involves an intuition of intrinsic value. (See "Aesthetic Experience and Moral Experience," Journal of Philosophy, Sept. 25, 1958, Vol. LV, pp. 837-846; "Comparative Aesthetics," Journal of Aesthetics and Art Criticism, Fall, 1965, Vol. XXIV, pp. 109-119; "The Aesthetics of Organism," Journal of Aesthetics and Art Criticism, Summer, 1968, Vol. XXVI, pp. 449-459.) "Beauty" is not merely "pleasure objectified" (George Santayana, The Sense of Beauty, p. 52, Charles Scribner's Sons, New York, 1896), but "intrinsic good objectified," now that we are acquainted with four or more kinds of intrinsic value. Objectification of intrinsic values (which aestheticians call "empathy") involves projecting intuited intrinsic value into an apparent object and then, normally spontaneously inferring that the value so projected exists in the real thing serving as a basis for the apparent object independently of the intuiting experience. Although critical training teaches that, in some fundamental respects, "beauty exists in the eye of the beholder," the natural tendency to function as naive realists persists.

When a mind is cluttered with multiplicities of factors calling for judgment and decision when faced with ethical choices, most people seem unable to remain critical about the subjective aspects and limitations of aesthetic (i.e., intrinsic value) experiences. The point being stressed here is that intrinsic values, which have their sole location in personal experience, are naturally projected as if existing in objects which appear, at least in part, to persist independently of such experiences. This is so, in part, because we tend to be aware that our value experiences are caused by real instruments (e.g., a grape in a salad) and yet fail to be sufficiently analytical under ordinary circumstances to differentiate the intrinsic and instrumental aspects in our value experiences.

The natural confusion inherent in value perception functions further as a confusing factor in ethical perspectives. The seeming reality of intrinsic values is supported not only by naive realistic, but also Platonic realistic (and consequent Christian theological) philosophies and by ethical theories which assert that axiological, aesthetic and moral rules hold universally and independently of individual or subjective differences. The unfortunate tendency, on the part of those who reject such realisms, either to deny the existence of all values or to claim that all values are subjective merely, often begets the hasty conclusion that, therefore, no generalization about either values or ethics are possible. But if, or since, many intrinsic values do exist within experience, it is not only possible but even relatively easy to make empirical, or experiential, observations and to draw general conclusions about them. Hedonism as a theory of both intrinsic value and right action is about as old as any other scientific theory. Theories about which kinds of instruments tend to produce enjoyed experience are many, and are inherent in the problems and conclusions of medical, commercial and theatrical enterprises. The financial successes of culinary, commercial advertising, and movie production occupations constitute evidence for the ability of people to generalize predictively about the kinds of value experiences that people will have under certain circumstances. Multiplicities of cultural, biological and personal differences do not cancel out observable facts about relative uniformities in human experiences. The task facing an ethicist in analyzing the multiplex factors and aspects involved in ethical situations is indeed complex. But the extreme impatience of those who want ethical scientists to come up with quick substitutes for traditional simplified codes (e.g., the "Ten Commandments") testifies to general ignorance of the intricacies involved. When the same people who deny the possibility of "instant physics" demand either "instant ethics" or abolition of ethics, it should be obvious that ethical science and ethical education is at a very low ebb.

In concluding this chapter, we gather together, and point out the significance for self and for ethics, of, the many ideas considered. The central thesis has been that a self is, or has, both instrumental and intrinsic value, both means to ends and ends-in-themselves. The intrinsic values experienced constitute a part of self. Their presence may be intuited, hence assured, even though we spend most of our time attending to other objects, especially to things that serve as instruments. If more-than-necessary devotion of self to objects as instruments, or to use of self as instrument, diminishes enjoyment of self as an end, perhaps we unwittingly pervert our efforts. If potential intrinsic good, by being actually unenjoyed or diminishedly enjoyed, because unattended to, is there by wasted, then perhaps we owe it to ourselves to devote more attention to appreciating ourselves as intrinsic goods, and to the specific kinds of intrinsic goods outlined in the present chapter. Increased enjoyment of self as intrinsic good may be an important part of what one most wants to have. Of course, if the so-called "Hedonistic paradox" recurs as Voluntaristic, Romanticistic, Anandistic and Organicistic paradox, such that you actually enjoy yourself as an intrinsic good more fully to the extent that you devote yourself to other things and persons and to instrumental goods, then perhaps you have only limited actual opportunity for maximizing your enjoyment of self as intrinsic good purified of practical interests.

Summary of Value Distinctions. I. Distinction between: (A) "a _thing_" (e.g., an experience) and (B) "its _value_." The terms, "thing" and "value," do not have the same meaning. One may speak of a thing without speaking of its value, and one may speak of the value of a thing in such a way as to differentiate such value from the thing.

II. Distinction between: A thing's (A) "_having_ value" and (B) "_being_ value." This distinction, like that between "substance" and either "attribute" or "quality" or "property," is a subtle one. When a thing _has_ value, its value may be somewhat different from it and thus somewhat external to it. When a thing _is_ value, such value is partly or wholly identical with it and thus partly or wholly internal to its nature.

III. Distinction between: (A) "_existence_" and (B) "_value_." If a thing may exist without value, the existence of a thing's value is an existence that is additional to the thing's existence as a thing without value. Hence we may distinguish between: (1) "the existence of a thing" and (2) "the existence of a (thing's) value." (We assume here that value cannot exist independently of things.)

IV. Distinction between: (A) "<u>intrinsic</u> value" and (B) "<u>instrumental</u> value." An "intrinsic value" is an "end-in-itself," i.e., a value which requires the existence of no other value in order to be a value. An "instrumental value" is a "means-to-an-end," i.e., a value which requires the existence of some other value (and ultimately of an intrinsic value) in order for it to be a value.

Relating this distinction to previous distinctions, we may further distinguish (1) "A thing and its intrinsic value." (a) "A thing and the intrinsic value which it <u>has</u>." (b) "A thing and the intrinsic value which it <u>is</u>." (2) "A thing and its instrumental value." (a) "A thing and the instrumental value which it <u>has</u>." (b) "A thing and the instrumental value which it <u>is</u>." (3) "A thing which has both intrinsic and instrumental value." (a) "A thing and the intrinsic value which it has and the instrumental value which it has." (b) "A thing and the intrinsic value which it is and the instrumental value which it is." (c) "A thing and the intrinsic value which it has and the instrumental value which it is."

V. Distinction between: (A) "<u>casual dependence</u>" and (B) "<u>teleological dependence</u>." "Teleology" is "the science of ends" and "teleological dependence" here refers to the dependence of "means" upon "ends", or of instrumental values upon intrinsic values. A thing having, or being, instrumental value depends, not for its existence as a thing but for the existence of its value, upon the existence of some intrinsic value (and upon the thing which has, or is, that intrinsic value). "Causal dependence", on the other hand, refers to the dependence of an intrinsic value upon whatever was instrumental in causing it to exist as an intrinsic value. Thus: (1) "Intrinsic value depends causally upon instrumental value." (2) "Instrumental value depends teleologically upon intrinsic value." Both depend for their existence upon the existence of the things which have such values.

VI. Distinction between: (A) "<u>actual</u> values and (B) "<u>potential</u> values."

VII. Distinction between: (A) "<u>subjective</u> values" and (B) "<u>real</u> values." A "subjective value" is one existing in a subject or valuer. A "real value" is one which does not depend upon the existence of a subject or valuer for its existence. (A subject, or valuer, may value itself as a value, and thus be both a valuer and valued.)

VII. Distinction between: (A) "<u>values</u>" and (B) "<u>value judgments</u>." Values <u>exist</u>. Value judgments are <u>judgments</u> about value.

IX. Distinction between: Judgments which are (A) "valuative" and (B) "evaluative." A "valuative judgment" here refers to judgments that values exist: "That is good." An "evaluative judgment" is one judging comparatively: "This is better than that."

X. Distinction between: (A) "judgments of value" and (B) "standards for judging." A "standard for judgment" is an ideal norm in terms of which values are judged comparatively. A "standard for judgment" is a prejudgment about judgments of value and one which functions as a standard for measurement of comparable values. Such standards may be personal or social.

XI. Distinction between: (A) "values" and (B) "oughts." (Here we go beyond mere "value distinctions" and need to distinguish further between "value distinctions" and "moral distinctions." We could further distinguish between "standards for judgement" and "standards for conduct.")

The distinction between "good" and "bad" has been presupposed; and another set of distinctions similar to those above should be noted relative to "bad."

Chapter VII

SELF-IMPROVEMENT

Can a self become better? An adequate answer to this question requires more than a simple "yes." Reflection leads to several other intimately related questions. First, if "to become better" involves "change," then we must ask: 1. What is change? 2. Can a self change? 3. What happens when a self changes? Secondly, "to become better" involves us in at least four other questions: 1. What do we mean by "better" and how do "better" and "best" differ from "good?" 2. Can intrinsic value change? Can a self's intrinsic good improve? 3. In what ways can a self's intrinsic good change and improve? 4. Do limits to self-improvement exist? Thirdly, these four questions have their negative counterparts: 1. What is meant by "bad," "worse," "worst?" 2. Can intrinsic evil change? Can a self become intrinsically worse? 3. In what ways can a self's intrinsic evil become worse? 4. Do limits of self-degeneration exist? Finally, we should ask: Do, and how do, possibilities for improvement and for becoming worse function relative to each other? Does improvement sometimes lead to degeneration, and does degeneration at times lead to improvement?

Can A Self Change? 1. Since "improvement" or "becoming better" involves "becoming" or "changing," insight into the nature of improvement will be adequate only if we grasp the fundamental nature of change. To change is to become different. Anything which changes becomes different. But, unless it "changes completely," i.e., from existing to not existing (after which there is no "it"), its change is incomplete or partial. Hence, anything which changes in some ways must also remain the same in other ways. To remain the same through change is to be "permanent" or "substantial." "Change by itself, apart from a background of identity, is impossible for the reason that where there is no underlying identity there is nothing to change." (A.E. Taylor, Elements of Metaphysics, p. 161, Methuen & Co., London, 1903.) However, "permanence is but a word of degrees." (Ralph Waldo Emerson, "Circles.") "In order to change, a thing must remain. If it does not remain, it has not changed, but something else has changed. Permanence involves enduring at last through different times. Thus permanence involves at least some change." (See my Metaphysics: An Introduction, pp 26-36, 138-139, 217-218, Harper & Row, New York, 1974.) "Change" and "permanence" are thus correlative and interdependent.

If to change is to become different, then there are as many kinds of change as there are kinds of becoming different. If to be permanent is to remain the same, there exist as many kinds of permanence as there are kinds of remaining the same. Some changes may be partly reversible. If you have become fat you may again become thin; but you cannot change back to the previous time and other circumstances before you became fat in the first place. All change seems partly irreversible because time, at least, is irreversible. Whenever anything which changes in any way "remains changed" in that way, its remaining thus is permanent. Such a change is a "permanent change." But also, when anything which embodies a permanent change in one respect later changes in some other respect, that thing, having such permanent change as part of its now-unchanging nature, involves such embodied permanent change as a part of it which remains through its further change. The longer a changed condition remains, the more permanent it becomes.

Of course, change may involve addition of something new, or subtraction of something old, or both. When one marries, one's change involves adding something to oneself which one did not have before. When a person loses a finger, this change involves loss of something previously possessed. When you change your mind, you may have to give up one belief or intention in order to acquire its opposite. Some changes seem to add more than they subtract, as when one earns more money than previously. Some changes appear to subtract more than they add, as when a mountain erodes. Some changes require equal gains and losses, in such cases as where you cannot become a day older without thereby losing a day from the life which you have yet to live.

Some changes occur quickly, even instantaneously, whereas others require longer periods of time. If each change or becoming different may be called "an event," we may distinguish between short and long events. Then not only are there as many kinds of events as there are kinds of becoming different, but an event lasts as long or as short as the time needed for a thing to become different in any respect. The event requiring weeks or months for the fracture to heal is long. A longer event is a more enduring, and relatively more permanent affair than a short event. But a longest event, such as the period required for you to come into existence, live your life and die, is still "an event" as far as the world is involved in the change consisting in the difference between your not existing, then existing, and then not existing.

Although much more may be said about the nature of change, enough questions have been raised and suggestions offered to illustrate the correlation and interdependence of change and permanence and the complexities involved in facing the question: "Can a self change?"

2. Is "self" a kind of thing which can change? One may develop an elaborate theory of the nature of change and still deny that a self can change. On the other hand, is a "self" a kind of thing which is, or can be, permanent? Since some say "no" to both of those questions, our own answer, i.e., that a self both changes in some ways while remaining unchanged in others, faces a double challenge. Replies to these questions have significance because different answers imply divergent courses of decision and action regarding what a person who seeks what is best for oneself ought to do.

Some contend that a self cannot really change because it consists in a simple, static, eternal soul which, having no parts, cannot lose parts, add parts or exchange parts, and thus cannot change. External attachments may come and go, but they are either illusory (as in Advaita Vedanta), or temporary (as with Jainism and Samkhya Yoga); or they may be permanent (as in dualistic Christianity). But the soul itself, no matter how much troubled by a permanent or changing body, is, in itself, eternal and unchangeable. Since it cannot change, there is nothing which one can, or ought to, do to change it. All oughtness pertains ultimately to freeing it from external conditions as much as possible, but such "freeing" is not a "change" in it as much as a change external to it. A soul so conceived can neither improve nor become worse in itself, though, paradoxically, it nevertheless somehow suffers from changed external conditions. Holders of this kind of view usually conceive "ethical" concerns as subordinate means of dealing with illusory, temporary or external matters, while idealizing as superior a faith in the existence of a soul in a pure state beyond the reach of time and change and beyond the realm of "oughts" and "ought-nots."

Others say self changes completely, because momentary and never the same twice Theravada Buddhism claims that all self-ideas are illusory, and that attachment to self, like attachment to other things such as body, wealth, friends, even God, constitutes a delusion-producing suffering. Behavioristic Materialists also see self-ideas, and all values, as evanescent epiphenomena in which an apparent self mistakes itself to be real, continuing and worth while. Such views also regard ethical concerns as illusory and superficial and even instrumentally evil, but, whereas Teravadins hope to end such illusion as quickly as possible, Behavioristic Materialists willingly enjoy a "jug of wine and thou" as long as possible.

Since we oppose both the view that self is utterly changeless and the view that self is either ultimately non-existent or merely momentary, we must maintain that self can both change and yet endure, both become different and yet remain the same, both genuinely grow, develop, decline and persist substantially. That is, a self may, even must, change in some respects in order to adapt and endure in other respects. A self actually exists. A self actually endures, at least for the period of its lifetime. A self actually changes, in many varieties of ways. Changes in a self may become permanent parts of a changed self. But no matter how long it exists, a self remains in some sense the same from the beginning to end. Change and permanence interdepend organically in constituting a self.

3. What happens when a self changes? It gains parts, or loses parts, or exchanges parts. It may become more complex when it gains, more simple when it loses, or variably more complex and simple as it gains, loses and exchanges parts or aspects. If added parts conflict with each other, as when having two ambitions, two jobs or two children, then a self may have to change its nature by expanding flexibly to maintain an enduring superior unification within itself of its conflicting parts. Persisting flexibility to withstand both internal and external changes is needed for survival. The varieties of ways in which a self may change and endure, already surveyed in a summary fashion in the chapters on "Self As Physical" and "Self As Social," need not be repeated here. But perhaps we should note that facts concerning the nature of change and permanence, the ability of, and need for, a self both to change and remain, and the ways, and problems involved in such ways, in which a self may change, all have bearings upon the nature of oughtness and self-obligation, at least as far as these changes and permanence involve changes and permanence in value.

Can a Self Become Better? Since a thing, or a self, might change without improving or getting worse, and since a thing, or self, might remain the same without improving or getting worse, the question "Can self improve?" involves something additional. If one holds the view that self is changeless, then it cannot become better or worse inherently. If one holds the view that self is non-existent, then no self exists to become better or worse. If one holds that self exists only momentarily, it hardly exists long enough to make questions of improvement or degeneration of much significance; even if, in such a view, one could steer a course to better future events, why do so, when some other, different, not-same self will reap the rewards? Since we believe that a self can change for better or worse, we find ourselves faced with the problem of trying to understand the nature of improvement, self-improvement, kinds of ways of self-improvement and limits of self-improvement.

1. What do we mean by "better" and how do "better" and "best" differ from "good?" Although the answers to these questions should be obvious from ordinary language usage, we may profitably point out here that all of the problems which plagued us previously concerning the nature of "good" recur or continue to annoy us when dealing with "better" (more good) and "best" (most good). The distinctions between intrinsic and instrumental values, between actual and potential values, and between a thing and its value, permeate problems involving "better" and "best." But if we have mastered them previously, we should have little additional trouble. A thing having potential instrumental good becomes better, i.e., acquires more potential instrumental good, when it develops more capacity (or opportunity) to serve in producing actual intrinsic good. When the sluggish motor in our car has been tuned, it "has improved" because it has attained a capacity to produce more enjoyment in us when we go for a ride. When a person's attitude toward a necessary task changes from one of reluctance to one of enthusiasm, the attitude (here regarded as an instrumental value) has improved. When, in doing a bit of work, your enjoyment increases, your actual intrinsic good is better than before the increase.

2. Can intrinsic value change? Each of the theories of intrinsic value already discussed (in Chapter VI), Hedonism, Romanticism, Voluntarism, Anandism and Organicism, claims that pleasure, enthusiasm, satisfaction, contentment and organic enjoyment, respectively, may be, and become, more or less and thus are changeable. The reader may observe, or recall from one's own past, how experiences do become more and less pleasant, interests more or less enthusiastic, desires more and less satisfied, contentment more and less complete, and how pleasures, enthusiasms, satisfactions and contentment have been more and less enjoyed together. Instrumental goods, which depend for their goodness upon their service to intrinsic goods, may be improved only if things having intrinsic good can have more such good. Of course, intrinsic value may change, at least in the sense that there can be more of it or less of it.

Can a self's intrinsic goodness improve? Can a self become intrinsically better? If, as maintained in Chapter VI, "Self as Value," a self is or has intrinsic goodness, and if, as we have just indicated, intrinsic good may change, at least the sense that there can be more of it, then it seems possible for a self's intrinsic good to improve. If by embodying more pleasures, enthusiasms, satisfactions, contentment and organic enjoyment within itself, a self is or has more intrinsic good, and if one or all of these can be increased, then a self's intrinsic good may be improved. Whenever you experience greater pleasures, enthusiasm, satisfaction or contentment, your self is or has more intrinsic good than before.

3. In what ways can a self's intrinsic good change and improve? Here again we must recall the constituents of self and consider how, or how far, intrinsic good may be experienced relative to each of them. For example, you are able to remember experiencing greater enjoyment upon becoming aware of more efficient functioning of any organ of your body. The pervasive aims of health studies and physical education programs in which you have participated were to improve your body not merely as an instrument for action but as an embodiment of more enjoyable feelings. You may review each of the kinds of experience summarized under "Self-Ideas" in Chapter IV, such as joining a group or playing a social role, in which you achieve a new status, or an additional way of being which you came to enjoy. You may think back to each of the kinds of desires, for esteem, love, adventure and security, considered in Chapter V, in which you attained additional satisfaction. Each "new level" of self that emerges may be an additional way in which you can enjoy being and thus experience more intrinsic good of your self.

Since your self endures as an organic unity of its many parts, aspects and levels, and since the enjoyment of being, with its pleasures and satisfactions, may, relative to each such part, aspect or level, increase in quantity, duration, intensity, quality, purity and "fecundity" (if we may extend some of Bentham's principles), your intrinsic good can improve in all these ways. More varieties of such ways should appear as other aspects or levels of self become revealed through Parts II and III of this volume. But since endurance and recurrence, etc., of intrinsic goods in one's experience, and thus in one's self, depend upon instrumental goods, the ways in which a self's intrinsic goods can improve depend upon the ways in which one can and does establish habits (capacities) and surroundings (opportunities) conducive to such endurance, recurrence, etc. The ultimate goal of ethics is to improve your self's intrinsic goodness as much as possible.

4. Do limits of self-improvement exist? Yes, of course. For limits to self, even though variable, do exist. And limits to each part, aspect or level of self exist, as well as limits to the number of such parts, aspects and levels which can be self-integrated. First of all, you have only a

certain amount of body. You cannot enjoy six arms and four legs. Although you may improve your muscular strength and speed, international Olympic contests dramatize the peaks of physical achievement beyond which few human beings can go. Although you enjoy two lungs and two eyes, as well as two arms, legs and ears, you can hardly enjoy two hearts, two stomachs -- to say nothing of three or four or five or more. Probably maximums of size, energy, age, etc., become familiar to students of physiology.

Total capacities for increase in social ingredients of self seem much less restricted than those for physiological growth -- especially for highly-socialized individuals. The numbers of groups, kinds of groups, levels of groups, which you may join, and thus join to yourself, seem greater than possibilities for physical increases. For you can add to yourself membership in another group when you cannot add to yourself another arm or leg. Yet, even here, capacities can be reached. Each group membership tends to require its quota of time, energy, money, or at least attention, and the quantity of things to which you can attend in a day, year or lifetime is not infinite. Both capacities and opportunities for group participation may become exhausted. So, even when increase in the social ingredients in your self improve enjoyment of your being a self with such social ingredients, and thus your being intrinsic good, limits to such expansion exist.

Conflicts among your desires, ambitions and extending interests compete with each other for whatever total amount of time and energy is available for disposal. Though persons differ greatly in versatility, adaptability and in ability to integrate multiple personalities, each eventually finds his capacity fully used up.

And limits exist for the amounts of pleasure (both in quantity, duration, and intensity; due to sensuous fatigue), of enthusiasm (which depends on limits of physical energy), of satisfaction (which can exist at one time or even at all of your times), and of contentment (which must be confined by length of time your bodily needs can remain unattended), to say nothing of time and energy required for attending to pains, frustrations and other sufferings which normally occur. Your ability to change, or add something new to your being for enjoyment, and your ability, or opportunity, to remain the same, or to enjoy unchanged being, both have termini. Even your willingness to accept things as they are, or are going to be, naturally comes to an end. If you willingly feel yourself identified with your family, corporation, profession, nation, mankind or even the universe, sooner or later, you will find conflicting factors disturbing such willingness. One who seeks and finds a beatific vision of his identity with God or the universe can hardly remain in such an ecstatic condition forever.

Limits to self-improvement do exist, though few of us have reached all of them. And these limits constitute limits upon self-obligation, which we have yet to discuss.

Can a Self Become Worse? Each of the four preceding questions has its negative counterpart.

1. What is meant by "bad," "worse," "worst?" Intrinsic evil, no matter how conceived, i.e., as pain, frustration, apathy, anxiety or organic suffering, may involve more, or most, such pain, frustration, etc. Instrumental evil exists as greater or lesser in proportion to the intrinsic evil it causes.

2. Can intrinsic evil change? Yes, there may be more or less of it. Can a self become intrinsically worse? Yes, a self may embody within itself more pains, more feelings, of apathy, anxiety, frustration and have its experience more occupied with attention to its sufferings. A self which embodies more such intrinsic evil thereby is intrinsically worse.

3. In what ways can a self's intrinsic evil become worse? Varieties include: (a) By embodying more of the four kinds of intrinsic evil just mentioned. (b) By increasing the quantity, duration, intensity, quality, purity and fecundity of such evil. (c) By experiencing such evil in more parts, aspects or levels of self. (d) By establishing habits ("character traits") which are conducive to recurrence or persistence of such evils, either directly or internally, through maintaining interests which conflict with each other, or indirectly, through habitually tormenting others who naturally reply in kind. (e) By seeking or remaining in an environment which recurrently induces suffering. (f) By increasingly demanding more for self, or others, than can be attained. Although these varieties of ways overlap, a multiple perspective provides us with a multiple approach to the basic moral problem of reducing intrinsic evil within ourselves.

4. Do limits of self-degeneration exist? Yes. When one prefers death to life he has reached a limit of tolerance for his existence as intrinsically evil. Self-destruction or, for that matter, destruction of self by others, puts an end to his intrinsic evil as well as to any intrinsic good. If one cannot die, but must "suffer utter eternal damnation," then we can only speculate as to whether it is possible for a self to become completely evil. Few willingly entertain this possibility, and, unless fear of it may serve somehow as a deterrent to evil tendencies, entertainment of it seems both

useless and unrealistic. Yet we may generalize that any highest level of pain, frustration, apathy, anxiety or organic suffering one can bear and still tolerate existence is the limit of one's own degeneration. Some persons reach their limits much sooner than others -- a violent tantrum or an overwhelming feeling of deficiency from a single loss serving as occasion for self-destruction. Others manifest great capacity for suffering, and one's capacity for suffering before reaching one's own limit may vary with time and circumstance, and with ideas regarding future prospects. It seems very doubtful that a person can become completely evil and remain so enduringly.

Interdependence of "Better" and "Worse". Intrinsic good and intrinsic evil can and do normally exist in the same person, even if not always at the same time. Although you may for moments be aware only of intrinsic goodness or of intrinsic evil, and although you may succeed in prolonging the periods of the former and in decreasing the durations of the latter, the naturalness of the intuiting both from time by the same self is evident to everyone. The normalcy for living things to experience both seems presupposed by those who picture an ideal place after death, "Heaven," where alone one can experience good without evil, and by those who project an ideal state beyond life, "Nirvana," which is beyond both good and evil. Since the same self can become both better and worse, "better" and "worse" depend upon that self both for their being and their becoming. But do they "interdepend?"

A person naturally grows. Growing may involve gaining more interests, enlargement of the being having such interests, and increase in the intrinsic good involved in such added being. But since you have only limited amounts of time, energy and attention, you must sooner or later find such expanding interests, and being, and goods, competing with, and conflicting with, each other. Whenever this happens, and when you become aware of such conflict as unpleasant, frustrating or otherwise harmful to your being, intrinsic evil comes to be experienced. In such situations, your becoming better, or increasing in intrinsic value, causes intrinsic evil, and some more of it than existed before. Hence, growth in intrinsic value may cause increase in intrinsic evil, or becoming better may cause becoming worse.

But also, healthy persons tend to learn from experience. When we discover that intrinsic evil follows from overdoing, from wanting more additional intrinsic value than we can attain without conflict, we may learn not to overdo by overdoing. We can learn not to want more new intrinsic good than we can manage without involving ourselves in additional intrinsic evil. When we have so learned, we deliberately try to diminish our growth in interests to the point where we can increase them without entailing harmful conflicts between them. Thus we can judge that our having become worse was instrumental to our becoming better, or at least better than we could have become without the instrumentally useful lessons derived from evil experience. Hence we conclude also that increase in intrinsic evil may cause increase in intrinsic good, or becoming worse may cause becoming better.

Of course, some of us learn more slowly than others, and all of us at times learn more slowly than at other times. We vary in moral ability, or intelligence. Some need to learn the same kind of lesson over and over again in each new type of situation, whereas others enjoy ability to "transfer their training" from one learning situation to another. Some, as children, master lessons which they profitably carry over into adolescent, marital, occupational and political situations. Others require the pains of relearning in each new personal and social context. Although it is true that we cannot improve more than we can improve, most of us have ability to become better than we have yet become. So long as this is the case, the problem of increasing our moral ability, or intelligence, both relative to insight and to either willingness or willfulness to do what is required, may be our most important moral problem.

Chapter VIII

SELF-OBLIGATION

"Obligation," "duty" and "oughtness" are terms with similar, if not synonymous, meaning. We shall attend here to their common significance. "Oughtness" consists in the power which a greater good has over a lesser good in compelling our choices. Although one ought to choose the better of two means to an end, the end or intrinsic value functions as the ultimate locus of such compulsive power. Hence, ultimately the power constituting oughtness consists in the superiority that one attainable intrinsic good has over another. Such power reaches its pinnacle in any greatest, highest or supreme good in any comparative situation. "The end justifies the means" because nothing else can. And the way in which one end is a greater good than another constitutes that demand upon our choices which exists as "oughtness." All other meanings of "oughtness," "duty" and "obligation" derive from this basis.

"Obligation" exists only when one faces alternatives. If, for any reason or for any period of time, you have no alternatives, either because you have achieved your goals and are occupying ourself with enjoying them or because you find yourself so situated as to be completely helpless, you have no obligation. However, such situations may be extremely rare, for you almost constantly face alternatives relative to degrees of willingness or unwillingness with which you accept your situation. Furthermore, you usually remain aware, even if only subconsciously, of your more-than-momentary being. Your semi-conscious concern for other-than-conscious aspects of your being, and for your future, in general even if not specifically, is suffused with such alternative attitudes as hope or resignation, or uncertainty or confidence, to say nothing of possibilities for fear, anger, resentment, or of eagerness and zeal, or of boredom. If you happen to be a helpless victim even of your own attitudes, then you have no oughtness regarding them. But when this happens, you are no longer a free agent. The question of the extent to which you function as a free agent (to be discussed in the following chapters) as against a mere mechanism itself constitutes an ought, and a most basic ought, whenever you have any choice in the matter. That is, insofar as you face the alternative of whether you ought to have more or fewer oughts may itself be your most important ought.

Having defined the nature of "oughtness" in general, we turn now to more specific kinds of oughtness. There are as many varieties of oughtness as there are varieties of alternatives. Without reviewing here the previously recognized distinction between "conditional" and "actual" oughts (See Chapter I), we will focus upon the perpetually bothersome problem of whether, and to what extent, we are obligated to others. Many believe that "obligations" are always to others, even only to others. When we do so believe, then to the extent that we have no interest in others, or have interests in competing against others, we tend to feel that we have no obligation to them. We may even feel obligated (without always being clearly aware of this feeling as obligation) to act disinterestedly or antagonistically toward such others. It may in fact be the case that one ought to oppose one's genuine enemies, and this "ought" is not something which one owes them, but is a debt which one owes to oneself. (Of course, if one's enemies can somehow benefit by one's opposition, especially in such a way that one can benefit by their benefiting from one's opposition, then one may have a further debt, not so much to them as to oneself.)

What is "Self-Obligation"? How do you owe yourself anything? How can you be indebted to yourself? This question does not refer to "paying back" anything to yourself, as one pays back borrowed money. Problems connected with reciprocal treatment will be considered in Chapter XIII, "Self As Just." It deals, rather, with recognizing and accepting yourself as being faced with alternatives relative to the existence of greater or less intrinsic good. Your debt is both to yourself and for yourself. It is to yourself because, and to the extent that, you yourself are the intrinsic good at stake. It is for yourself because, and to the extent that, you yourself are an intrinsic good to which or for which something can be done since only that which is, or has, or will be or will have, intrinsic good can have anything "done for" it. Instrumental good, as indicated earlier, depends for its existence upon its service to some intrinsic good.

You are self-obligated because you are an end-in-yourself with potentialities for continuing or increasing (or discontinuing or decreasing) your intrinsic good. Where the alternative of existing or not existing occurs, you ought to prefer the existence of intrinsic good just because intrinsic good, or greater rather than less intrinsic good, is the ultimate basis of oughtness. A self is an inherently obligated being just because it is or has intrinsic value which can be endangered or improved. The fact that you can be improved by your own actions, if and when you can, constitutes self-obligation. All of the ways in which a self can become better or worse, as noted in the previous chapter, constitute areas of self-obligation whenever one is confronted with a choice between alternatives.

The limits of choosable self-improvement and self-degeneration constitute limits of self-obligation.

The nature of self-obligation is more than a general kind of thing for it depends upon the specific nature of self; and since, as noted earlier, each self may vary, and many selves may differ, in their extent and complexity of being, what constitutes self-obligation varies somewhat from person to person and time to time. Consider for example a person who happens to be a parent who has lost a child. His being, and enjoying being, a parent exits as a part of his nature and intrinsic good While the child lives, the parent ought to aid in preserving and improving his child (who is also an intrinsic good) because he owes it to himself to preserve and improve that aspect of himself constituted by his being, and enjoying being, a parent. When the child dies, the parent loses his being, and enjoying being, a parent, with whatever being and enjoyment or sorrow that status may entail. He may now cherish a memorial and enjoy or suffer whatever being and awareness this new status brings. A person whose nature and circumstances remain mostly unchanged for long periods retains relatively stable self-obligations. But one who changes rapidly or often thereby acquires versatile self-obligations. If one has any choice in the matter, the question of whether he can develop ability to change his nature and value quickly and frequently may itself be not only a matter of self-obligation but a most important one.

We shall not review here details of the complex nature of self, with its multiplicities of parts, aspects and levels, each of which may have its own being and enjoyability. But we may need a reminder that the persistent problem of retaining self-integration in the face of growing complexities of goods, and of the obligations they involve, itself constitutes a major self-obligation. Whenever we acquire new goods, whether in the form of having new friendships, new institutional memberships, new wealth, new skills, or whatever, we add new obligations. Even apart from questions of social obligation, which have yet to be discussed, we may repeatedly face the problem of retaining integrity or enduring resilience. During childhood and youth one may revel in an abundance of untapped resources for growth. But maturity and old age bring many to their limits of healthy self-expansion. Not until we confront ourselves as having undertaken too much do we realize that we have overreached our capacity for growth. When we become too tense, harried, distraught, confused, desperate, and especially when we become consequently weakened and less able to perform our already-integrated functions, we have not merely extended, but distended our self. Children and youth, or whoever has not yet reached full capacity, are self-obligated to grow some more. Mature and aged persons, or whoever can add, or even maintain, energy-consuming functions, only at expense to their integrity and resiliency, have reached their limits and have become self-obligated not to add to but perhaps subtract from their cluster of active goods which, when retained, conflict with each other and with the superior good of personal integrity.

For example, one who has no children perhaps ought to have children, whereas one who already has more children than one can support ought to have no more. One who has little wealth perhaps should seek more, but it may be that one who owns more wealth than one can protect from thieves or use efficiently ought to have less. One who enjoys few interests normally should acquire more; on the other hand, one who has more interests than can be pursued with some satisfactory degree of depth perhaps ought to withdraw from enough of them to escape a condition of pervasive superficiality. Self-obligation is thus complex and variable, and so one may be self-obligated to be aware of and sensitive to such complexities and variations in self-obligation.

Since "oughtness" originates in intrinsic good, in facing a choice of alternatives between intrinsic goods, and in the power that a greater has over a lesser intrinsic good in compelling such choice, a comparison of each of the aspects and theories of intrinsic good should prove rewarding. Insofar as intrinsic good consists in pleasant feeling, Hedonists correctly assert that "oughtness" should be defined in terms of choosing pleasure rather than pain, or pleasure rather than no pleasure, or the most pleasure rather than less pleasure, whenever relevant alternatives present themselves. One is self-obligated to choose the greatest possible pleasure from among alternatives present or in prospect, for one thereby promotes oneself as a pleasure-embodying being, or as an intrinsic-good being, as much as possible. Insofar as intrinsic good consists in satisfaction of desire, Voluntarists properly contend that "oughtness" involves prompting desire and satisfaction, fostering satisfaction and preventing frustration, and encouraging the most satisfaction, whenever opportunity and capacity permit. Existence endows us with a self-obligation to choose the greatest possible satisfaction now or in the long run, for we thereby reenforce ourselves, and existence insofar as it actualizes itself in us, as satisfaction-incarnating beings, or as intrinsic-good beings, as much as we can.

Insofar as intrinsic good consists in feelings of enthusiasm, Romanticists rightly insist that "oughtness" consists in endeavoring to be vigorous, eager, buoyant, and to avoid feelings of depression, hopelessness and lethargy, whenever possible. You are self-obligated to exert your will, your impulse, your passion, and to fight monotony, mechanical habits and inhibiting feelings of guilt, when you have any choice in the matter. Insofar as intrinsic good consists in contentment, Anandists appropriately insist that "oughtness" implies seeking to achieve the most complete quiescence possible by eliminating all desires, anxieties, and disturbances. Each self is inherently self-obligated to master and suppress all desireousness as much as possible, either by stilling completely all influences from bodily life, as in Raja Yoga, or by replacing willfulness by complete and spontaneous willingness, as in Zen.

Insofar as intrinsic good consists in "organic enjoyment," Organicists more comprehensively claim that "oughtness" encompasses and incorporates at least some of each and all of the foregoing "oughts" together with an ought regarding their harmonious but variable integration in a resilient enduring self. That is, "oughtness" pertains not only to alternatives between more or less pleasure, satisfaction, enthusiasm and contentment but also (1) to alternatives between whatever more or less of intrinsic good may be involved in choosing between (a) a pleasure and a satisfaction, (b) a pleasure and an enthusiasm, (c) a pleasure and a contentment, (d) a satisfaction and an enthusiasm, (e) a satisfaction and a contentment, (f) an enthusiasm and a contentment, and also (2) to alternatives between enjoying one's being with all of these ingredients variably intermingling in a "come what may" fashion and deliberately focusing one's attention exclusively upon a pleasing sensation or an exciting desire. "Oughtness" comprises choosing not only between quantity, duration, intensity, quality, etc., of enjoyment, between present and future enjoyment, between kinds of intrinsic good ("pleasures," "satisfactions," etc.) enjoyed, but also between seeking "more being" to be enjoyed (which may become more than one can enjoy) and "more enjoyment" of the being which one already is (which may result in disability to obtain or retain enough more being, e.g., food, health, wealth, security, needed to continue such enjoyment).

For example, consider your self going to a carnival. Carnivals are designed to produce pleasures, enthusiasms, and satisfactions (but not much, if any, contentment). Part of the complexity of the organicist theory of self-obligation may be illustrated relative to some choices typically faced by a circus-goer. Normally one approaches a big circus with some limitations regarding money, time and energy. If you are young, wide-eyed and overflowing with vigor and enthusiasm, lack of money may be your chief vexation. If so, then you must estimate how to divide your resources between side shows and main attractions, between sensuous pleasures (popcorn, peanuts, candy), thrills (roller coaster, ferris wheel, dark tunnel), astounding marvels (two-headed calf, magic tricks, fat man), pride of prowess (marksmanship, guessing games, strength-testing machines), and between pursuing your own preferences and yielding to requests by your friends. In the rush of excitement, few can or would care to if they could, distinguish between "pleasant feelings," "enthusiasm" and "satisfaction of desire." All intermingle kaleidoscopically; in such circumstances comprehension of "chaos-integrity issues" regarding self is doubtless beyond normal ability.

But you may be able to discriminate between your desire to see a particular show now and your desire to be able later to say that you had been, and had enjoyed being, at that show. Later, at least, you can distinguish between your satisfaction in having been there and the pleasing taste of mustard and pickles on your hot dog. Furthermore, you may notice a general air of excitement pervading not only the atmosphere but your own spirit, even when you do not actually participate in each gay, gaudy, giddy delight. An enjoyment of your own being in "just being there" may be more obvious when noting other youngsters dejectedly standing on the outside looking longingly in.

You can hardly enjoy yourself at a carnival without some abandonment of yourself to its attractions. Thus there is a sense in which you ought to do so. Yet also, limits exist beyond which you ought not go in reducing your whole nature and welfare to that of a carnival-goer. Sane selves expect to exist tomorrow also and retain sufficient prudence to prevent undue debts, hangovers and jeopardy to life and friends. Children whose parents provide for their morrow have less reason for caution. Oldsters, whose vexations consist less in lack of money than in lack of energy, tend to be more aware of enduring goods, such as strength for tomorrow, consideration for friends, and unwillingness to be misled by trivial deceits, farces and frivolities. Retention of overarching perspective marks maturity. Yet you ought not to go to a carnival if you is unprepared to enjoy something of its demand for gullibility.

The issue at stake so far as Organicistic self-obligation is concerned has to do with how far you should permit yourself to be pulled in either of two polar directions: abandonment to momentary attractions, pleasures, thrills, excitements on the one hand, and retention of permanent welfare ideals permeating your awareness while at a carnival, on the other. What one ought to do at a carnival, or at any time, depends upon apparent alternatives regarding prospective enjoyment of intrinsic goods, now and in the future, or regarding present thrills versus anticipatable satisfactions.

Variations in perspectives must be expected relative to youth and age, amounts of time, money and vigor, and both insight into and actual abilities regarding responsibilities for future goods. An irresponsible adult may rightly abandon himself more wholeheartedly at a carnival than a responsible child. Oughtness is relative. But common kinds of conditions of such relativity remain to be noted.

Negative oughtness, or "ought-not-ness," consists in choosing the least of two or more prospective evils whenever such option exists. Intrinsic evil, Organicistically conceived, has been described as "organic suffering," which includes unpleasant feelings, feelings, of frustration, feelings of apathy, and feelings of discontentment. Instrumental evil exists in whatever aids in producing such feelings. One ought to choose and to act in such a way as to prevent or reduce present and future occurrence of all such evils insofar as one can. The Organicist view of ought-not-ness thus incorporates aspects from Hedonistic, Voluntaristic, Romanticistic and Anandistic views of negative oughtness. It refuses to reduce the nature of such negative oughtness to either of the four aspects alone but at the same time recognizes that any one of them may dominate the oughtness facing one in a particular situation.

You are self-obligated, then, to enjoy the intrinsic goods (whether distinguishable as pleasures, satisfactions, enthusiasms, or contentment or as undifferentiated organic enjoyment) embodied in your being, and to avoid incorporating intrinsic evils (whether discerned distinctly as pains, frustrations, apathy, or anxiety or suffered as general misery), as much as you can.

Finally, we should consider the question as to whether it is better to be non-ethical (beyond good and evil and beyond oughts and ought-nots) than to be even all-good or to-have-done-all-that-one-ought-to-do. Here is a question, and a lesson, urged upon us by Anandists. But we must distinguish between "non-ethical" (or "amoral") in the sense in which we have no choice among alternatives and "non-ethical" in the sense in which we have chosen, or ought to choose, to be "non-ethical." Some Anandists claim that it is better to be beyond all good and evil than to be all-good. The Nirvana idealized in Madhyamika's <u>Sunya</u>, Advaita's <u>Atman</u> and Samkhya's freed soul (<u>purusha</u>) all exemplify this claim. Whenever the strain of conflict between one's oughts and ought-nots becomes experienced as an intrinsic evil judged to be greater than the good which can come from doing what one ought, then, if one has the alternative, one ought to choose to escape from such strain by entering an amoral status.

By doing so you thereby surrender an essential part of your normal self -- your free will, your power to choose, your morality. To surrender your morality in the interest of amorality may, on occasion, seem, and be, the most moral thing to do. But to do so completely, i.e., forever and for all future occasions, constitutes a kind of suicide, i.e., moral suicide. To do so is to become no longer a "person" or "self" in its full sense. From an Organicist viewpoint, you ought to try to ascertain when it is better to be amoral, even completely amoral, and when it is better to be moral, even completely moral -- even if you must thereby choose ("Existentially") to choose some evil. In sum, at times one ought to want to be amoral, at times you ought to want to be moral, and at times you must choose between wanting to be moral and wanting to be amoral; and this latter choice itself may be your most ultimate kind of choice, your "highest" option, yet it may become a common-place option for one living at an Organicistically "high level" or morality.

What is Social Obligation"?   In popular usage the term "social obligation" suggests return of courtesies, such as repaying a call or an invitation by your new neighbor. But in the present context, "social obligation" refers generally to obligations which you as an individual have to all others who have or will become in any way involved in your own obligations to yourself. That is, "social obligation" is here conceived as an extension of, or rather as an essential part of, self-obligation. The extent to which your nature and welfare and enjoyment of intrinsic good depend upon, or interdepend with, the nature, welfare and enjoyments of intrinsic goods by others, is the extent to which your own self-obligation involves social obligation. Another meaning of "social obligation" will be used in Part II, Chapter XXII, where organized groups, such as a nation, may be regarded as having obligations both to its citizens (Does a nation have obligations to minority groups?) and to other groups (Does the United States have obligations to assist "developing countries?").

Oughtness or obligation, we have said, exists whenever we have a choice between alternatives and consists in the power which a greater good has over a lesser good in compelling our choice. The ultimate basis of oughtness exists in intrinsic good. Self-obligation exists whenever you are aware that choosing and acting upon one rather than another alternative embodies in yourself greater intrinsic good now or is instrumentally conducive to eventual embodiment in yourself of such greater intrinsic good. To the extent that you are social, i.e., have group memberships and social roles as parts of yourself (see Chapter IV, "Self and Social"), and experience "organic enjoyment" relative to such parts, you have self-obligation pertaining to whatever options occur for increasing or decreasing intrinsic good relative to them. The problem of knowing the extent of the social parts, aspects and levels of your nature continues permanently to be both significant and variable. It is significant because your social aspects are <u>essential</u> to your nature. Social, psychological, biological and even physical scientists progressively uncover additional kinds of dependence. It is variable because you may actually change with respect to your dependence upon others for your enjoyment of intrinsic good and, what is equally important, you may waiver in your knowledge and awareness of such dependence.

Unfortunately many highly dependent persons suffer from an illusion of independence, an illusion fostered normally in anyone whose annoyance with social restrictions magnifies itself into an intolerable bogey, and fostered additionally by cultural ideas of "individualism," especially "rugged individualism," in situations where conditions permitting and causing such individualism have ceased to exist. But also some who possess ability for greater independence fail to discover and experience the intrinsic good enjoyable in actualizing such condition of being. Your capacities for developing self-enjoyment and thus self-obligation may be stunted in either the direction of too much independence or too much dependence. Neither independent nor dependent being exclusively serves as a basis for enjoyment and obligation. For you may desire more independence and then enjoy feelings of satisfaction when it is acquired, or you may desire more dependence and enjoy satisfaction when this is attained; and you may desire more interdependence of self and others, or more versatile interplay of dependence and independence, and appreciate these when achieved.

Marriage exemplifies interdependence in which two persons normally enjoy acquiring a social status, both in the surrounding community and relative to each other, which constitutes a part, aspect or level of both persons as beings. In addition to other, perhaps more obvious, joys and sorrows of marriage, the experience of being married, or of having a married condition as a part of one's being, occurs as something to be enjoyed. The custom of anniversary celebrations offers aid in directing attention to the enjoyability of such condition, something more useful later in marriage after each has come to "take the other for granted." Interdependence in marriage involves fluctuation in kinds and degrees of dependence and independence, both daily and over longer periods. Mutual dependence for experiences of intimate emotions, not merely for interstimulation but for joint consummation of orgasmic ecstacies, heightened by sympathetic or, better, empathetic, rapture, should be quite obvious. But even unbounded bliss subsides, physiques become fatigued, we must work to eat, and life requires, for example, some husbands to lift heavy burdens and some wives to suckle children in ways such that each must do one's work alone. The differing joys experienced in achieving feats of strength and in nurturing a child constitute husband and wife as beings also different in kind with private kinds of intrinsic-good appreciations. Anti-nepotism laws, which signify unfortunate results of permitting marital prejudices to interfere with corporation policy decisions, illustrate practical need for husband and wife to seek some goods separately. However, even greater goods may be enjoyed by a man who appreciates the more complex personal enhancement emerging from being both dependent upon and independent of his wife and dependent upon and independent of his corporation for different, but nevertheless organically interrelated intrinsic goods. Additional multi-leveled aspects of being enrich a self, provided additions do not overtax one's ability to integrate them or produce conflicts of goods which force one to embody more intrinsic evil.

Self-obligation involves social obligation to the extent that one's own intrinsic goods intertwine with those of others -- as they do, both in intimate mutualities and in economic-political systems complexly organized for the efficient mass production needed for high standards of living. To the extent that a self may become more secure, more substantial, as well as more rich and complex, through accepting and using manageable opportunities for increased social obligation, one may be self-obligated to do so. Intricacies of ways in which one's own self-obligations interdepend with self-obligations of others have yet to be explored.

Principles for Choosing. Do principles for choosing exist? Some say, "Yes." Some say, "No." Some say, "Maybe."

1. Affirmers may be divided for convenience into two groups: "extremists" and "moderates." "Extremists" claim that some universal principles for choosing necessarily exist. They may point out the long and devious historical struggle of mankind from chaotic, uncertain, superstitious, fearful Animism to orderly, sure, deductive and confident Rationalism. The remarkable discovery, which reached a climax in Greek philosophy, of universal necessary laws of existence, whether exhibited in nature or persons or God, has been hailed as final achievement of human

superiority over all other animals. "Man is a rational animal." Such a view involves a problem for humans, namely, that of discovering such universal and necessary laws and of explaining how such laws can be.

Some Rationalists, such as Aristotle, Augustine, Calvin and Spinoza, conceive one uncaused, self-existing God as perfectly rational. Creations, including persons, may imperfectly embody or reveal God's complete rationality, resulting in immorality. If persons were as perfectly rational as God, they would conform completely to universal and necessary moral principles. Accurate expressions of God's "Will," which is identical with his "Reason," provide principles for choosing, in morals as in mathematics, which permit no exceptions.

Other Rationalists, including atheistic Mechanists, inherited similar ideals of Rationalistic determinism. "If our existence is based on the play of blind forces and only a matter of chance; if we ourselves are only chemical mechanisms, how can there be an ethics for us? The answer is that our instincts are the root of our ethics and that the instincts are just as hereditary as is the form of our body. We eat, drink, and reproduce, not because mankind has reached an agreement that this is desirable, but because, machine-like we are compelled to do so. We are active, because we are compelled to be so by processes in our central nervous system; and as long as human beings are not economic slaves the instinct of successful workmanship determines the direction of their action. The mother loves and cares for her children, not because metaphysicians had the idea that this was desirable, but because the instinct for taking care of the young is inherited just as distinctly as the morphological characters of the female body. We seek and enjoy the fellowship of human beings because hereditary conditions compel us to do so. We struggle for justice and truth since we are instinctively compelled to see our fellow beings happy. Economical, social, and political conditions or ignorance and superstition may warp and inhibit the inherited instincts and thus create a civilization with a faulty or low development of ethics. Individual mutants may arise in which one or the other desirable trait is lost, just as individual mutants without pigment may arise in animals; and the offspring may, if numerous enough, lower the ethical status of a community. Not only is the mechanistic conception of life compatible with ethics; it seems the only conception of life which can lead us to an understanding of the source of ethics." (Jacques Loeb, The Mechanistic Conception of Life, p. 31, University of Chicago Press, Chicago, 1912.)

"Moderates," on the other hand, may regard some principles as universal but not necessary, and some as very general but not universal.

Empirical studies by sociologists and anthropologists reveal a "universal culture pattern" (Clark Wissler, Man and Culture, p. 74, Thomas Y. Crowell, New York, 1923.) which, however caused, prevails everywhere, thus providing a basis for moral standards available to everyone. For example, although monogamy is not practiced universally, no culture exists without some system for regulating marriage.

2. Deniers also may be divided into "extremists" and "moderates." "Extremists" claim that no bases for principles of choosing exist. Some of these emphasize obvious differences observable as prevailing among people and their goods. Each value-experience is unique, hence incomparable; thus no basis exists for comparing or judging or choosing. Some stress illusoriness of values and of principles; thus any supposed basis for judging is really illusory. Some complete determinists say we have no freedom, hence no freedom of choice; thus no principles for free choice exist. Some believers in free choice assert that submission of choice to principle is to surrender freedom; thus choosing to choose by principle is choosing to surrender choice, so the very idea of a principle for choosing is practically self-contradictory. Some Linguistic Analysts reduce value judgments to "emotive sentences" and these, being "non-factual," must be excluded from the realm of factual judgments. So, many different schools of thought agree in denying the existence of any genuine bases for principles of choosing.

"Moderate deniers" admit that there may be some ultimate bases for generalization but insist that we mortals find life just too complicated to systematize. It is impractical to undertake the most futile endeavor to discover reliable principles of uniformity for value-judgments; even though ideally there might be, in actual practice there is no "science of ethics." Even if we could reduce all choices to choices under principles, the task is too enormous; it would be an unbearable burden, and a greater evil than any good that might come from it. Besides, there is no need to try, since Nature (Tao) is wiser than persons and provides for all our needs anyway. (See my edition of Tao Teh King by Lao Tzu, pp. 47-55, 86-91.) Providence, whether natural or divine, supplies all that is needed for life and its fulfillment. Superimposing artificial principles upon Nature's self-sufficient plan merely leads persons away from Nature's way. Just as all other animals and plants come into being, live out their lives, and die, without setting up and appealing to artificial principles for choosing, so human beings, also creatures of Providence, can, and should, do likewise. So "moderate deniers" agree that, even though there may be bases for making moral generalizations, either it is not worth our while, or actually evil, to do so.

3. "Maybe" covers a wide range of view holders unwilling to be drawn toward either extreme. Both of the claims, i.e., that some universal principles for choosing necessarily exist and that no bases for such principles exist, remain dubious though discovery of such principles may be possible and, if so, effort expended in this direction may prove worth while. This range, which shades gradually into the two varieties of moderates just mentioned, includes both those tending toward more skepticism, emphasizing doubts as to whether we can or cannot discover such principles, and those tending to prefer pragmatism, willingly accepting the challenge to try out proposals regarding principles to see whether or not, and to what extent, such proposals do work.

4. We find ourselves sympathetic to the pragmatic "maybe-ers." Science itself is essentially pragmatic in nature. That is, on the one hand, it retains a degree of tentativity regarding its most firmly established conclusions and, on the other, it entertains, even if only playfully, the most absurd hypotheses, but as evidence mounts for or against hypotheses, including ethical hypotheses such as Hedonism, Voluntarism, Romanticism, Anandism and Organicism, it takes them more seriously. The types of evidence sketched in previous chapters suggest workable distinctions between intrinsic and instrumental values, actual and potential values, and pleasures, satisfactions, enthusiasms and contentment as intrinsic goods. Granted the existence of intrinsic good and evils, more and less of these, and oughtness as power of greater over lesser goods, then some bases exist for further explorations regarding principles for choosing.

Persons are by nature choosing beings. This fact appears as obvious as anything about persons. This trait of choosing, to say nothing about "choosiness," seems universal both in the sense that it occurs in all persons and in each person most, if not all, of the time. Even when not choosing, a person often appears to be choosing not to choose. The need for choosing exists within human nature to the extent that survival and satisfaction depend upon such choice. Of course, we choose in accordance with such principles before we discover them to be principles. Yet, just as we sometimes fall off cliffs, even though we naturally tend to avoid falling off cliffs, so we sometimes choose wrongly, even though we naturally tend to choose rightly. Knowledge of, and awareness of principles for choosing should enable us to choose rightly more often.

Both of the views, that principles for choosing necessarily exist and
that no principles for choosing exist, have some basis in fact. Persons do
choose and must choose just because persons are faced with alternatives,
and the conditions which make them choosing beings involve whatever
principles inhere in those conditions. Yet also, many situations calling for
decision are so intricate, so pervaded with obscure causal factors, and so
unique, that it is impossible for us to discover all of the principles actually
operating and to judge clearly what is actually best. And in some
situations where we could so judge if we could study long enough, such
study is neither possible, nor feasible, nor worthwhile. Thus we often face
decisions as to whether we ought to try to choose between looking for
and not looking for principles for choosing. This problem of choosing
whether to choose not to choose may be a most persistent one for anyone
seeking to do what is best for oneself in the long run.

Whoever has time enough to make a study of ethics should try to
discover for oneself whether and what principles for choosing exist. The
remainder of the present chapter will be devoted to exploring several
aspects of this problem selected for separate treatment. We shall
endeavor to state some most general principles and to formulate them as
items for a most general code. But first let us consider an issue
concerning which widespread misunderstanding exists, namely, absolutism
versus relativism regarding ethical principles.

"Absolutism" versus "Relativism". People commonly contrast
"absolutism" and "relativism" in ethics as if they were contradictory
opposites, implying that if you are an absolutist you cannot be a relativist
and if you are a relativist you cannot be an absolutist. However, the
incorrectness of this common view is easy to demonstrate, if we but pause
to examine it a bit more carefully.

1. "Absolutism" is said to hold that standards are universal and
unchanging and hence exactly the same for all. But observe an ambiguity
in the meaning of "exactly the same for all." It may mean (a) "exactly the
same for all regardless of circumstances" or (b) "exactly the same for all
in exactly the same circumstances." Or worse, it may be ambiguous with
respect to whether and how much such circumstances are expected to be
alike.

2. "Relativism" is said to hold that standards are relative to different
particular and changing circumstances. But observe certain ambiguities
in the meaning of "relative to." (a) Standards are sometimes said to be
relative to each culture or each century or each group, but, at the same

time, absolute and universally binding within that culture, century or group. This view has been called "cultural relativism," and may be illustrated by the well-known saying, "When in Rome do as the Romans do." (b) Standards are sometimes said to be relative to each individual, but at the same time absolute for the individual. ("Each man is a law unto himself." "Each man must be true to himself.") (c) Standards are sometimes said to be relative to each moment, and thus, at the same time, absolute for that moment. Thus the most extreme relativist involves himself in a predicament which is hard to distinguish from the most obviously true form of absolutism. To say that each moment for decision is self-contained or has its standard for judgment contained entirely within itself rather than related to and dependent upon other situations, because other situations differ from it, is no different, for practical purposes, from saying that standards are exactly the same for all persons in exactly the same circumstances when no two circumstances can be exactly the same. Thus complete relativism is a kind of absolute relativism. And the just-mentioned complete absolutism is a kind of relative absolutism.

If we have observed, in the foregoing, that each kind of relativism is involved in its own kind of absolutism, and that "absolutism" is ambiguous until it is further defined relative to the extent to which such circumstances are intended to be alike, we may conclude that one can hardly be an absolutist without also being to some extent a relativist or be a relativist without also being in some sense an absolutist. If so, then we do not have a clear grasp of the "absolutism-relativism" issue until we can formulate clearly the ways in which both absolutistic and relativistic aspects are present in each situation. We propose that the following is a more adequate statement than either "absolutism" or relativism."

3. First, we submit as obvious the view that, insofar as things or circumstances are alike, we have a basis for generalization and, insofar as things or circumstances differ, we do not have such a basis. Things and circumstances are both alike in some respects and different in others, although many of us develop predilections for noticing the similarities and ignoring the differences while many of us tend to see the differences and overlook the similarities. We tend to see what we look for. Things are alike in being things, and different in being different things. Furthermore, things, and circumstances, may be grouped together in "kinds" on the basis of their having certain similarities in common. And things of any kind are alike in being things of that kind, and yet different in being different things of that kind.

Next, we submit as also obvious that standards are both universal and unchanging in some respects; for insofar as persons and their circumstances are the same, what is right for one person or in one circumstance may differ from what is right for other persons or in other circumstances. It should be noted that this view incorporates all of the foregoing five statements into its own single, and at the same time more general and comprehensive, statement by means of the more precise variable "insofar as." To keep this more general and comprehensive view in mind is to have a profounder insight into, and a more powerful grasp of, the nature of ethical situations. It states a most general principle, and one that remains relevant to all situations in which other, still-to-be-considered, principles also apply. This principle may be used to formulate an item in a most general code: You ought always note, as well as you can, how much situations are both alike and different when judging whether you ought to decide to act in one situation as you rightly decided to act in another previous situation.

This third view is seen by Organicists both to follow from, and in turn to support, their general tenets. Although relativism and absolutism differ from each other in some essential respects, they also depend upon each other for their meaning and nature. Each is true in its positive assertion, i.e., that rightness merely is relative insofar as situations differ and that rightness is absolute or universal insofar as situations are alike, but each is false in its denial of what is true in the other, i.e., that rightness is relative even when circumstances are the same and that rightness is absolute or universal even when circumstances differ. The apparent omnipresence of both similarities and differences provides bases both for a reasonable search for principles for choosing insofar as choosing situations are the same and for a reasonable skeptical expectation that right choice cannot be reduced entirely to matters of principle because, and to the extent that, situations differ.

Some Principles Stated. To the extent that persons and their circumstances are alike, bases for generalization exist. The purpose of the present section is to state and examine some very general principles proposed for choosing between goods. These principles may vary in degree of obviousness. The universality of their applicability may be tested by different persons with variable degrees of success. Hence, they are proposed here as hypotheses for the reader's consideration. But, to the writer, they seem both intuitively obvious and testable without exception. They will be grouped for convenience into six groups.

A. *Principles Applying to Both Intrinsic and Instrumental Values.* Our first general principle, formulated as an item in a most general code, is that: *Other things being equal, when faced with a choice between two alternatives, one of which is good and the other evil, a person ought always to choose the good alternative.* The principle consists in the good (ultimately, the intrinsic good) being the ultimate locus of (teleological) power for compelling our choices. The code item is a statement of a rule for choosing which has its basis, and explanation, in this principle.

The phrase, "other things being equal," may need some comment here. It applies not only to the principle, and code item, under consideration but to all the principles for choosing proposed here and, indeed, to all scientific principles. Every scientific principle is, or should be, stated or interpreted, as a conditional ought (See Chapter I), or the applicability of every scientific principle depends upon whether or not, and to what extent, circumstances are actually alike. To neglect what should be, as far as possible, an ever-present awareness of the conditional nature of universal scientific principles is to be in danger of inferring mistakenly. Whoever falls into the error of assuming that scientific principles have an absoluteness greater than actual, i.e., apply regardless of circumstances rather than apply only insofar as circumstances are the same, judges falsely. Your judgment may not be morally wrong if you have not been faced with a choice between alternatives; but your judgment may nevertheless result in evil consequences to the extent that you have been misled unwittingly to affirm a false conclusion. The conditional nature of scientific principles, and the willingness to remain tentative required by the scientific attitude, persist as continuing conditions of applicability of scientific principles. However, this need for tentativity, both in formulating and stating principles and codes for choosing, which should carry over into situations where moral decisions must become categorical, need not reduce the apparent obviousness and testability of such principles and codes as holding within the conditions involved in such conditional nature of scientific principles.

A second general principle and general code item pertains to alternatives consisting in greater and lesser goods and to alternatives consisting of greater and lesser evils. This will be considered in three aspects. The first aspect may be stated as a code item as follows: *When faced with the problem of choosing between two alternatives, one of which is good and the other better, other things being equal, one ought always to choose the better.* The second aspect may be stated as a code item as follows: *When faced with the problem of choosing between two alternatives, one of which is bad and the other worse, other things being equal, one ought always to choose the bad rather than the worse.* The third aspect, which combines and extends the first two aspects, may be stated as a code item: *When faced with the problem of choosing between two or more alternatives, some of which are better than others and some of which are worse than others, other things being equal, one ought always to choose the most good and least evil possible.* These three aspects, stated as code items, have their explanation in the general principle that of two goods (ultimately, two intrinsic goods), one of which is better than the other, the greater goodness of the one (whether pleasure, satisfaction, enthusiasm, contentment or organic enjoyment) has within itself the (teleological) power to compel our will to choose it, and that of two evils (ultimately, two intrinsic evils), one of which is worse than the other, the greater evil of the one (whether pain, frustration, apathy, anxiety or organic suffering) has within it the (teleological) power to compel our will to choose to avoid it.

We might, at this point, note that the first principle and code item stated above has been incorporated into the statement of the third aspect and its principle of explanation. The inclusion of simpler principles, or codes, in more complex principles, or codes, does not eliminate them, though it may eliminate need for enumerating them. Rather, such inclusion indicates not only that complex principles depend upon simpler ones but also that simpler ones which exist as statements based on partial similarities between situations involve, and are involved in, the more complex principles needed to complete their own nature and contribution to an interpretation and codification of general principles for choosing which is adequate to account for the more complex similarities existing between situations. Although each of several simpler principles for choosing may be intuitively obvious in itself, such intuitive clarity does not depend upon exclusive isolation; the nature of each such principle may depend upon others in such an intimate way that one can intuit their interrelations as obvious also. The obviousness may appear, upon reflection, to function as an automatic presupposition of most unreflective thought, decision and action. To "common sense," they may seem so obvious as to be unworthy of deliberate attention. "Common sense" disparages the philosophical quest for "first principles" because what is "perfectly obvious" cannot be made any more obvious by being singled out for discrete attention. However, the kind of obviousness which satisfies unreflective "common sense" hardly quiets scientific curiosity for discovering and explicating "first principles." Yet, also, since complex explication of principles may leave a person actually so amazed and confused by the task of trying to take them all into consideration, especially in moments requiring quick decision, one may rightly choose to rely upon "common sense" rather than try to calculate a right decision in the face of complexities needing a battery of mechanical computers to retain both all the principles and multiplicities of factors which should be taken into consideration when, to some degree, it is false that "other things" are "equal."

B. *Principles Pertaining Primarily to Intrinsic Values.* The options confronted with respect to the problem of choosing among alternative intrinsic goods (a problem that does not arise to one wholly immersed in enjoyment of intrinsic good) have to do with actualizing potential intrinsic goods or with more fully appreciating intrinsic goods only partly actualized. If, as we have observed, intrinsic goods may be experienced as pleasant feelings, satisfactions, enthusiasms, contentment and their variable inclusion in organic enjoyment, then rules for choosing, insofar as they can be formulated, pertain both to each of the four to the extent that they differ from each other and to organic enjoyment insofar as it variably embodies each of the four within its own variable being. Full exploration of the problems involved would require more investigation of the nature of pleasure, satisfaction, enthusiasm and contentment than we can enter into here. Although general principles peculiar to each of them may be formulated, we will limit our suggestions mainly to general principles which apply to all alike.

In discussing *pleasant feeling* as intrinsic good in Chapter VI, we developed our treatment of Hedonism beyond the scope intended for that Chapter and anticipated, in part, what needs attention here. *To the extent that pleasures differ in "quantity," one ought, when faced with the problem of choosing between greater or lesser quantity, other things being equal, always choose the greater quantity. If pleasures differ in "duration," one ought, when faced with the problem of choosing between longer or shorter durations of a pleasure, other things being equal, always choose the longer-lasting pleasant feeling. Where pleasures differ in "intensity,' one ought, when faced with the problem of choosing between a more intense and a less intense pleasure, other things being equal, always choose the more intense pleasure. When pleasures differ in "quality," one ought, when faced with the problem of choosing between a higher-quality and a lower-quality pleasure, other things being equal, always choose the higher-quality pleasure.*

Now since, during a particular period in which prospective pleasures are to be experienced, pleasures may have both quantitative, durational, intensive and qualitative aspects, the issue normally becomes one of whether to choose quantity versus duration, or duration versus intensity, or intensity versus quality, or quantity versus quality, or duration versus quality, or quantity versus intensity, or rather, between more complex (e.g., quantity-intensity versus duration-quality) alternatives. Since situations normally also contain awareness of objects or object-complexes and activities or activity-complexes, choice-problems regarding the above-outlined alternatives seldom appear so sharply defined. Vagueness, uncertainty, even ignorance, regarding such issues leaves us usually victims of whim, impulse or inclination. Nevertheless, the foregoing principles for choosing among pleasant feelings should appear, upon reflection, as naturally reasonable conditional oughts. Although "other things" are seldom if ever "equal," awareness of the availability of such principles may provide both additional assurance (and enjoyment in being a person who can, if he chooses, choose on principle, which enjoyment itself may be experienced as an intrinsic good) and actual assistance whenever issues do occur in sharpened form. The principles are significant also because they carry over into decisions regarding the making of instruments. Ought we manufacture instruments that produce more quantity, duration, intensity or quality of pleasures? These principles bear also upon how we feel that we ought to treat our friends, for we might rightly choose to tickle a child, praise a youth, evidence fidelity to a spouse or sit quietly conversing about life with an oldster, whereas reversing such options could have quite different effects.

We extended our discussion of *feeling of satisfaction* and Voluntarism also beyond the intended scope of Chapter VI in anticipation of present needs. Satisfactions too may differ with respect to quantity, duration, intensity and quality. That is, some choice-situations appear as differing both relative to greater or lesser quantity, longer or shorter duration, more or less intensity and higher or lower quality, and relative to the interrelations of these differences to each other. An intense versus an enduring satisfaction, for example, may present itself as a primary issue, not merely on particular occasions but also in choosing, and rechoosing, a pattern for living. Each of the types of alternatives outlined above for pleasure situations may reappear for satisfaction situations, insofar as pleasant feelings and feelings of satisfaction are alike in these respects. But differences also appear because desiring may be accompanied with an enjoyed quality of anticipatory satisfaction. And changing circumstances of life, such as those peculiar to vigorous children, to uncertain youth, to hard-working middle age and to retired oldsters, require shifts in the enjoyability of intense versus high-quality satisfactions and pleasures which also condition each presented choice, requiring dependence upon hunch or habit or indifferent submissiveness relative to the interdependence of these distinguishable kinds of intrinsic good also.

Enthusiasm is felt as more or less sustained or intense and so, if one has any choice regarding prolonging or intensifying such feelings, the greater intrinsic good enjoyable thereby obligates him to do so. If some types of enthusiasm involve efforts which result in quick or prolonged exhaustion of energy, or endanger your life and further enthusiasms, then you ought avoid them if you have an alternative for producing less quick or less prolonged exhaustion. Prospects regarding recurrence of enthusiasms may be decisive oughts in deciding whether or not to marry. The object of your desire may determine the quality as well as endurance and intensity of your enthusiasms, for when you have a cause to live for, such as national liberation, racial justice, or anti-poverty legislation, you may be more spontaneously inspired to act more eagerly and urgently and unreservedly than without such cause.

Contentment also may be experienced as more or less pure or prolonged or profound. So any obviousness regarding whether more or less of the intrinsic good involved from alternative courses of action thereby constitutes self-obligation. Negatively, if you can reduce or eliminate exhausting anxieties by a noon nap or an afternoon nip, you may then be obligated to do so. Those finding comfort and reassurance through moments of prayer ("Saying grace before meals"), a daily hour of prayer ("family altar"), a weekly "day of rest" (often with church services) tend to experience efforts in such directions as self-obligations. The Japanese Tea Ceremony aims at inducing contentment. One may achieve degrees of relaxation from even the merely physical aspects of Yoga, from recurrent attention to the fact that "desire for what will not be attained ends in frustration" (See my Philosophy of the Buddha), and from "living in Zen" (See my The World's Living Religions, pp. 206-221, Dell Publishing, New York, 1964). If you can acquire a feeling of confidence about your course in life, whether by attaining more secure circumstances, by "thinking things through" to assured convictions, or by adopting a more yea-saying attitude, then you may be obligated to do so to the extent that more contented aspects of your life thereby involve enjoyment of greater intrinsic good. As your self becomes increasingly multi-leveled (See Chapters III and IV), you may face problems of depth psychology generating choices between whether it is more important for you to maintain confidence and contentment at the lower or more profound levels of your being while enduring surface disturbances in your daily activities or whether you should permit each anxious confrontation to overwhelm your mentality completely. Frequent consultations with an understanding friend, a minister, or a psychiatrist may constitute self-obligations of those who do not easily retain enduring feelings of assurance regarding the more fundamental aspects or levels of their lives. The pervasive feelings of contentment involved in living by firm convictions tend to involve such significant amounts of feelings of intrinsic good that one naturally seeks to settle one's doubts as soon as one can.

Although the instrumental evils involved in a dogmatist trying to impose his ideas upon unwilling auditors are so well known as to be almost universally abhorred, the intrinsic good of contentment inherent in feelings of knowing that one's own views are true is such that one is self-obligated to seek such contentment whenever one can.

Organic enjoyment both involves or consists in the foregoing four types of enjoyment and involves or consists in enjoyment of their variable interdependence. In unreflective practice, it tends to be indistinguishable from them. But distinction of it from them, and of them from each other, arises from, and serves, the need for differentiating the relative goods of pleasures, satisfactions, enthusiasms and contentment and of choosing between them. If pleasures have greater intrinsic good than satisfactions, or satisfactions greater intrinsic good than pleasures, for example, then one ought, other things being equal, to choose pleasures over satisfactions, or satisfactions over pleasures, as the case may be. If one actually experiences more intrinsic good in pleasures as a child, in enthusiasms when young, in satisfactions when middle aged and in contentment during old age, then these unequalizing factors need consideration in a more comprehensive, dynamic life-perspective in terms of which one ought to formulate one's moral rules. Varying circumstances, including changing capacities and opportunities, may need to be faced with different specific attitudes and rules; though the wisdom of attaining and maintaining a general "attitude toward life" of meliorism as against extreme (unrealistic) optimism or undue (unnecessary and self-suffering) pessimism also needs consideration and effort.

The foregoing principles for choosing pertaining primarily to the intrinsic goods have as the common explanation of their code items the self-evident principle that intrinsic good is its own "reason for being." A thing which is an end-in-itself requires no other "reason for being," no other teleological explanation, even though its causal, conditional and compositional explanation may be infinitely complex and necessarily uncertain. *To the extent that anything is an end-in-itself, it ought to be appreciated, whenever one is faced with the alternative of whether to appreciate or not to appreciate it and "other things" are "equal."* If we remain unaware of things as ends-in-themselves or unaware of options concerning whether to or not to appreciate them, they are beyond our opportunity, or capacity, for appreciation. But by becoming aware of intrinsic good as the ultimate locus of all good and of all obligation, and aware of our own ability to increase our appreciation of such good, we thereby become "more moral," more obligated, and a being with more potential enjoyment of intrinsic good, than otherwise. Part, and a most important part, of the purpose of studying ethics is to increase one's own actual intrinsic good through developing awareness of one's ability to increase one's feelings of self-obligation regarding actualizing one's potentialities for enjoying one's being as intrinsic good. Increased self-obligation is something which, when one becomes acquainted with its nature and consequences, one ought to want as much as possible. This, indeed, is ultimately "what one most wants to do."

Practical limits, including needs for attending to necessary instrumental goods, however, require attention for choosing among instrumental goods and between instrumental and intrinsic goods. Since intrinsic values cannot exist without instrumental values also, choosing to attend to instrumental values and for choosing between instrumental and intrinsic values, also constitute a part of "what one most wants to do." Part of the significance of the Organicistic view may be found in its own thesis that one ought always to resist the temptation to reduce the ultimate bases of self-obligation to either intrinsic or instrumental goods alone, since both teleological and causal factors are essential to the existence of good and self-obligation.

C. *Principles Pertaining Primarily to Instrumental Value.* First, since no enjoyment of intrinsic good can exist without life and since no life can exist without the instrumental causes and conditions essential to its nature, one needs to give attention to those instrumental goods which are necessary for life. General code item: *When faced with the problem of choosing between means which are essential to life and means which are not essential to life, other things being equal, one ought always to choose the means which are essential to life.* The reason or principle underlying this code item is that more intrinsic good will exist if life exists than if it does not exist. (If the life expected will be one of greater evil than of intrinsic good, however, then, other things being equal, one ought to choose means essential to ending such life.)

Secondly, by applying our "second general principle and code item" cited above (i.e., other things being equal, one ought always to choose most good and least evil possible) to problems pertaining primarily to choosing among instrumental values, we may note some typical kinds of issues relative to which we can state some typical sub-principles and sub-codes. Three of these will be noted, namely, those dealing with permanent versus transient instruments, those dealing with productive versus unproductive instruments, and those dealing with efficient versus inefficient instruments.

1. *When faced with the problem of choosing between two instruments, one of which is more enduring or more lasting as a potential instrumental good, other things being equal, one ought always to choose the instrument with the more enduring good in preference to the one with the less enduring good.*

2. *When faced with the problem of choosing between two instruments, one of which is more productive, in the sense that it is useful in the production of more instruments which can produce still more instruments, etc., which function as potential instrumental goods, other things being equal, one ought always to choose the more productive in preference to the less productive.*

3. *When faced with the problem of choosing between two instruments, one of which is more efficient, in the sense that is produces, directly or indirectly, more intrinsic good than it involves intrinsic evil in its production, and the other of which is less efficient, other things being equal, one ought always to choose the former.*

Regarding each of these three general sub-codes we may note that, although distinguishable, they are also similar in pertaining to more-versus-less instrumental value, in overlapping with respect to the instruments to which they apply, and in finding their justification in the common underlying principle which consists in one's long range interests or in what is best for one's self in the long run where "best for self in the long run" means greatest enjoyment of intrinsic good. Each is a form of the principle which Bentham called "fecundity." Each has a negative counterpart which together may be stated as a general code item: "Avoid waste." All may refer to instruments existing either outside or inside self; i.e., to things existing external to self ("opportunities"); and to character traits, habits, virtues, or to both ("abilities") and their fitness to each other. These three codes may be stated together as: *When faced with the problem of choosing between two alternatives, one of which increases and the other of which decreases one's abilities -- in the long run -- other things being equal, one ought always to choose the former.* All may be involved in a shift in the ratio of significance of the permanent versus the transient, or the productive versus the unproductive, and the more versus the less efficient production as your life proceeds; for if you have much life left to live, you may rightly be more concerned about enduring productive goods than later in life, unless, and to the extent that, you expect yourself to live on, in any of your levels of being, as identified with your children, your creations, your nation, your culture, mankind, or ultimate reality itself.

We cannot reemphasize too often the significance of the phrase, "other things being equal," for these principles may in actual application conflict with each other. For example, sometimes endurance (of delicately designed chinaware) should be preferred to efficiency (rapid washing of dishes) whereas at other times efficiency (in doing dishes with disposable paper or plastic dishes) should be preferred to endurance (involving washing, storing, protecting, repairing). Likewise, sometimes productive goods (machines for making machines) should be preferred to unproductive goods (machines for making decorations already in surplus) whereas at other times unproductive consumer's goods (food and clothing needed for survival) should be preferred to productive goods (machines for making machines whose products cannot be used until after the present generation of people is dead). The issue of whether to concentrate on production of "producer's" goods versus consumers' goods," facing "developing nations" seeking rapid industrialization, is a matter of social policy which has its analogue in personal problems in which one constantly faces the issue of how much of one's resources to spend in current fun and how much to save or invest for future safety. Since "other things" are seldom "equal," these general codes and sub-codes state only "conditional oughts."

Thirdly, another issue regarding instrumental values has to do with the relative certainty or uncertainty that a potential instrumental good will become actualized and result in actual enjoyment of intrinsic good. This issue is primarily "epistemological," i.e., concerned with knowledge, truth and certainty, rather than primarily "axiological," i.e., concerned with the nature of values. But it is axiological and ethical also to the extent that the rightness of one's choice in seeking to actualize the greatest amount of intrinsic value depends upon probabilities regarding prospects. Ethics, rightness, self-obligation and principles for choosing all depend upon epistemological conditions because such conditions are parts of the "other things" that may or may not be "equal." Thus, "being moral" involves not only "knowing thyself" in some adequate measure but also "knowing something about the nature of knowledge," including probability theory, and something about the nature of all the "other things" which may or may not be equal in relation to typical judging situations. The importance of knowing is part of "the importance of living."

This third issue may be formulated as a code item: *When faced with the problem of choosing between two instrumental goods, one of which is more sure to result in an actual intrinsic good and the other of which is less sure, then, other things being equal, one ought always to choose the former.* For example, a knife that is known to be sharp and sure to cut should be preferred to one that is dull and which may or may not cut, other things being equal. Or a brand of product that has always pleased should be chosen in preference to a new brand which is as yet untried, other things being equal. A kind of activity which has always yielded enjoyment should be favored as against one which sometimes does and sometimes does not bring enjoyment. This issue and these examples have negative counterparts, of course. For example, a kind of activity which has always resulted in boredom should be avoided in preference to a kind of activity in which prospects regarding boredom remain uncertain, other things being equal.

D. *Principles for Choosing Between Intrinsic and Instrumental Values.* Three such general principles will be distinguished.

1. The first may be formulated as a code item as follows: *When faced with the problem of choosing between two alternatives, one of which is an intrinsic good and the other of which is an instrumental good, one ought, other things being equal, always choose the intrinsic good.* The phrase, "other things being equal," is important here especially because the conditional ought being stated is highly abstract, and because a seeming

instrumental good is not actually an instrumental good unless it actually results in an intrinsic good. Thus, if the intrinsic good involved in this instrumental good also becomes part of the perspective within which the alternatives are viewed, then the problem becomes that of choosing between one intrinsic good on the one hand and an instrumental good together with its potential intrinsic good on the other. However, many actual choices must be made between an immediately enjoyable intrinsic good and obtaining or retaining instruments whose prospects of fruitfulness remain uncertain. Here the issue of certainty versus uncertainty regarding instruments resulting in actual intrinsic goods becomes paramount. For example, one may feel a need for deciding between spending his last now-available dollar for a highly-praised movie, the enjoyment of which is immediate and self-terminating, as against spending it for an otherwise unobtainable highly-rated book which he may never find time to read. Of course, since "other things" are seldom "equal." Pride in owning such a book as well as prospective discomfort arising from needs for caring for it, storing it, dusting it, moving it, guarding it against theft, may be factors.

The foregoing discussion, focusing upon difficulties in taking the principle into consideration as such in actual decisions, should not becloud its basicness to value theory and ethics. The principle is always inherent in the distinction (and in the need for distinguishing) between intrinsic and instrumental value in the first place. Hence, insofar as one can choose between an actual intrinsic good, which is an end in itself, and an instrumental good, which does not have its end in itself, one ought to choose the former because intrinsic good both is the ultimate basis of choice and is intuitively apprehended as ultimate or as an end in itself whenever its nature is clearly recognized. Intrinsic good is "the end which justifies the means," and thus ought always to be preferred to the means, other things being equal.

2. The second general principle, which may seem to contradict the first, is really a necessary supplement to it. Whereas instrumental good depends upon intrinsic good teleologically (intrinsic good is the end for which instrumental good is the means), intrinsic good depends for its existence upon instrumental good causally. Hence, to the extent that an intrinsic good cannot exist without those instruments and their goods as causes of it, one must treat the instruments and their goods as prior to the intrinsic good to be caused. This principle may be stated as a general code item as follows: *When, and insofar as, instrumental good is causally*

prior to intrinsic good, one ought, other things being equal, always choose the instrumental good or means to an end (thus obtaining both means and end) as against an end, or intrinsic good, which does not, because it cannot, exist without the means to it. These two code items do not contradict each other because the phrase, "other things being equal," contained in each of them signifies, in part, that the factors stated in the other are thereby being taken into account.

3. The third general principle incorporates the first two into a more comprehensive statement. As a general code items it may be formulated as follows: *When faced with the problem of choosing between two alternatives, one of which consists in both intrinsic good and instrumental good and the other of which consists in either intrinsic good or instrumental good alone, one ought, other things being equal, always choose the former.* Reference here is to three situations, the first of which involves both an intrinsic good enjoyed as an end-in-itself and an instrumental good which may lead to another intrinsic good, the second of which involves an intrinsic good enjoyed as an end-in-itself without an instrumental good which may lead to another intrinsic good, and the third of which involves an instrumental good which may lead to an intrinsic good without any immediately enjoyed intrinsic good as an end-in-itself. When faced with a problem of choosing among these three alternatives, one ought, other things being equal, to choose the first because greater intrinsic good is in prospect than in the other two.

E. *Principles for Choosing Between Intrinsic and Instrumental Values Where Production and Consumption of Instrumental Values Are at Stake.* Using the term "enjoyed" and "not enjoyed" to refer to experiences in which intrinsic goods are present and absent, respectively (principles relative to intrinsic evils will be neglected here), we suggest the following for consideration.

1. *When faced with the problems of choosing described in the following, one ought, other things being equal, to choose the former: a. Productive activity which is enjoyed and productive activity which is not enjoyed. b. Consumptive activity which is enjoyed and consumptive activity which is not enjoyed. c. Activity which is both productive and consumptive and enjoyed and activity which is both productive and consumptive and not enjoyed.*

2. *When faced with the problem of choosing described in the following, one ought: other things being equal, choose the former: a. Productive activity which is enjoyed and consumptive activity which is enjoyed (i.e., equally). b. Non-consumptive activity which is enjoyed and consumptive activity*

which is enjoyed. c. Activity which is both productive and non-consumptive which is enjoyed and activity which is both consumptive and non-productive which is enjoyed. One ought to choose the former in each case because, in addition to the enjoyments, presumed to be equal, instruments which may have good later are produced, not consumed, or produced and not consumed, respectively.

3. Still more complex situations exist which, because the same in some respects, provide a basis for formulating principles. Some of these involve "diminishing returns"; and there is a sense in which all "laws of diminishing returns" are moral laws insofar as instrumental values are involved. The first has to do with diminishing returns (i.e., actual intrinsic goods enjoyed) resulting from increased production of instruments. *When a point has been reached at which additional production can result in no more enjoyment, an "ought to produce" turns into an "ought not to produce," other things being equal. (I.e., do not make instruments which can never be used, when no enjoyment can come from making them.)* The second has to do with diminishing returns resulting from increasing consumption of instruments. *When a point has been reached at which additional consumption of instruments yields no more enjoyment, an "ought to consume" turns into an "ought not to consume," other things being equal. (E.g., do not eat more candy now if taste buds are completely saturated or appetite is perfectly satiated.)* The third has to do with diminishing returns resulting from both increasing production and increasing consumption of instruments. *When a point has been reached in the production and consumption of instruments yields no additional enjoyment, as "ought to produce and consume" turns into an "ought not to produce and consume," other things being equal.*

F. *Principles for Choosing Between Actual and Potential Values.* Since actuality of intrinsic good is the ultimate locus or power to compel our choices, any power that a supposed potential intrinsic good has for compelling our choice exists ultimately in its actuality. Hence, the obviousness of this basic principle for formulating a code item: *When faced with the problem of choosing between an actual intrinsic good and a potential intrinsic good, one ought, other things being equal, to prefer the actual to the potential.* However, we seldom face a problem which occurs in precisely this extremely abstract form. In fact, if the potential is a "real potential" (i.e., one that will in fact result in an actual intrinsic good) and not merely a "conditional potential" intrinsic good, then if the potential and the actual goods are equal, other things being equal, except that time may be considered as an insignificant factor, it may make no difference whether one enjoys the actual intrinsic good now or the actual intrinsic good which the "real potential intrinsic good" must actualize in the future. If the potential intrinsic good is merely "conditional," or if a person is uncertain as to whether the potential intrinsic good is "real" or "conditional," then, other things being equal, one clearly ought to prefer the actual to the potential.

Since the applicability of the foregoing code item depends upon whether the potential intrinsic good is "real" or "conditional," perhaps a code item relative to this distinction may be found more useful. However, the high degree of uncertainty often accompanying problems concerning judgments about "conditional" and "real" potentially tend to make issues of certainty versus uncertainty of great significance here. Since a "conditional potential intrinsic good" is one which <u>would</u> become <u>if</u> all other needed conditions cooperate and since a "real potential intrinsic good" is one which <u>will</u> become <u>because</u> all of the needed conditions will cooperate, the existence of intrinsic good is assured in the latter and not in the former case. Thus, *when faced with the problem of choosing between a "conditional potential intrinsic good" and a "real potential intrinsic good," one ought, other things being equal, always choose the latter.*

Derivable code items relative to instrumental values are implicit in the foregoing. But we shall stop our present discussion with a summary which should prove suggestive for further independent consideration, though it will result in a welter of confusion if one is unable to keep constantly in mind at each step the necessary condition for adequacy of principles derivable when and insofar as "things are alike," namely, "other things being equal." *When faced with the problem of ordering one's preferences relative to the following items, other things being equal, one should prefer first actual intrinsic good, secondly, real potential intrinsic good, thirdly, actual instrumental good (which involves real potential intrinsic good), fourthly, real potential instrumental good, fifthly, conditional potential intrinsic good, and finally, conditional potential instrumental good.* However, since "other things" are seldom "equal," and since one may be faced with problems which are primarily causal in nature, one may find occasion for reversing this order of preferences; for to the extent that nothing can become actual which was not first potential and to the extent that a greater quantity and variety of conditional potential instruments increases the richness, etc., of potential intrinsic goods, prudence may dictate concern for increasing varieties of conditionally useful instruments in the absence of more than probable assurance that some new and better actual intrinsic good will result.

Finally, we suggest that *if and when one is faced with the problem of choosing between alternatives, one which consists in both actual and potential intrinsic goods and the other of either actual or potential intrinsic good alone, one ought, other things being equal, always choose the former.* This suggested code item should hold even if the potentiality is only "conditional" or whether one is uncertain as to whether it is "conditional" or "real."

We will conclude our consideration of "conditional oughts" by observing some difficulties in applying them. Does having very general, even universal, principles and code items, each of which is a conditional ought, help in choosing rightly, as when, for example, he must decide whether to marry Jane or Jean? Of course, one should choose greater quantity, duration, intensity and quality of pleasures, satisfactions, enthusiasm, contentment and organic enjoyment, but how can one predict life-long prospects? Of course, one ought to choose what is necessary for existence, but one can exist without marrying and at the moment Jane seems as necessary, or as unnecessary, as Jean. Of course, one should choose a more enduring over a less enduring, a more productive over a less productive and a more efficient over a less efficient instrument, but Jane seems to be about as healthy and able and skillful as Jean. And of course, one should choose certainty over uncertainty, but in one's present state of indecision he may be as certain, or as uncertain, about the one as about the other. How, in such a circumstance, can the foregoing general principles be of any help?

Or the situation may be, and usually is, still more complex than just pictured. Jane may be more exciting, Jean more loyal. Jane may be more vivacious, Jean more healthy. Jane may be a shrewd spender, Jean a thrifty saver. Jane may be more beautiful, Jean a harder worker. Jane makes friends easily; Jean keeps out of trouble. If these and other alternative virtues appear to balance each other, then to what principle for choosing may one appeal?

If gripped in a state of undecidability, one may then be faced with the problem of choosing to remain in such a state or in getting out of it by any means available. It is customary, in dealing with this problem as a theoretical problem, to cite the story of Buridan's ass who reputedly starved to death between two equally attractive piles of hay because he could not make up his mind which of the two to eat. One may, of course, "flip a coin," or choose not to choose but "let nature take its course" and see which of the two succeeds in tipping the balance in some practical decisive action.

General codes may be of little use if one waits until pressured into an immediate decision-situation. General principles in ethics, as in any other science, have only a conditional utility; and just as such principles in physics and biology may be expected to prove useful in solving problems of engineering or medicine only when the "other things being equal" are known, so one needs to know that other things are equal where application of general ethical principles is concerned. Each particular decision-situation has some unique aspects which make appeals to principles only partly appropriate. Their use, then, may prove to be the greatest when (1) planning one's life, (2) formulating and establishing habits of choosing and (3) devising more specific codes.

1. Awareness of, and knowledge of, general principles of values and of obligations should make a great difference in planning one's life. Now life can hardly be planned completely, and some decide, even rightly, not to plan their lives. But most of us recognize that some planning may be better than none. In reflecting upon the nature and purpose of one's own life and how to conduct it so as to get the most out of it, knowledge of fundamental principles can be most useful. The issue, for example, of whether one shall decide to be primarily an absolutist or a relativist may be settled by appeal to general principles. The question of whether or how much one will devote oneself to long-range versus short-range interests can be decided intelligently only by appeals to general principles. Solution to the problem of whether one ought to seek simplicity or indulge oneself in rich complexities of tendencies may be aided by knowledge of general principles. And such issues as whether one shall emphasize spiritual versus material, or active versus passive, or romantic versus rationalistic, or humanistic versus technological, or ends versus means, types of life endeavors may be resolved with the help of general principles. Although not all of the major kinds of self-obligation will be brought into view until we have finished Parts II and III of this volume, surely by now the importance of discovering and employing general principles of choosing in formulating one's philosophy of life should be clear.

2. Habits of choosing (and in a sense all habits are habits of choosing) may be acquired unreflectively or from very early instruction. "Give me the boy to train," said Roman Catholic Cardinal Gibbons, "and I care not for the rest of the world, for the boy of today will be the rest of the world

tomorrow." (See also John B. Watson, Behaviorism, p. 262, W.W. Norton, New York, 1925.) Yet nevertheless, some habits can be modified, and you may even develop the habit of modifying your habits whenever you discover a better way of behaving. The more self-reflective and self-controlled you are, the more you will deliberately choose to modify your habits in accordance with those principles which seem to you to bring about what is best for yourself in the long run. If, and because, it is better to establish habits when you have more opportunity for thinking through what is probably best for yourself in the long run, you ought to establish them then. Formulating and establishing a best set of habits of behavior, and of choosing, is part of what one most wants to do. At such times, knowledge of general principles for choosing may be most useful.

3. Can and should more specific codes be devised? If you continue to be rankled by antagonisms to codes imposed upon you by others, you may not be amenable to considering this problem. If you remain an unreflective relativist, you may habitually respond negatively. But it should be obvious to one who has followed our preceding discussion that the problem of choosing is amazingly intricate and that any practical aids will be most welcome. The more we penetrate into the nature and complexity of principles for choosing, the more we hope for simplified codes to guide our everyday decisions. When you are able to think through a decision-situation in light of all available factors and principles, we can hardly urge you to depend upon a code. But most of us most of the time are unable to think through such situations. Hence formulation of practical codes, if and when possible, may be part of what we ourselves most want to do.

The present volume deals with general ethics (individual, social, final) rather than with specific areas of ethics, such as medical ethics marital ethics, business ethics, professional ethics, etc. Practical conduct seems to necessitate formulation of codes for common practice within each area. Each specific kind of business, such as automotive, grocery or clothing, or each specific branch of business, such as accounting, production or sales, tends to demand its own specific code of conduct. Each of these more specific areas of code-making involves both its own general principles, based upon common kinds of behavior and decision situations within the area, and the most general principles common to all kinds of behavior and choice situations which we have discussed above. It is a mistake to believe that specific ethical principles and codes do not involve the more general ones. They may be presupposed as too obvious to state. They may be rediscovered by studying the needs of specific areas. But when they are forgotten, and when specific conditional oughts are misstated as categorical oughts, moral trouble lies ahead. Codes are made for persons, not persons for codes. And the ultimate reason for specific codes consists in what is best for persons in the long run; and the purpose and function of statements of the most general principles for choosing is to clarify what is best for persons in the long run.

Summary of Principles for Choosing. Other things being equal:

A. *Principles applying to both intrinsic and instrument values:*
1. Choose good in preference to evil.
2. Choose better in preference to worse:
    a. Choose better in preference to good.
    b. Choose bad in preference to worse.
    c. Choose better in preference to worse.

B. *Principles pertaining primarily to intrinsic values:*
1. Choose greater in preference to smaller "quantity."
2. Choose longer in preference to shorter "duration."
3. Choose greater in preference to lesser "intensity."
4. Choose higher in preference to lower "quality."

These may apply to pleasant feelings, satisfaction, enthusiasm, and contentment, both relative to each distinctly, to two or more or all, and to "organic enjoyment" as variably including all the others.

C. *Principles pertaining primarily to instrumental values:*
1. Choose those necessary for existence in preference to those not necessary.
2. Choose more enduring instruments in preference to those less enduring.
3. Choose more productive instruments in preference to those less productive.
4. Choose more efficient instruments in preference to those less efficient.
5. Choose instruments more sure to produce actual intrinsic values in preference to those less sure.

D. *Principles for choosing between intrinsic and instrumental values:*
1. Choose intrinsic in preference to instrumental values (teleologically).
2. Choose instrumental in preference to intrinsic values (causally).
3. Choose both in preference to either alone.

E. *Principles for choosing between intrinsic and instrumental values where production and consumption of instrumental values are at stake:*

  1. a. Choose productive activity which is enjoyed in preference to productive activity which is not enjoyed.

      b. Choose consumptive activity which is enjoyed in preference to consumptive activity which is not enjoyed.

      c. Choose activity which is productive and consumptive and enjoyed in preference to activity which is productive and consumptive and not enjoyed.

  2. a. Choose productive activity which is enjoyed in preference to consumptive activity which is enjoyed (i.e., equally).

      b. Choose non-consumptive activity which is enjoyed in preference to consumptive activity which is enjoyed.

      c. Choose activity which is both productive and non-consumptive and enjoyed in preference to activity which is both consumptive and non-productive and enjoyed.

  3. a. Choose to produce no more instruments than can be consumed enjoyably.

      b. Choose to consume no more instruments than can be consumed enjoyably.

      c. Choose to produce-consume no more instruments than can be consumed enjoyably.

F. *Principles for choosing between actual and potential values:*

  1. Choose actual intrinsic value in preference to potential intrinsic value.

  2. Choose real potential intrinsic value in preference to conditional potential intrinsic value.

  3. (Two summaries for ordering preferences are omitted here.)

  4. Choose actual and potential intrinsic value together in preference to either actual or potential intrinsic value alone. Failure to keep in mind that the phrase, "other things being equal," introducing the above summary, is intended to be an integral part of each of the items in the summary will result in misinterpretation. Each of the principles for choosing is intended as a scientific hypothesis about a conditional ought understood as applying universally to relevant choices whenever all other things are equal.

Chapter IX

SELF AS AGENT

Four intimately related topics will now engage our attention. They have to do with (1) "agency" or action, especially with how one acts as a "moral agent," (2) "intention," both intended action and intentions as actions, (3) "responsibility," including responsible action and being a responsible agent, and (4) "freedom," including being "a free agent" or having "free will" or "freedom of choice." Each of these four topics has its opposite, e.g., "patiency," "unintended action," "irresponsibility" and "unfree action." The fourth of these topics will constitute the following chapter. Although each of the first three may be sufficiently distinct and sufficiently significant to deserve more extensive treatment, they are grouped together here for convenience.

Agency. 1. *What is "agency"?* An "agent" is one who acts or a power that acts. The term "agency," as used here, ambiguously denotes both (a) any particular action or acting or exertion of power and (b) the general nature of acting (since the more awkward terms, "agentness" or "agenticity," have not achieved common usage). Right acts or moral actions involve agency. So exploration of the nature of agency should provide further insight into the nature of morality.

If we accept a fundamental definition of things, including agencies, we may say that "a thing is what a thing does" and that "an agent is anything which acts." The way an agent acts constitutes the kind of agent it is. Action involves an actor. Whether the actor is temporary or permanent may be judged by whether it acts permanently or temporarily. If an action continues, it appears that a substantial agent is involved. Now a substantial agent may act either, or both, dynamically, i.e., in such a way as to change or produce changes, or statically, i.e., in such a way as to remain the same or to keep things unchanged. Thus we may have both dynamic agents and static agents or, of course, organic agents, i.e., those that change in some respects and remain the same in others.

"Agency" has its direct opposite in "patiency." Just as an "agent" is something that acts or is active so a "patient" is something acted upon or passive. Ignoring "self-activity" wherein an agent acts upon or within itself, we may note that most action involves "interaction" between two or more things in which each thing functions both as an agent that acts upon other things and as a patient being acted upon by other things. Interaction entails not only acting upon and being acted upon by other things but also "reacting" or acting again after having been acted upon.

Such "reacting" constitutes a thing as being a "reactor" or a "reagent." "Reagency" involves both agency and patiency for, in acting again after having been acted upon, a thing must have been a patient or receiver of action in order to respond to such received action. When an agent acts and reacts continuingly or recurrently, it functions as a substantial agent or reagent. If it ceases to react or respond, it thereby functions as no longer substantial or ceases to function as an agent or reagent.

When an agent manifests continuing ability to respond, especially in ways that are regular and can be relied upon, it is said to be "able to respond" or to be "responsible." (Ethics, or science generally, would be impossible if there were no responsible agents or reagents, for generalizations regarding activity are possible only to the extent that reagents react in the same ways to similar ways of being acted upon.) But, likewise, continuing and reliable reagency involves continuing and reliable patiency (or "re-patiency") for a thing can hardly be expected to react in the same way if it does not, or is not able to, receive action in the same way. Patiency and reagency are so intimately interrelated that it may seem artificial to differentiate between them. Substantial agency is "organic" in the sense that its agency, patiency, reagency and "re-patiency" continue interdependently while it continues to interdepend with other organic agents with which it interacts. Resiliency, or ability to react not only to being acted upon by different things or by the same things in different ways, is necessary for continuance in being in a dynamic world. Resiliency is part of the fuller meaning of agency, or at least of the agency needed for science and ethics.

2. *Self as agent.* Are you an agent? The answer to this question is easy. Not only do you function as an agent, but, because you act in many different kinds of ways, you have many kinds of agency or are an agent of many kinds. How do you know? Intuitively. By observing your self acting, reacting, and interacting. Although some indirect actions take a long time, as when one operates indirectly through letters and memory, other reactions occur so directly and immediately that they are experienced as action-reaction gestalts. A vivacious tussle between two alert boys may engage many varieties of physical interaction all within the grasp of one act of attention.

Thus we discover our own agency, for we find ourselves already acting when we stop to ask the question: Are we acting, or are we agents? Apparently we were born active and act as long as we live. To live is to act. If George Herbert Mead is correct (See Chapter IV), then we also have agency thrust upon us by others who treat us in such a manner that we become forced to react, and we discover in observing our reactions that we function as actors. The more others hit us, coax us, blame us, shame us, the more we respond "willfully." We develop habits of action, some due to hereditary bodily structure and functioning, and some due to conditions prevailing in our environment. Such habitual patterns of action or reaction lead us to observe ourselves as substantial agents, but, further, we discover that our own agency is something over which we may have considerable control. Not only can we will to move our arms, but also we can will to will or to intensify or mollify our will. Children play at groaning or screaming, at first for the purpose of discovering just how much variation in intensity their own agency can produce. Finally, we imagine new ways of acting and try them out to see whether or not we can act in these new ways. The pragmatic method, i.e., of trying something out to "see if it works," serves as the method we naturally use to discover our own agency, our kinds of agency, and the extent and limits of our agency. Such experimentation is part of the way in which a self discovers both that it is, and what it is, and how much, e.g., how complex and enduring and resilient, it is.

Having discovered our own agency, and our ability to increase or decrease it, we may discover other things about it.

(a) We can initiate action. Not only do we, by "exercising our will," increase or decrease our activity, but we may will to stop acting or, having stopped acting, we may will to act again. Regardless of the necessary physiological and other conditions, we do seem to be able to initiate action, or to begin to act spontaneously. Here again, one may experiment deliberately. One may try to act. One may, when acting, try not to act. One may will. One may, when willing, will not to will. Although agency need not be, yet it may be, both self-starting and self-stopping.

(b) We can initiate action more frequently. We can initiate more enduring action, as we commit ourselves, or commit our intentions, to carrying out a plan of action for an hour, for a day, for a marriage, or "for eternity." We can initiate degrees of intensity, as when we become demanding, utterly devoted, overbearing or "throw a tantrum." We can seek greater complexity of action, as when we act and interact both within ourselves and with other persons and things in very intricate ways; that is, we may create more interaction or more organic interaction.

(c) We can discover the need for patience; and that we have ability to increase or decrease our patience, and initiate patience in ourselves, and sometimes in others.

(d) We can discover not only the extent of, but also how to extend, our agency. First we learn to point our finger, then to use a stick as a pointer, and then to ask another person to point out something for us. When we act in such a way as to get others to act for us, or "to act as our agents," we have extended our own agency through them. Sometimes agencies become institutionalized, as public or private corporations, thereby extending the effectiveness of persons acting as citizens or of persons acting as owners. For example, when the postman delivers mail to my door, he is acting not only as a person himself but also as an agent for the district postal system which functions as an agent for the national postal system which is an arm of the national government which is a collective agent for its citizens, including me. Thus the postman not only acts upon me by handing me a letter but acts for me as a citizen of a society which employs him for this purpose. Or the insurance claims adjuster who calls upon me represents and acts for a local insurance adjustment company which acts as an agent for several insurance companies, one of which is a mutual insurance company acting as an insuring agency for me. We may discover that we can initiate extension of our agency through institutionalized groups by becoming members of existing groups or that we can initiate new institutionalized groups by forming new companies; companies may be formed by agreement of wills, and one may will to induce others to will to agree to form a company, thereby initiating additional or extended agency of and for oneself.

(Although you may never know as clearly as you wish the answer to the question, "What am I?" you surely continue to be somewhat aware of the fact that your own spontaneous action, as well as your willing or unwilling passivity, involves an implied inference that action involves an actor and that you can discover, in part, the kind of actor you are by the kind of acting you do, by acting more or less frequently, more or less enduringly, more or less intensely or more or less complexly. You are an agent, and your actions, immediate or remote, are, as yours, parts of you.)

3. *Kinds of agency.* Limiting consideration of "kinds" here to those which are parts, aspects or levels of an individual self, we may note, generally, that there are as many kinds of self-agency as there are ways of acting. We cannot enumerate all of these here. But attention to the following may prove rewarding. Distinguishing ways of acting in which different parts, aspects or levels of self act from the ways in which different things are acted upon (or kinds of causal agency from kinds of effects), we shall focus attention here only on the former.

An outline of such kinds has already been provided for us in the foregoing chapters or, for that matter, in all three parts of the present volume. For each chapter in Part I deals with one or more ways in which a self is an agent; e.g., a self acts as good, acts as improvable, acts as obligated, acts as owner, acts as just, acts as conscientious. And each chapter in Part II deals with one or more ways (a) in which a self's groups act as agents for him, e.g., his family's acting as improvable extends his own interest in improvement, his company's acting as owner may extend his own acting as owner, his nation's acting as just may extend his own interests in injustice, and (b) in which a self acts as agent for his group, e.g., he acts as his family's "head," he acts as his company's officer, he acts as his nation's citizen. And each chapter in Part III deals with one or more ways (a) in which his universe acts as agent for him, e.g., by providing conditions for continuity and growth, pervasive justice, and both unlimited futures and final satisfactions, and (b) in which a self may also act as agent for his universe or God in bringing about its growth and justice and final satisfactions, as well as hope for the future, here and now. Agency, or interagency, is much more rich, complex and organic than we can elaborate here. We shall limit our review primarily to those kinds of agency suggested in Chapters III and IV.

As "physical," a self has a body with hands and feet and so one acts as a grasper and walker, with cells (e.g., blood cells, and one acts as a bleeder or as one who should prevent bleeding), with molecules (and one acts as a being which can be vitalized by vitamins or devitalized by poisons). A self's body has weight and so one acts as heavy or light in ways which take gravity into consideration, has size and one acts as large or small in ways in which one takes the sizes or openings into account when one tries to go through them, and has shape and one acts as tall or short in reaching for objects. A self possesses a biologically-inherited body, and acts as an animal, but as a person, not as a cow, bird or snake, and acts as a being with biological interests, such as those in eating, excreting, breathing and reproducing. A self may identify itself with its clothes, land, tools and house, and act as a "well-dressed" person, as a land owner, as a skill possessor and as a house-dweller. A self has a brain, a nervous system and sensory organs, and acts as a thinker, rememberer, seer, speaker, hearer, toucher, etc. All the constituents of self as physical may enter into a self-as-agent and when they do, they constitute a part of its agency.

As "social," a self has group memberships and social roles and one may act, and at times does act, consciously and intentionally as aware of each. When you use your family name you act as a family member. By attending school you act, for example, as a seventh-grader. By stopping for a "Stop" sign you are acting as a member of your community. By paying income or social security taxes or by driving on federal highways, posting a letter or receiving social security benefits, you are acting as a citizen of your country. By punching a clock, manipulating a company machine or drawing a company paycheck, you are acting as a company employee. Each role you play in each of your groups, as a teacher, pupil, customer, clerk, employer, employee, foreman, typist, cashier, accountant, machinist, repairman, researcher, architect, physician, nurse, driver, voter or whatnot, constitutes yourself as a social agent, an actor in a social situation, and thereby also constitutes such social action as part of yourself as agent. If your pride, friendship, adventure and security depend upon your social skills, your acting as a specialized functionary in a complex social organization constitutes your self as actively interdependent with the various other parts of that complex social organization. Your own action as a continuing, reliable functionary and the permanent, dependable functioning of others in such stable, complex organization organically interdepend, and this interdependence enables you to act as a specialized agent in, and for, such organization as an agency.

As "cultural," a self, in speaking, functions as a representative of a linguistic culture, and one who speaks bilingually acts as an agent of two linguistic cultures. One who is aware of cultural histories, e.g., of the history of Western civilization or of Hindu or Chinese civilizations, may deliberately act as a Westerner or a Hindu or a Chinese; or if one has appropriated fundamental elements from each, one may act as a "citizen of the world." As a person grows in cultural riches one becomes capable of acting in more ways or of increasing the kinds of agency which embody themselves in his activity. He may become a highly flexible and multi-leveled agent, acting, all within a moment, as a hand-waver, a parent, a citizen and a bilinguist, in saying goodbye to a son departing by plane.

Of course, you may act against other persons, e.g., against your parents, against your community, against your employer, against your country, and against the restrictions imposed upon you by your culture, your social role and the responsibilities attached to your social skills. You may find the different levels of your own personality, such as your interests in your family, your corporation, your city, your country, your union, in conflict with each other. And you may act in conflict with yourself. Some of your acts against yourself may be manageable, just as you get over an attack of indigestion. But sometimes you find yourself overwhelmingly confused, distraught, uncertain, and act as a confused, distraught and uncertain agent. If there is virtue in being a well-integrated, resilient, facilely-adaptive agent, one will seek to keep his different kinds of agency from clashing too much with each other. One may, at times, act primarily as a person with parts, or with only one part, as when one works all day as a company clerk (a part which has many subparts, of course); but there are times when one must also act as a whole. Acting as part and as whole need not be inconsistent, so long as one remains an organic whole, i.e., a whole in which one's various parts depend upon each other and together upon oneself as a whole. Thus a self has organic agency when and to the extent that it continues to act as a whole interdependent with its parts without suffering from a need for devoting itself too much to acting as, or through, or for, any one of its parts.

4. *Values of agency.* In addition to the good and bad effects, or instrumental values, of one's actions, the intrinsic good of enjoying being includes enjoyment of being active or being an agent. Although we cannot say that "being an agent" necessarily involves "being an intrinsic good," just as we cannot say that being, i.e., more being, necessarily is intrinsic good. For one may act or react negatively, painfully, or indifferently. But enjoyment of being an agent is a variety of enjoyment and as such exists as intrinsic good. Enjoyment of agency, claimed by Romanticists as a kind of intrinsic good far superior to that of satisfaction, appears to be automatically presupposed in spontaneous activity, witnessable in bouncing and cooing infants and intuitable as such in one's own experience if one will but pause long enough to attend to it.

If you can enjoy your agency, may you enjoy all of the kinds of agency mentioned in the preceding section? May each of your kinds of agency, each part, aspect or level, be enjoyed as such? Can you enjoy acting as a parent, as a clerk, as a machinist, as a citizen, as well as an athlete, eater, seer, lover, hater? When you add to your functions, through joining new groups or accepting new social roles, do you thereby increase your actual or potential intrinsic good? You may enjoy new agency. You may enjoy enduring agency. You may enjoy organic agency as interdependence of your old and new agencies as well as those interdependencies previously mentioned. But when you overact, you may find yourself or others acting against you, or you may deplete your energy so exhaustively that you cannot recover effective or enjoyable agency immediately. Agency may involve intrinsic and instrumental evils also, for you may suffer, and act as sufferer.

Whenever you have any choice in the matter, i.e., when you face an alternative of whether to be or not to be an agent, or to be or not to be more of an agent, or whether to be or not to be an agent with more parts, aspects or levels of agency, you confront an ought or obligation. The values involved in these alternatives may be either intrinsic or instrumental or both.

(a) If agency is enjoyable, and if more enjoyment exists when one enjoys more agency, then one ought to act more or deliberately initiate more action. Questions of quantity, duration, intensity and quality recur relative to this kind of enjoyment of being. Ought one to act oftener, other things being equal? Ought one to act more enduringly, i.e., as a more enduring agent or in such a way as to experience more enduring enjoyment of agency, other things being equal? Ought one to act more intensely, or as a "more active agent," other things equal? Ought one to act as a "higher quality agent," e.g., as illustrated by the just-mentioned "specialized functionary in a complex social organization" who nevertheless retains a highly-integrated, resilient, organically-unified personality, other things being equal? Ought one's being, or not being, more active vary from time to time at each level; and ought such variations themselves be matters of deliberate agency, for an imbalanced agency of self as physical or mental, as individual or social, as familial or national, as monolingual or bilingual, may itself be significant moral question, judged in terms of possible maximums of enjoyment?

(b) Insofar as agency produces results, good or bad, for self or others, obligation also exists when one faces alternatives. One ought to be an instrumentally good agent, and this oughtness occurs and recurs at each level of self-as-agent, when alternatives appear; and consequences recur relative to frequency, duration, intensity and quality of resulting intrinsic values. However, one ought not to overact, when overaction exhausts action or begets destructive counteraction. One ought not to act against one's employer so as to lose one's job, against one's country so as to lose one's citizenship, against one's spouse so as to lose one's family, or against one's body so as to lose one's life, when these remain fundamental to one's existence and nature and prospects for continuing enjoyment. One ought to know when to stop acting, or to act passively, for best results -- to say nothing of the enjoyment of being patient, a kind of enjoyment regarded as a supreme intrinsic good by many Asian idealists. Interdependence and interagency which produce consequences reciprocally multiply results for good or ill and magnify opportunity and capacity for effective agency by self.

Intention. 1. *What is "intention"?* You know, as well as anyone, what an intention is. You consistently judge others as blameworthy or as blameless for producing harmful results, depending upon whether you believe that they did or did not intend to produce those results. You excuse yourself from blame for evil effects which you did not intend. You feel that you can honestly take credit for good results which you did intend to bring about. Yet, when asked to define, clearly and simply, what you mean by "intention," you may hesitate, falter and wonder, not without good reason, just what intention is anyway. For several problems must be faced and settled before we can be sure that we genuinely comprehend its nature. In what follows we shall begin to explore some of them.

a. Some say that we intend only when confronted with a problem of choosing between alternatives. Such a view implies that whenever we face no alternatives, or have no choice, or do not decide, we do not intend. Intentions come into existence when alternatives and choices and decision situations occur, and they cease when these disappear. But, we may ask, when one is enjoying comfort, is one perfectly satisfied, is one confronted with no problem, does one not intend to continue that way, even though one does not consciously recognize any decision problem regarding possible alternatives of continuing versus not continuing in that way? Critics of our first view may assert that as long as we live consciously, we face alternatives, at least the alternatives of wanting to continue or of caring not whether we continue, and the alternatives of whether we willingly or unwillingly accept our circumstances and prospects. Some would add, further, that we are always dialectically involved in the choice of whether we intend to accept ourselves as intending beings or intend to reject our capacities and opportunities for intending. You will have to choose, and intend, for yourself which of these, or other, alternative views regarding whether we are always or only sometimes faced with alternatives. In any case, the problem here considered involves us in the question of whether a decision and action upon it can ever be wholly intended.

b. Are actions always either intended or unintended exclusively, or may they be partly intended and partly unintended? Although at times we may distinguish sharply between intended and unintended actions, more often, especially upon reflection, we tend to become unsure whether they can be differentiated clearly. Let us, for convenience, consider four possibilities and examine each: (1) Wholly unintended action. (2) Partly unintended action. (3) Partly intended action. (4) Wholly intended action.

(1) Is action every wholly unintended? When your stomach rumbles, for example, or when you choke or cough or sneeze, you may believe your behavior to be purely physical or mechanical or wholly compulsory and thus not intended. You may have been pushed by someone or by a falling object which caused you to harm another accidentally. You tend to believe that accidental responses are unintended. You may be sitting carefully with your knees crossed and find that an accidental tapping stimulates your automatic reflexes ("knee jerk") in such a way as to tip over an ink bottle or to press an alarm button. You may jump with fright at a loud crash and spoil a complex mixture or an expensive painting. You may fall asleep and discover later that your unconscious body movements caused damage. All such kinds of action may be thought of not only as unintended but as wholly unintended.

(2) Many, perhaps all, actions are partly unintended or involve unintentional aspects. We recognize that often, when we decide and act deliberately, we cannot foresee all of the consequences. Sometimes these consequences in fact turn out to be quite different from what we wanted. For example, we choose to travel rapidly, but not so fast as to produce an accident. That is, we "didn't mean to" cause some of the effects resulting from an intentional act. Again, sometimes we feel forced to choose and act in ways which we prefer not to. For example, supposing that I want to aid a temporarily stranded woman in a circumstance where my approaching wife will misunderstand my motives, I may feel forced to refuse to give such aid. I intentionally refuse to aid, even though, and because, I desire to promote aid. Or, I may feel forced to carry out the orders of a superior officer when I believe evil will result. In fact, any time we intend to act to produce good results which might have been better if we could have acted otherwise, we intend to act without assenting to, and thus without fully intending to produce, such less than best results. Finally, we may distinguish between "conscious," "unconscious" and "subconscious" factors in our decisions, the latter being not wholly intended. That is, subconscious tendencies, however acquired, become factors in our preferences which enter into our decisions and intentions even though we might choose otherwise if we became aware of them as such. To what extent can a person be held responsible for his

"subconscious" intentions when he would not have these same intentions if he became fully conscious of his circumstances?

(3) Although it may appear that "partly intended" actions exist whenever "partly unintended" actions occur, we shall here emphasize some different aspects. First, we may distinguish between "permissive intent," where one intends to "let nature take its course" without interference on our part, and "insistent intent," where we deliberately choose to influence the course of events. When you intend to do nothing about a situation, are you or are you not intending? Is not an intention not to act as much intentional as an intention to act? Refusal to assent or act may be as deliberately stubborn as any affirmation and overt action. Furthermore, can you ever intend not to intend? If you deliberately decide not to decide, are you not responsible for the consequences of such a decision? Can you escape responsibility by choosing not to choose? If you allow yourself to be used to produce an evil result, are you not partly responsible for the result to the extent that you intended to permit such use?

Secondly, we may feel quite unsure about results but believe that some action is needed anyway. We then assent only partially or tentatively. In fact, as we become more fully acquainted with the complexities of life, we tend to realize that we can never take into consideration all of the factors involved in decision situations. Do we then fully intend to act in partial ignorance of consequences or do we only partly intend? We often find ourselves called upon to decide, and act, with reservations or only "half-heartedly." "Come along to the dance with me this evening. You may not have an exciting time, but at least you won't be completely bored." "This isn't the job you wanted, but it's better than none."

Thirdly, at some time our feelings of commitment become more intense than at others. Do our intentions differ in degree as our enthusiasms vary in intensity? If so, then a weak, sick or starved person, whose physiological condition prevents a vigorous response may actually have his intentions determined by them. Do hyperthyroid persons intend more, more intensely, more fully than hypothyroid individuals? To what extent do temporary or permanent physiological factors influence the partiality or wholeness of your intentions? And what bearing do these conditions have upon the rightness and responsibility for your decisions and actions?

(4) Can an action ever be wholly intended? First let us ask what is meant by "wholly intended." Four suggestions occur for consideration. Some say an action can be wholly intended (a) only if it exists as the

intention of the whole person, (b) only if it results in action, (c) only if one intends to accept full responsibility for the consequences willingly, and (d) only if one is completely free in making one's choice. Since "responsibility" will be considered in the third part of the present chapter and "freedom" will be explored in the following chapter, consideration of these latter two suggestions will be postponed.

(a) If an action can be called "wholly intended" only when it involves the whole person, then what is "the whole person"? The meaning of "whole self" varies with different philosophies of self, as we have seen, so what is connoted by "wholly intended" will differ. A review of the suggestions offered in Chapters III and IV, should reveal that one's self may be conceived as complex, multileveled, dynamic and variable. If so, then the meaning of "wholly intended" action will entail these many complex, multi-leveled, dynamic and variable factors which constitute a "whole self." Once the nature and constitution of self is decided upon, then we may face two other questions.

First, does your "whole self" participate in intending, or is your intending a function of some particular or specialized part of your self? Does your body intend? Does your mind intend? Does your "spirit" intend? Does your essence, energy, elan, will, or any other supposedly specific part of you, do your intending for you? Or, do you, i.e., your self as a whole, with all of your parts organically integrated, intend? The issue is significant if you are to regard your whole self as responsible, for where recompense for injury, "blame" and "punishment" become relevant, the intending part or parts alone, on the one hand, or the self as a whole, on the other, may be "held responsible." Some punishers punish the body. Some punish only the will (repentance is sufficient). Some put the whole self to death. The rightness and wrongness of some actions depend upon intentions, and intentions are functions of either a part of the self or of the whole self. Does your whole self act when you intend and act upon your intentions?

Secondly, do you commit your whole self, present and future, in deciding to act? Is your intention "complete" as soon as you have reached a conviction and feel committed to carrying out your intention? Does "complete"mean complete for the moment, complete for a lifetime, complete forever regardless of circumstances; or can you intend completely and still reserve the right to change your mind, moments, weeks, years or decades later? Is it possible for your conviction to be so complete that it can never be changed; or is every intention subject to change? Can you commit your whole self in any intention?

We have proceeded, thus far, by assuming that an intention may be regarded as single. We may have several successive intentions, but each is different. On the one hand, if we consider the matter, we may see that our intentions often, perhaps always, overlap. For example, I intend to sit at this table, because I intend to eat dinner, because I intend to obtain nourishment, because I intend to work hard and live long. Intentions not only overlap; they may also serve each other hierarchically. I intend to sit in this chair partly because I intend to live long. Intentions may be interdependent; for it may be that I can carry out my intentions to live long only through having other specific intentions, such as the intention to sit in this chair, in order to do what is needed to promote such long life. Now, when I intend, on any particular occasion, do I commit all of my other intentions partly; do I then commit part of my intentions completely; or is the matter of "all" and "some," and of "partly" and "completely," itself a dynamic and variable condition of living and intending? What do we mean by saying that an action is "wholly intended?"

Sometimes, when we see a person in a fit of anger, having a tantrum, or doggedly pursuing a course of action which we know he will regret later, we say, "He is beside himself." He does not have his larger, fuller or long-range interests in mind, even though his present intention seemingly consists in a consuming insistence upon acting in a violent manner. In such a situation, we tend to believe that his true intentions are not those which he would, and will, assert if and when he understands himself and his own interests more fully and clearly. Can you really intend what you will later regret? If so, then rightness and wrongness may be related to your "true intentions." Do your "true intentions" differ from the intentions of your "whole self?" Can some part of your self intend for your whole self?

If the ultimate good is intrinsic good and if your "true intentions" consist in getting the most of what is good for yourself, then your true intentions can hardly be determined apart from what is most good for yourself. Not only do different metaphysical views of the nature of mankind and the universe vary with respect to what and how much such intrinsic good is available to you, but, if holding one such view rather than another itself makes a difference in the amount of such good attainable, then one ought to hold that metaphysical view which makes life actually most worth while. One who conceives oneself to be God's creature may believe that one's true intentions are those that God has for him. One who conceives his ultimate nature and value as identical with intentionless

Brahman may believe that all intention is illusory except the intention to achieve intentionlessness. One who thinks of himself as a materialistic mechanism enjoying moments of evanescent self-consciousness and pleasure may regard intention itself as evanescent, momentary, self-deceptive and futile. And one who feels himself to be a romanticistic urgent impulse may intend only that he continue unendingly as a self-perpetuating, self-willing, impulsive intender.

But no such simple solution satisfies the Organicist who sees self as both momentary and enduring (with both momentary and enduring intentions), as both conscious and subconscious (with conscious and subconscious intentions), as both private and social (with both independent and shared intentions), as both local and cosmic (with intentions regarding his own house, his nation and his universe), and as both complete and incomplete in different respects (and thus with intentions to remain satisfied with some achievements while intending both to work for new attainments and to want some more ever unfinished future). Although there is a sense in which each intention is the intention of one's whole self, since self as an organic unity cannot eliminate its unity from any particular act of intention; yet also there is a sense in which each intention is only a part of one's self, for no complexly organically unified self can reduce all of its nature, and "true intentions," to any one of its intentions. But also any particular intention, as an actual part of self, is a "true part," and it is a "true intention" provided it intends itself to be only such a part and not a deliberate or ignorant negation of all the other parts, and values, of self. A self's intention is most wholesome when a self knows its particular intention to be a particular intention of a self with other greater and smaller intentions that may be promoted (or thwarted) by acting upon it. Hence, one intends responsibly only to the extent that he takes his other values, intrinsic and instrumental, into account; and, as social and cosmic in nature, a self intends responsibly as a "whole self" only to the extent that he includes the goods of others and of the cosmos in his account of "his other values."

(b) If an action is "wholly intended" only when the intention ends in action, then we should notice some different kinds or degrees of action. Distinguishing between covert and overt action, we may think that our intention is complete as soon as our mind is fully made up even though we engage in no overt action. You may intend to act provided such action involves no trouble, without intending to take the trouble to act. Or, you may fully intend to act if an appropriate opportunity arises, even though it never does. Or, you may begin an action without continuing it, or you may continue it up to the last phase without finishing it. Furthermore, after you have started to act you may discover some unanticipated factors that cause you to change your course of action somewhat. Now must you carry out your act precisely as first intended or may you modify your intentions as you go along? Does "wholly intended" mean only at first intended or may it include modified intentions, even completely changed intentions as when you change your mind and reverse your direction?

2. *Intention and agency.* Are you first an agent which then intends? Or do you intend to be an agent? Are you first an actor, discovering yourself already in existence as acting, and then intend to continue acting, either carrying out previous actions or deciding to modify yourself and embark on new actions? Or are you an intender that moves your self into action by the strength of your intentions? Do your intentions have causes or do your intentions cause? Whoever differentiates agency and intention into two separate kinds of being finds difficulty in reintegrating, or even interrelating them. But if you accept your agency as constituting your intention and your intentions, whether merely as incipient actions or as fully carried out through action, as constituting yourself as agent, you should feel no difficulty in behaving as an organically unified entity. You may experience conflicts between your intentions and your actions only if you fail to recognize that you may have conflicting intentions resulting from competing values all of which are your own when you have a greater richness of opportunities than you have capacity for exploiting. You become a choosing, intending, self-obligating being only because you have more values than you can enjoy, and there is a sense in which rightness of action arises only because you must act as a chooser among alternatives and it is these occasions requiring choice which constitute you an intender or an intending agent. In this sense, you are an agent who becomes an intender. Yet, having discovered your power to decide between alternatives, and thus to determine the course of the future, you may so enjoy experiencing such power that you actively intend to continue and even to increase the intentionality of your agency. This is, you may also intend to be an agent and intend to be an intender.

3. *Self as intender.* Are you an intender? Are you, by nature, an intending being? Part of the answer to the question asked earlier, "What am I?" may be found in discovering organic relations between agency and intention, as just noted, and between self and intention. Although, surely,

a self consists of more than intentions, can you be a self without intentions?

Responsibility. Are you responsible? For what? To whom? How do your responsibilities arise? What difference does it make, if any, whether or not you are responsible, and what, if any, responsibilities do you have? These questions constitute the five topics for exploration in the present section.

1. *Are you responsible?* Or do you *have* responsibilities? Can you be responsible without having responsibilities? Can you have responsibilities without being responsible? What is "responsibility" anyway? We select five kinds of factors for consideration in answering these questions.

First, we often judge others as "to blame" for evil consequences of their actions, or, at least, of actions resulting from their intentions. A person is said to be responsible for any effect that one deliberately causes. Implied here is the view that a person is in some sense a free agent, and an originating source of action. If you merely transmit mechanically some force which causes ill effects, you do not normally blame yourself as responsible for the result. But when you yourself intend these effects, you recognize your own self as a responsible agent in producing them.

Secondly, "responsibility" means, literally, "ability to respond." When you have in fact influenced results, your ability to respond in such a way that you recognize your influence, and your responsibility for such influence, constitutes yourself as a responsible being in this sense. If you can and do accept the fact of your agency, you function as a responsible being. If you cannot or do not recognize yourself as an intending and causative agent, then you are spoken of as "irresponsible."

Thirdly, you may recognize yourself as responsible for causing evil consequences without being willing to "make amends." Where the principle of reciprocity and justice are expected to prevail, then when you respond normally in such a way as to give as you receive or to give in return value commensurate with value received, then you respond justly and behave as a responsible person. But whenever you become unwilling to repay a just debt or to restore a deliberately caused loss, you may properly be considered an "irresponsible" person, in another meaning of this term.

Fourthly, you may be responsible in all of the foregoing senses and still be irresponsible in another sense. For, even when you intend to be the cause of results, and recognize that you are the cause of such results, and are willing to repay for damages you have caused, you may still be unable to make restitution. If you have killed a man, how can you restore his life? You are unable, i.e., unable to respond in such a way as to make restoration; hence you are "irresponsible." Or, if you deliberately set fire to a \$500,000-dollar building when your total assets are less than \$1,000, you are "irresponsible." In this sense, responsibility involves capacity to deal with the situation.

Finally, your living in a group, whether family, municipal or national, for example, involves you automatically in certain conditions inherent in the interdependence of your welfare with that of others. Group decision about allocation of responsibilities to be borne by individuals generates assignment of such responsibilities. Whether you have been specifically chosen for a particular service or whether you share in some normal, even standardized, moral duty, you function responsibly when you satisfactorily perform the assignment. But you will be regarded as irresponsible, relative to such group assignments, if you cannot, or do not, or will not perform them. In this sense, you may be regarded as responsible for actions which you did not initially originate and did not intend.

Having surveyed five senses of "responsibility," we may now ask again, "What is responsibility?" and "Are you a responsible person?" If you do not accept all of the five senses as applying to yourself, why not? If you do, then you recognize that responsibility may entail more than mere intention and intentional action. Choice is deliberate, yet life is too complex to comprehend completely. Hence, some risk occurs with almost every choice, including each choosing not to choose. If, in any decision and action, you know there will be many results which you cannot foresee, some of which may be evils beyond your capacity to remedy, you may be acting as a partly irresponsible person. If you cannot act without being willing to be responsible not only for the results you intend but also for some which you do not intend, do you not intend to be irresponsible for some of what you cause but do not intend? To the extent that you become aware of such circumstances, do you not become responsible for intending to be somewhat irresponsible?

Another "side of the coin" has to do with the fact that you were not entirely responsible for coming into existence in the first place. That is, you were not, originally, responsible for your being born either as a (partly) responsible or a (partly) irresponsible being. Some, especially those bearing their responsibilities uncomfortably, who seek to unload their responsibilities whenever possible, will see here an escape. They are, originally and hence ultimately, not responsible for their condition; hence they should not be blamed, no matter what they do. However, enjoyment of continuing irresponsibility is not a birthright, for if you have no responsibilities, you have no rights and cannot properly complain if any person or circumstance harms or destroys you. Only by achieving some degree of responsibility do you become a person, and only by choosing and intending to become a more responsible person do you acquire both abilities and rights to more and continuing enjoyment of goods. Some of the issues at stake here have yet to be demonstrated, but the question, "Are you a responsible person?" has both a "Yes" and a "No" answer, and the further knowledge of the kinds and degrees of both responsibility and irresponsibility in your nature may well be a part of what you most want to acquire.

2. *For what are you responsible?* For intrinsic value. Since things that have intrinsic value may perish and since, whenever you have a choice between alternative courses of action in which one or another, and more or less, intrinsic good is at stake, you may cause the survival or perishing, the realization or wasting, of intrinsic good, you are responsible for such causation. Since obligation consists in the power that a greater good has over a lesser good in compelling our choices, you are responsible for your obligations, both for intending when choosing and for acting when carrying out your intentions regarding such obligations. Just as all of your obligations are primarily self-obligations, so you are responsible for the existence of, and optimization of, your own intrinsic value so far as you have any choice in the matter. Since you are essentially social and since, and to the extent that, your own intrinsic enjoyment may be enhanced by means of social cooperation, including interest in, sympathy for, and enhancement of, the intrinsic values of others, you are also responsible for all obligations involved in such choices as you have relative to the existence and optimization of intrinsic goods of others. If there were no intrinsic values, or if intrinsic values could not be changed in any way by your actions, you would have no responsibilities relative to them and, I think, no responsibilities at all. Your abilities, both opportunities and capacities and the fitness of these to each other, to increase or prevent decrease of intrinsic goods constitute your responsibilities. You are responsible for such increase and diminution of decrease, as long as you have a choice in the matter and power to act upon your decision.

3. *To whom are you responsible?* You are responsible, first of all, to yourself. Because your own intrinsic values are constantly at stake, you are responsible to yourself for their continuance. Perhaps we should have asked "To <u>what</u> are you responsible?" The answer then would be "to

intrinsic goods," for they and their precariousness function as the ultimate source of responsibility. But since your own intrinsic goods are the primary locus of your own interests, they function as the teleological source of your responsibilities. Since you are also inherently social and depend upon others for the realization of your self as social, you are responsible to such others for the continuance and improvement of their intrinsic goods. Now if you happen to be disinterested in others, your obligations to them may seem to cease. But few persons are able to live safely in isolation from others, and in an increasingly populated, increasingly interdependent world, the number of such persons tends to become smaller still. Although some persons have been so negatively conditioned as to fear and hate all others, the empirical generalizations based on the experiences of most persons tend to substantiate the conclusions that most of us will get more joy out of life if we increase our interests in others up to a certain point. Such increase in interests in others brings with it increased obligations, and responsibilities for such obligations, to the others as far as the status of their intrinsic goods can be influenced by our decisions and actions and so far as our own intrinsic goods depend upon our continued interdependence with these others. Persons who have little insight into the ways of optimizing their own intrinsic goods through their social opportunities tend to have a weak sense of responsibility to others. The more you become aware of enhanced enjoyment of your own being resulting from your becoming more highly socialized, the more you almost automatically acquire increased interest in, and increased feelings of responsibility for, the well-being of others.

4. *How do your responsibilities originate?* Since responsibilities have their source in intrinsic goods, in the power which greater good has over lesser good in commanding our assent, and in actual choices between alternative courses of value-creating or value-preserving activities, responsibilities originate in the same way in which these come into being. Your responsibilities, as yours, emerge into being in the same way, and at the same time, that you yourself evolve into existence as a responsible self. If this did not happen all at once, e.g., at birth, but did, does and will happen gradually and under varieties of circumstances, then your responsibilities originate gradually and variably. For example, you do not become responsible for keeping out of the way of automobiles until you become aware of dangers to yourself; you do not become responsible for support of your child until you become a parent; you do not become

responsible for the safety of your nation until you become aware of yourself as a citizen. A review again of the aspects, phases and levels of self surveyed in Chapters III and IV may reveal something of both the processual character and the multi-complexity of origins of your responsibilities.

Here, perhaps, we should notice how each of the five senses of "responsibility" outlined above originates. To the extent that you are responsible for whatever consequences you cause, your responsibilities of this sort are caused by whatever causes you to be a causing being. In the sense that you become responsible whenever you accept the fact of your agency, your responsibility in this sense grows out of your awareness of yourself as a free agent and your willingness to accept yourself as such. Insofar as being a responsible person requires a willingness to repay for injury which you have caused, your responsibility originates in whatever way such willingness arises. When responsibility consists also in ability to restore damage, then your responsibility has its foundation in whatever has produced the means you have with which to make restitution. Those responsibilities that become yours by virtue of your becoming a socialized being, e.g., friend, parent, citizen, owner, or officeholder, arise from your socialized nature and from the particular group-decision policies inherent in the groups to which you belong. Thus, since your responsibilities are of many kinds, they have many sources. Over some of these you may have control; e.g., you may decide whether to join an additional group or you may or may not deliberately acquire additional wealth and greater willingness. But some responsibilities have become yours simply because you exist as a good being whose precarious existence involves some self-obligation to put forth the effort needed for continued existence.

5. *Why are your responsibilities significant?* What difference does it make, if any, whether or not you are responsible and which, if any, responsibilities you have? Selecting only a few aspects of ways in which deliberate assumption of responsibility may be significant, we will relate responsibility to the nature of self, to self-esteem, freedom, authority and, indeed, to intrinsic value itself.

First of all, to be human is to be responsible. You can hardly accept yourself as a human being without recognizing some degree of responsibility as inherent in your human nature. You cannot be a self, a person, without acknowledging yourself in some way responsible for yourself and your values. To the extent that your own existence and continued enjoyment of intrinsic goods depends upon your recognizing and consenting to take some responsibilities for such survival of good, you must accept yourself as such and thereby accept such responsibilities as are involved. Not only must you assent to having some minimum of responsibility in order to be a person, but the kind of person you becomes depends in part upon the kinds of responsibilities you embrace.

Secondly, since you tend to esteem independence somewhat, and since independence involves some responsibility for self-management, you may regard yourself more highly as you become more responsible for your own self and values. But, also, social esteem, esteem by others, is something most people admire, and thus your acceptance of responsibility not only for your own welfare but also for that of others puts you in an admirable position. Although no precise correlation exists between bearing responsibility and admiration, generally speaking the more responsible you are, the more we have to recognize your significance as an authority and as an owner or possessor of the ability to carry such responsibility. "This may well be the age of those who believe that responsibility rather than success is the measure of man." (Peter F. Drucker, Landmarks of Tomorrow, p. 59, Harper, New York, 1959.)

Thirdly, responsibility involves freedom of choice. Hence it presupposes such freedom. There is a sense in which the more responsibility you acquire, the freer you are; although there is another side to this matter, since genuine responsibility requires that you act in accordance with your decision. But you deliberately compel yourself to act not only momentarily but continuingly upon your decision, thereby continuing to act freely. Of course, if you assume more responsibility than you can bear, so that fulfilling one obligation involves failing in another, your own assumption of too much responsibility makes you unfree. But, within the limits of your ability, failure to accept responsibility for doing, or being, or enjoying what is good makes you less free than you otherwise might be.

Fourthly, one who has responsibility thereby tends to have authority. Responsibility and authority should be commensurate with each other. One who lacks authority, or ability, to fulfill an obligation does not really have responsibility in its fullest sense. Assumption of responsibility for being a parent, for example, automatically endows one with authority to deal with the value problems which arise from parenthood. One who accepts responsibility for public office thereby attains authority appropriate to this task. People who accept responsibility for your welfare necessarily obtain whatever powers over you as are needed to fulfill their duties. You may become more authoritative as you become more responsible.

Finally, when you find yourself enjoying being a person, being esteemed, exercising freedom and being an authority, you can recognize such enjoyment as itself an intrinsic good. When greater responsibility brings "more personality," then more esteem by self and others, more freedom of choice and more freedom to determine, and more authoritativeness may yield greater enjoyment or greater intrinsic good embodied in your self. Those who become aware of the enjoyment involved in self-appreciation of being a responsible person tend to want to become still more responsible. The more responsible you become, the greater your self becomes and the greater your goodness becomes, both instrumentally, as an agent useful in preserving or creating such goods, and intrinsically, to the extent that you enjoy your status as more responsible. Part of the marvelous authority attributed to Jesus by his followers may be accounted for by his apparent willingness to "accept responsibility for the sins of the whole world." You can discover for yourself that you acquire increased ability as you accept increased responsibility for the welfare of others. For, just as when someone does something which is good for you and you like such goodness from him, so you yourself may be accepted by others as a person with power to produce good to the extent that you accept responsibility for doing such good for others.

If enjoyment of intrinsic good is the goal of life and if assumption of greater responsibility involves you in enjoyment of greater intrinsic good, then achievement of greater responsibility is part of what you most want to do. However, since there are limits to human and personal capacity, you should not wish for more responsibilities than you can bear. We may generalize, I think, and say that a young person, whose capacities are still developing, should seek to become more responsible, a mature person should seek to maintain responsibilities and assume no more than one can handle, whereas an older person, whose powers are declining, should deliberately choose to relinquish some of his responsibilities. In fact, once awareness of ability, freedom and responsibility for increasing and decreasing responsibilities occurs, one may thereby become responsible for increasing or decreasing them. Responsibility, like agency, intention, freedom and other moral traits, is organically related to self. The kinds and amounts of responsibility you have constitutes, in part, the kind of self you are.

Chapter X

SELF AS FREE

Are you free? The obvious answer to this question, especially in light of constant harping on the subject of freedom in politics, literature and life, is "Yes." However, anyone who has thought very much about the problem of the nature of freedom discovers that it is so fraught with ambiguities and subtleties that becloud perspective that it becomes more puzzling as one penetrates farther into it. Part of the difficulty lies in the fact that there are several different kinds of freedom as well as many theories of the nature of freedom. Each new outlook, for example, must somehow demonstrate that freedom can be explained in its terms; hence new metaphysical theories tend to result in new theories of, and thus meanings of, freedom. We shall have to circumscribe the topic somewhat in order to deal with only a few of its complex factors at a time.

Since ethics, as a science investigating the nature of oughts and obligations, can exist only if the freedom of choice presupposed in voluntary decisions exists, a "Yes" answer to our question is required. You can be ethical only if you are free. A science of ethics can exist only if the freedom of will and freedom of choice involved in deciding between alternatives exist. However, to say with assurance that you are free does not, in itself, reveal what freedom is. The first problem confronting us, then, is to explore the nature of freedom, since opposing views concerning the nature of freedom may result in conflicting implications for the nature of free choice, obligation and rightness.

What is "Freedom"? 1. *Kinds of Freedom.* Although there may be some common features of meanings of freedom in all fields of investigation, such as physics, metaphysics, logic, politics, psychology and ethics, we should notice, first of all, that differing emphases occur in the ways by which the problem is dealt with in them. As an example of physical freedom, we may cite a mechanical pulley fastened to its axle as being free to revolve only when its axle revolves, as being free to turn on its axle only when unfastened, as free to slide along its axle if unrestricted, as being free to tip sideways when removed from its axle, and to be "free-falling" when unsupported in any way. Logical freedom is freedom from contradiction, for in logic we say that what is contradictory "cannot be" and hence is not free to be. Political freedom may be of many sorts, such as freedom from control and freedom to control, and freedom of speech, press, assembly, equal treatment before the law, etc.

We propose not to indulge here in a comprehensive survey of meanings of freedom in all fields, but merely note that our limiting the use of the term "freedom" to meanings relevant to ethics does not exhaust the problem. You may be free in other ways than those involved in making decisions. But we will restrict our concern here to those meanings of freedom which appear to be involved in making moral choices. Having divided our volume into Part I, "Self," and Part II, "Society," and our treatment of "freedom" into Chapters X, "Self as Free," and XXV, "Social Freedom," we will postpone consideration of "political freedom" to Part II. Here we focus attention upon that "freedom of will" which is presupposed in "freedom of choice."

2. *What is "Freedom of Will"?* "Will" is a general term that includes in its meaning what is meant by "wanting" and "desiring" and by such more specific urgings as longing, wishing, yearning, demanding, insisting, hating, fearing, asking, grasping, hoping and being exasperated. "Will" is present in both "willfulness" and "willingness." "Will" is presupposed in "will not" and its variations such as refusing, rejection, renouncing, rebelling, revolting and repulsing. We shall use the terms "will," "desire" and "want" as synonyms for present purposes.

"Freedom," as already indicated, is "ability to do what you want to do." At least, this general meaning of the term will be used here and is proposed as something common to all of the theories of freedom to be explored in the following. But first we will analyze and explicate more fully what is meant by "ability to do what you want to do." Each of the terms in this definition is, as logicians say, "a variable involving many values."

a. "Ability" includes both "capacity" and opportunity." Distinguishing between "internal" abilities and "external" abilities, we choose to call the former "capacities" and the latter "opportunities." If, when sitting in a room with an eight-foot-ceiling, I desire to jump up twenty feet, I am unable to do so because the ceiling prevents me. But I am also unable to do so because I lack the muscular energy. Hence I am doubly unable. I am unfree to jump in this way because I lack the opportunity and because I lack the capacity. All of my opportunities and capacities together constitute my "abilities," in the sense in which this term is used here.

b. The verb "to do" may be replaced by the verb "to get" or "to be" or any other verb in any tense. That is, you are "free" whenever you are able to get what you want to get, or to be what you want to be, or to become what you want to become, or to eat what you want to eat. When the verb "to do" is replaced in its first occurrence in the definition by another verb, such as "to get," it should be replaced in its second occurrence by the same verb, i.e., "to get," in order to keep the meaning clear. When the second occurrence seems redundant, it may be omitted; but it should not be omitted whenever doubts about it may arise. Since you cannot do or get or be something without the thing, status or activity denoted by a noun and whatever adverbs and adjectives are needed to describe such doing, being or getting, the verbs referred to here involve all of the nouns, etc., needed to describe the doing, being or getting which is wanted.

c. "You," in this definition, means your self. Now, as we have seen, the term "self" has a wide range of meanings. Both what constitutes your self and what, at any particular time, you mean by "self" may be somewhat different from your constitution and meaning at another time. To the extent that this is so, what is meant by "freedom" defined in terms of your ability to get what "you" want to get may, or must, vary as the meaning of "self" varies. But, also, to the extent that there is something which remains throughout all of your self's existence and throughout all of your uses of the term "self," "freedom" so defined remains the same in meaning. The nature of self is being explored throughout Part I of the present volume.

d. "Wants" may be of any sort, whether momentary and trivial or enduring and profound. Previous discussions of the nature of self and its basic needs, interests, wants, and their operation as apparently single whims and as life-long, systematic, multi-leveled, multi-valued plans, are presupposed here. One's wants may be vague or clear, conscious or subconscious, selfish or highly socialized. Intrinsic values serve as the basis of wants. And one's "true intentions" surely constitute most of what one wants.

e. "What," or more generally, "whatever," you want refers to the most-described wants. But we may add here that "what"may refer to anything, whether described by a noun or verb or adjective or adverb, as indicated above, and even whether describable or indescribable; and it may be particular or general, and for yourself, others or the cosmos.

So far as the present chapter is concerned, then, "freedom" means "ability to get what you want to get." This meaning is regarded as more general than the meanings yet to be described in the following theories, and thus as a meaning which may be recognized as presupposed by, and common to, all of them.

Theories of Freedom. Seven distinguishable theories, and some of their subvarieties, seem worth noting here. Each has its negative counterpart or theory of "unfreedom."

1. *Absence of restraint.* The most common and most obvious meaning of "freedom" is a negative one: "absence of restraint." If someone has tied your hands or imprisoned you, you feel unfree. If someone has prevented or prohibited you from doing what you had intended to do, you experience limitations upon your freedom. Since we feel unfree whenever we feel restricted, we naturally conceive freedom as release from such restrictions. When we generalize about such release, we tend to idealize freedom as complete absence of all restrictions whatsoever upon our actions. Then we include not only physical limitations, such as bars and locks, but also social prohibitions, such as legal and moral demands, among the restraints which make us unfree.

Unfreedom typically is thought of as a purely external matter. Things or people or laws outside ourselves restrict us. But things existing inside ourselves do not, because they are parts of us. However, little reflection is needed to discover that inner limitations, such as lack of knowledge, skill or energy, inhibitions, or conscience, may restrain us as effectively as external limitations. Your incapacity to act prevents your action more often, perhaps, than lack of opportunity. When we become aware of the fact that inner limitations restrict us as truly as outer, then we tend to generalize that freedom consists in absence of all restraint, whether from inner or outer. All that prevents us from doing what we want to do makes us unfree.

However, when we thus regard whatever frustrates our desires as making us unfree, we tend to ignore the role of our wants in making us unfree. You may wish to be locked in a room so as not to become involved in troubles with others. You may wish to remain ignorant of certain issues so that you will not be called upon to deal with them. Hence limitations, merely in themselves, need not necessarily frustrate us and make us feel unfree. Limitations make us feel unfree only when we want them removed or when we have desires that cannot be fulfilled as long as they exist. But our wants themselves may make us unfree. Whenever we want what cannot be obtained, our wants themselves serve as source of our frustration and, thus, of our unfree situation. For example, whenever you have two wants such that, if you fulfill the one you must frustrate the other, and if you satisfy the other you must disappoint the one, either one of your wants makes you unfree to satisfy the other.

Whereas we so commonly attend to the objects of our desires and frustrations that we overlook our desires themselves as causes of unfreedom, we may attain increased enjoyment of life felt as free from frustration by intentional restriction of our wants so as to bring them more clearly in line with what we are likely to get. Once we more fully realize that our own wants serve as sources of frustration, we may tend to generalize that the fewer desires we have the freer we feel.

This latter view has appealed to many Hindu, Jain and Buddhist thinkers as the clue to all evil. The source of human unfreedom is entirely inner, they believe. If you can free yourself from your desires, you will experience no frustration and feelings of unfreedom. The Raja Yogin seeks complete freedom through complete extinction of desire. This view, that the source of unfreedom is wholly inner and a matter of having wants, is about as reasonable as its opposite, i.e., that the source of unfreedom is entirely outer and consists only of restrictions producing frustration. But there is a saner solution to the problem of enjoying more feelings of freedom than either complete absence of external and internal restraints or complete elimination of desires. This consists in wanting, but in modifying your wants more closely to what you can expect to get. (See my Philosophy of the Buddha, Chapters 1, 4, 6.) Whenever you want what you are going to get, you automatically feel free. One does not have to eliminate desires, but only those desires which will be frustrated, in order to achieve feelings of complete freedom.

Another usually-overlooked predicament involved in understanding "freedom of choice" is that choice occurs only when one faces alternatives. Now when the alternatives referred to are both good, i.e., equally good, we have two goods both of which we want but not both of which we can have. Thus we want more than we can get whenever we have either opportunity or necessity for choosing between alternatives. It follows that we must be frustrated whenever we have to choose, because we must give up at least one of the desired alternatives. Noting this, some who have achieved a degree of satisfaction come to the conclusion that what they most want is not more freedom of choice but more freedom from choice. Freedom from choice frees one from the frustration involved in having to give up one or more desired alternatives. Not having choices consists in lack of "freedom of choice" only if one happens to want to face choices. Having to make decisions which one prefers not to have to make causes one to be more frustrated and hence to feel more unfree. When you want to be freed from having to choose, you are as truly restrained from satisfying your wants when you are forced to choose as you are by any other kind of restraint. This kind of freedom may not be obvious to younger persons who feel that most of their unfreedom is due to impositions upon them by others, but the more that responsibilities for making decisions devolves upon older, parental and administrative persons, the more significant does this kind of freedom become.

2. *Indeterminism.* If only voluntary action is considered ethical, then involuntary action is considered nonethical or beyond the range of ethics. The difference between voluntary or willful action and involuntary or unwilled action is often thought to be that involuntary action is caused by something other than our will. Whatever is caused is determined by its causes, and the view that actions are determined by their causes is called "determinism." When one considers voluntary and involuntary actions as opposites and identifies involuntary acts with determined acts, one may easily (even if mistakenly) infer that one must identify voluntary acts with undetermined acts, and that one must subscribe to "indeterminism," the view that some actions occur without being determined by causes, in opposition to "determinism," the view that all actions are determined by their causes. The typical reasoning involved here holds that what is caused or determined is unfree, so what is free must be uncaused or undetermined. Freedom, then, consists in being undetermined. Your will is free when nothing causes its action. Your choice is free when nothing compels you to choose one alternative rather than another.

However, anyone who holds this view is plagued with difficulties, if he spends very much time reflecting about it. It presupposes the existence of something in the world that is undetermined. Thus, in effect, it denies the assumption, "nothing happens without a cause," which is commonly believed to be a necessary presupposition of the physical sciences, to say nothing about those who use it as an argument for the existence of God. Anyone who asserts that some undetermined being exists in the world then finds that he has to give some account of how the world can exist with both determined and undetermined beings in it. Many have sought a solution in "dualism," the view that there are two different kinds of beings in the world, matter, which is determined, and spirit, which is undetermined. Spirits alone have undetermined wills. This solution works, provided one is not too critical of one's assumptions. When one is asked: "Are spirits uninfluenceable?" one must admit some influence upon, and hence some determination of, spirits. The problem of how both determined and undetermined things can exist together has been shifted from "the world" to "spirits;" but here the problem remains to be considered all over again. Those who believe that spirits can think, hence reason, recognize rational determinants within spirit. If interaction exists between spirit and matter, e.g., as soul and body, then material causes, e.g., pain, hunger, pleasing sensations, etc., must be able to produce spiritual effects. The typical difficulties encountered in metaphysical dualism (See my _Philosophy: An Introduction_, Chapter XIII.) leave this attempt to account for indeterminism quite unsatisfactory.

Other attempts tend to meet a similar fate. Some seek to maintain freedom of will as undetermined being by denying the existence of matter entirely. Some give up trying to explain the situation and settle for an ultimate mystery. Recently, the appearance in physics of Heisenberg's "principle of indeterminacy" has led wishful thinkers to jump to the conclusion that "at last, physics justifies the assumption of indeterminacy in nature." However, since Heisenberg's principle has to do with our inability to obtain data regarding both the position and velocity of subatomic particles, and thus with "indeterminacy" in the sense of our inability to decide, rather than with the existence of anything as uncaused, the mistaken identification of these two different meanings of "indeterminacy" with each other constitutes a very crude type of mistake. This mistake illustrates the length to which some go in trying to justify their wishful thinking about freedom as indeterminacy.

Another difficulty encountered by the present view is an apparent inconsistency appearing in conflicting assumptions. Part of the reason for believing that we have freedom of will is that we wish to influence, i.e., to determine, the course of future events. If we will to produce certain good effects but are unfree to determine the outcome because indeterminism rather than determinism prevails, then we cannot do so, and this reason for wanting freedom of will and freedom of choice disappears. We not only want to determine things but also the ideas and wills of other people. We desire to help others help themselves. But we cannot do so unless our wanting and acting, depending upon deterministic principles, can cause their will to want what is better than what is worse for them. Thus an appeal to indeterminism as justification for freedom of will appears to be self-defeating. Freedom of choice is of value only if determinism exists, or at least enough of it for a choice to determine which of two courses of action will follow.

A main source of the difficulty in the indeterminist view may be found in a typical mistake involved whenever reasoning takes opposites for contradictories. "Free" and "unfree,' "uncaused" and "caused," and "indeterminism" and "determinism" are opposites. But they are not necessarily contradictories, for these terms may denote aspects of the same things rather than characteristics of things divided by an excluded middle. That is, a thing may be completely caused, in the sense that it is a product of nothing but its causes, and still have some unique aspects, that were caused to be there but which did not preexist in the causes, that enter into its causation of consequences. (See below, "The Freedom-Determinism Controversy.")

3. *Self-determinism.* By "freedom" we sometimes mean self-determination or self-causation. When my actions are determined by causes outside of myself, I am unfree. When they are determined by causes inside myself, I am free. Here the primary opposition is that between inner and outer causation. We find this usage also in political affairs, when we speak of "the self-determination of peoples." Those governed by other peoples are unfree; those who govern themselves are free. No indeterminism is required by this view. A self and its behavior may be completely determined and still be free. Freedom consists not in freedom from determination but in self-determination. One's desires may be caused. One's will may be caused. One's choices may be caused. But so long as the causes are one's own, or are parts of one's own self, one is free.

An important issue regarding this view centers about the nature of self. As we have seen previously (in Chapters III and IV), the nature of self is not always clear. If some clear-cut boundary between self and not-self existed, then the line between free and unfree behavior could be clearly drawn. But insofar as self varies somewhat in nature and extent, what constitutes self-determination also changes. If, for example, I oppose myself to clothes, when they inhibit my action, they seem to cause me to be unfree. But when I consider my clothes as mine, as parts of me as a well-dressed, self-respecting person, then when they inhibit my action I do not blame others for making me unfree but accept the inhibition as self-caused and thus as in no way causing me to be unfree. If you can expand your conception of self to include your family, your community, your nation or mankind, then you may expand the range of ways in which you can be caused and still feel free. But as you restrict your conception of self to exclude your body, your past, you memories, your reason, then when any of these influences you causally, they seem to make you unfree.

4. *Fitness of capacities and opportunities.* Distinguishing again between two kinds or aspects of "abilities," namely, those considered inside our selves as "capacities" and those thought of as outside of self as

"opportunities," we may discover that there is a fundamental sense in which "freedom" consists in the fitness of "capacities" to "opportunities" or of "opportunities" to "capacities" or, rather, in their fitness to each other. If "freedom" means "ability to do what you want to do," you can have such ability only if you have both the required "opportunity" and the needed "capacity." Consider, for example, a situation in which someone has made you a gift of a violin. You now have an opportunity to play a violin but you remain unfree to do so because you lack the needed skill or capacity. If, after acquiring the capacity for playing the violin, someone steals it, then you become unfree to play it for lack of opportunity. Thus, neither opportunity nor capacity alone is sufficient for freedom.

Consider, further, two persons, the first having great capacity and equally great opportunity and the second having small capacity and equally small opportunity. There is a sense in which the two are equally free, as we say, in "quality," even though they differ in "quantity" of freedom. When you have a given capacity and an equal opportunity, then if either your opportunity increases without increase in capacity or your capacity increases without increase in opportunity, you become less free "qualitatively," because you now have either an opportunity which you are unfree to use because you lack the needed capacity or a capacity which you are unfree to use because you lack the needed opportunity, without becoming less free "quantitatively." When you have an opportunity for which you lack capacity, then increasing your capacity to equal your opportunity makes you both "qualitatively" and "quantitatively" more free. When you have more opportunity than capacity, then if you lose opportunity so that it becomes equal to your capacity, you become more free "qualitatively" without becoming less free "quantitatively."

Concomitant increase in both capacity and opportunity makes you more free "quantitatively" without increasing your freedom "qualitatively." Concomitant decreases in both capacity and opportunity makes you less free "quantitatively" without decreasing your freedom "qualitatively." Decrease in either capacity or opportunity without concomitant decrease in the other makes you less free "quantitatively" (because you are unable to use the one without the other) and "qualitatively" (because you then have an ability, whether capacity or opportunity, which you are unfree to use because you lack the other). Increase in either capacity or opportunity without concomitant increase in the other makes you less free "qualitatively" (because you then have an ability, whether capacity or opportunity, which you are unfree to use because you lack the other) without increase in freedom "quantitatively" (because you are still unable to use the one without the other).

We have, thus far, neglected to examine the important roles of both (a) awareness and (b) desire, in considering the view that freedom consists in fitness.

(a) To the extent that one is unable to will, choose or act without awareness, awareness is an essential condition of freedom of will, freedom of choice and freedom of action. Is awareness a "capacity" or an "opportunity?" Perhaps, since we normally think of our awareness as subjective or inside ourselves, we more often regard it as a "capacity." If awareness is part of your capacity, lack of awareness functions as lack of capacity. Then, if you lack awareness of an opportunity, such lack causes you to be unfree to make use of it. If, however, you become aware of an opportunity which you already have, you thereby become more free in the sense that you now acquire a capacity needed in order to make use of it. On the other hand, if you feel your lack of awareness as due to external causes, such as a curtain that blinds your vision or a panorama of interesting spectacles that constantly occupies your attention, you may regard it as a lack of "opportunity." "If only I had time to think of that! But, too many distractions!" Regardless of whether awareness appears as a "capacity" or an "opportunity," it is an essential part of your "ability" without which many of your other "abilities" cannot function. Hence, awareness itself is an essential factor in that fitness which constitutes "freedom" in the present sense.

(b) Desire may also function as an "ability" in the sense that lack of desire may prevent you from making use of your other capacities and opportunities. If you have been elected or appointed to an office or paying position but are unwilling to perform its duties, you remain thereby unfitted for this position and become unfree to hold it. You may own a violin, thus having an opportunity to play it; you may be a skilled player, thus having a capacity, but still have no desire to play it. Thus your having a desire to play which is fitted to this circumstance frees you to play, whereas lack of desire to play involves you in a lack of ability in the sense that you lack something which is necessary to enable you to play actually. Desire to make use of your other abilities is itself a factor in your ability and in your fitness or unfitness to make use of these abilities and thus a factor in making you free or unfree, in the sense that "freedom" consists in "fitness." Desire operates in this way not only negatively, i.e., where lack of desire to use your abilities makes you unfree, but also positively, i.e., where presence of desire to do what you have no ability for doing makes you again unfitted and hence unfree, in this sense. When desire, functioning as a "capacity," is unfitted to "opportunity," you are unfree. When such a desire disappears, so that absence of desire is then fitted to absence of opportunity to satisfy such desire, you become again "fitted" in this respect and hence "free" in this sense.

5. *Submission.* Although, from some points of view, submission in any sense is regarded as surrendering freedom, there exist many different views that remain all alike in holding that "freedom" consists in subordination of "the lower" to "the higher" or in submission of one's lesser interests and values in service to one's higher interests and greater values. These views agree that intrinsic good is the ultimate source of need, desire and obligation, and that one naturally most wants what is best. The views differ regarding what is best and what needs to be done in order to attain it. Seven such views will be noted.

Perhaps the most well-known of these is that which presupposes an all-knowing and all-good-willing God who both knows and wants what is best for you. When your will differs from the will of God, i.e., from what God both knows and wants what is best for you, then what you want is not as good for you as what God wants for you. You may believe that you want what you want, because you lack full awareness of what is best for you and thus what you really want. If you can learn from bitter experience or from reliable teachers that you do not always know and want what is best for yourself, because of your ignorance, and that you can change to "always knowing and wanting what is best for you" by submitting your desires to what you know to be the will of God for you, then you become free. That is, you become free to realize your best interests or highest desires because you surrender your desires to satisfy your less-than-best interests or lower desires. This view is sometimes stated as becoming "free from sin" or "saved." "Saved" here means that one's highest values are assured of realization and "sin" means that one prefers to follow "evil ways," i.e., to satisfy desires that are less than the best. Many who differ regarding their picture of the goal of life and how it may be achieved still agree that one can attain complete freedom in this sense only by "surrendering one's will completely to the will of God."

Rationalists, especially extreme rationalists, who see the universe and minds as ultimately completely rational and only the completely rational as completely good, idealize surrendering one's irrational impulses to the dictates of one's reason. Unreasonable behavior not only leads to bad results but it is bad in itself, whereas reason, being good in itself, makes reasonable behavior the embodiment of such good-in-itself. Plato, Aristotle, Augustine, Aquinas, Calvin, Descartes, Leibniz, and Spinoza, to name only a few rationalistic philosophers, subscribe to this doctrine in one way or another. The view that freedom consists in subordinating one's unreasonable impulses to rational control may be illustrated by logical or mathematical reasoning. Two plus two equals four. If you should happen to prefer that two and two equal five and proceed to act impulsively upon your preferences, you would soon get into trouble, especially in trying to collect debts. Only if you willingly submit your inclinations to the demands of mathematical and logical reasoning can you attain what is right and good and best for you. Your mind is free to think correctly only if you submit it to the rule of logic. Your self is free to act correctly only if you submit your behavior to the rules of rational conduct.

Romanticists take an opposite view of what is ultimate in the nature and value of the universe and self. The world is alive, vital, willful, and persons are vital impulses expressing a portion of a divine will permeating, nay, constituting, the universe. Desire is the source of a person's being and value. The thrill of creating a thing of beauty by wanting it so, the feeling of power in prolonging kaleidoscopic fantasies into unending dreams, the exaltation of over-generous giving, of violent damning, and of replacing ugliness with beauty or beauty with ugliness, all inspire a self with spontaneous enthusiasm. Not satisfaction, which puts an end to desire, but desirousness itself is felt intuitively as its own joyous excuse for being. If what inhibits desire, arouses a more intense desire, then it is good, for it increases the strength of one's vigor. Cessation of desire, weakness, fatigue, indifference -- these are the real evils. As long as you are desiring, you are free. When your strength or ambition or zeal are gone, your freedom to live, to be fully alive, terminates. However, this view, too, involves submission. Here you must submit to your own impulses. Only when you submit completely to each ecstatic whim, each brutal demand, each amorous wish, each lustful gulp, each greedy grab, each carefree cry, can you be completely free. "What we finally mean by a free man is one who finds himself chained to his own will." (Richard Rothschild, Paradox, the Destiny of Modern Thought, p. 104, R. Smith, New York, 1930.)

Hindu Vedantists picture ultimate reality as perfectly quiescent Nirvana. Only that which is completely peaceful, undivided, undisturbed and indifferent is real. Both the universal Brahman and the subjective Atman exist really only as pure, undifferentiated, thoughtless, will-less bliss. Whatever arouses desire (such as the Romanticist's impulse), or disturbs the mind with distinctions (such as the Rationalist's inferential reasoning), or causes the soul to look for salvation through something outside itself (such as the theist's will of God) deprives the soul of its freedom to remain in perfect peace. Yogic efforts to eliminate all attachment to things, objects, laws, loves, beliefs, memories or desires are required in order to reattain the freedom to be one's true ultimate self. The efforts required for yogic practices may seem little like submission. Yet one must devote oneself wholeheartedly, hence submissively, to one's task. But the very zeal with which one bestirs oneself may nullify one's efforts, because one can make progress toward the quiescent goal only as one pursues one's way even more quiescently. One must submit one's will willingly to will-lessness. Only then can one be completely freed from whatever prevents one from gaining that bliss of Nirvana which is the highest value, the greatest good.

The Taoist, Lao Tzu, conceived nature as good, both the world as nature and the nature of each individual person or animal. When each thing follows its own inner nature, all goes well. When a person starts meddling in the affairs of others, one finds resentment and gets into trouble. To impose upon others and to be imposed upon by others leads a person away from oneself. The only way to be freed from trouble is to submit completely to one's own inner nature. When one's inner nature calls for more air, one breathes more deeply. When it calls for sleep, one simply goes to sleep. When it calls upon one to excrete, one excretes. In this way, one is free to be oneself. Submission to one's own true (i.e., inner) nature frees one from becoming artificial (i.e., interested in natures other than one's own).

Sociologists and political scientists may be forced to become more fully aware of the social nature of persons. To the extent that society, whether one's family, one's state, one's nation or one's corporation, becomes interested in one's welfare, it seeks to prepare political, economic and cultural conditions most suited to one's well-being. But it can promote your welfare only to the extent that you cooperate with it. It cannot serve you unless you let it. If you revolt against it, violate its laws, become a criminal, you make yourself unfree to enjoy its benefits. Those who see that one's greater good is what is provided for one by his society tend also to see that one gains freedom to enjoy such good only to the extent that one submits to accepting its services. Of course, different people and conceptions of society may prevail; some plan their welfare in greater detail and some demand more complete conformity to its established patterns. But all views that hold that greater good is to be found in and through society believe that submission of the individual to acceptance of whatever is required in order to obtain that good is itself a kind, indeed, a source of freedom.

Organicism, at this point, may observe that each of the kinds of submission of lower to higher self may provide its own kind of freedom. To the extent that there is some virtue in the contentions of each claimant (and surely there is some), there is then a further need for submitting to the fact that there are these many ways of attaining freedom through submitting. Organicism claims that submission to, acceptance of, and action in accordance with, this fact may be a still more superior kind of submission than any of the others because it deliberately incorporates all of the other kinds of superiority within itself. It does so without insisting that if one of these kinds is really superior than all the others must be inferior to it. It believes that those who are free to find many different kinds of higher values are freer than those who find freedom only through one kind of higher value. It agrees that submission of lower values to higher values is a genuine kind of freedom. But it claims that those who believe that any one of the proposed superior values is alone superior thereby become unfree, and would make others unfree, to pursue such superiority as may be found in each of the other kinds of superior values. Hence, submission to the fact of a multiplicity of kinds of superiority is a still higher kind of superiority to the extent that it provides more freedom than any one or two of the others alone.

6. *Agency.* According to this theory, freedom consists in willingness to accept oneself as an agent, as an originator of action, or as a prime mover. This theory may be explored in three levels.

First, an agent is anyone or anything which acts. To act is to cause results. So whenever you cause results you are an actor or an agent. How, one might ask, does being an agent differ from "self-determinism" as discussed above? To the extent that you merely transmit causal influences from elsewhere, you may serve as a caused cause. You are part of a causal system which is such that some of the system operates within you; when you regard the causes as your own, then you are self-determined, and hence, in this sense, free. But you are not an originating cause; you are merely a transmitting cause. You serve as a mechanical agent. But you are not a "free agent."

Secondly, in order to be a "free agent," you must not only be a cause of results but you must also regard the source of your causation as within yourself as an originator. Now you might be an originator without knowing that you are or without wanting to be. If you do not know that you are an originator, you can hardly regard yourself as being a free agent relative to such origination. If you do not want to be an originator, you may reject your agency as being free and regard your action as something forced upon you against your will. You can be a "free agent," in the sense intended here, only if you both know that you are and that you want to be an originator. Your wanting may be merely permissive rather than insistent, i.e., it may consist in willingness rather than in willfulness. But conscious, or at least subconscious, assent to being an agent is required in order to be functioning as a free agent.

Theorists habitually thinking merely in terms of universal determinism have difficulty in comprehending how agency can ever be regarded as spontaneous. Yet those who acclaim the present idea of "free agency" often believe that you can intuit your own agency. You exert yourself into being, or if not into being, at least into acting. Your will to be or your will to act is a self-willed will. Although one may will to will, etc., dialectically, most holders of this theory believe that you can intuit your own will as self-starting, as self-caused, as self-originating. Freedom as agency consists in ability to do what you want to do because the wanting itself is self-originating as well as because willing is itself a most basic kind of ability. "Free agency" is self-enabling. Hence, a "free agent" is free no matter what the results of one's action. You may be unfree in the sense that you do not get what you want but you are still free in the sense that you are the self-enabler, or self-originator, of your wants.

You are free in this sense whenever you accept yourself as a prime mover. You may even mistakenly believe that you are an originator; but if you accept yourself as an originator, then you accept yourself as free in this sense. As long as your willingness to so accept yourself continues, you continue to be such a free agent. Those who doubt their own intuitions of free agency may use the pragmatic methods: they may try to will, i.e., to will to will or originate will, and see whether or not they succeed. Repeating the experiment, if experiment is needed, should convince them that they can will merely by wanting to. And, in the process, they can obviously intuit whether or not they are willing to be such a willer.

Thirdly, this theory may become expanded through the addition of another characteristic. Perhaps it then becomes an additional kind of theory. If you alone are the originator of your actions, are you then responsible for your actions, and, indeed, alone responsible for your actions? Furthermore, are you not also responsible for the results of your actions, for the effects of which you are a cause? Does not your willingness to be a prime mover involve a willingness to be responsible for the results of which you are the originating cause? If so, then whenever you exhibit some unwillingness to be responsible for the results which you cause, does this not imply that you somewhat refuse to accept yourself as a free agent? Does not your unwillingness to accept responsibility for the consequences of your own action imply that you are unable to do what you want to do -- unable to do because you are unable to want, or freely will, to accept yourself as a self-originator of your doing? In this third level of exploration, we find freedom consisting in agency where agency involves a willingness to accept oneself as the responsible originator of causes which have effects. Whoever is willing to be responsible for the consequence of self-originated actions is a free agent.

7. *Organic freedom.* Organicism aims to incorporate all of the positive proposals about self as free expressed by the previous six theories. It rejects all of the negative assertions in each theory which deny the positive proposals in other theories. How Organicism does this is shown in the following.

Organic freedom involves ideas of absence of restraint, both external restrictions and internal limitations. Although inner and outer are opposites, and what is outer may restrain what is inner, what is inner may also restrain what is outer; and it takes both inner and outer restraints, supplementing each other, to constitute all of our restraints. But also whatever things, such as locked doors or lack of energy, which make us unfree when they frustrate our desires may be means to freedom when they help to satisfy our desires, as when we desire isolation from intruders or relief from onerous tasks. Hence absence of restraint sometimes frees us and sometimes makes us unfree. Furthermore, not only do we feel unfree when restraints frustrate our desires, but desires themselves, whenever we desire what we cannot have, are, in effect, self-frustrating and hence sources of our feelings of unfreedom. Freedom from desire, in such circumstances, is as truly a kind of freedom as freedom of will. Finally, freedom of choice, between two alternatives both of which are desired but only one of which can be attained, entails frustration of one of the two desires, i.e., that desire for whichever alternative cannot be obtained. Hence, freedom conceived as having more desired alternatives from which to choose also entails unfreedom conceived as failing to attain more of the desired alternatives offered. Hence, Organicism sees the many pairs of opposites, inner and outer restraints, which may both frustrate and satisfy our desires, which desires may make us free or unfree depending on whether we want what we can get, including situations in which our desires for more alternatives involve more frustrations. Both of each pair of opposites is needed in the full picture of the nature of freedom, and whenever we neglect or deny one of any pair we suffer from a one-sided view of the nature of freedom, even freedom conceived as absence of restraint.

Indeterminism, conceived as complete absence of determinism, or causal determination, is rejected by Organicism as merely negative. However, the idea that determinism and indeterminism must be regarded as contradictory views is also rejected, as will be indicated in discussing "the freedom-determinism controversy" below. Hence, there is a sense in which indeterminism, conceived as determined indeterminism, plays a subtle role in the idea of organic freedom.

Organic freedom includes self-determinism. Furthermore, it includes self-determinism in a system conceived positively as completely determined, though not where such complete determinism, in some positive sense, negatively rules out all possibility of indeterminism in any other positive sense. Again, for demonstration we must refer to the discussion of "the freedom-determinism controversy" below. But also, since variations in conceptions of self entail changes in conceptions of self as free or unfree relative to such self-determination, all of the dynamic variables involved in the nature of self, as explored in earlier and later chapters, enter into the conception of organic freedom as inclusive of self-determinism.

Freedom thought of as fitness of capacities and opportunities not only is accepted as part of the idea of organic freedom but is in fact a product of Organicistic thinking. The theory, stated as if conceived independently because it expresses and emphasizes certain aspects of the problem of freedom which are recognizable as distinguishable, arose out of earlier shapings of Organicistic thinking, including recognizing awareness and desire serving either as capacities or opportunities, depending upon how they function relative to an organic self's needs.

Although the idea of freedom as submission of lower to higher self seems obvious as a general kind of freedom, the existence of conflicting theories about which aspects of self are higher serves to provide Organicism with a more complex, more organic, conception of what is higher in a self. For example, recall the controversy between Rationalism and Romanticism regarding which is the superior good, reason or will?

Both are aspects inherent in human nature. Both are goods instrumentally and serve as constituents in feelings of appreciation. Now when our enjoyment of being rational is taken as an intrinsic good, it serves as a kind of standard in terms of which other goods, such as the zest enjoyed in experiencing irrational impulses, are judged and found wanting. Whenever you regard willful impulses as irrational, will is then rated as a lower aspect of self, and you can become free to do what is best for yourself only by submitting your will to your reason. However, there are also times when a desired goal becomes endowed with its experienced value only through the depth or intensity of our longing for it. When our intellect throws doubt upon the ultimacy of the value experienced in such longing, its effect is negative, and especially when its reasonings are trivial, picayunish, one must regard one's own reason as possessing inferior value. One becomes free to pursue and achieve the higher value of his "heart's desire" only by submitting his reason to this enduring impulse. Reason and will, each in its own way, serves as a basis for what is higher in self. Whoever would rule out one, merely because one at some time favors the other, impoverishes oneself. If you can retain a dynamic integrity of self by enjoying first one and then another of your many value-aspects as superior, each in its own way, you can experience a kind of value superiority in such flexibility which is greater than the value superiority which limits itself to only one of its value aspects as alone superior. Submission of a tendency to pursue only one of these alone to that superior value-experience in which each and all may be enjoyed in its proper time and turn is, of course, submission just as truly as any other kind of submission. And its kind of freedom is at last just as much a kind of freedom as any of the limited kinds of submission outlined previously.

Experiencing the feeling of agency may indeed be experienced as a feeling of freedom. You are free to feel yourself acting as a free agent to the extent that you willingly accept your agency as your own and your self as a responsible agent. When such feeling of agency is intuited, it appears as self-evident. However, such feeling of being a prime mover in this sense in no way implies that one's feelings or one's willingness are uncaused. One's being _caused_ to feel free need in no way detract from one's being caused to _feel free_; the feelings felt are genuine and the agency exercised may be genuine. Again, the Organicistic reasons for this view will appear below. But, we may add, conceiving self as multi-faceted, multi-leveled and multifunctional involves the emergence of appreciation of, and acceptance of, one's self as being multi-agential and as having many kinds of freedom even merely as a free agent.

The Freedom-Determinism Controversy. Disputants about whether we are free or determined often agree in presupposing that freedom and determinism are contradictories. That is, if you are determined, then you are not free; if you are free, then you are not determined. Given this presupposition, the alternatives usually seem to be: (1) You are completely determined; hence you are not free. (2) You are free; hence you are not completely determined. (3) You are dual, having a part (soul?) which is free, and a part (body?) which is determined. A study of the history of this controversy will reveal that all of the three views remain unsatisfactory.

(1) The view that you are completely determined is alleged to be supported by the natural sciences. But the conclusion that you are therefore completely unfree must be rejected in the light of intuitive evidence of your own free agency which is as ultimate in the way of evidence as any other intuitive evidence that is required to serve as the basis for scientific theories.

(2) The view that you are free, hence undetermined, although supported by intuitive evidence, appears to undermine the principles of universal causality ("Nothing happens without being caused to happen") and of the uniformity of nature (given the same set of causes again, we will get the same set of effects again) upon which the sciences depend.

(3) The view that you are dual, though popular, is fraught with so many difficulties that it hardly seems worth considering. For, in addition to facing the difficulties encountered by both of the foregoing views, it encounters problems of explaining how that which is completely free can transform itself from a free into a determining being, how that which is completely determined can be determined by that which is free, and how that which is free can be completely free and still be influenced by that which is completely determined, or by other free persons. Holding that a soul is completely undetermined turns out to be unsatisfactory, since a soul should be self-determining, i.e., its earlier decision should have some influence upon its own later condition; also, if a soul is rational, it is involved in a rationalistically determined system. But if a soul is also determined, then there are two different kinds of deterministic systems (one within soul and one outside soul in body) which must somehow be reconciled and yet be kept different, and also the problem of how determinism and freedom can be reconciled within a soul presents us with

our original predicament all over again. (For a classical example of the typical dualistic contentions and of typical difficulties in dualism, see my Philosophy: An Introduction, Chapter 13.)

A better, even if less usual, way to deal with the controversy is to attack the common assumption that freedom and determinism are contradictories. "The position to be defended . . . is that both those who deny all freedom and power of personal choice and those who deny determinism are taking false positions. This is not an 'either-or' issue . . . (but) a 'both-and' problem . . ., both may be not only compatible but reasonably held at the same time." (H.H. Titus, Living Issues in Philosophy, Third Edition, p. 172, American Book Co., New York, 1959.) Since the controversy involves metaphysical presuppositions, solution to the problem requires postulation and examination of a metaphysical scheme that both explains how determinism and freedom can exist together without contradiction and remains adequate in dealing with all other kinds of metaphysical problems. We choose to present a theory of causality that will show how both freedom, conceived as uncaused causation, and determinism, conceived as caused causation, may be universal conditions of all nature, not merely of persons. Although such uncaused causation does not in itself constitute free will, the difficulties preventing acceptance of both of the foregoing alternatives will disappear.

Our argument involves two somewhat unusual conceptions of the nature of causation: (1) Causation necessarily involves novelty.   (2) Causation is always multi-leveled.

1. When causation is conceived in terms of mechanical "resultants," i.e., where the effects are already contained in their causes and where the causes are carried over completely into their effects, the results are, in principle, perfectly predictable. According to this view, every formula should represent all the causes together as exactly equal to all of the effects: $C = E$. In the causal process, nothing is gained and nothing is lost as far as the total energy in the causal situation is concerned.

When causation is conceived in terms of "emergents," however, something new emerges which could not have been predicted. "The whole doctrine of emergence is a continued protest against mechanical interpretation." (C. Lloyd Morgan, Emergent Evolution, p. 7. Williams and Norgate, London, 1923.) "The orderly sequence of natural events historically viewed, appears to present, from time to time, something genuinely new. . . . But if nothing new emerges -- if there be only regrouping of pre-existing elements and nothing more -- then there is no emergent evolution." (Ibid. p. 1.)   Interpreting Morgan's distinction between "resultants" and "emergents," we may say that, in mechanical causation, "there can be nothing new in the world, unless it be simply a new arrangement, a new collection, a new association of material elements." "Such happenings as are said to be new sums -- as in mathematics when 5 and 7 are added together for the first time, the number 12 is said to be new, but there is nothing in 12 that was not already implied in 5 and 7. Or, when one billiard ball is hit by two others, the motion imparted to it is new for the balls, but the motion, the kind of behavior, is not a new kind of behavior. The amount and direction of motion could have been predicted precisely if the direction and motion of the other two balls had been known. And there is nothing in the moving ball which could not be explained directly as a result of the motion and direction (and other similar factors such as slope of surface, air resistance) of the other two. The motion of the billiard ball is explainable as the resultant of the motion of the other two balls." (See my Philosophy: An Introduction, p. 214.) Emergent causation involves resultants, but it involves something more. "When carbon having certain properties combines with sulphur having other properties, there is formed, not a mere mixture, but a new compound, some of the properties of which are quite different from those of either component. Now the weight of the compound is the resultant, the sum of the weights of the components; and this could have been predicted before any molecule of carbon-bisulfide had been formed. One could say in advance that if carbon and sulphur shall be found in any ascertainable proportions there will be such and such weight as resultant. But sundry other properties are constitutive of emergents which could not be foretold in advance of any instance of such combination." (Morgan, op. cit., p. 3.) Furthermore, each emergent then functions as a new causal agency. The emergent (which includes resultants) causes effects that are effects both of the old, or predictable, causal ingredients and of the new, or unpredictable emergents. Thus genuinely new ingredients enter into causation whenever emergents arise. (For a fuller account of the nature of emergents, see Chapter 18 of Philosophy: An Introduction.)

Organicism absorbs the emergentist doctrine of the occasional emergence of novelty and supplements it, first by extending the idea of emergence of novelty to every causal situation, and then by recognizing that a somewhat, but not exactly, corresponding loss or cessation also occurs in each causal process. Each causal event involves both "caused causation" in the sense that effects are caused by causes which are resultant effects of causes and "uncaused causation" in the (too easily misunderstood) sense that effects are caused by causes which are also newly emergent effects of causes. "Determinists are correct in asserting that each cause-effect situation involves complete determination of effect by cause in the sense that the effect is caused to be what it is entirely by its causes. That is, only its causes cause it. If anything else caused it, this something else would be included among its causes. Furthermore, there is nothing in the effect which was not caused by its causes. Yet, even though this be true, it is also true that each effect is in some sense new and different as compared with its causes. The crux of the difficulty lies partly in the usual tendency to oversimplify what we mean by the cause and the effect. For symbolic convenience we often use the symbolism: C --> E. Such symbolism tends to presuppose that cause and effect are merely simple or single unitary entities. If so, then if they equal each other, or if the effect follows wholly from its cause, we have a kind of identity of cause and effect. But surely we do not intend that cause and effect should be exactly identical. In fact, when we examine more fully what we mean, we discover that each existing cause and effect is really a complex of causes and a complex of effects. Each effect is really the effect of a multiplicity of causal factors or influences from a number of different entities. Each effect is an entity which then functions as a cause of a multitude of influences upon many other different entities. Thus a minimum symbolization of the situation involves something like the following:

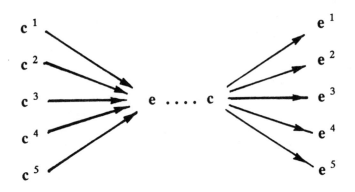

"Insofar as each effect is one effect, i.e., has some unity or wholeness about it, it is substantially different from the multiplicity of its causes. This difference is not only a difference of the effect from each one of its causes taken singly, but also a consequence of the fact that it is one although they are many. That is, c^1 cannot be the sole cause of e, for c^2, c^3, c^4 and c^5 are also its causes. Likewise c^2 cannot be the sole cause of e, since it must share such causation with the other causes. Likewise for c^3, c^4 and c^5. If e if the joint effect of the five c's, there must be something about it which is contained neither in any one of its causes taken singly nor in all of them collectively, because their collectivity involves a manyness, and an external relatedness of each from the other, which does not exist in the effect. Thus although, on the one hand, the effect is completely caused in the sense that its nature is what it is because of its causes; yet on the other hand, there can be no causation without causes causing effects in such a way that each effect involves something that was contained neither in any one of its causes taken singly nor in all of them taken together as an externally related collection. This something in the effect which was not contained in its cause is, in a sense, uncaused. If being caused means that there is nothing in the effect that was not already in the causes, then this something, which was not in the causes, is uncaused." Something similar should be said about each cause having multiplicity of effects where, again, the unity of a cause is destroyed through dispersion into its effects and is contained neither in any one of them singly nor in all of them separately, although, of course, the cause is also preserved insofar as its causality is carried over into its effects. "The effect, as an existing entity, in turn functions as a cause of other effects. Insofar as its effects are a result of its causes, it is a caused cause. But insofar as its effects are a result also of it as uncaused, it is an uncaused cause. Thus, not only is determinism true, in the sense that each effect is caused by nothing but its causes, but also indeterminism is true in the sense that there is something about each effect which, through entering into subsequent causation, did not exist as such in its causes." (Philosophy: An Introduction, pp. 245-246.)

Hence causation, in every instance, involves both 100% determinism, in the sense that every effect is caused to be what it is by its causes and nothing but its causes, and at the same time an aspect of indeterminism in the sense that something exists in the effect which did not preexist in its causes. If there is a proper sense in which a thing is said to be "free" when its own agency involves an undetermined aspect in the above sense, then all things are caused to be free, in this sense. But since all things are also caused, and caused to be causers, they are also, and fundamentally, determined or unfree, in these senses. Hence, determinism and indeterminism, in the senses indicated, are ever-present aspects of causation; and determinism and indeterminism, in these senses, are not contradictory, but inherently supplementary in nature.

Establishing the metaphysical coexistence of determinism and indeterminism in causation, and of an uncaused aspect in all further causation, does not in itself establish identity of such uncaused aspect with the experienced sense of agency or of free will. In fact, there is nothing incompatible in the idea of complete determination of will that is caused to feel completely free. The feeling of freedom is an intuited feeling. Belief in complete determinism results from intellectual inference. The foregoing argument is presented here for the purpose of refuting those mechanists who claim to prove that freedom is impossible because will is determined and that, therefore, the case is closed. The argument reopens the case, perhaps permanently. Similar argument could be used against the other alternatives cited above: (2) You are free; hence you are not completely determined. (3) You are dual; having a part that is free (and not determined) and a part that is determined (and not free). A "both-and" metaphysics and logic eliminates metaphysical necessity from "either-or-but-not-both" arguments.

2. Causation is also always multi-leveled. Citing for convenience only one simple hierarchy, we may note that our galaxy is a whole composed of stellar systems, that our solar system is a whole with planets as parts, that our earth is a whole with multifarious kinds of parts, including societies of men, that each society is a kind of whole of which each member is a part, that each person is a whole with bodily organs as parts, that each organ consists of cells as parts, that each cell is a whole made up of molecules as parts, that each molecule is an entity which has atoms as parts, and that each atom is a whole having electrons and other subatomic particles as parts. Some investigators have seemed interested in explaining phenomena only in terms of causal antecedents within one of the above-noted levels. Biologists once thought in terms of cells producing cells; but eventually they became aware of, and interested in, the molecular factors in heredity and environment, and then in the roles of atomic and subatomic particles in cell constitution and causation. But also the roles of bodily, psycho-physical, social psychological, geographical, solar and cosmic factors gradually became known and taken into account in understanding and explaining the nature and causes in cell behavior.

Causal formulas involving equations intended to depict the principle of the uniformity of nature that were limited to uniformities supposed to exist at any one level have had to be revised to take account of the causal influences of causal factors existing primarily at other levels that have effects that may appear as non-uniformities when viewed merely from within any one level. The principle of the uniformity of nature should not be surrendered merely because causation is discovered to be multi-leveled; but one should recognize that, the greater the number of different kinds of causes, including causes from different levels, the greater the amount of novelty and uniqueness that may be caused to exist in every effect occurring in any of the levels. The more novel and unique any entity is caused to be, the more it acts as a novel (uncaused and undetermined in the above sense) and unique agent.

The principle of the uniformity of nature, let it be remembered, does not assert that nature is merely uniform in such a way that it exhibits no differences. The principle states that, when a given set of circumstances (causes) produces a given set of effects, then, whenever exactly the same set of circumstances occurs again, exactly the same set of effects will occur again. The principle, in itself, does not say that exactly the same set of circumstances will ever occur again. The Organicist principle, which we may name "the principle of the organicity of nature," asserts that all things are both alike in some respects and different in some respects. Insofar as things are alike in their recurrence, the principle of the uniformity of nature holds. Insofar as things are different in their recurrence, the principle of the uniformity of nature does not hold, but the principle of the uniqueness of each entity in nature holds. The principle of the organicity of nature incorporates both the principle of the uniformity of nature and the principle of the uniqueness of each nature as polar opposites inherent in all natures and in all causation.

When a self is conceived, not as a timeless and unchangeable soul, but as an organic whole integrating many levels of being and of causal determination within its own nature, the multicomplexity of its dynamic uniqueness provides plenty of opportunity for many varieties of uncaused causation to function aspectivally as inherent in its nature.

Establishment of multileveled determinism does not in itself demonstrate identity of such uniqueness of agency and what is experienced as "free will" and as "freedom of choice." But it further clarifies the picture in such a way as to further render implausible the mechanistic hypothesis that complete determinism, in one sense, implies the impossibility of indeterminism and freedom, in any other sense. The more unique a person's agency is, the more one may be regarded as one's own. But the more complex the causes of a person's agency, the more complex one is as a person; a person's caused agency is, in another sense, as much one's own as one's uncaused agency. One does not cease to be oneself merely because one's self has been caused. One does not cease to be oneself merely because one's self is unique. If one is both caused and unique, then one's agency and one's will are both determined and free, in different senses at the same time, and all the conditions needed to account for the assumption of freedom of will and freedom of choice apparently presupposed by ethics may be seen to be explained.

Self as Free. Self is free, then, not only physically, politically and volitionally, as mentioned earlier, and free not only in the senses of having some absence of restraint, some indeterminism, some self-determinism, some fitness of capacities and opportunities, some submission of lower to higher self in various ways, some willingness to accept oneself as an agent, and some organic interdependence of these different kinds of freedom, as summarized above, but also free as a unique, novel being, not merely simple but also multi-complex, having a dynamic uniqueness that is continually caused as a consequence of many levels of causal factors entering into the production of one's unique being, as suggested in the foregoing section. Freedom is many-faceted, multi-phased, vari-aspected. A self may be free and/or unfree in all these ways, even all at the same time; even though one's mental and attentive powers may be unable to remain continuously aware of more than one or two of them. Each way has its own role to play in a self as an end-in-itself, as an intrinsic value. Each way, as it functions more or less significantly, comes to constitute, and in this sense determine, the particular nature that a self has. What is best for a self in the long run, and thus what is right for a self to do, in the way of seeking to become more free or less free in any or all of these senses, is multi-complex, dynamic and somewhat fluctuating.

Selecting for further emphasis the sense in which a self is a free agent and, more specifically, the sense in which it is a responsible agent because it accepts its agency and its responsibilities as its own, we may further explore an aspect of the nature of "intention," consideration of which was postponed in the last chapter. There it was said that a sense exists in which an act is wholly intended only if it is completely free. But now, having discovered how complex the nature of freedom is, and that freedom is not incompatible with determinism, we can say that, while there may be a sense in which an act is wholly intended, this sense must not be regarded as ruling out many other senses in which the same act is not wholly intended (even wholly not intended). For example, you did not, prior to your own existence, intend to come into being. In this sense, your whole being and all of the intentions that arise within it, were wholly unintended by you; and this sense of being and acting in a wholly unintended way continues to be an aspect of your being even though you remain, deliberately or unwittingly, unaware of it. Reappraising the situation as one in which a person can never be wholly free in a way that rules out all causal determinism, the extent to which you can be wholly free in one limited sense still remains an option, one that many find desirable.

To the extent that you are free in the sense that you willingly accept yourself as an agent, you have some latitude regarding how much you will consider yourself as an intending or as an unintending, and as a responsible or as an irresponsible, being. You can observe the kinds of lives lived by those who consider themselves responsible and by those who consider themselves irresponsible. Or, better, you can recall, or experimentally observe, those occasions when you regard yourself as responsible and those when you regard yourself as irresponsible. You may then conclude what kind of being you prefer to be. Since there is a sense in which a thing is what a thing does, you can, in this sense, become a responsible being by accepting yourself as, and acting as, a responsible being. Of course, since there are times when your opportunities for being responsible and your capacities for bearing responsibility change, if you try to be responsible in times or ways when you lack opportunity or capacity, then you will fail. You may hastily generalize that, therefore, you never had opportunity or capacity for being responsible. Or, when you try to be irresponsible, at times when both the opportunity and capacity for a certain responsibility are present and actually yours alone, again you fail. Again you may hastily generalize that there is no escape from freedom, no escape from responsibility. But, just as there is a time for sleeping and a time for waking, so there are times for accepting responsibility and times for accepting irresponsibility. And just as some are more sluggish and others more agile in shifting from sleeping to waking, so some are more lethargic and others more spontaneous in acquiring and discarding their sense of responsibility. The issue of choosing between responsibilities, and how much of each, you should seek to embody may be among your most important oughts. You not only may intend, but you may also, dialectically, intend to intend, or intend not to intend. And, to the extent that such dialectically deeper intentions condition and predetermine your more superficial intentions, devotion of deliberate attention to your more basic decision as to whether you will prefer to be a more intending being, and a more responsible being, or a less intending being, and a less responsible being, may well be a most important factor in determining actually how free or unfree you become as a responsible agent.

Since all of the foregoing discussion is far too complex to keep in mind all of the time, you will, for convenience, seek some simpler formula for your personal guidance. By contrast, the simple moral rules handed down to you by others, and against which you may have revolted as something imposed upon your personal freedom, may now be viewed as desirable instruments for freeing you from being required to make the weighty decision about what you ought to do in the face of a self and world multi-suffused with multi-complexities. All this is a matter that each must decide for himself. But we suggest recalling the general definition of freedom, one common to all of the other meanings we have discussed, as ability to do what you want to do. This is at once a seemingly quite simple and clear definition that also contains within it ambiguous "variables" ("ability" and "want" and "do) that may take any or all of the various kinds of factors discussed in the chapter as "values."

Your self is determined. Your self is free. Your self is determined in many ways and may enjoy many kinds and levels of freedom. The important issue is not whether or how much you are free or determined. Rather, it is how free you want to be. If you want to be more free than you can be, then you are unfree to be free in this way. If you want to be less free than you can be, then you are unfree to be unfree in this way. But if you want to be as free as you are, in any or all of the multifarious ways in which you are free, you are already free to be free in these ways. Thus, you have a large measure of freedom to decide how free you want to be.

Chapter XI

SELF AS SOVEREIGN

What is Sovereignty? Although we more often meet the term "sovereign" in connection with political affairs, and we can understand fully the meaning of "sovereignty" only through a study of the history of political theories and practices, the term has a basic relevance to the nature of self. No only must any sovereign, such as a king or president, be a person, but, insofar as societies are democratic, each person has some socially-recognized sovereignty. Sovereignty pertains to power of control. One who has sovereignty has power to control. Such control may be either or both power to control others and power to control oneself. An absolute sovereign presumably would have complete power over both himself and all others. However, in practice, sovereignty is naturally limited in many different ways. Sovereignty tends to be distributed among people, either among a few or among many. Furthermore, since there are different kinds of situations or functions over which control may be needed, there are different kinds of sovereignty. Again, presumably, an absolute sovereign would possess all such kinds of sovereignty. But, since no one person can know or do everything, even an absolute sovereign would have to delegate some of his powers to others, and thus in effect distribute some of his sovereignty.

In contemporary industrialized, urbanized and somewhat democratized societies, complex interdependencies require complex and multi-leveled division of labor, responsibility and authority. Not only do we distinguish between levels of control, such as that within a family, within a community, within a state, within a nation and at the world level, but also between kinds of control within levels, such as legislative, judicial and administrative, with various branches in each area. Within any complex organization, such as a university, for example, division of labor into teaching each of many subjects, building maintenance, record keeping, public relations, student affairs and dealings with trustees requires distribution of responsibility and authority. One cannot adequately exercise control without appropriate authority. Such authority is sovereignty. Increase in the number of specialists of various sorts, each with his own area of responsibility and power to decide and carry out specified duties entails increase in the numbers of kinds of authority, and sovereignty, needed in a society.

Discussion of the kinds and levels of sovereignty belongs properly in Chapter XXVI. Here we wish to indicate both the significance of sovereignty for self and of self for sovereignty. Each person who acts as a functionary in any group must be able to distinguish between his power to act as an officer for his group, therein exercising delegated group sovereignty, and his power to act as an individual, thereby exercising individual sovereignty. Although, in a sense, all sovereignty, or certainly all socially-recognized sovereignty, has a social source, since groups are composed of individuals, the sovereignty belonging to a group belongs to it by virtue of its being made up of individuals upon whom it continues to depend. So, in one sense, sovereignty is social in origin; but in another sense sovereignty is individual in origin. Furthermore, even individual sovereignty is social in origin, to the extent that an individual comes into being, is molded by, maintained by and controlled by his groups; but also social sovereignty, of all kinds, has an originating and enduring basis in the individuals who function as group members. Recognition of the interdependence of individuals and their groups, and of individual and group sovereignties, should not prevent us from directing our attention first to the nature of individual sovereignty as such. Not only do national constitutions provide guarantees for individual rights, but the rightness of national constitutions rests upon rights inherent in the nature of individually. What, then, is "individual sovereignty?"

Individual Sovereignty. "Sovereignty" means self-control. What self-control consists of depends upon what self is. Does an individual have power of self-control? If so, in what does such power consist? Having surveyed the "freedom-determinism controversy," we have a background of doubts and of positive proposals regarding the extent to which a self is caused or determined, hence controlled by antecedent and external factors. The natures of sovereignty and of freedom are interdependent, both socially and individually. Can an individual have sovereignty without freedom? Can a person have power of self-control without being free to decide upon and direct one's own actions? A full exploration of the nature of individual sovereignty would involve a review of the nature of agency, discussed in Chapter IX, and of the various kinds of freedom, discussed in Chapter X. Here we must be satisfied with exploring a few aspects of the problem.

The nature of self-control is not merely a metaphysical affair, presupposing the existence of a self, with some uniqueness as well as some history, with some power of self-causation as well as living in a world which causes it, with some permanence as well as some changeableness, but also an epistemological and axiological affair. Power of self-control is hardly genuine unless a self has some knowledge: some understanding of itself, its own nature, its future, its values, and both what is good for it and how to attain such good. Power of self-control is hardly genuine unless a self has some value, some future value which is at stake in action; for control, including self-control, is valueless, worthless, useless without some purpose, some end-in-view, some intrinsic value that can be attained or maintained. Hence, the issue of the nature of individual sovereignty is essentially also a moral issue. In order to be genuinely sovereign, an individual must be or have intrinsic good that is somehow at stake in his behavior in such a way that his own power of self-control to decide and act will make some difference in the future.

Sovereignty is good because some human goods are at stake. Individual sovereignty is good, but only because it enables the individual to increase or maintain intrinsic value or to decrease or prevent intrinsic evil. Thus, you need to know what your goods are before you are capable of exercising intelligent self-control. You may, of course, have the power to destroy yourself, to mislead yourself, to degrade yourself. Sovereignty, thus, may also be evil, but it is evil also because some human goods are at stake. Since, among individual evils, having too many desires, such that they compete with each other and produce frustration, as well as having too few desires, such that too many of one's potential intrinsic goods remain unactualized, both kinds subvert one's sovereignty. Both the existence and the exercise of individual sovereignty depends upon having goods, knowing that one has goods, and being willing to act in such a way as to attain and maintain them. Sovereignty involves a willingness to act, to accept oneself as an actor or agent, and as a chooser or decider of courses of action which have a bearing upon future value. Hence, sovereignty does not exist apart from goods, and sovereignty is itself a good, first an instrumental good in whatever sense it promotes or prevents obtaining and retaining intrinsic goods, but perhaps also an ingredient in the intrinsic goods of those who enjoy being free and self-controlled. One may also need to be, and enjoy being, controlled by others; but this is another question. Yet it is not entirely others, for, as social, a self may be able to obtain and retain some of its intrinsic goods only through the interdependence of sovereignties, i.e., through both controlling and being controlled by others insofar as cooperatively-realizable goods are at stake.

Chapter XII

SELF AS OWNER

Problems concerning the nature of ownership, private or public are properly regarded as primarily problems in social ethics. Yet, except for those views of ownership which regard all that is owned as being owned either by a state as opposed to individuals or to a God as opposed to man, ownership is regarded as something that, directly or indirectly, characterizes individuals. To the extent that ownership is individual, it is the individual self which owns. There is a sense in which individual ownership is a basic condition of all social ownership. And exploration of this sense is a proper part of individual ethics.

What is "Ownership"? What, basically, do we mean by "ownership?" Ownership pertains to whatever is one's own. If anything is one's own, then one owns it. You own whatever is yours or whatever belongs to your self. Since conceptions of ownership involve conceptions of self, different views of self yield different ideas of ownership. Here we can explore only three kinds of issues among the complexities of aspects of self serving as bases for different conceptions of self: a. Self as static vs. dynamic. b. Self as individual vs. social. c. Self as simple vs. complex.

a. Does a self exist only at moments or does it endure continuingly? If only momentarily, then ownership by a self can only be momentary. If enduringly, then may one not own enduringly? If you endure for a while and then cease, does not your ownership endure for a while and then cease? If you remain everlastingly, do you own everlastingly? Of course, if you are complex, enduring in some respects and ceasing in others, your ownership may be both enduring and ceasing in these different respects. Temporarily, one may own an apple or a theater ticket, and cease to own them after the apple is eaten or the performance is over. You may buy and sell some things, and thus acquire and lose some ownership. But are not also some things owned as long as one lives: your own body, for example, or your parents or your citizenship? May you own things even after you are dead? Some societies institutionalize rights of an individual to "will" one's fortune and effects to others, or protection of reputation from defamation after death. A deceased person's "estate," a social fiction functioning as a stubborn fact, may continue to be regarded as "his" or "her" or "his own" or "her own" even years after he or she is dead.

The foregoing suggestions, relating to whether a self is conceived to be static or dynamic, and in what ways, have bearing upon what one ought to do regarding ownership. If your self, and hence your ownership, is merely temporary, then your oughts regarding such ownership are merely temporary. If your self, and hence your ownership is enduring, even everlasting, then your oughts regarding such ownership may be enduring, even everlasting. If one's self is both static and dynamic, in various ways, then some of one's oughts pertain to enduring ownership, some to temporary ownership, and some also to problems regarding which of these two kinds of ownership is better. If enduring ownership of goods yields enduring enjoyment, then enduring ownership of such goods ought to be sought. Of course, if some goods, such as a pleasing smile or tasty tidbit, can be owned and enjoyed only momentarily, then one's oughts regarding owning them can be, and should be sought to be, only momentary. However, if, by recalling pleasant experiences, you can re-enjoy them, then if you have, or own, a good memory, you have, or own, all the goods thus kept in memory. A good memory may thus be among the best assets which one owns.

b. Does a self exist as a unique, isolated and self-controlled individual that only externally enters into association with others, as extreme individualism claims, or does it exist as a created, perpetually nurtured and sustained member totally dependent upon some higher being, whether State, Society or God, as totalitarianisms claim? Or does a self exist as interdependent, both partly unique and self-contained and partly dependent upon larger entities within which it shares much in common with other selves? Individualists conceive selves separatistically and thus consider ownership as exclusive. If a thing is yours, then it is not mine. Totalitarians see selves as submerged parts of a Totality, more owned than owners, but owners nevertheless. If God or the State or the Race is ours, then it is mine as much as it is yours. Organicists understand self as social, and thus see ownership as inclusive as well as exclusive. While some things are yours alone, others -- many others -- are ours. Joint ownership is ownership. People fluctuate regarding how much what they own is individual and how much what they own is owned through sharing ownership with others.

Furthermore, each person may be owned as well as owner. For example, a mother's child is her own child; hence the child is owned by the mother. But also the child's mother is its own mother, and hence the mother is owned by the child. Here, ownership is mutual. Again, when a person is a citizen of a nation, the nation is his nation, and thus he owns it; but also he is one of his nation's own citizens, and thus it owns him in a way in which it does not own the citizens of foreign nations. Again, such ownership is mutual. However, a merely cursory observation of the numbers and kinds of things and ways in which a person owns and is owned will reveal that, except for those relatively few things which he owns exclusively (such as clothes and shoes, body and ideas, name and reputation), most of them are owned by him only partly. Most ownership is complex and, perhaps unfortunately, the more complex our social and political interdependencies become, the more complex such ownership becomes; and, consequently, the more complex does a self become even merely as owner. If I own my body, my parents, my children, my other relatives, my community, my state and my nation, my car and my house, my college and my students, my profession and my colleagues in it, my corporation and its officers and clients, my church and its members, my club and its properties, etc., then not only do I thus partly own so many things but also I am partly owned in so many different ways. Furthermore, here also fluctuation occurs not only relative to the numbers and kinds of ownership but also to degrees of ownership; for when there are three members of my family who thus own the family home, then when there come to be five members, ownership is distributed among five rather than merely three. But, of course, in an intimate family, each in a sense owns the other and one may not be impoverished by such a smaller share in home ownership. However, as the dependent personalities of children grow into more interdependent and then to more independent conditions, preference for, and needs for, more independent and more exclusive ownership develop. Wise parents recognize growing needs in their children for becoming increasingly self-sufficient and thus, in a very fundamental sense, less owned. The perpetually repeated revolt of youth, somewhat analogous to the bitter repetitions of antagonisms attendant upon the struggle for independence by colonies, present plenty of evidence for cycles of development regarding how much a person is willing to be owned as well as is willing to own. The adolescent who revolts against being too much owned by his parental family often soon falls in love and pledges undying love in marriage, entailing both owning and being owned by not only his spouse but also his children.

Ownership of material things, such as machinery or buildings or land, serves only as a part of the ownership complex constituting self as owner.

c. Is self simple or complex or does a self somehow retain unity and simplicity throughout its growing, variable complexities? Is a self always a single simple whole, which owns and is owned simply and wholly? Or is a self always complex, such that its parts own and are owned somewhat independently of each other and of their whole? If we consider, for a moment, dualism, the relatively simple view that a self consists of two parts, soul and body, then we may ask: Does the body have (own) a soul? Does the soul own its body? Does the body own some parts (fingers, blood, urine) that the soul does not own; does the soul own some characteristics (eternality, simplicity, ideas) that its body does not own? Or, if a body has (owns) a soul of its own, does it also own the soul's parts (e.g., ideas), etc.? The point is that, if a self exists as both whole and parts, then it may enjoy, or at least experience, with or without joy, two or more kinds of ownership, that which it owns as belonging to its parts and that which it owns as belonging to its whole. For example, if your hand is your own and your status as a spouse is your own, you own both; but also if your life (i.e., as a "whole") is your own, do you not now also own your life? You may lose your hand or your spouse without losing your life; and you may lose your life without your body losing its hand or without losing your spouse who continues to own your name, property and children in memory of you.

Although, in light of the amazing complexities that appear as we further study a few of the aspects of ownership, we might wish that ownership were actually as simple as individualists and totalitarians (e.g., anarchists and communists) depict it, if ownership is really multi-complex, we can hardly feel that we have faced up to reality unless we try to understand the complexities of ourselves as owners as we actually are. How a self can retain wholeness, and continuing ownership of such wholeness, through its increasing multiplicity of parts becomes even more amazing as we explore the many levels of self as social. Whereas I own my clothes personally, I own my home and car through my family group, my water supply and sewage disposal system through my city group, my highways and colleges through my state group, my postal system through my national group. Individualists fight multiplication of levels of groups because each new level of group ownership subtracts from what each individual can own exclusively. Totalitarians reluctantly participate in multiplied levels because each level of ownership detracts from the completeness of ownership by the whole. Organicists welcome new levels of ownership when and if they increase the amount of ownership by individuals. But as both capacities for ownership vary, so some ought to seek more levels of ownership (including ownership of and by a world federal state) whereas others, or other persons at other times, ought to withdraw their interests in owning more than they can actually integrate into the wholeness of their personalities. Some (women more usually) rightly retain integrity through devoting more attention to problems of ownership of and by their families; some (men more often) rightly retain integrity by devoting most of their efforts and energies to problems of ownership within or through their business profession. But focal emphasis of most of one's active functioning as owner in some areas or levels of life should not eliminate persisting latent interest in all other levels of self as owner which actually are one's own.

Importance of Ownership. Although "ownership" pertains to anything that is one's own, you are concerned about ownership only because it is of value to you. Whatever is good, or well, weal or wealth, is or has value. Ownership of material wealth, i.e., of things that serve as instrumental goods, is important because it serves one's ends or intrinsic goods. Ownership of health, reputation, attitudes and memories also serve as instrumental goods. But likewise, to the extent that you enjoy not only each of these things or traits, your intrinsic good is enhanced. Of course, if you suffer from ownership, of things or traits, then they constitute instrumental evils and you, while suffering, experience more intrinsic evil.

Those who consider ownership as pertaining to things external to self and its intrinsic value tend to regard such wealth as instrumental merely. But those who consider ownership as being inherent in the nature of self, i.e., that ownership is an integral part of a self, regard such ownership as part of the being which, when enjoyed, is itself enjoyed as intrinsic good. If the latter view is correct, then you become richer not only instrumentally but also intrinsically when you participate in more levels of ownership. Insofar as "a thing is what a thing does," a self is an owner of, and through, in all of many ways and levels. To the extent that your enjoyment extends to all of these ways of owning, the richer your own intrinsic value becomes, in addition to the ways in which these different ways instrumentally contribute to the other intrinsic values you enjoy through satisfaction of your interests in family life, community life, national citizenship, professional security, etc. Ownership is important, then, both because the instruments owned serve as instrumental goods and because enjoyment of owning is an additional intrinsic good in itself.

Furthermore, you may enjoy being owned. Normally, people desire to "belong." People join groups, whether churches, lodges, professional societies, urban, state and national citizenship groups, recreational groups, or by marriage into a family group. Those who enjoy being owned, desire to be owned in whatever way will bring to them the most enjoyment: a man marries a woman whom he thinks will continue to love him (i.e., own him as a lover); you, when you have a choice, seek to belong to more popular, more powerful or more high-rating groups, for you thereby feel that you will enjoy such membership, or being owned as a member of such a group, more. Being disowned is experienced often as a form of being despised. Ostracism and exile traditionally have been regarded as among the severest forms of punishment. Of course, people who dislike being owned, because they believe that to whatever extent others own them they do not own themselves, prefer freedom from being owned, including freedom from being owned at all levels of ownership. Complete anarchy (meaning freedom from ownership as well as from control) is an ideal of such persons. But, to the extent that people find themselves actually intricately interdependent, they may enjoy experiencing themselves not merely as owners but also as being owned in many kinds of levels of ways.

Part of the importance of ownership consists in its being foundational to "rights" and "justice," topics to be considered in the next chapter. "Rights," as we shall see, pertain to ownership rights. If you cannot own, then you have no ownership rights. If you have many kinds and levels of ownership, then you may have many rights, some relative to each of the kinds and levels. Justice, whether "distributive," i.e., pertaining to distribution of wealth through wages, inheritance or taxes, or "retributive," e.g., repayment for damage, presupposes that a self is an owner; and the numbers of kinds of justice which one can rightly participate in depend upon the numbers of kinds of ownership one has or can have.

If ownership is thus related to your intrinsic goods, through enjoyment of owning and of being owned, through possessing a wealth of instrumental goods that lead naturally to intrinsic goods, then ownership, and more kinds and levels of ownership, is part of what you most want and constitutes an aspect of your greatest oughts. There is no more fundamental question in ethics, and in life, than ownership. Ethics is concerned with what is good and how to get it, but "how to get it" includes as part of its meaning "how to own it." To the extent that life is dynamic and one's needs, opportunities and capacities for enjoyment change, what is best for a self in the way of ownership changes from time to time. Some ought to seek to own more; some ought to seek to own less. Ownership has its negative side, which we have not explored here: disengagement from owning instrumental evils, whether guns, bad habits, ill health, antagonistic attitudes or debts, and choosing to terminate some kinds of ownership may be among one's most important oughts.

Chapter XIII

SELF AS JUST

Do you have any rights? Would you like to escape all duties? Why be just? Do you expect justice? Do you deserve anything? The present chapter, which perhaps should be divided into two or even four chapters, deals with four intimately interrelated concepts: rights and duties, and justice and grace. A thorough exploration of any one of them would lead us into all of the problems of ethics; hence each is a central, crucial and categoreal ethical concept.

Rights. What are "rights?" Distinction needs to be made between those rights which have been assigned to you as a person by your groups and those which you have prior to such assignment. How does a group obtain the rights which it assigns to individuals, and from where does it obtain its right to assign such rights? Surely group rights derive, at least in some fundamental part, from rights which individuals have prior to, or as foundational to, such groups. We postpone until Chapter XXVIII discussion of both rights that groups have as groups and rights that individuals have as a result of group memberships. Here we shall explore the more basic question: how do rights originate in persons as individuals? What, then, are such rights and how do they originate?

Are rights something inherent in life or are they acquired? Surely you have no rights until you exist? Did you have a right to come into existence before you existed, or before there was a "you"? If existence is not a right prior to existence, is existence a right after one comes into existence? Do you have a right to live after you are alive? If not, how can you acquire any lesser rights, such as a right to own property or to protect yourself? If so, how did you acquire this right? If you do acquire your rights do you acquire them all at once or gradually? Do you evolve or attain rights in the same way and at the same time that you acquire your life? Are you fully alive at conception or do you acquire your life gradually, first through foetal development dependently within your mother's womb and then through birth and separation from your mother? (Roman Catholics apparently regard an individual fully existent at conception and as having rights such that its mother's use of birth control methods which destroy a fertilized ovum is considered as murder. Others regard a person's nature as evolving gradually both within and beyond the womb; bodily movements and incipient consciousness are late developments within the womb, and despite its yelling, a newborn babe has little real capacity, intelligence or selfhood, and hence very little in the way of rights. It must be nurtured and protected, cared for and trained, during months and even years before it acquires a sense of dignity and worth, responsibility and "moral accountability." Since we acquire abilities gradually, we acquire the rights pertinent to those abilities gradually. A child of two may have a right to be fed, but surely he has no right to employment or to hold responsible public office. Different views of the nature of life, i.e., whether it is fully existent at conception or develops gradually through several years, have a bearing upon whether a person acquires rights all at once or only gradually.) Are all of our rights "given" to us, i.e., acquired without any intentional effort on our part, or must we "earn" some (or all)?

While you are pondering your own views on these questions, I wish to propose an answer. Rights involve values. If there were no values there could be no rights. These values, ultimately, are intrinsic goods. If there were no intrinsic goods, there would be no rights. Rights are intimately and ultimately related to intrinsic goods. Different conceptions of the origin and nature of intrinsic values have varying implications for views of the origin and nature of rights. But regardless of differing details about the origin and nature of intrinsic value, we may generalize that intrinsic value is its own "excuse for being." Intrinsic goods are ends-in-themselves. They are the "final" goods or ultimate loci of good. Hence, it is the coming into being of intrinsic good, and of a person as an intrinsic good, that is the basis for rights. Insofar as you are an intrinsic good, you are your own end-in-itself and your own justification, or self-justification, for being and for having the rights inherent in and stemming from such intrinsic good.

If you somehow come into being all at once, and your intrinsic good emerges all at once, then your rights may also be acquired all at once. Of course, if you are eternal, an eternal being with eternal values, must you not also have eternal rights? But if you come into being gradually, your intrinsic good, and consequently your rights, come into being gradually. We observe this growth after birth. Genetic psychology, child psychology, adolescent psychology, psychology of learning, all testify to stages of growth in capacities for, and achievements of, awareness, appreciation and enjoyment of different levels of perception, conception, ownership, responsibility and active roles in social groups. We have already referred, in previous chapters, to many levels of personality and the many levels of intrinsic good that result from them. The gradualist theory implies that a minute kind or level of life has only relatively minute intrinsic good and hence only minute rights, though real and conditional potentialities complicate the picture. It implies also that a magnificent personality, accomplished, multi-faceted and multi-leveled, appreciating and being responsible for many varieties of complex interdependencies -- such as a national president, a brilliant scientist, a productive literary genius, or a profoundly wise philosopher -- may have relatively more rights than ordinary people. Danger lurks in a gradualist theory due to ease of misunderstanding by hasty generalizers. But you can, if you desire to do so, draw out some implications of a previously-stated principle: insofar as persons are alike, we have a basis for generalization: what is right for one is right for all, and, likewise, what are rights for one are rights for all. To the extent that those who are different have abilities to become alike in intrinsic good, they may have rights relative to such abilities; but also the many ways in which persons who are alike have abilities to become different or unique in intrinsic value, they may have differential rights relative to these abilities.

Of course, if rights are acquired, they may be lost, either partially, through diminution, or completely, through destruction. A person may lose ownership of a house which burns down, a parent or child who dies, a job through business failure, as well as a limb which is amputated or one's vitality which is sapped through illness or old age. Do you have any rights after death? If, after death, there is no "you," how can a "no you" have rights? Here again, different views on the nature of a self, whether as an eternal soul or an evanescent consciousness, have different implications. You may have devoted friends in whose memory your being and imputed goodness persists, and thus have imputed rights, such as wishes carried out or memorials kept in perpetuity. And you may live in a society that legally assigns rights to carrying out of "wills" and against defamation. If abilities, and consequent intrinsic good enjoyments of those abilities, decline gradually, one's relevant rights may diminish likewise. An aged person who must spend half of each day in bed no longer has a right to full-time out-of-doors employment, and societies rightly recognize needs for compulsory retirement plans.

My proposed answer implies that you have certain human rights due you by your very existence as a possessor of intrinsic good. If you then want to know what these rights are, I must first give a general reply, namely, that, other things being equal, each intrinsic good is its own basis for its own kind of right. If the good is a momentary pleasure, then your right to enjoy it may last for only a moment. Of course, if you have some enduring capacity for enjoying repeated pleasures, rights relative to this capacity are inherent in it. If you are an enduring good, enjoying life, for a life-time or for eternity, you thereby have a basis for enduring rights. But, just as intrinsic goods, and the capacities for enjoying them temporarily or enduringly, do not normally exist in isolation, so your rights exist in conjunction with, interdependent with, and at times in severe conflict with, each other. To the extent that this is so, you have conflicting rights, such that attainment or maintenance of one involves failure to attain, or destruction of, others. Hence, if you have more rights than you can realize, do you not actually have a right to all your rights. That is, to the extent that your values, value-potentials, and, consequently, your rights conflict with each other, each tends to diminish the ideal fullness of the others. Even when temporarily isolated from others, a person who can enjoy playing a piano and enjoy playing a trombone does not have a right to enjoy playing both at the same time; just as there are limits to your capacities for enjoying intrinsic goods, so there are limits to your actual rights, quite apart from socially-enacted legislation about rights. So, my proposed answer implies that you lack certain rights due to your very lack of existence or the lack of existence of any particular kind of intrinsic good or capacity for having that good.

We have not yet discussed the question of whether a person has any "earned" rights as distinguished from those acquired by virtue of one's existence and intrinsic good. Here, our answer must be "Yes," though recognition of earned rights should not prejudice us against belief in the existence of unearned rights, just as recognition of the existence of unearned rights should not be an excuse for ignoring or denying the existence of earned rights and the need for earning such rights. If you cannot experience some intrinsic good, such as enjoying a warm fire or a delightful opera, without performing the instrumental tasks needed for chopping wood or for buying the ticket, then you may have no right to such enjoyment. Whatever goods cannot be achieved without your own effort do not belong to you as a right without such effort. In fact, you may or may not have a right to earn other rights, whether socially recognized (as when one has a right to attend school to earn credits to earn a degree to earn a job to earn advancement) or not.

Having rights constitutes a part of what a self is, and the kinds, amounts and levels of such rights determine the kind, size and complexity of a self as a right-possessing being. Thus, your concern about the nature and value of yourself may automatically generate interest in your rights as yours. Concern for protecting your rights or for earning other rights may be among your most important oughts. You are rightly concerned about your rights.

Duties. What is duty? Duty consists in what is due or owed. Your duty consists in what you own. Owing involves obligation. What is owed is always, basically, some value. Although we sometimes speak of what we owe as a "debt" which we ought to "pay," the "payment" referred to is moral, not merely monetary, and pertains to values of all kinds when we are defining "duty" generally. In this broad sense, "doing one's duty" and "paying one's debts" have equal significance. Why this is so will be clear only if we recognize that we have two, or four, kinds of general duties.

First, we need to distinguish duties to self from those to others. Too often we think only of duties to others. Duty involves value, and ultimately some intrinsic good -- one's own intrinsic value, of course. Your intrinsic goods, their creation, maintenance and increase, constitute the ultimate basis of your duty. Since you are essentially social, you have duties to yourself to be and do whatever is needed to assure the creation, maintenance and increase of your intrinsic goods in and through your social extensions. Consequently, you have duties to yourself as social. If you lack an adequate conception of yourself, you will fail to comprehend why you have, and should do, your duties.

One of your first duties is to try to discover more about your own self and in what ways it is social. We keep in mind here the distinction between those aspects of self as social which grow naturally out of its capacities and opportunities and those which have been institutionally assigned to it by established groups. Your own duties as a socially interdependent being do not always correspond exactly with those conceived and enforced by your group's officers; hence the issue of how to promote such correspondence remains a continuing problem of social ethics, as we shall see in Part II. But you have duties, not so much because they have been assigned to you by others, but mainly because they grow out of your own intrinsic goods and your natural interests in preserving and magnifying them. To the extent that you can do this only through group organizations functioning by means of established standards and authorized officials, you have a fundamental interest in conforming to these standards and accepting the official requirements as the best means to your own ends. So, although we may distinguish two kinds of duties, those to self and those to others, duties to self are foundational to duties to others, even though, in popular practice, too many become aware only of demands made by others as "duties."

Secondly, we need to distinguish duty to enjoy from duty to repay. The second of these two depends on the first, even though too often we become aware only of the second as duty. Since intrinsic good is its own excuse for being, its own end-in-itself, its own justification, it is that which you ought to seek to enjoy. It is the ultimate source (not the cause, but the goal) of obligation and, consequently, of duty. When intrinsic good goes unappreciated, such good has been wasted. The self-evident worthwhileness of enjoyment of intrinsic good automatically generates a feeling of obligation to enjoy it, and to maintain and, if possible, to prolong or increase enjoyment of it, whenever distractions by need for attending to other values do not interfere. This feeling of obligation constitutes our basic duty. It is the basis of all other duties. Your first duty is to realize your intrinsic goods, to exploit your opportunities and capacities for enjoyment and appreciation of this life, both in general and in all of its richness of detail.

However, since your existence and intrinsic goods may be temporary and since your opportunities and capacities for enjoying them are in fact limited by circumstances demanding your attention to means and to choices among ends and means, you are faced also with duties to repay. Different parts of a self interdepend and compete, so exploitation of opportunity for enjoying one kind of good may retard, diminish or destroy opportunity for enjoying other kinds. For example, you can hardly watch a theater performance and play basketball at the same time. Furthermore, when you devote all of your energies to theater-watching and none to basketball, you may unbalance yourself. If so, then when you have attended the theater too often, you may owe it to yourself, i.e., you may have a duty, to play basketball more often. The concept of a "well-rounded life" involves the idea that life normally contains many kinds of value-exploitation opportunities within it, and when you exploit some of them too much and others too little you owe it to yourself to "repay," i.e., to exploit the others as much as they deserve. Likewise, of course, to the extent that ends depend upon means, when you have attended so much to enjoying ends that you have neglected attention to supplying what is needed for prolonging or restoring such enjoyment, you thereby develop a duty to yourself to pay more attention to these means.

We should notice that the two foregoing distinctions cut across each other. That is, you may have duties both to yourself and to others regarding enjoying and enabling others to enjoy, and duties both to yourself and others to restore imbalances of the kinds just noted. Or, you may find that your duty to enjoy intrinsic goods is one that you sometimes need to share with others, as well as something private, and that your duty to restore balance among competing goods ought also to be shared.

Furthermore, since people exist interdependently, their needs for repayment take reciprocal forms. That is, to the extent that people interdepend, they owe it to each other to assist each other in promoting shared enjoyment and in allowing private enjoyments in some proportion. It is here that the issue of the demandingness of duties becomes annoying, frustrating and antagonizing.

To repeat, not only do you have a duty to yourself to create, maintain and consume intrinsic goods but, to the extent that you interdepend with others, you also have similar duties to others. And not only do you have a duty to repay to any one of your many kinds of goods for neglect of it, but also, to the extent that your own goods interdepend with those of others, you have a duty to permit, and to encourage, others to repay themselves. Included in the foregoing are duties which people owe each other. Not only ought a student who has gone to a movie on Wednesday night repay himself by studying on Saturday night, but also if he has asked a roommate to keep quiet so he can study for an examination, he ought to repay by remaining quiet when his roommate needs to study. It is in this latter area where we find that one person's rights constitute the basis for another person's duties. Reciprocal relatedness of rights and duties has its basis in intrinsic goods. Consequently both differences and similarities in the intrinsic goods of different persons have bearings upon the reciprocality of their duties. Yet also, both similarities and differences in the ways in which people have been, are, or are expected to be, useful to each other affect their duties to each other. Verbal or legal promises constitute a part of the picture, but these must appear to be founded upon genuine mutuality of interests if they are to be judged warranted.

Focusing attention specifically upon the duties which persons have to each other, we should observe why one person's rights become another person's duties. If you have a right to a share of anything, such as a meal, a room, and income, a professor's time, or control of public policy, this right is actually yours only if you actually share in it. But if another takes your share, consumes your portion of a meal, for example, you cannot have your share. Do you have a right to what cannot be? What happens to your rights when others do not do their duties? What happens to your right to share a meal when another eats it? It disappears, unless, somehow, the person who has been negligent in one's duty to leave your portion for you is willing and able to repay with some substitute value; where such willingness or ability is absent (e.g., when a dog eats your meal), your right disappears. If this is so, then rights, or at least some rights, depend for their existence and attainability upon

whether or not others do their duties. Conversely, the rights of others
who interdepend with you can be actualized only if you remain able and
willing to do your duty to them. Where resources abound, such as fresh
air out-of-doors, you can actualize your rights without depending upon
others. But where resources are limited in ways such that if one person
overconsumes, others must suffer shortages, then the actuality of your
rights to a share depends upon others recognizing and dutifully respecting
such share.

As a self, not only do you have rights, thereby being a kind of being
that has such rights, but also you have duties, and you are, by the nature
of your social interdependence, a kind of being that has such duties.
Rights and duties vary, sometimes momentarily, such as those regarding
occupying space on a crowded sidewalk or in heavy traffic, sometimes
over a lifetime, such as those pertaining to health, citizenship or marriage,
and sometimes contingently, as when opportunity (with its rights and
duties) to become president of the United States depends upon earlier
establishment of motivation and tendency through success or failure in
local student elections.   Your duty to yourself includes, surely,
understanding the nature of duty, of yourself as by nature dutiful, and of
what happens to yourself when either you or others fail to do their duties.
"And now we may perhaps also be able to understand more clearly why
the formulating of one's philosophy is one's first moral duty." (Richard
Rothschild, Paradox: The Destiny of Modern Thought, p. 103.)

Justice. Minimal exploration of ideas of justice requires distinguishing
between two kinds of justice, "distributive" and "retributive," and
clarification of two concepts, "equality" and "deservingness." Justice has
to do with values, or good and evils. So "distributive justice" names those
problems that occur when goods or evils are divided among people. For
example, when a person dies and his estate is divided among heirs, or
when an unsteady hand cuts a cake at a children's party, questions of
equality and deservingness regarding how portions shall be allotted
constitute issues of fairness or justice. These exemplify distribution of
"goods." Distribution of "evils" is illustrated by division of chores, such as
who among children shall wash the dishes, who will sweep the floor and
who will empty the trash, or by systems of taxation, involving variations
in property evaluation, location of differentials in income tax rates, and
which products, sales or imports shall be taxed and how much. Likewise,
"retributive justice" names issues involved in returning goods and evils that
have been given or received. One should be paid a fair wage. One

should pay one's debts. One should repair damage that one has caused. "Retributive justice" requires reciprocation of goods or evils. Both distributive and retributive justice are plagued with problems regarding "fairness," including how to assure equality among unequals, and "deservingness," especially in the face of doubts as to whether anyone deserves anything at all.

1. Distributive justice relates to each self in two ways, i.e., as receiver and as giver. a. Does a self get its "fair share" of whatever is coming to it? Does it obtain its proper portion of benefits being bestowed? Such justice, or injustice, has two further aspects: justice means receiving "all" of one's full share; to the extent that you do not receive your full share, you receive unjustly. But does it not also mean receiving no more than one's proper portion? That is, whenever you have received more than your share, have you not also received unjustly? And, whenever you willingly receive more than your share have you become unjust -- an unjust receiver? Furthermore, does your willingness to receive unjustly, i.e., more than your distributive share, retributively justify your deserving to receive unjustly, i.e., less than your distributive share? b. Does a self give justly? Does it distribute its gifts justly? Again, two aspects appear. When giving, do you see to it that each of those to whom you give obtains his full share? If you neglect to see that justice is done to others even in your giving, are you not to this extent unjust? But also, when giving, do you assure yourself that each of those to whom you give receives no more than his full share? If as a giver you distribute in such a way as to allow some to receive more than their share, are you not, as a giver, unjust in this sense, even though you may in fact be a generous giver in giving much more than you have received? Does your willingness to permit some of your recipients to receive unjustly justify retributive deservingness to receive unjustly?

Already it should be clear that "justice" is a many-sided characteristic. But we would be unjust in our treatment of this topic if we failed to indicate how much more complicated even distributive justice becomes through recognizing "levels" of gifts. A person naturally experiences many levels of receiving and giving. Biologically, you receive genes from your parents and give genes to your children. Physiologically, you receive food and air and in return excrete and exhale. Psychologically, you receive sensory stimuli, admiration and ideas, and you stimulate, despise and propound. Socially, you receive associates, companions, enemies, and you associate, accompany and endanger. Culturally, you receive language and institutions, and you speak to others, passing on or modifying mores through your own ways of behaving toward others. In more detail one gives and receives, justly and unjustly, through casual, family, community, state and national groups, for example. Justice, even distributive justice, is a complex, universal, multifaceted, multi-leveled condition of selfhood. Those issues regarding social justice to be considered later in Chapter XXVIII are only samples of particular kinds of justice. Their overwhelming importance to those immersed in them may make them appear to be the only kinds. But the problem, "Is a self just?" remains inadequately comprehended until one becomes aware of how omnipresent and multi-aspected justice is. Lest one become dismayed at the prospect of even knowing how to be just, we mention, before proceeding to further complications, that an attitude of genuine ever-willingness to be just may resolve most of your psychological difficulties about being just.

Distributive justice involves equality. Yet, people are unequal not merely in a few but really in very many ways. Age, size, health, wealth, experience, memory, incentives, understanding, tastes, environment, etc., make us different, hence unequal, in multitudes of varieties of ways. How is equality, hence justice, possible? Although it is easy to generalize that insofar as people are alike they can and should be treated equally, what generalization is implied regarding how to treat people when they are unlike? Basically, justice requires that we treat people alike insofar as they are alike and differently insofar as they are different. When a cake is cut at a party, should older children receive bigger slices? Or shall cake-cutting distributive justice require treating all alike despite some obvious differences? Shall each person be justly entitled to only one vote, or do the wiser deserve greater influence in deciding social policy? Problems of inequality are complicated not only by differences in capacities of individuals but also by differences in opportunity. Sometimes people with weak qualifications are sought when many job vacancies exist; but other people with strong qualifications are shut out when jobs are scarce. Our "founding fathers," no matter what their qualifications, had opportunity to vote on the Constitution itself, but we seldom have opportunity to vote even on a minor amendment. Shall Johnny, who deserved to "lick out the pan" because he helped prepare the cake, still deserve his fair share of the cake even after his stomach is already stuffed? Does one's receiving one kind of share affect what constitutes justice relative to other kinds of shares? How can justice ever be equal when the value of presumably fixed units of any good, ten dollars, for example, varies even with the same person at different times, for when one is young and poor, ten dollars seems a huge sum, whereas after one has achieved financial success, this same amount may appear as a trivial tip. The problem of how to deal justly with others when faced with multitudes of inequalities plagues us perpetually in making ethical decisions. Again, constant anxiety about exactness in justice will cause us endless misery, especially as we more fully comprehend the varieties of inequality among unequals; but an ever ready willingness to accept the just consequences of our own injustices makes possible a pervasive sense of calm and confidence that justice will prevail -- not a picayunish justice computer-calculated to minutest details, but a broad and sufficiently abundant justice in which our undeserved gift of life is viewed as so great that we can only feel ashamed when we quarrel about tidbits. Whoever feels the world unjust to him should recall the poet's wisdom: "I was without shoes, and I murmured; until I met a man without feet."

2. Retributive justice also has two aspects: how one repays others for what one receives and how one expects to be repaid by others for what one gives. Some people seem much more concerned with one rather than the other of these two aspects, or kinds, of justice; is not this unequal concern itself a kind of injustice? May such injustice justly beget reversed injustice?

a. When you seek to pay your debts, i.e., to repay others for what they have given you, you face certain problems. First, the issue of whether equality is possible recurs. Even where debts are contracted in terms of seemingly fixed units, such as a thousand-dollar loan on a house, inflation and deflation of both the value of dollars and of the house make exact justice impossible. Work and wages can never be precisely correlated. Shall wages be calculated on bases of time spent or of effort put forth, or whether the work is primarily that of "brain or brawn," of effort to accomplish or actual accomplishment? Where exact equality of repayment is impossible, how just should you try to be?

Secondly, people differ in their deservingness, not merely regarding distributive but also regarding retributive justice. Sometimes college administrators believe that justice requires paying a teacher with several dependents more than a single person even for the same work. If issues regarding distributive justice interfere with attempts at retributive justice, how can one know how to be just? Issues regarding retributive justice also sometimes interfere with distributive justice, as when dividing the party cake one judges that Johnny was rude so deserves the smallest piece. It may be that people who already have more of wealth or wisdom do not have the same rights to repayment or retaliation as those who have less. We judge that, although little Tim hit big Joe, Joe should not have struck back because he is older and should know better.

A third problem, more serious than the first two, but following from them, is "Why should I try to be just?" Some say: "If exact justice is impossible, no justice is possible, so why try to be just?" Of course, where you are forced to repay, whether equally or even more than you have been given, you will have to do it. But where you are not forced to repay, why do so? Here one's beliefs about the values of acting justly will depend upon the extent to which you have faith that the principle of reciprocity operates with general reliability. For those who accept schemes with cosmic guarantees, such as the Indian belief in the inexorableness of Karma, the Jewish-Christian-Islamic doctrine of the perfect justice of God, or the Confucian faith that appropriate reciprocity is nature's best way, may be motivated to act. But too many persons, especially these days, who have abandoned faith in traditional schemes, must have newer and more current reasons for believing that they ought to want to be just when they are not forced to be just. Examples of the impossibility of exact justice, of the kinds pointed out above, are obvious to everyone.   Young children early learn about such examples. Furthermore, the more complex our life and society become, the greater the numbers and kinds of inexactitude that normally occur. By remaining alert to opportunities where such inexactness occurs, you may find increasing numbers of ways for getting without giving. Why should not a person become smart? If there are ways of "beating the game," why not make use of them? This view not only is widespread but is publicly recognized and even encouraged: give-away stunts, from television quiz shows to trading stamps, from gambling casinos, race track betting and lotteries, to winning a free prize merely by registering. Yet, if you assent to the rightness of receiving something for nothing, by registering your name for a free lottery, do you thereby assent to the rightness of injustice, and thereby forfeit your own right to demand justice, at least relative to the circumstances surrounding the lottery? Some are "willing to take their chances."

What reply should be given to those who earnestly ask: "If I can beat the game and get away with it, why shouldn't I?" This question, more technically formulated, is: "If I can be unjust and still receive justice, why should I bother to be just?" We need not repeat the threats of those who promise eternal damnation; people who heed these threats do not earnestly ask our question. Our answer is designed for, and can be expected to appeal only to, persons recognizing the nature of self as involving many levels of intrinsic goods inherent in complex, dynamic, megalopolitan interdependencies. It is summarized in the following three arguments.

(1) First, both intuitively and from ordinary experience, you can realize that one who "beats the game" becomes "fair game" for beating. Where the issue is simple, as when one secretly steals from a transient whom he will never meet again, we can only appeal to his conscience; but our earnest questioner may still be developing his conscience. However, where the issue becomes complex, the stakes become higher, so much higher that, when a person understands what he is doing in terms of multiplicities of his values, he will recognize how foolish he is to jeopardize greater values for the sake of a lesser good. We illustrate the issue by a single example. But adequate comprehension of the varieties and extent of actual complexities can come only through a study of the various social, economic, political and psychological sciences -- a task essential in elementary, secondary and college educational programs -- the pursuit of which now largely replaces earlier "religious" instruction as the locus for shaping value comprehension and value conviction. When these studies fail to provide adequate insight into a person's genuine values, bases for appeal to individual prudence regarding his own best interests are missing.

Consider a college student, displeasing his parents because pursuing a course of study opposing their ideals, financially distressed because forced to pay extra costs beyond his control, persistently annoyed by his needy roommate to whom he cannot repay a long-standing small loan, faced with failure in a course, in his college career and in awaiting employment because he lacks time to prepare a required paper, out of a job because he questioned his employer's unethical business practices and about to be deserted by his fiancee because he cannot compete with a more affluent competitor. A discarded paper of the kind needed falls into his hands. A miraculous solution to a perilous set of problems unjustly pushed upon him! Retyped with suitable modifications, the paper, its quality already certified by an instructor's grade, should bring desired results. Who will know the difference? The paper is due tomorrow. There is just time enough to recopy. The values at stake, i.e., copying portions of a discarded paper versus success in college, career and marriage, seem clear. One acts rightly when one intends to produce the best results, involving sacrificing lesser values when such is necessary to the attainment of greater values. If, somehow, the issue could end here, as is often the case in fiction and in dreams, ethics would be simple, and rightness of behavior, even if not reducible to ten commandments, would still be relatively easy to manage.

However, despite the immensity of the values at stake, one is short-sighted if he fails to be aware of the presence and importance of other values which are being risked. These may be discussed relative to two possibilities, his being caught and his not being caught.

His chances of being caught must enter his calculations. Some instructors are noted as "easy marks"; here the risk seems less. Yet an instructor too has values at stake in guaranteeing his college and his students an honest amount of genuine achievement in his students; if he fails, he endangers his career, marriage, and public self-respect. He too must have worked out techniques of both providing freedom of action by his students and assuring himself that the work is genuine. For example, merely by adding or subtracting a book from a bibliography or changing the wording of a standard question, an instructor can often detect the vintage of papers submitted to him; and an experienced instructor knows that he is a fool if he does not set such traps for cheaters.

His (i.e., the student's) rating with intimate friends, such as roommate and fiancee with whom he has shared his vexations, is at stake, for they will want to know how his miraculous recovery occurred. When his intimates discover that he is willing to sacrifice his ordinary principles of honesty when he faces a crisis, they then come to realize that his honesty with them may be superficial also. If he does not lose his friends entirely, he experiences diminished trust. A person who finds himself distrusted either accepts such distrust as justified, in which case he has less respect for himself, or rejects it, in which case he mistakenly feels that the world is treating him unjustly, thus mentally preparing himself to justly treat the world unjustly, and develops further self-pity, a spirit conductive to constant griping which both cripples his confidence and makes him a nuisance to others. Loss of trust by one's intimate friends is one of the greatest tragedies that can happen to a person. The values at stake here are inestimable.

His future, academic and professional, is jeopardized. For discovery may result in expulsion from college. This even blacklists him forever, since colleges now uniformly require record transcripts from all previous educational institutions, and experienced employers demand a full account of all years and months spent during each earlier period of employment and education, together with the names of employers and educational institutions. Most of us are familiar with the expensive, painstaking, thorough investigations needed to screen applicants for U.S. "classified" positions. We are less familiar with the fact that most large corporations find it necessary to invest heavily in effective personnel practices, employing experts whose function it is to provide assurance that its employees are not merely competent but also reliable. A cheater who gets caught faces greatly-reduced employment opportunities and, should he nevertheless be hired, a position of limited responsibility with prospects for continued surveillance. In a simpler society, a person may fail in one community and yet succeed in reestablishing himself in another. But in complexly interdependent megalopolitan living, the cost of failure by unreliable personnel is too great to permit people of dubious honesty to become established in positions of responsibility. A person who expects to live, and to advance, in our kind of society now misunderstands himself and his value if he fails to comprehend the necessity for establishing an unblemished record for reliability.

His self-respect, which should be among his most important values, is threatened by every temptation to be unjust. Self-respect involves many ingredients. We mention three kinds. First, even in one's utmost privacy, sheltered from most intimate companions, a cheater finds that he has to face up to himself as deficient, whether in dreams in fear-infected day-dreams or in attempts at honest self-evaluation. A person who knows himself to be a cheater cannot respect himself as much as one who knows himself to be honest. One may try, even with some success, to hide such a shortcoming from others; but his own subconscious processes will not allow him to remain forever unrealistic about his condition. Those who manage somehow to dull their consciences thereby also induce diminished conscientiousness generally in ways which take their toll through shortcomings in other occasions.

Secondly, even the most jovial and carefree cavorting with one's intimate companions may become subtly pervaded by distrust after they have discovered, or even merely suspected, one of cheating. Snide humor about one's reliability cuts deep into one's self-respect, sometimes deeper than intended, for, as one recalls the supposedly-hidden reality, his fear of discovery and disesteem unconsciously draws the cutting edge further inward on his wave of emotion. One cannot respect himself as much when his most intimate friends, those whom he most trusts to esteem him for his true worth, despise him, or even merely seem to when his own gnawing uncertainties magnify his fears into horrendous clouds of self-contempt.

Thirdly, even in one's most assured, front-polished public associations, psychological slips subtly suffuse one's attitude and language, revealing in minute degrees, awareness of lack of utter reliability. If a man cannot trust himself, he cannot expect others to trust him. And the very uncertainty infecting his own attitude regarding his reliability conveys itself unwittingly to others. If, as a result, one's actual social, economic and professional position is reduced, his self-respect as measured in terms of standards for these also suffers. Thus, in innumerable ways a person's whole outlook on life and his chances for happiness may be at stake when he cheats.

Finally, his self-enjoyment, hence his intrinsic good and the essential worthwhileness of his life, are at stake. For much of a person's enjoyment of life consists in his enjoying being the kind of person that he is. When he knows that he has realized ideals that both he and others admire, he rightly and confidently enjoys himself as a being who embodies these ideals, and his enjoyment is sure, steady, pervasive and persevering. But when one finds that he is morally deficient, especially when he believes his deficiencies to be due to decisions resulting from his own folly, he may spend much of his time, waking and dreaming, trying to hide from his own reality; each attempt to hide involves him in another lie, for his turning his face away from the facts about himself amounts to another way of lying to himself about his condition. If one can realize what a large percentage of his time becomes spent in running away from himself, trying to escape, even if only subconsciously, from the evils he believes to be embodied within him, one who is tempted to cheat will attribute great weight to the evils therein. People who have learned the hard way, i.e., who cheated and then experienced for themselves the psychological rewards in self-disesteem, do not need to be told that "honesty is the best policy." A man who can say to himself, with warranted conviction, "I am just," can enjoy a self-evident intrinsic good of the kind that constitutes his own life as most worth while.

(2) Our second argument reviews and endeavors to refute a fallacious hasty generalization upon which lack of faith in the general reliability of the principle of reciprocity often rests. The hasty generalization, as previously stated, is: "Exact justice is impossible; therefore no justice is possible" It appears more convincing when occurring as a shorter, more ambiguous assertion: "Injustice exists; therefore justice does not exist." The fallacy becomes clear when the argument is put in traditional syllogistic form: "No (injustice) is (justice); Some (injustice) (exists). Therefore no (justice) (exists)." What follows, logically, from the two premises is that "Therefore, some (justice) does not (exist)." When you become aware that "Some (injustice) (exists)" warrants inferring only that

"Some (justice) does not (exist)," you realize that the task of deciding when and how much injustice, as well as when and how much justice exists, remains a continuing problem. The hope for an easy solution, abandonment of all belief in and concern for justice, is unwarranted. Instead of concluding "Why should I be just?" one is left with the more difficult and perpetually annoying question, "When and how much should I be just?"

A counter-argument, not proving that one should always be just but serving as further evidence that no easy solution is in prospect, may be stated as follows. "If the principle of reciprocity works, the when others are unjust to me, I justly reciprocate unjustly to them." Correct. But it follows also that, if you justly reciprocate unjustly to them, then they too justly reciprocate unjustly to you, etc. Hence, following this line of argument and action, a future of perpetual series of injustices is all that you can expect. In such a prospect, your rights all disappear, for the existence of your rights depends upon some reasonable expectation that others will do their duties justly. Thus, in effect, if you act upon the belief that you have a right to be unjust to others you beget, for yourself a situation in which you come to have no rights at all. Justice too is justly reciprocated, and one who believes and acts upon the faith that the justice achievable through trust in the general reliability of reciprocity is more worthwhile than the injustice justly achievable through reliance on it, stands a chance of reaping some degree of justice, whereas the disbeliever has only injustice in prospect. Our counter-argument proposes a wager, reminiscent of Pascal's. Given a world of pure chance, bet on the following issue. In which kind of a world would you fare better, one in which you are assured of complete injustice or one in which you may obtain some, even just a little bit, of justice? By betting on the former, you have everything to lose, and by betting on the latter, you have something to gain. Granted that the actual world is not a world of pure chance, the argument points to the lack of clarity in the fallacious argument: "Others are unjust to me, so why should I not be unjust to them?" If you reason in this way you are actually unjust to yourself if you thereby replace a future prospect of some justice with a future prospect of no justice.

(3) Our third argument has to do with evidence for the reliability of the principle of reciprocity. Here, we must appeal to experience and to experiment. Detailed exposition will not be presented here; this matter has already been explored in Chapter V. If you have neglected to observe how the principle operates in your own life, you should stop and take

time to do so. That it works negatively, you can recall without much effort. That it works positively, you can recall also if you are willing to look without deliberately blinding your eyes. If you cannot, for any reason, recall, you can try to assure yourself through deliberate, controlled experiment. You may be able to enlist the help of another in checking your observations and recording results. Exact justice cannot be expected, as we have repeatedly stated; but unpredictable increments, that should also be included in your records and calculations, occur often enough, usually, to counterbalance obvious injustices which also normally occur. The appeal to your own experience is our final appeal. We argue that if you fail to recognize an amazing degree of reliability for the principle of reciprocity, you have failed to observe your own experience with persistence and objectivity.

b. When you expect to be repaid by others for what you have given them, you face certain other problems in addition to those just surveyed. Let us direct our attention here specifically to how it is possible for one to be repaid equally in circumstances where people are essentially unequal. An obvious example exists in the relationships between parents and children. Parents cannot expect their children to repay them for their services. (Earlier rural children were often able to do this by producing more than they consumed before leaving home, but in megalopolis, repayment, which does sometimes occur, is a rare exception.) But the principle of reciprocity operates more broadly: should a parent expect his children to repay him any more than he repaid his parents? Again, varieties of complications affect different situations differently, so expectations should leave room for great flexibility. The most that a parent can hope for is that his children will treat their children as well as he treated them, and will expect no more repayment from their children than he expected from them. Similar examples obvious to all may be observed in host-guest, teacher-pupil and employer-employee relationships. The world is full of "have and have-not" situations wherein genuine differences determine how the principle of reciprocity may be expected to operate. You fail to appreciate fully the nature of the Golden Rule until you recognize the superiority of the Confucian formulation: treat each other as you would be treated by each person if you were that person. Only then will you feel that you are being justly repaid by others who, because genuinely different, cannot repay you except through expressing, perhaps only by their way of living, a willingness to repay you through trying to be as just in their situation as you would try to be if you were in their situation.

Grace. The term "grace" has both broader and narrower meanings. Unfortunately, perhaps, the narrower meaning is better known. Broadly speaking, grace exists whenever one has received more than one deserves, regardless of whether the source is impersonal or personal. Narrowly speaking, only persons (including God as a person) can be gracious. We will use the term in its broader sense which is, of course, inclusive of the narrower. The terms "grace" and "justice" are commonly paired because "justice" pertains to what is deserved while "grace" refers to more than is deserved. "Justice" consists in getting exactly what one deserves; "injustice" consists in getting less than one deserves; "grace" consists in getting more than one deserves. Of course grace, like justice and injustice, has two aspects: getting and giving. You are "just" when you give exactly what you owe; you are "unjust" when you give less than you owe; you are "gracious" when you give more than you owe. Hence a discussion of "grace" is a natural extension of problems inherent in the nature of justice.

The distinction between distributive and retributive justice has implications for understanding the nature of grace. Grace too may be "distributive" (received and shared by many who do not deserve) and "retributive" (reciprocated by being as gracious to others as others have been to us). Each of these kinds of grace involves us in dialectical problems.

Grace may be said to be distributed whenever two or more persons receive more than they deserve. One may ask what, if anything, does a person deserve? Prior to being born, did you deserve to be born? Being born, do you deserve to live? Living, do you deserve to receive goods, such as food, shelter, clothing, associates or happiness? Who can say that, distributively, you deserve anything? Is not the gift of life itself, regardless of its source, a matter of sheer grace? Some, having received a gracious gift of life, somehow believe that, since they received it, they deserve it. Furthermore, some of these believe that "the world owes them a living," and even become anxious about receiving their share, or more their share, of the world's goods. When a bounteous universe distributes among people goods that they do not deserve, greedy persons naturally inquire: "Am I getting my fair share?" But how can you honestly ask whether you are receiving your full share of grace? If grace consists in more than one deserves, how can one ask: "Am I getting my full, i.e., deserved, share of what I do not deserve?" Yet, there is a sense in which one does deserve more than one deserves. In order to make this clear, we cite an example. You continue to live, and you learn to trust empirical methods of understanding the nature of persons and the universe and of predicting the future course of events from past experience. If you did not deserve to be born but were born, and did not deserve to live but do live, and do not deserve the goods you receive but do receive them, you may, on the basis of past experience, predict that you will continue to receive them. Although multiplication of receipts of undeserved goods does not make them any more deserved, the question of whether such undeserved goods are being distributed equally is a fair question that may properly face everyone who is curious, and not merely those who are greedy. If there is to be grace at all, or if there will continue to be more grace, the question of whether it is fairly distributed is as legitimate as the question of whether justice itself is being distributed justly. In fact, it is the other side of the same question now being discussed in terms of grace, or more than one deserves, rather than in terms of distributive injustice, or less than one deserves.

Grace may be said to be retributed whenever you are as gracious to others as others have been to you. Although, on the one hand, grace and justice are opposites, yet they are also interinvolved. When you have received graciously, you tend to want to be gracious. And when you have been gracious, you often hope, even learn to expect, that others will be gracious to you in turn. If you believe that, when you have been gracious, you justly deserve reciprocated graciousness, you infer that grace should involve justice. In fact, since people enjoy being gracious (and such enjoyment is intrinsic good), may one not only enjoy being gracious himself but justly owe to others opportunity for them to enjoy being gracious to him? Hence, being gracious may constitute an important part of what one most wants to be, though being just, regarding permitting others to enjoy being gracious and just, may also constitute part of what one most wants to be.

Chapter XIV

SELF AS CONSCIENTIOUS

Do your have a conscience? What is a conscience? Do you have a single conscience or many consciences? Why is conscience important in ethics?

What is Conscience? Although everyone knows intuitively what conscience is, the long history of efforts to explain its nature in terms of the presuppositions of different philosophies and of the perspectives of specialized sciences has produced in many minds a state of confusion. We try to clarify the problem by surveying eight typical theories, classifying them relative to the traditional issue of whether conscience is innate or acquired.

1. Three different theories agree that conscience is essentially innate. That is, at birth a child has all of the necessary conditions of conscience present in its being, even if still in undeveloped form. The particular form which conscience takes as the child develops may be wholesome or unhealthy, but conscience as a faculty, function or ability has its essential nature already present at birth. These three will refer to conscience as something (a) "theologically implanted," (b) "biologically evolved" and (c) "axiologically inherent."

a. Best known, perhaps, is the view that conscience is theologically implanted. God created persons and placed within them a sense of right and wrong. Conscience is sometimes spoken of as "the Voice of God" somehow dwelling within each person. If persons will but listen to, and heed, its commands, they will act rightly. Sometimes it is only a "still small voice;" sometimes it overwhelms one with frightening fear or feelings of shame. Persons who habitually attend to other things may lose their abilities to hear it; but persons may deliberately cultivate their abilities to listen to it just as they develop their other senses and ways of knowing. One of the purposes of prayer is to exclude distracting factors so that a person can concentrate upon listening to this voice of God.

Problems arise for those holding this theory when they find that God seems to speak differently to different persons and to the same person at different times. How can persons be sure that what they hear is the voice of God and not, for example, the voice of the Devil? Debates continue among theorists and doubts continue within individuals. But two schools of thought have developed regarding one aspect of the issue of consistency. One says that God, being eternal, implants the voice of an eternal, unchanging message that is essentially the same for all persons and all times.   Variations must be explained in terms of faulty development of a person's ability to hear, or to failure to listen carefully or of listening to the Devil instead.   The other conceives God as taking a direct interest in each person, thus speaking to each in a way suited to his problems and circumstances.   It is a mistake to regard what God says to a particular person at a particular time as a universal law holding for all persons at all times.   A third view, popular with Romanticists, should also be mentioned: God, as the principle of life within us, is rich in vitality and speaks to us through the varieties of impulses inspiring our vivacious appreciation and vigorous actions; God himself is that vitality which conscientiously refuses to be restricted by rigid formalities such as social customs or logical deductions, much less by eternal commands that leave us imprisoned, dead, sterile and bored.   God lives within us as impulsiveness, serving as all the conscientiousness we need.   Hence, conflicting conceptions of God continue to result in divergent views regarding how his voice speaks to us and what it has to say.

b. Some believe that conscience is the "voice of the Race" which has evolved biologically. Some speak of it as the "voice of the herd." Freud calls it the "collective unconscious." Each species, in order to survive, develops inheritable tendencies that enable its young to adapt through innate response patterns. These are called "instincts." Each individual, human as well as animals of other species, is born with innate tendencies acquired from biological ancestors. When a person goes counter to these, one becomes afraid. Although each may also acquire habits of one's own, conscience consists basically of those that have been inherited. Some instincts are fully present in babes at birth, such as fear of falling or fear of loud noises, whereas others require a longer period to mature, such as the mating instinct. Those who claim that conscience is acquired should realize that whatever part of it is acquired results from modifications in the basic instincts rather than beginning from nothing or than being something attached to a person from the outside, like clothes which one puts on to keep him warm.

c. Each child at birth has needs, wants, desires. Fulfillment of these is good. Some desires, especially in children and adolescents, are strong but trivial and temporary. Some pertain to more enduring goods, such as desire for a long, healthy, happy life, for higher education, for well-rounded development, for marriage, children and professional achievement. When awareness dawns that, in achieving some trivial good, you are so acting that you are jeopardizing some deeper value, then the feeling that occurs to you may be called "conscience." "Conscience," says

DeWitt H. Parker, "is the voice of the profounder wish-level." Not only does oughtness consist in the power that a greater good has over a lesser good in compelling our choices, but conscience is the feeling of obligation which occurs as we experience such compulsion. Conscience is not something innate that tells us specifically which particular objects are good; it is something general that operates whenever we become aware that we have chosen, are choosing or are in danger of choosing, a lesser rather than a greater good. Thus your conscience may bother you when you slight your friends, or when you become lazy at a time when unrecurring opportunity "knocks at your door." Conscience occurs not only when you fear that you are choosing lesser goods, but also, perhaps even more violently or dramatically, when you fear that you have chosen the greater evil. Conscience, then, is that innate tendency, not merely for preferring greater over lesser values, but also for fearing to fail in making such choices or in acting wisely upon them.

2. Three other theories agree that conscience is acquired. We will speak of conscience being acquired (a) "naturally," (b) "socially" and (c) "intellectually."

a. All human beings, like other animals, are naturally subject to stimulus-response conditionings. When a child is stimulated by some light or sound and responds by reaching toward it, if the result is pleasing he may continue toward it or repeat his reaching. If the response is painful, he will withdraw. When he initiates action that results in pain, he is inhibited. Some inhibitions are momentary; others become habitual. Physiological psychology provides us with "laws of learning" related to positive and negative conditioning. Now conscience consists in the feeling of fear of evil consequences believed likely to follow from acting upon any impulse or tendency to act. Although conscience is primarily negative, i.e., is fear of evil consequences, it may also function positively, i.e., as fear of failure to attain more enjoyable consequences. But it is always negative in the sense that it involves fear. Inhibitions and conditioning therefrom are all acquired after birth. Although much of our conditioning may be accidental, education, whether provided by parents or teachers, is wise when it is designed to condition children to develop habits conducive to their long-range pleasures. "Spare the rod and spoil the child." Of course, we now have "progressive"methods of providing more intricate kinds of conditioning. But conscience, in any case, is acquired naturally by conditioning; and the differences between the consciences of different persons may be explained as due to their varying experiences producing inhibitions.

b. Some regard conscience as purely social. Ethics pertains to relations between people, not to private desires or fears. Conscience originates in social experience. You discover that others approve or disapprove your behavior, and conscience consists in your developed fear of social disapproval. Conscience is fear of what people will think. Only after you have been punished by some person for doing what that person thought ought not to be done does conscience arise. Group mores, to say nothing of laws and police, courts, jails and capital punishment, constitute prevailing beliefs about proper taboos. As you grow up in a community, you learn to acquire the group's fears as your own. Conscience consists in acquired awareness of fear of failure to conform to the mores or abide by the taboos. Although introspectively you may not be able to distinguish between a fear caused by personal experience with physical objects (such as bumping your head when arising under a table) and a fear caused by social disapproval, conscience consists in those fears derived from social conditioning only. Those who hold this theory may presuppose the physiological mechanisms discussed above as underlying social conditioning, but they limit what is properly meant by "conscience" to the results of social conditioning.

c. People acquire ideas and ideals, in addition to other kinds of conditioning from physiological and social sources. Ideas about how things work, how nature functions, and how to get what is good serve as bases for beliefs about how one ought to act. Ideals, as ideas of high or of the greatest values, function as goals of endeavor and as goods that we ought to choose to realize. Some ideals arise out of personal dreams of what one would like to have or be. Some have been inherited from our cultural ancestors whose dreams have become institutionalized for us. Whenever our intellect seeks to understand and explain, then some system of ideas, some interpretive scheme, is constructed to provide for us an answer to our questions about the nature and goodness of life. When such a system has been accepted, when reason deduces what we ought to do, whether in general or in particular situations, then we experience feelings of obligation to do as reason commands. When you assent to logic or mathematics as reliable ways to knowledge, then if you reach a "wrong answer," you feel that you ought not have reached it and that you ought to find the "right answer." Although many have come to regard mathematics as morally neutral or as lying outside the realm of ethics, these terms, "right and wrong answers," originally had, and really continue to have, value and obligational connotations. Your conscience, as a feeling of fear that you will not get what is best, bothers you when you perform a textbook exercise, to be sure. The system may be a theological system, a legal system, a nationalistic cultural system or a methodological system. Having accepted the premises and the validity of deductive inferences, you then feel obligated to assent to and act upon the conclusions. Such feeling of obligation is conscience acquired through reasoning. Extremists may admit "natural" and "social" conditions only if these fit within their rational scheme. Moderates may see intellect-motivated conscience as supplementary to "natural" or "social" origins.

3. Surveys of theories of the nature of conscience remain superficial if they leave the impression that conscience must be either innate or acquired but not both. Of other theories, we mention only two.

a. Some thinkers, regarding "innate" and "acquired" as opposites, believing that each person normally has two different kinds of conscience, namely that which is innate, such as the voice of God, and that which is acquired, or learned from personal experience. You may be so impressed with the difference between these kinds that you will call one "conscience" and insist on giving the other some different name. Yet both involve feelings of fear which, merely as feelings, can hardly be distinguished from one another. Their differences seem to be ideational, either with regard to how the obligation is conceived or how the fear is believed to have originated. Persons inheriting a system of ideas describing these kinds of conscience as different, automatically involve the system-differentiating ideas in their conceptions. Since conflicts may occur between these two kinds of conscience, you must either suffer uncertainty from such conflict or seek some ideal as to how to resolve it through regarding one as superior to the other. This type of theory, which may be called "dualistic," includes many varieties, depending upon which of the foregoing six theories are adopted.

b. Although conscience is simple, simply a feeling of obligation to choose the greater good or a feeling of fear that one has not chosen that greater good, it is also complex, a complex organic entity having complex sources, complex functions and complex variabilities needed to adapt to life's multi-complex circumstances.

The sources of conscience are both innate and acquired. You cannot acquire what your inherited nature will not permit you to acquire, so all you acquire develops from and modifies innate capacities. Each person is born with desires that entail goods and evils as satisfactions and frustrations, for example. Greater and lesser goods, and evils, emerge from having more enduring needs; hence choices between such goods or evils occur; thus a person is born with an inherently ethical nature. Each person inherits biological tendencies from parental, racial, human and animal ancestors, including   many levels of genetic instinct and the physiological mechanisms which make frustration, conditioning, habit formation and patterns of response-associated fears possible. How much geological, solar, astronomical and other cosmic factors serve to predispose one's inner sense of oughtness remains speculative; one's nature could not have originated outside of the total universe, so to the extent that cosmic tendencies function inherently in one's sense of oughtness remains an open question; doubts must continue regarding claims that one has "heard the voice of God" giving specific directions in clear detail, though one who fails to appreciate some feelings of identity with possibilities for goodness in the rest of the universe may predispose oneself to unhappy loneliness or egotistical misery.   Complexes of chemical and physical, including subatomic, causal processes also condition the existence and nature of conscience in ways which may properly be called innate.

But conscience is also acquired, naturally through all conditionings, positive and negative, socially through active participation in various kinds and levels of groups, and intellectually through whatever conceptual systems one inherits or constructs. Although the distinction between innate and acquired sources of conscience remains useful and should be kept clear, awareness of the complex ways in which inherited and acquired factors interact as conscience develops should make us realize how highly organic, or intricately interdependent, the various factors constituting conscience become in even a young child. The myriads of ways in which these factors intermingle in an active megalopolitan adult are marvelous to behold.

Thus an adequate answer to the question, "What is conscience?" must take into account the "some truth" expressed by all of the foregoing theories, each of which remains inadequate because, and to the extent that, it neglects the "some truth" in each of the others.

Pervasiveness of Conscience.   Since conscience is your feeling of concern for your values, experienced as fear that you have done less than what is best, it functions whenever awareness of doing or having done less than the best occurs. You may enjoy life at times without being aware that your values, or opportunities for greater values or possibilities for diminished values, are in any danger. Whenever possible, you ought to seek to be free from such danger and fears of danger; hence you ought, whenever possible, to free yourself from feeling conscientious, for concentrating attention upon the goal of life is better than to worry about means whenever life permits. But most of the time we must be aware of our values and dangers to them, so most of the time we must be conscientious. Some not only enjoy (experience intrinsic good) while working (devoting themselves to means) but also enjoy being conscientious. Even though conscience is felt as fear, alert, efficient attentiveness to each occasion for choice, decision and action with feelings of mastery may be enjoyed. Highly conscientious people usually enjoy being conscientious; when this is so, such enjoyed conscientiousness is experienced as intrinsic value. Of course, when we suffer severe pangs of conscience, we experience evil, sometimes so great that we may even contemplate suicide. Where the value issues at stake are small, conscience may remain unnoticeable and transparent. We become inured to recurring unpleasant feelings when we know about their inevitability (e.g., an injectionist who may suffer excruciating feelings during nurse's training becomes immune to discomfort of patients after months of experience). We become extremely disturbed and intensely conscientious when our major goods, such as our life, property, occupation, reputation or marriage, are suddenly threatened. Conscience and conscientiousness vary, then, somewhat in proportion to the apparent differences in danger to our values. Its presence is pervasive, though it calls attention to itself usually only when its functioning as our feeling of oughtness bestirs emotion enough to be noticeable.

Being so pervasive, conscience may operate relative to any of a self's values. If we review all of the aspects of self sketched in preceding chapters, we may recall how conscience operates when any part of ourself as physical or self as social is endangered. Every kind of self-interest, whether pertaining to esteem, love, adventure or security may, and at sometime or other does, disturb our conscience. Awareness of neglect of opportunities for self-improvement or for prevention of deterioration ("Clean your teeth twice a day; see your dentist twice a year") causes us to worry. Not only may each occasion for choice present us with feelings of obligation, but awareness of possible, or of seemingly authoritative, principles for choosing may intensify or complicate the operations of our conscience; indeed, any appreciation of the usefulness of principles for choosing may cause conscientious search for such principles, or annoyance with the frustrating effects of codes may lead us to hope conscientiously that no such codes or principles rightly exist. Acceptance of self as agent intimately interdepends with conscience, for feelings of agency, or of power to act in ways which affect values, are part of the source of conscience, and conscience itself is felt as self-compulsion which automatically urges one into action; you intend to be conscientious and you conscientiously intend, and you are responsible for being conscientious and conscientiously carries out your responsibilities. Not only do you conscientiously seek to maintain your freedom (whether to choose or from choice) and to establish restrictions that tend to assure greater actual freedom, but also your very feelings of freedom may function as goods that you fear to lose, thereby serving as sources of your conscience. If sovereignty is multi-leveled and you pursue your values through controlling and being controlled at many levels of social control, then your conscience itself must be capable of functioning as feeling of obligation at each of these many levels and respond as a complex organism to enrichment from the varieties of value inherent in each of the levels. Insight into "levels of democracy" and "democracy of levels" reveals how intricate are the sources of conscience. Since ownership has to do with anything, i.e., any good, which is your own, such ownership is a basis for conscience, and you conscientiously seek to acquire and maintain such ownership as is actually best for you. Knowledge of rights and duties creates conscience accordingly. You seek justice for yourself and seek to be just to others conscientiously; and your conscience may bother you when you discover that you have graciously received more than you deserve or when you have failed to be sufficiently gracious to others. Intelligence, as we shall see, is conscience operating efficiently.

Importance of Conscience. Not only is conscience, as your feelings of obligation, as pervasive as your personal choices, but it serves as foundational to "social conscience," to be explored in Chapter XXIX, which refers to something pervasive relative to "society" (Part II) and its goods and choices, and as foundational to fulfillment of the purposes of life itself (Part III, "Satisfaction"). In part, you are constituted by your conscience. You are what you are by virtue of the sensitivity, maturity and adequacy of your conscience. "A man is known by the problems he keeps," or by the issues with which he conscientiously occupies himself. A person whose conscience troubles him much over trivial things thereby demonstrates himself to be a somewhat trivial person. A person whose conscience commands him to be effectively concerned with the problems of men, in his neighborhood, nation or the world, automatically thereby becomes more of an influence for greatness and thereby embodies greatness within himself.

Ethics is concerned with what is best and what one ought to do in order to obtain it. Oughtness consists in the power that a greater good has over a lesser good in compelling our choices. Conscience is our feeling of oughtness. Although conscience calls attention to itself only when our reactions to choice situations become so emotional that such emotion itself becomes a disturbing datum of experience, our feelings of oughtness permeate the whole range of the kinds of choices presented for us to make. Since such emotion disturbs our attention usually only when negative or naggingly prolonged, we become more familiar with conscience as a feeling of fear, and since our choices involving differential consideration for the welfare of ourselves and others are more likely to be accompanied by fears appearing to be caused by external and persisting demands, we become especially aware of social sources of such negativity and nagging. However, when we realize how broadly and generally our conscience is based, we recognize that, actually, following your conscience is what you most want to do -- because conscience, properly trained and attuned, is nothing more than the voice of your best interests. Whoever mistakenly conceives one's conscience as merely a fear of punishment (which, additionally, is itself a kind of punishment as long as its fear is present in experience) regards it as an evil to be gotten rid of as soon as possible. But when one discovers that "obeying one's conscience is what one most wants to do" is a self-evident truth when stated tautologically (conscience is the feeling that one ought to want to do what it takes to get what is best; therefore one who wants to do what it takes to get what is best wants to follow one's conscience), then one regards it as a most treasured possession and capacity which one desires to keep alert, flexible and intricately trained. To the extent that you regard your own welfare as interdependent with that of others, you will wish to help others discover how broadly-based their consciences are and to train and attune them to creating and maintaining richer surpluses of social goods.

Chapter XV

SELF AS INTELLIGENT

Are you intelligent? What is intelligence? Does becoming more intelligent mean that one has become better morally?

What is "Intelligence"? "Intelligence" is a term with many meanings, ranging from "the sublime to the ridiculous." We shall survey a few of these for the purpose of clarifying the problem and of indicating how each meaning has a somewhat different bearing upon ethics.

1. Basically, "intelligence" is a synonym for "wisdom." Wisdom consists in having attained the goal of life. No person is wise until he is happy. The wise person both understands the nature and purpose of life and enjoys its values. A wise person not only knows how to live but also is not unduly disturbed by not understanding that which is beyond his understanding. A wise person knows that happiness is life's end-in-itself and that understanding is a means to that end, not an end-in-itself. Wisdom consists not in knowledge or understanding merely, but in being happy and in having used such knowledge to attain happiness.

2. Secondly, and derivatively, "intelligence" is a kind of "ability." As an ability, it is, basically, the ability to attain happiness or the ability to achieve the goal of life. As such, it involves whatever understanding is needed in order to achieve such ends, both understanding of what is the goal of life or of what constitutes happiness and of the means needed to attain it. Fundamentally, it is the ability to not mistake some part of life for the whole of life, or to see how the value of life as a whole is present in some or all of its parts. It involves ability to distinguish between means and ends and to subordinate means to ends, even when the ends are to be found primarily in means-activities.

3. Since intelligence, in the foregoing senses, involves the use of the means needed to attain the ends, it includes ability to use means. Hence, when focusing attention upon means, as we do so much of the time, we rightly employ the word "intelligence" in referring to such ability. Unfortunately, preoccupation with this meaning of the term "intelligence" tends to make us forget its more ultimate meanings. Here we are concerned with ability to understand and choose between ends whereas the foregoing meaning pertained primarily to ability to understand and choose among means, which involves, of course, ability to distinguish between ends and means.

Two kinds of ability may be distinguished relative to means: (a) ability to understand how to use the means and (b) the ability to choose the better means. Although these tend to go together, we discover that some persons develop prodigious intellectual insights in some fields of science and technology and acquire complicated technical skills without becoming able to make wise practical decisions even in those fields. Sometimes a will to choose is lacking, sometimes whim, passion and prejudice interfere, sometimes fear of possible failure, of misjudgment or of displeasing superior officers cripples one's power to take responsibility for decision. That is, one may be prudent but lack know-how, and one may have know-how but lack prudence. Both know-how and prudence are kinds of abilities. Each is a kind of intelligence. And one who seeks to be more intelligent will try to attain not only more of each but also more of both in ways that support each other.

Each of thee kinds is complex and various in its nature. (a) Not only is understanding of means essential to intelligence, but some admire "understanding," "intellect" and "reason" so much that they come to regard "intelligence" as primarily, if not exclusively, a matter of "intellect." Although "intellect" has been variously conceived, some believe its function to consist primarily in understanding forms and their relationships. Hence a study of logic and mathematics is regarded as essential to development of intellect. Ability to make clear distinctions, sharp divisions, exclusive differentiations and to comprehend complex systems of relations is idealized. However, also, ability to see similarities, especially of the subtlest sorts, and to generalize even regarding sparse examples of uniformities is also essential. Furthermore, ability to observe indefiniteness and ambiguity and to generalize about these, as we learn especially from Hindu philosophies, and ability to apprehend mutual immanence and complementarity in opposites, as we learn from Chinese philosophers, may be an important ingredient in intellect also.

In addition, "understanding" may include knowledge of feelings and of processes. There are romanticistic as well as rationalistic ideals of understanding means. Knowledge of temperament, sentiment, emotion, sensation, frustration and satisfaction, and how to produce, control or diminish these, all constitute part of understanding means. Acquaintance with physical, social and emotional processes and practical experience, giving one insight into "the feel of things," serve as kinds of understanding. Knowledge of when and how to stop, e.g., automobiles, courtship, ambition, and sympathy for others, is necessary to intelligence.

(b) Prudence too is complicated. It also is a kind of "reasonableness." The distinction between our present two kinds of intelligence was conceived long ago. On the one hand, some regard "reason" as ability to deduce or to understand formal relationships, quite independently of all considerations of value. On the other hand, we also say: "When faced with a choice between two goods, one of which is better than the other, what is the reasonable thing to do? To choose the better of two, of course." Here "reason" refers to ability to choose the better of two goods. Here "reason," "prudence" and "intelligence" become synonyms. However, knowledge of goods and of how they differ is not sufficient for prudence; and you must also be willing to choose and to take responsibility for your choices, and sensitivity regarding degrees of willingness and variabilities in one's capacity for bearing responsibilities is needed here.

4. Another meaning of "intelligence," that may or may not presuppose the foregoing meanings, has to do with ability to adapt. One common definition of "intelligence" is "ability to adapt to relatively new situations." This conception grows out of studies in biology and experimental psychology. The goal of life is regarded as survival in a world where life, constantly threatened with extinction, must "struggle for existence." Only "the fit survive." Those beings which survive are "intelligent." Those which perish are not. Since species develop inheritable instincts, innate habits of response which enable even the young to survive, such instincts constitute a fundamental part of such "intelligence." However, since each living being must constantly face new threats to its existence in an ever-changing world, those species, and members, which can overcome their innate habits and develop new abilities to respond in such a way as to survive in such new situations are "more intelligent" than those which do not. However, to define "intelligence" as "ability to adapt to relatively new situations," as "advocates of progress" tend to do, ignores another side of adaptive situations. Conditions in the world not only change but also at times, even for long times, remain the same. A being that can adapt to relatively new situations but which becomes bored, weakened, or deteriorated when conditions remain enduringly the same, may perish also. If the goal is survival, then "intelligence" consists in "ability to adapt," but such ability includes ability to adapt to unchanging situations as well as to changing situations.

This meaning of intelligence, although apparently originating in biological studies, has been extended to all areas of life and refined in many ways. Pragmatists, especially William James and John Dewey, interpret "intelligence" as ability to solve problems. They have in mind, of course, primarily practical problems or actual problems. Since life sometimes provides us with a surplus of energy and free time, we may even invent artificial problems, either those in games, as in checkers or chess, or those in the theoretical sciences, such as mathematics or physics, which may or may not later prove useful in solving practical problems. In fact, much of our educational experience, as in laboratory science courses, or in theme composition, comes to be devoted to solving artificial problems. The purpose of such experience is to help us to improve our abilities to solve such problems in a way regarded as preparatory to solving the actual problems which we expect to face later. "Progressive" educators believe that children learn to solve practical problems better by coping with actual rather than artificial problems, and that intelligence develops more rapidly thereby. Children should be faced with, and allowed and urged to decide for themselves, actual ethical problems rather than merely provided with codes or fictional ethical examples. For Pragmatists, all practical problems involve values, and hence intelligence is essentially ethical in nature, and the best way to improve intelligence is to grapple with actual ethical problems.

Although "intelligence" defined in terms derived primarily from biological struggles for survival through adaptation has been extended by Pragmatists to ability to deal with all problem-solving situations, such problems tend to be regarded not only as particular but also as temporary. However, we wish here to emphasize that, although facing questions about the nature and goal of life, what constitutes intrinsic good and to what extent shall one devote himself to end-values as against means-values, etc., always occurs at particular times, these are among a person's most important practical problems, and that "intelligence" as ability to adapt, and to solve problems, properly includes ability to deal with these problems. Hence, although one who defines "intelligence" as ability to adapt and solve problems may not always have "intelligence" in our first three meanings in mind, we here wish to assert that one's definition is inadequate until one does so.

As we shall see in Chapter XXX, "intelligence" as just defined serves as a basis for "social intelligence," or the ability of groups to solve their group problems including, or even especially, their moral problems. Whereas solutions to problems adopted by a group needing to adapt to certain circumstances tend to become established and institutionalized, when circumstances change so that solutions to previous problems no longer serve present problems, the institutions (whether mores, laws or organizations) enforcing those solutions need to be given up or modified if the group is to remain intelligent, i.e., able to solve its problems. Moral codes need to be adopted whenever they serve as useful instruments for aiding social adjustments; but also they need to be abandoned or reformed whenever their use ceases. A group is "intelligent" only when it keeps its codes efficient and discards or revises them as soon as their usefulness declines.

Another extension of meaning for the word "intelligence" has occurred relative to problem solving. Since problem solving requires ingenuity in suggesting new hypotheses to be tried out as possible solutions, something called "creativity" is needed. Now creativity has become idealized, not merely as a means to solving problems, but as a kind of good in itself. That is, just as men have come to idealize "art for art's sake" so they have come to idealize "creativity for creativity's sake." It is true that you are more creative when you are more intelligent because your problem is one that demands creativity in order to be solved. And when you practice creativity in art and other artificial problems, you may indeed acquire greater skill and improve your intelligence by doing so. But the question of whether creativity merely for the sake of creativity can be regarded as constituting intelligence is open to doubt, except where persons find enjoyment, hence intrinsic good, in such creativity as their mode of seeking and living in the goal of life. Enjoyment of artistic creativity as the goal of life, for those whose luxurious conditions permit, may indeed constitute intelligence. But, even in a land and time of increasing luxury, most people must still find their goal of life closely allied with enjoyment experienced in solving practical problems and regard themselves as intelligent in proportion as they succeed in such practice and in enjoying the process and the result.

5. Finally, since problem solving abilities occur not merely in solving particular problems but also as general latent capacities to solve similar problems in similar ways, intelligence as general problem-solving ability is something that people have investigated extensively. The need for predicting success in education, business or research has led to designing tests of adaptability. First, many specific kinds of abilities were tested and finally tests for general ability, called "general intelligence" and measured by a scale giving an "I.Q." or "intelligence quotient." The accuracy and adequacy of these tests continues to be questioned, and one is cautioned to use them judiciously and always in conjunction with other kinds of evidence. Test makers must consider many other factors in designing their tests, such as need for reducing the tests to printed material, rapid taking and rapid, even machine, scoring, mass use, secrecy, etc., so that few tests are given under ideal conditions. No one is more aware of the inadequacies of intelligence tests than the experts who design them. Yet, use of these tests has become so common and use of the term

"intelligence" in connection with them has become so wide-spread that the other, more basic, meanings of "intelligence" tend to be forgotten. Disgusted cynics complain: "Intelligence is what intelligence tests test." Those who believe that problems in mathematics and logic are most typical of problems tend to employ artificial problems in these fields in such tests. But "social intelligence" tests have also been designed and provide indices of a different kind of ability. Further improvements in the design and use of such tests are to be expected. But we have yet to see a test that adequately predicts development of "intelligence" as "ability to attain happiness," involving understanding of the nature and goal of life and how to attain it.

Since all of the foregoing meanings properly apply to the word "intelligence," an intelligent person will be able to discriminate which meaning is intended in each context where the word is used.

Ethical Intelligence. When "ethics" is taken in its popular narrow sense of "conformity to the mores" and "intelligence" is viewed as rating on an "intelligence test," correlations between "being ethical" and "being intelligent" may be very small. But when "ethics" is regarded as concern for what is good, i.e., for the goal of life as including the most enjoyment of intrinsic goodness, and when "intelligence" is regarded as the ability to attain the goal of life, happiness, then the meanings of these two terms not only overlap but become practically identical. The purpose of a study of ethics is to increase one's intelligence. Then nature and purpose of intelligence is to help to become "more ethical" or to attain more of what, in terms of available intrinsic values, one ought to attain. Hence, ethical living is intelligent living and intelligent living is ethical living.

Since this notion of "ethical intelligence" is all-inclusive in its scope, it involves concern for the whole of one's life as well as for each of the various parts. It includes concern for a person's interdependence with others and thus for those matters of "social intelligence" pertinent to each person which we have yet to explore in Chapter XXX. It includes concern about what is final or highest in life as well as about lesser intrinsic goods and the multitudes of means thereto. Hence, ethical intelligence is inseparable from religion conceived as the quest for, and attainment of, the goal of life. "The ethical," "the religious" and "the intelligent" are not three exclusive classes of things, as we may tend to think when we structure our thoughts in terms of a class-logic; rather they are three distinguishable aspects of all phases of life where intrinsic values are at stake. Aspectival differences include: you are "religious" when you are questing for a goal of life, you are "ethical" when you are doing what you ought to do, and you are "intelligent" when you are able, and exercises your ability whenever suitable occasion occurs, to do what you ought to do in pursuing the goal of life. "Religion, so conceived, involves ethics and "ethics," so conceived, involves religion, and both involve intelligence. That is, one is most religious when one is most ethical, and one is most ethical when one is most religious. And, one is most religious when one is most intelligent, and one is most intelligent when one is most religious. Unfortunately, these assertions do not apply to all meanings of the terms "religion," "ethics" and "intelligence," and misquoting these statements out of context is likely to cause great misunderstanding.

A self's intelligence is a part of it. You may become more or less intelligent -- in each of the above ways. Becoming more intelligent is, surely, part of what you most want to become.

Chapter XVI

SELF AS ORGANIC

Pausing for an overview, we may note some general conclusions which seem warranted if the views expressed in the previous chapters are accepted. The function of Part I has been to explore some of the more obvious aspects of the nature of self for two purposes: (a) To try to understand and formulate a view of the nature of a self and its values which serves to clarify reasons why a self automatically involves wanting what is good for it and to know what it can, and ought to, do in order to obtain such good. Or, why a self is by nature ethical, and some of the ways in which its ethical nature manifests itself. (b) To try to show what kind of an individual basis exists for social ethics. Since too many theories of social ethics presuppose an oversimplified conception of the nature of individuals, they fail to be adequate for taking account of the complex needs and values of individuals. Of course, to the extent that individuals are social products, our study of the nature of individual selves remains incomplete until we have explored the natures of groups and observed further complexities in the ways in which individuals are influenced by them.

Aspects of Self. First, let us review and summarize together the various aspects of self surveyed in the foregoing chapters. Distinguishing between self as apparent or knowable and self as unknown and even unknowable, we realize that, despite what seems obvious about ourselves and the increasing knowledge available to us through the sciences, some aspects of self remain beyond understanding and hence must continue to be left out of our explicit account of its nature. Despite these persisting areas of obscurity, we know enough about self to be overwhelmed by its intricacy, complexity and variability.

You intuitively presuppose that, as a minimum, a self exists as the doer of what you do, as both the agent or enactor of your deeds and the recipient of actions by other persons and things upon you. It is that which desires, wants, wishes, intends, decides, chooses, accepts, rejects, commits and experiences problems, frustrations and satisfactions. It is something which is aware of itself and of others and of interactions between itself and others. Its growing or fixed distinctions between "me" and "mine" and between "mine" and "not mine" contribute to its fortunes in its interrelations with others; and its survival and prosperity depend upon whether or not its self-interestedness manifests itself in altruistic or selfish ways. Its interests in a social world constitute it a social being and serve as a basis for its having an ethical nature.

A self is essentially physical; even if it may sometimes somehow transcend its physical nature, its functioning as an ethical being cannot be separated from its physical conditions during its lifetime. A self cannot function either as a continuant or as an interactor in our physical and social world without acting as, and through the instrumentality of, its own physical body. In addition to the more obvious knowledge that a self has of its body through extending its arms, wiggling its fingers, and suffering pains and bruises from falling and bumping, and through eating and excreting, sleeping and waking, seeing and hearing, we now have all of the various sciences to supplement and extend such knowledge. Astronomy gives it a solar and planetary location and an infinitesimal size and duration in the vast stretches of space and time. Physics reveals the nature of its mass, weight and size and how it operates in accordance with laws of motion and the principles of mechanics, optics, and electronics. Chemistry describes its molecular contents and processes as conditioned by peculiarly organic compounds constituted by amazingly complex atoms and subatomic particles. Biology describes its hereditary nature, molded through aeons of struggle for existence and survival through adaptational mechanisms which, despite their success in producing and maintaining us, remain precarious and bring us, as individuals, eventually to our deaths. Physiology analyzes its cells, organs, and systems (skeletal, digestive, glandular, muscular, circulatory, respiratory, nervous, reproductive, etc.) and the processes and principles involved therein. Physiological psychology examines our sensory-motor systems, including our visual, auditory, gustatory, olfactory, tactile and kinaesthetic sensations and our brain, explaining how sensations, feelings emotions as well as perception, conception, memory, imagination and thought occur. A self is, or is conditioned by, all of these kinds of things, and by their variable and complex interdependencies producing a uniquely identifiable body despite exhibiting uniformities described by the many sciences as common to all human bodies.

A self is essentially social, both in origin and nature and ideals. An infant depends upon a father for conception and a mother for birth and some kind of nurse for early care and survival. Infant and childhood roles, whether provided or demanded, mold a person's idea of oneself. You discover yourself through the actions of others upon you and your attempts and successes or failures in your efforts to react toward them. Your "me" develops first and then your "I," according to G.H. Mead. You imitate others, your parents, siblings, neighbors, school chums, popular idols and heroes in fiction. "One can no more organize his personality independently of a group than he can be born without a mother." Your language, occupation, marriage, recreation and religion are all derived from, and involve, others. Both the general patterns, whether as mores, laws, science, literature, art or religion, which structure the minds of all persons, or the peculiar personality traits which emerge from one's particular roles as second son of Jay Clay, tall basketball captain of Grant High School, left-handed trumpet player in Flagstaff Scout Troop II Band, junior clerk in the Third Street Hardware Store and second beau of the daughter of wealthy Marcus Smythe, which shape one self alone, have essentially social natures. The very nature, purpose and goal of life, with ideas of values depicted in terms of public esteem, financial success, social security and of exciting and comfortable surroundings, come to us at least partly through suggestions by others. So a self is social, not merely in origin and nature, but also in ideals as to what constitutes its own self-fulfillment.

A self by nature has wants, needs, interests, desires. Some of these are alike in all persons, or sufficiently so that generalizations about them are scientifically possible. W.I. Thomas suggests as a minimum classification that all selves desire to be esteemed and not despised, to be loved and not lonely, to be entertained and not bored, to feel secure and not afraid. Many of these desires are necessarily social and, when so, ten principles may be formulated regarding factors involved in how to control our happiness. When our desires affect others we depend on these others and their responses to our interests. In order to induce them to cooperate, we must do what they require of us as a price for their cooperation. We like to be served by them. When we attain what we like, we want more of what we get, and too often more than what others are willing to give. By insisting on getting such more, we undo our welcome and diminish or destroy that willingness, thereby endangering our likelihood of further service. A principle of reciprocity may be discovered to work with general but strikingly variable reliability, usually reflecting our own sincerity or lack of it. We have power to initiate operation of the principle, negatively and positively, in order to induce others to assist in the satisfying of our needs, and to the extent that we remain aware of this power we can exercise considerable control over our own happiness. Multitudes of philosophers and psychologists, each in his own way, have formulated advice regarding how wise self-interest devotes itself unselfishly to large measures of altruism. Fritz Kunkel depicts as well as anyone how "egocentricity begets egocentricity" and Jesus has expressed as well as anyone why you should "love thy neighbor as thyself." (See Fritz Kunkel, Let's Be Normal, Ives Washburn, New York, 1929.)

A self is good, intrinsically good, and a self is evil, intrinsically evil. Such goodness consists in pleasant feelings, satisfaction of desire enthusiasm and contentment or in any successive or organic combination of these. Such evil consists in pains, frustrations, apathy anxiety, and in fear of death or destruction, and in any felt collection or coalescence of them. Since these vary in quality and quantity, in intensity and frequency, in simplicity and complexity, in clarity and subtlety, in depth and breadth of our self-engrossment in them, and in temporal evanescence and enduring permanence, they often elude intellectual grasp. Our naive but natural attempts to objectify them in things or persons or symbols leave us puzzled by their subjective variability. Our sophisticated attempts at an explanation entice our hopes for clarity and enlightenment but normally leave us baffled cultists. A self is variably both good and evil intrinsically, and it is both victim and partial master over its fortune and value fate. But intrinsic value depends upon instrumental values and control over these depends upon understanding and insight into the value-producing mechanisms abounding in the world and in persons. Difficulties in distinguishing between a thing and its value, intrinsic and instrumental value, actual and potential value, subjective and objective values, value experiences, value judgments, evaluations, socially-formulated norms for value judgments and obsolescence regarding such formulations, all becloud our picture. But if you are a shrewd observer, you will know whether your own scheme for depicting your value-predicament is bringing you enjoyment or misery and whether or not you need further ventures investigating alternative schemes.

A self can change, becoming better or worse, intrinsically and instrumentally, within limits. When you have within you ability to improve yourself or to prevent your deterioration, you have an obligation to do so. Why? Because obligation, oughtness or duty consists in the power which a greater good has over a lesser good in compelling our choices. Regarding each actual intrinsic good, one ought to judge that it be maintained or repeated, other things being equal. Regarding each potential intrinsic good, one ought to judge that it be actualized, other things being equal. You owe it to yourself to optimize your intrinsic goods and minimize your intrinsic evils. You ought, of course, to seek, create and maintain whatever instruments are needed for this purpose. Since a self is complex, it owns a variety of values, not all of which can be fully achieved or permanently maintained. Hence, one must choose among them. Insofar as realization of a greater variety of values may involve an added increment of riches, one may be obligated to seek some balanced or well-rounded scheme for selecting among values to be realized. However, depth of appreciation of any one complex value may also have a claim to superiority over great breadth which permits only superficial depth in any one of them. Hence the problem of balancing breadth with depth persists for many as a crucial problem. Some, whose energies or opportunities are actually limited, wisely choose to realize more restricted varieties of values. To the extent that a self is social, one ought to consider one's social abilities, both opportunities and capacities, for realizing social values among one's primary oughts. Since a self includes levels of physical, psychological and social existence and value, it may owe itself realization of some values at each of many levels, even some balanced realization of values among such levels, though again each person may find his greatest social values in some rather than in other levels. A self is a bearing with obligations to improve itself in various ways as much as it can.

The issue, how to know what are one's value potentialities and what are one's obligations regarding them, is complex and fraught with uncertainties. Personal experience, advice from friends, knowledge gained from the sciences, wisdom proclaimed by the sages and religious leaders, local mores and popular opinions expressed through press, radio and television all have roles to play. Exposed to multifarious varieties of suggestions, megalopolitan personalities become overwhelmed with confusion and, often nowadays, assent to chaotic relativism simply because no one of the many suggestions seems sufficiently certain. But if the absolutism-relativism issue can be partially resolved, by keeping in mind that scientifically observable generalizations are warranted insofar as persons and situations are alike but not to the extent that persons and situations are different, individuals can hope that further search regarding reliable generalizations may be rewarding. Some principles for choosing, which seem obvious enough in their completely general form, have been proposed here. In themselves, they provide no solution to particular problems, but knowledge of them, and use of them in attempts to think through particular problems, may save one from errors due to hasty generalizations, from some kinds of unclear thinking and from surrendering to hopelessness too soon. One who knows that institutionalized codes have their bases in principles for choosing becomes more able to evaluate critically traditional or legislated codes in terms of these principles and to prepare for himself, in times when he has sufficient leisure for reflection or under the stress of persisting provocation, codes for guidance in times of crisis. When you can improve your chances for realizing greater intrinsic value in some recurring types of situation by preparing recallable advice to yourself, then you owe it to yourself to do so. Here is one sense in which a self is a kind of being which ought to have an ethical code. Of course, in areas where understanding and evaluation remain beyond your competence, you may owe it to yourself to seek and accept the advice of others who are experienced in both techniques and value know-how.

A self can hardly choose, with or without principles or codes, unless it has a power to choose. Each self is an agent which tends to accept itself as more or less an initiator of consequences even of various kinds and levels of consequences for itself and for others. Such acceptance involves intention of volition, though issues regarding whether you regard yourself responsible for all, including unforeseen, consequences and whether you commit your whole self, or your self wholly, in any or all intentions remains somewhat unclear. To the extent that a momentary whim, wish, passion or angry demand represents your "true intentions," you rightly commit your will; but a self's rich, complex, multi-leveled, enduring and evolving cluster of values cannot be kept fully in mind at all times. You can hardly express your "true intentions" without considerable caution. Some deliberate effort to survey and weigh your major goods usually is needed before you can be sure that your present judgment is one you will also later regard as true. Although agency and intention may at times be irresponsible, normally you tend to accept yourself as responsible for your choices and, so long as you have the requisite abilities, for the consequences of your decisions and actions, even being willing to repay for damage to others which you unwittingly caused. When you realize that your are responsible primarily to yourself and your intrinsic goods and for their achievement and preservation, you more willingly accept such responsibility as your own; when you realize that you are essentially social in various ways, you also willingly accept your social responsibilities as your own, even though doubts continue to plague you as to precisely what are your social responsibilities and how important they are relatively among your goods.

A self which intends and acts responsibly is free in many different senses. It is free to will. It has freedom of will. It may even, at times, enjoy freedom from will. Except for those who conceive freedom as indeterminism, and indeterminism and determinism as contradictories, freedom and determinism may be regarded as not incompatible. If whatever happens is caused to happen, then if you are free, you are caused to be free; but freedom which is caused is none the less freedom. The freedom which we normally desire is not freedom from causation but freedom to cause. It is ability to do, or cause to be done, what we want to do, or cause to be done. This is true in general, regardless of whether we conceive freedom as absence of restraints, self-determinism, fitness of opportunities and capacities, submission of interest in lower values to interest in higher values, accepting oneself as a responsible initiator, or as organically involving two or more of these kinds of freedom together.

A self is also sovereign to the extent that it exercises self control. You have as many kinds and levels of sovereignty, most of them partial rather than complete, as you participate in influencing the system of control and are controlled by it in ways which you really want to be. You are owner in all of the senses in which you recognize things as your own. You may own some things exclusively, but most of your ownership, especially that attained through the various levels of groups in which you participate, is partial and shared with others. You not only own but are owned, and the more you participate in groups, the more you belong to or are owned by others as well as the more you own such others as your associates. Although some of what you own may be valueless, much of what you own, and most of your proper concern about ownership, is good, i.e., intrinsic good, or has good, actual or potential, as instrumental to creating or maintaining your intrinsic goods.

A self has rights and duties. It has duties to others because they have rights and others have duties to it because it has rights. Where two or more people are involved, one person's rights constitute the basis for another's duties. However, in addition to rights and duties which are politically assigned and to those which appear as customary and as arising from mutual consent of unorganized persons, some of which are earned as a result of service, there are basic rights and duties inherent, even innate, in a person's coming into existence as a being having intrinsic good and in evolving emergently higher types of intrinsic good. Although some rights and duties are "inalienable" since they are the same in all persons because persons are alike in being persons and in having intrinsic good, some rights and duties differ, since one who earns more than another, by whatever kind of service to others has a right to the more which one earns. Furthermore, one who acquires specialized abilities to appreciate (symphonic music, theoretical physics, interlinguistic interpretation, athletic superiority, etc.) may thereby acquire specialized rights and duties. But all rights and duties that have been acquired can also be lost; for you may lose your ability to hear, you may lose your earnings when death and bankruptcy eliminate your creditors, and you may lose your life. In addition to having social rights and duties, you may find that you owe it to yourself to ascertain that some of your goods which have rights, so to speak, to actualization and enjoyment are not destroyed by your overdevotion to other goods; that is, you have a duty to yourself to give some attention to all of your goods. Some persons who believe they have duties only to others neglect duties to themselves.

Also related to rights and duties are justice and grace. Justice pertains to giving or receiving what is deserved. When you receive less than you deserve, you have been dealt with unjustly; when you give less than you owe, you are unjust. When you receive more than you deserve, you have been dealt with graciously; when you give more than you owe, you give graciously. Justice and grace are of two kinds: distributive, involving the division of goods among persons who may or may not have earned them, and retributive, involving repayment of goods for goods received. Justice, which involves quality, becomes enormously complicated because difficulties exist in trying to decide how to determine when equality prevails among unequals. Equality prevails among unequals to the extent that their inequalities are taken fully into account. All people are alike in some respects and different in others. Justice involves treating people equally in ways in which they are alike and unequally in ways in which they are different. To the extent that two persons are unique, justice prevails when each appropriately receives unique treatment.

Grace too may involve justice, for one who receives graciously may, desiring to be just, want to reciprocate graciously. When you realize that you did not deserve to come into the world in the first place, you may regard receipt of whatever justice you get as really also a matter of grace. Undeserved living in a world of rights and duties exemplifies receipt of grace. Correlativity of rights and duties exemplifies justice. You have a right to justice only if you are willing to be just; you have a duty to be just if you believe that you have a right to justice. You have no right to grace except when you have first been gracious and when you believe that you have a duty to be gracious at least to those who have been gracious to you. Rights, duties, justice and grace thus all interdepend. A self's complexities include these interdependencies and these, having no existence apart from selves, interdepend with selves. A self is conscientious. Conscience is an omnipresent feeling of fear, wherever values are at stake, that one will fail to attain what is most good. It is our feeling of oughtness manifesting itself whenever we become aware of threats to our goods. As all-pervasive, it appears to some to be the foundation of all ethics; some even try to reduce ethics to simply following one's own conscience. This view is correct, when conscience is conceived broadly enough, including both innate and acquired aspects; those who deny that either of these aspects is inherent in conscience must account for what is denied in other language having similar meanings. Difficulties in capturing the nature of conscience, which is experienced generally as a feeling of fear but not generally in terms of uniformly definable sets of ideas, has led to a plethora of descriptions suited to different philosophical schemes. Some insist that conscience is essentially innate. These differ, however, regarding whether it is "theologically implanted" (voice of God), "biologically evolved" (voice of the herd), or "axiologically inherent" (voice of a greater value claiming precedence over lesser values). Some insist that conscience is basically something acquired. These differ, also, regarding whether it is acquired "naturally" (as negative conditioning through stimulus-response mechanisms), "socially" (only from other persons, culture, including mores), or "intellectually" (from accepted theoretical explanations, whether logical, scientific, theological, nationalistic or cultistic, from which we deduce implications for right actions). Exclusivistic contentions favoring either innate or acquired theories are rejected by both Dualists and Organicists. Dualists contend that conscience is of two completely different sorts, innate and acquired; they tend to prefer different names for these two sorts, and may vary regarding which of the foregoing six explanations they prefer. Organicists see the innate and acquired aspects of conscience as interdependent. We cannot acquire what we do not already have some innate basis for acquiring, and innate conditions, not merely instincts but also size and weight, vitality and vigor, and general and specific varieties of hereditary intelligence, all are among the innate factors conditioning conscience. But acquired factors influence both individual and cultural development. For what persons acquire will influence which of their inherited factors become further developed, and inherited factors can be passed on to progeny only if individuals acquire the additional adaptive abilities needed for their particular circumstances. Thus a complex of interdependencies produces and sustains self as conscientious.

A self is intelligent, more or less, in several ways. Intelligence, variously conceived, is (1) wisdom, or happily enjoying life as an end-in-itself, (2) ability to attain the goal of life, (3) ability to understand and use the means to life's goal and prudence in choosing to act upon the better means (4) ability to adapt, both to relatively new and to relatively old situations, and (5) ability to score highly on intelligence tests. Ultimately, intelligence pertains to knowing what is good and how to get it, not merely temporary and trivial goods but ultimate and enduring goods, including the greatest goods of life, and not merely know-how but understanding, conviction and commitment regarding one's oughts or obligations. In its broadest and deepest meaning, "intelligence" is something all-pervasive and is essentially equivalent with ethical living, in the broadest and deepest meaning of the term "ethics."

Conclusion: A study of "individual "ethics" reveals that a self is organic. That is, on the one hand it is something simple, unique, integrated and persisting while on the other hand it is a complex of many multi-leveled interdependencies. These multiplicities constitute and determine the particular kind of uniqueness which each single self manifests. As unitary, a self is a substantial entity possessing its multiplicity of interdependent traits as characteristics. In so far as these characteristics are shared by other selves, generalizations about the nature of selves are possible. Many such generalizations have been selected for exploration in the preceding chapters. Each common trait has been observed to involve a complex of multi-leveled interdependencies, and each such observation may be regarded as a conclusion. But also, all of these aspectival traits exist interdependently, constituting a self an interdependency of interdependencies.

Although some will regard such amazing complexity as cause for abandoning concern for mastering ethical principles, either retreating to pessimism, accepting custom, submitting to impulse and whim, or planning to wait until confronted with a problem to decide what ought to be done, others will meet the challenge by trying to develop a complex and dynamic but principled approach to ethical problems. One may observe that, when self-interest, value, obligation, conscience and intelligence, for example, are conceived as omnipresent aspects of self, they not only overlap and interdepend but also parallel each other in such a way that insights relative to one provide insight also into the others. Discovery of a matrix of similarities provides clues to easing the problem, since solutions worked out relative to conscience or intelligence may serve as aids in dealing with problems regarding self-interest or obligation.

Furthermore, separation of treatment of individual and social ethics here may both show how certain kinds of problems which first appear independently at either an individual or a social level later become recognized as analogous in fundamental ways. Decisions concerning what you believe that a group ought to do about a particular problem may provide insight regarding how you should decide relative to an analogous personal problem. The complexities of interdependence between individual and social ethics we have yet to demonstrate. But here we may say, in general, that awareness of additional complexities can provide us with additional insights useable in many areas rather than being merely added tasks with which we are unequipped to deal. Conceiving self as integral as well as complex prepares us for seeing ways in which societies attain and retain integrity despite the diversities in their members and other-group relations. Discovery that groups require minimums of integrity and principles for maintaining such integrity may shed light upon how much integrity, and interest in principle, each individual may need to survive and prosper. Self is organic. Society is organic. Self and society are organically interrelated.

Why be moral? As suggested in Chapter I, this is what you most want to be. The method of demonstrating such a conclusion has been to show that it is something of a tautology. That is, a self can be known to be ethical by its very nature when we observe that it is or has intrinsic good at stake in its choices and actions and that it naturally most wants what is best for it. When oughtness is observed to consist in choosing and doing what is best, then one must conclude that doing what one ought and doing what is best for self in the long run are synonymous. When being moral consists in doing what you ought to do, then being moral, in this fundamental sense, is just what you most want to be.

PART II

SOCIETY

Chapter XVII

SOCIAL ETHICS

Social ethics presupposes the existence of groups and pertains to what is good for groups. Each group is concerned for what is good for itself and about what ought to be done in order to attain or keep that good. A group acts rightly when it intends to produce the best results for itself in the long run. What, then, is a group? A group consists of persons, two or more, aware of having common interests. On the one hand, the nature of groups is so obvious, since we live in groups almost all of the time, that any attempt to give a formal definition seems superfluous. Yet, on the other hand, the question "What is a group?" like the question "What is a self?" presents us with baffling paradoxes and varieties of uncertainty, when we seek to fix an answer with finality. We must leave to sociologists the problem of grappling with general definitions and accept, for convenience, one offered recently: A social group is "a number of persons whose relationships are based upon a set of interrelated roles and statuses whose relationships are based upon a set of interrelated roles and statuses, who share certain beliefs and values; and who are sufficiently aware of their shared or similar values and their relations to one another to be able to differentiate themselves from others." (Ely Chinoy, Society: An Introduction to Sociology, Random House, New York, 1961, p. 82.)

Although a group is not a person, for it has no human body, brain or mind, it is made up entirely of persons and their interrelationships and so serves the purposes of persons and shares with persons certain aspects of personality. We choose, in this text, to point out many analogies between individuals and groups of individuals and between individual ethics and social ethics. The extent to which groups and individuals are alike will continue to be debated among theorists. Some speak of a "group mind" (See William McDougall, The Group Mind, and John E. Boodin, The Social Mind, especially Chapter IV) and one has recently examined "The State as an Organism, as a Person, and as an End-in-itself." (H.J. McCloskey, Philosophical Review, July, 1963, Vol. LXXII, pp. 306-326.) We locate intrinsic value primarily in individuals and their feelings. Since social groups have no existence apart from individuals, individuals and their feelings are always present when groups exist. Hence, in this way, groups always involve intrinsic values. But they have no actual intrinsic value apart from individuals. Yet, even so, just as we judge the other persons, and sometimes animals, to have intrinsic value which we ourselves do not directly experience, so we often judge that a group is a kind of substantial entity and a locus of intrinsic value. Even though such value is imputed, a group may function as if seeming to have such value really through our functioning relative to it as if it had such value. Hence, functionally, or "behavioristically," groups seem to have intrinsic value and other characteristics of persons. They have them, we believe, as a consequence of their being composed of persons, dependent upon persons, and functioning as extensions of persons. We shall, in the following, employ ordinary language usage in referring to groups. Common sense, in English at least, regards a group as an "it" which can think and choose and act in such a way as to do, or fail to do, what is best for itself. A group too can "act rightly or wrongly" and have desires, needs, intentions, attitudes and commitments. But such intentions and acts are never separate from intentions and acts of individual members who constitute, or in some special way represent, the consensus of the group. Although we shall speak of groups acting wrongly, even in relation to some of their own members, such groups and wrong action never exist apart from some individual members who also share in, and are in some fundamental way responsible for, such action.

A group is not a person and a person is not a group; hence person and group are opposed. Yet a group is nothing apart from persons and is an extension of persons, so each group is a supplementary opposite of its members, not something antithetical to, or contradictory to, its members. Conflicts between a person and his groups occur partly as conflicts within a person himself, for a person always has more interests than those which are served by any one group. A major and continuing ethical issue facing each group is how much of each member's time, energy and total welfare shall be engaged in interdependence with it; conflict of interest appears both when a group demands too much and when it serves too little. Consequently the nature of each group may itself be more or less tenuous and fluctuating in its relations to each particular member. Yet the needs of individuals for group membership and for stable, useful and efficient groups assures the perpetuity of some groups, and the greater the needs which a group serves and the greater the efficiency with which it serves, the more enduring it tends to be.

Whenever members becomes aware of their common nature and interests, they tend to think and act in terms of those interests. Then all of the kinds of problems surveyed in Part I tend to recur relative to each group. In order to demonstrate the extent of analogous problems and analogous solutions between individual and social ethics, we have deliberately first separated and then correlated topics by chapters. Both

similarities and differences between individuals and groups must be kept
in mind as we proceed.   To ignore the differences is as serious a
shortcoming as to overlook similarities. Let us review, chapter-wise, some
analogies.

A group is dependent upon its members even as a self is dependent
upon its physical body. Different kinds of persons, young and old, male
and female, energetic and weak, generous and stingy, conscientious and
carefree, adaptable and stubborn, all contribute to the complicated sets
of conditions upon which a group depends. Levels of interests and needs
within members, regarding food, health, esteem, money, security, all
variably serve as foundations for groups. Yet each group somehow
maintains some central unity, some persisting wholeness, some simple
integrity, despite all of the divergent varieties of ingredients in the
individual and collective make-up of its members.   The various
antagonisms between members function as parts of the nature of each
group also. Hence each group involves a multicomplex dependence upon
its members even while its members depend upon it to serve some of
their own complexes of needs.

A group does not exist in isolation from other groups but interdepends
with them also and in various ways. Not only do groups depend upon
groups of the same kind, nations upon nations, states upon states,
communities on communities, families upon neighboring families, at least
for non-aggression and for peaceful and constructive cooperation in
matters of common interest, but also upon sub-groups and super-groups
of many sorts. A nation depends upon its member states, a state depends
upon its numerous communities and a community depends upon its
families, to mention only some more obvious examples. Even a four-
member family may contain several subgroups: parents versus children,
females versus males, father and daughter prefer sports while mother and
son prefer reading. But also children even as a group depend upon
families, families as groups depend upon communities, communities as
groups depend upon states, and states as groups depend upon nations.
Hence each group interdepends with groups of at last three different
levels. Each of these other groups provides influencing conditions upon
which or within which a group depends for its own nature, roles and
functions and, indeed, the success with which it performs its own functions
for its members. Some groups come into self-conscious existence as a
consequence of the existence and attitudes of other already-existing
groups: "Albuquerque has a ball team; why doesn't Santa Fe?" Some
groups mold their own policy after those of other successful groups:

"Their college offers a wider variety of majors than we do; we ought to improve our variety." Some groups come into existence as a consequence of culturally established laws: "Your high school will be accredited only if you provide for physical education classes." Hence groups are social not merely in the sense that they are composed of two or more persons but also in the sense that they automatically interdepend with other social groups.

Groups too may become selfish. But here we find new dimensions of selfishness. (a) A group may be selfish relative to its members. That is, it may demand more time, effort and loyalty from some or all of its members than it has a right to demand in light of its service to them. This selfishness may function through the attitudes of the group's leaders without being shared by all members or it may be present in the group's spirit which is shared in by all members in periods of group self-consciousness and enthusiasm. That is, in addition to selfishness which an individual may express in relation to another group member as an individual, and to another group member as a member of the group (requiring him to do more than his share of the group's work), and to the group as a group (seeking more than his share of the group's benefits), a member may participate in approving the group's selfishness, either relative to its members or to other groups as indicated below. These, then, are all dimensions of selfishness in which a person may participate. (b) A group may be selfish in relation to other groups of the same kind or level. States may have competing interests, such as those of Arizona and California over rights to water from the Colorado River. Nations may treat each other unfairly through tariff wars. (c) A group may be selfish in relation to a subgroup. A state may tax selected extraction industries such as uranium mining or certain consumer classes such as large families by excise or sales taxes. (d) A group may be selfish in relation to a higher group within which it is a subgroup. Some states, for example, may deliberately fail to perform needed services for its citizens so that the federal government will pay the bill.

All such kinds of group selfishness may involve problems regarding group esteem and group security, even if not love or adventure (except for sport or war). The ten principles cited in Chapter V may apply also to group tendencies. A thorough test of these principles would require trying them out in all of the dimensions of possible group selfishness just outlined. Although all of these dimensions are avenues through which an individual may express one's own selfishness, complications occur due to the indirect ways in which the effects of such selfishness redound. Such indirection may lead less cautious enthusiasts to endanger themselves unwittingly. Furthermore, less selfish members must share in suffering from the reciprocated consequences of group acts motivated by the wills of more selfish members. Problems regarding collective responsibility for the misdeeds of representative members of a group became appallingly complicated, so much that those inclined to escape facing responsibilities even more quickly seek excuses for evading group moral problems. But guarding against such willingness to escape may then become a primary moral duty of each group.

A group has values, in several senses. (a) It consists of persons, each of which is an end-in-itself or is the locus of one or many intrinsic values. In whatever sense persons as intrinsic values belong to a group, that group has those persons and their values as constituents. But persons also have instrumental values, in serving themselves and each other and the group; their skills, ownership, intelligence, etc., which function in them as members of the group thereby function as instrumental values possessed by the group. A group of wealthy citizens, for example, may be thought of as a wealthy group in whatever way their wealth is at the disposal of the group. (b) A group is useful, or instrumentally valuable, to its members in whatever way it serves them. Each different kind of group will have a different kind of service, hence some different kind of value, for its members. (c) When a group functions as if the locus of intrinsic good, it is something to be admired, appreciated and regarded as good, even as good-in-itself, a characteristic already noted in the second paragraph above. Even though the intrinsic value is imputed, its functioning as such in the minds of its members who, as patriots, for example, at times regard its goodness worth dying for, constitutes a behavioristic reality which its members and other groups must respect. (d) In addition, each group may have something popularly called "social values." What this vague general term means may be illustrated best in community groups. People have ideas or ideals about how they and others in their group should behave. These ideas, when established in practice, are called "mores" technically, or "customs" more loosely. They serve as standards both for behavior and for judgment. They tend to be stable, though they also tend to fluctuate like fashions and fads and even, in periods of group excitement and violence, manifest themselves as group will. They may be tabulated by anthropologists and public opinion pollsters. Sometimes called "public opinion," they powerfully influence individual behavior and serve as a primary means of social control. Despite the fact that they appear, under our analysis, to be superficial rather than fundamental values, they are most important practically because they are the value ideas occupying the minds and shaping the motives of individuals. Too many theories try to reduce ethics to mores, a tendency found among sociologists and anthropologists, especially those specializing in demography and idealizing science, including social sciences, as "value-free." Regardless of how this issue is settled among theorists, groups do have values in the sense that mores serve as standards for behavior and judgment, and these do function behavioristically as realities constituting part of the nature of each group. Not only do some groups consist of members who hold conservative or radical views, but we also speak of such groups as "conservative groups" or "radical groups."

Groups are evil also. They not only (a) consist of persons who are evil in the senses discussed in Chapter VII but also (b) may fail to serve their members well and even destroy some members through capital punishment, (c) become regarded as the locus of intrinsic evil (more evident in out-groups endangering us inimically, such as militaristic nations which come to be judged as "foreign devils"), and (d) embody "low" standards of conduct which bring degeneration to their citizens or war with their neighbors. Crime, corruption, immorality, destruction, all are imputed attributes of the group in which these characteristics prevail as traits of their members.

A group can be improved through the improvement of its members, of its members' service to it, of its service to them, of its service to other groups of the same kind or level, to subgroups and to those groups of which it is a part. Groups have obligations to themselves which become manifest as obligations to their members and to other groups with which they are related and, of course, to the members of those other groups. Groups act and hence function as actors or agents; they act through their members and especially through officers or leaders, though also, when the actuality of a group has established itself as something habitual in the minds of its members or in the minds of members of other groups, it may continue to function through its effects in those minds without specific volition, effort or consciousness on the part of leaders; groups act responsibly, in various senses, holding their members and officers responsible and being held responsible by their members and by members of other groups.

Groups are free, more or less, in several ways, not only because several kinds of freedom exist, as outlined in Chapter X, but also because groups provide freedoms for their members, are free to serve their members, and are free to serve other groups of various kinds and their members; unfreedoms, of course, exist also in all of these various ways.

Groups are sovereign in whatever sense they have self-control; not only do they serve as areas of sovereignty for their members and have some control over their members, but they may control as well as be controlled by other groups of the same kinds or levels, by their subgroups and by groups of which they are parts; of course, sovereignty is normally restricted and partial, and groups may be characterized by lack of sovereignty also in all of these various ways. Groups own not only their members and their relationships to other groups, but also rights delegated to them relative to property ownership and even rights to apportion ownership rights among their members.

Groups are just or unjust, gracious or ungracious, and have rights and duties. Since rights have their ultimate locus in intrinsic good, group rights depend ultimately upon the rights of individual selves with their inherent, if variable, values. But since each group's nature is limited to only some of the goods of each of its members, i.e., those shared in common by them, its rights are thereby limited also. Yet, despite these limitations, each group normally has a complex of rights, and duties, relative to its members and other groups of various sorts. When the multicomplex relations of each group are compounded with the multicomplex relations of each of its individual members, the problem of the nature of rights and duties will seem unmanageable if we do not retain some simplicity or perspective regarding the fundamental nature and locus of rights and duties in individuals. But also the task of deciding upon and acting upon rights and duties of groups cannot be handled merely in general; each particular right and duty needs to be attended to in its own way by specific decision and actions of each group member, often guided by, even coerced by, appropriate officials of the group. Larger and more intricate groups depend increasingly upon representative and authoritative officers; consequently problems relating both to the rights and duties of such officers and to other members grow in significance and in acuteness whenever failure occurs. As people become more socialized in multiplicities of ways, issues of social justice and, indeed, social grace, occupy larger roles in the lives and natures of individuals.

Groups have consciences. Of course, only persons have consciences, but when persons share concern about common goods which may be endangered or improved, they manifest conscientiousness as group members and naturally insist that their group officials manifest such concern conscientiously. Groups in which the consciences of the members, and, especially, the officers, are sensitive, alert and efficient may themselves be described as conscientious, for such groups then function behavioristically as if conscientiousness characterized actions of the group as a group.

Groups have intelligence. Of course, only persons have intelligence in the sense of consciously endeavoring to adapt to problem situations and in the sense of enjoying happiness as the goal of life. But to the extent that groups maximize these endeavors and enjoyments in their members, they too may function as if, and be described as, intelligent. Groups act, both through their officers and through the responses of their members, in ways more or less conductive to survival and happiness of their members; those which do survive and solve problems and conduce to happiness thereby behave as if, and hence are, more intelligent than those which do not. Social intelligence, involving all levels and kinds of groups, may become a larger part of each individual's intelligence as individuals become more socialized.

Why be moral? Or, now, why be concerned about group morality? Since morality pertains, ultimately, to what is best and what ought to be done in order to attain what is best, being moral is what one most wants to be. Hence each group also naturally wants what is best for itself as a group, and when each group has multiplex relations and relevant goods, what is best for it has multitudes of aspects. A group's main moral concerns focus primarily upon the welfare of its own members, of which it consists and without which it cannot maintain itself. But the welfare of its members may only partly depend upon, and waver relative to, it; hence its own nature and service, and what constitutes what is best for it relative to each member, may be very dynamic and tenuous. Furthermore, to the extent that a group depends upon its relations to other groups, especially when its existence is threatened by competition with them, what is best, and hence of greatest moral concern, may pertain to these relations. Thus, the question, "What is morality?" involves something which is itself variable and dynamic, so much so that individuals may feel overwhelmed and incompetent. Yet, since your morality pertains to your own goods, including your greatest goods, you cannot evade any of your moral concerns without denying something that is fundamental to yourself. If you choose, as an easy or lazy alternative, to let others make your decisions for you and take care of you as they choose, then you behave as a little child and should have no cause for complaint if you come to be treated as such. As a mature and able person, you want your groups to be moral because their morality is a fundamental part of your own.

Chapter XVIII

SOCIETY AS DEPENDENT UPON INDIVIDUALS

Analogy. A self depends for its existence and nature upon its body, organs, cells and other parts as continuing conditions. So likewise a group depends for its existence and nature upon its members and their natures (minds, bodies, organs, needs, habits, interests, skills, insight, etc.) as continuing conditions. Change in the members of a group, whether through loss or gain of members or loss or gain of any of their parts, such as health, wealth or willingness to cooperate, etc., affect the nature of a group and may determine its perpetuation or cessation, just as changes in a self's body, organs or cells may modify its nature and chances for success or failure. Since all analogies break down when pressed too far, we must use restraint in employing this one. But a general similarity does exist between how a self as a functioning whole depends upon its parts and how a group as a functioning whole depends upon its members as parts. Such dependence involves also an analogous interdependence; for the ways in which the members of a group participate, cooperatively or rebelliously, wholeheartedly or with cautious reserve, depends upon how well their interests appear to be served by that group, just as the health, energy and efficiency with which a self's bodily organs serve one depend upon how much concern one has given to their well-being.

Our analogy is not merely a factual one but also involves values. It is, for our purposes, basically an ethical analogy. That is, just as the existence and nature of the goods which a self enjoys depend upon the well being of its bodily conditions (including sense organs, nervous system, glandular system, sustained consciousness or vivacious will), so the existence and nature of the values enjoyed by a group (through the enjoyments of its members) depend upon the abilities, willingness and actual attentiveness with which its members function as group members. Instrumentally, of course, the analogy seems quite clear. The various ways in which a group depends upon its members serve as instruments to its existence and nature, and as instrumental values in whatever way these instruments eventuate in enjoyments of individuals as members of the group. These enjoyments of individuals <u>as members of a group</u> constitute the intrinsic goods of that group. It is the group, as a group, which, behavioristically, functions as the locus of those intrinsic goods experienced by the persons functioning as members of that group. Or, the interfunctioning of persons as group members and the functioning of a group as an active extension of those persons thereby function as enjoyment of intrinsic goods by that group. Our analogy breaks down in that the locus of the intrinsic goods of a group exist always as enjoyments experienced by persons. Yet, in the sense that no social groups can exist apart from persons and their conscious experiences, our basic analogy involves only a continuingly dependent kind and degree of independence for groups. When all things can exist only by being interdependent in the first place, any independence we talk about must be conditional and contingent. When people become antagonized by their groups, they tend to hate them and seek to separate themselves from them. Sometimes they succeed, and then interdependence ceases; but sometimes they can only minimize their interdependence with such group. But when they experience hatred toward a group, they thereby embody it as an intrinsic evil in their experiences. It continues to function and to exist in them negatively. Only when persons completely forget a group does it cease to function as an existing and value entity in them. Thus, behavioristically, groups have intrinsic value, contingently and dependently, just as individuals have intrinsic value, contingently and dependently upon their bodily parts.

Our analogy has ethical implications. For, as we have already seen in Part I, wherever intrinsic values are at stake, duty, obligation or oughtness exist. A group has obligations. It has them, first of all, to the individuals who are its members in the sense that, and to the extent that, they are its members; the point here is that, especially in specialized groups, the duty of a group to its members is limited, basically, to those ideals which its members share in common. A group must also respect its members as individuals, and hence also has limited rights corresponding to such limitations in duties. The duties and rights of a group remain inseparable from those of its members or exist as duties and rights of its members as members. Increasingly intricate societies naturally evolve greater number and kinds of specialized groups each involving its own quite strictly limited functions, duties and rights.

Groups Exist. Despite the obviousness of group existence, many persons will seek to deny the existence of groups, and consequently of group rights and duties. How do groups exist? Even though continuingly dependent upon individuals for their existence and nature, they do exist behaviorally and do so with sufficient endurance to be spoken of as substantial. In fact, some groups, such as a nation, a denomination or corporation, endure longer and hence are more substantial, than some or even all of their members. A nation may last for several centuries while all of its citizens live for less than one. Groups perform functions, hence act as substantial agents. Groups are the objects of action, recipients of effects, receivers of praise and blame, possessors of wealth. They may be receivers or payers of taxes. Groups have power, both over their own members and in relation to other groups. They may even cause individuals to come into being (by subsidizing births) or cease to be (through war or capital punishment). Thus they are centers or sources of causal efficacy.

Groups have location, some occupying a definite geographical area, such as a state or county, some identified by an established headquarters and a specific address, some merely by the presence of their members in whom they have their being. Different kinds of groups, each performing its own kind of function, have different kinds of existence, power, location, and duration. Groups may also own and be free, just and gracious, and have sovereignty, intelligence and conscientiousness, and thus function substantially as possessors of all of these characteristics. The existence of groups seems beyond doubt to anyone who investigates the matter carefully, as well as to all of us in our more uncritical moments when we automatically presuppose existence of the groups of which we are members. "The social state is at once so natural, so necessary, and so habitual to man, that...he never conceives himself otherwise than as a member of a body....people grow up unable to conceive as possible to them a state of total disregard of other people's interests." (John Stuart Mill, Utilitarianism). The ways in which groups exist, however, is not always so clear.

Groups Depend. Groups depend on members. But how? Both for their existence and for their nature.

No groups can exist actually without members. What a group is and some of the ways in which a group depends have been discussed already in Chapter XVI. These will not be repeated here. But we wish to stress the need for keeping in mind that, despite their substantiality and powerful agency, groups continue to exist and function only through the continuing awareness and willingness of individuals to function as participants in them. Of course, buildings, constitutions, ordinances, books, etc., may be created to remind us of our willingness to participate. So the existence of some groups, such as memorial societies, may depend also upon mechanical instruments which prod our memories, upon buildings and conveyances which make assembly possible, upon a postal system which enables sending of notices of meetings, upon officials who earn their living by bearing responsibilities relative to maintaining memorials, and upon laws which protect memorial rights. When all members of a group cease to exist, the group thereby ceases to exist. But also, when all members of a group cease to be aware of the group, it ceases to exist, except insofar as there are potentialities for its being revived in awareness. And when all members of a group cease to be willing to accept membership in the group (except when forced), the group ceases to exist as an active agent. Thus, basically, groups are completely dependent upon individuals for their existence.

Groups depend upon members also for their nature. The nature of a group consists in what it is or does. Hence, observation of the different kinds of functions which groups perform reveals their natures, or "whatnesses," and thus how they differ as kinds of groups.

Groups vary in numbers of members, in mobility, i.e., whether members remain the same or change rapidly, in whether members are alike or different, in whether they perform few or many functions for members, in whether they perform the same functions for all members or different functions for different members, in whether they perform functions rather continuously or only occasionally, e.g., once in a lifetime, etc.

The natures of groups vary as the needs and wants of individuals differ. Hence the natures of groups are involved in how individuals differ in capacities or incapacities, in their age, sex, size, health, temperament, training and dreams, in their willingness or unwillingness to have groups perform functions for them, in their insight, or lack of it, regarding what a group can do for them and what is required of the individual as a member of it. Such insight, which may be more difficult to acquire as groups become more numerous, complex and specialized, is fundamental to group existence. Groups depend upon the presence in individuals of understanding what responsibilities are needed and willingness to accept responsibility both for having functions performed for them and for doing what is needed in response or repayment by the group.

The natures of groups vary in morale, or in the sense of loyalty which members have as a consequence of awareness of the values which their groups have for them. Loyalty to a group, which grows naturally from the self-interest an individual has as a member aware of its value to him is something necessary to group existence. ("In so far as one identifies himself with a whole, loyalty to that whole is loyalty to himself; it is self-realization, something in which one cannot fail without losing self-respect." (Charles Horton Cooley, Introductory Sociology, p. 62. Charles

Scribner's Sons, New York, 1933.) The natures of groups vary with the varieties and intensities of loyalties of their members. Some loyalties occur naturally, as when a person is born, reared and protected in a family, tribal or national group. Some must be instilled and maintained by artificial methods, such as enrollment, propaganda, contract, and official pressure.

Hence groups depend for their existence and nature upon the fact and character of their interdependencies. The functions which groups perform for their members and the awareness and willingness of individual members to have those functions performed for them interdepend. These functions vary, for groups may depend much more upon some members than upon others; and some members are much more dependent upon a group than other members. The varieties of ways in which members cooperate and compete relative to a group's services affect the nature of such interdependence and hence the nature of the group.

When we realize how tenuous are the bases for the existence of groups, we may wonder how so many of them can remain so substantial and function so effectively. The variability and evanescence of awareness of, attitudes toward, and willingness to accept responsible membership in, groups seems to be a very unstable foundation for groups. It is true that some groups, such as casual groups, movie groups, college class, groups may be quite evanescent. Yet, wherever there are actual social needs, these attitudes must occur, and the substantiality of groups has a continuing basis in the substantiality of these individual needs. We cannot here repeat consideration of the ways in which each self is fundamentally social. (See Part I, especially Chapters IV & V.) But we should keep in mind the nature, mechanisms and principles of developing and maintaining "we-feelings." (See Fritz Kunkel, Character, Growth and Education, J. B. Lippencott, Philadelphia, 1938, and Alfred Shutz, Collected Papers II, Studies in Social Theory, 3rd Ed., M. Nijhoff, The Hague, 1971.) And we should be aware of ethical implications of this tenuousness and of these mechanisms.

A point needing emphasis here is that groups ought to be concerned about their health as groups, even as individuals need to attend to physical health. Just as a person must care for his body against ills of deterioration, so a group often needs to give attention to the conditions which are necessary to maintain its existence and effective functioning. That is, it must keep its members aware of it, interested in it, loyal to it, and responsible for it. A mother, for example, in caring for her children tries to have them regard and treat each other as brothers and sisters. A nation may wisely encourage its school children to "pledge allegiance to the flag and to the republic for which it stands" every morning. Colleges use intercollegiate sports competition as means for promoting a spirit of unity.

Implications of the tenuousness of group existence for ethics include need for maintaining awareness of certain oughts. Groups, like individuals, have certain oughts that are fundamental to their existence, namely, those that have to do with their existence, nature and health. Whoever becomes responsible for the continuance of a group immediately thereby acquires, in addition to one's other oughts, those obligations necessary to insure existence and proper functioning of the group. Sometimes these obligations must be concerns of all members; sometimes they are delegated to specific officials. However distributed, these obligations must be met if the group is to exist.

Since a group cannot exist or function independently of its members and their interests or values, a group ought to be concerned about the welfare of its members. Its oughts and their oughts interdepend. Some groups depend on individuals much more than their individual members depend on them. This is true, for example, of corporations, audience groups, and casual groups. But also some individuals depend on some of their groups much more than those groups depend on them. The dependencies of an infant on its family, a native on his tribe, a citizen on his nation serve as examples. Hence, not only do a group's oughts interdepend with the oughts of its members; but oughts vary, and consequently there may be considerable variations in the ways in which these oughts interdepend. But such variability does not constitute mere relativity. Insofar as such different groups are alike relative to such oughts and such interdependence, we have a basis for generalization about them. Even generalization about variability remains generalization rather than mere relativity. So, although the kinds of similarities may be somewhat more difficult to discover as society becomes more megalopolitan, bases remain and the need for discovery of them may thus become all the more urgent for those concerned with social ethics.

Chapter XIX

SOCIETY AS INTERDEPENDENCE OF GROUPS

In the previous chapter, we emphasized dependence of groups upon individuals. In the present chapter, we stress how each group depends also upon other groups, sometimes for its existence, usually for some part of its nature.

Thus, we continue to explore certain analogies between groups and individuals. Wholes and parts interdepend. Not only do wholes depend upon parts but parts depend upon wholes. For those to whom this generalization is not immediately obvious, we state it more fully: Not only does a whole of parts depend upon its parts in order to be the whole that it is, but also each part of a whole depends both upon the whole in order to be a part of that whole and upon all of the other parts without which that whole could not be as it is. A person depends upon one's bodily organs and each organ depends upon the continuing function of one's body as a whole; but also a person is part of a family as a social whole and depends upon all the other members of this family in constituting that group of which one is a member. Likewise, a group, such as a family, depends upon its members, while each member can be a member of that family only if there is such a family as a whole; but also a family group depends for its existence in a tribe, community, city or nation both upon the existence of that group and upon all of the other families needed to constitute it as such a group. Thus far, the analogy is clear.

To the extent that groups are like individuals in these ways, certain like consequences follow for ethics. Each group has interests. These may be thought of as self-interests. Although a group does not have a "self" in the same sense that a person is or has a self, it is regarded, both by its members and by members of other groups, as an entity with a nature and needs which function as interests. It does not have consciousness, desires and enjoyment of intrinsic values apart from those of its members; yet in whatever way it behaves as a substantial unity embodying in the interests of the persons who are its members, it may be thought of as if having such consciousness, desires and enjoyment. Although we speak of a "group itself," its interests are never separable from those of its members, for they are interests of its members; however, since its members are persons having other interests also, conflicts may exist between an individual's interests as a member of a group and his other interests. So, although in general a group's interest remain inseparable from those of its members, sometimes a group must protect its interests against those of an individual whose other interests are antagonistic to it, and sometimes an individual must protect one's other interests against those of one's group when antagonism occurs between them. Among the ethical implications of the whole-part relationships inherent in the nature of groups are those involved in deciding and choosing what is best for a group when such a partial conflict of interests exists. (Newsworthy examples appear whenever an owner of private investments which stand to profit from government favoritism assumes a public office in which his decisions will have a bearing upon such favoritism.)

But our concern here is primarily with how groups interdepend. Whereas some groups, such as geographically isolated communities, remain relatively independent, some other groups, such as a local barber's union or a school district, are very dependent. "Two general types of communities may be recognized, the independent and the dependent. As with most dichotomies, this classification is a first approximation to an adequate description of differences. Independent and dependent classes of communities should be thought of as comprising two parts of a continuum which measures degree of independence.   If complete independence is represented on a scale by -1, and complete dependence by +1, then all communities which fall below an indistinct "midpoint" -- the 0-point -- comprise the independent class, and all that fall above the 0-point make up the dependent class. Differences between communities, in other words, are conceived as quantitative rather than qualitative in character. Furthermore, it is entirely probable that (extreme) polar types on the scale of independence are nowhere to be found.   Complete independence may occur from time to time, but only under extraordinary circumstances. On the other hand, complete dependence of a community is illogical, for the very concept of community implies a separate identity." (Amos H. Hawley, Human Ecology, A Theory of Community Structure, p. 222. The Ronald Press Company, N.Y., 1950.)

Such partial independence and partial dependence together constitute interdependence. Great varieties and degrees of such interdependence complexify the problem of understanding the nature of interdependence and ethical implications thereof. But possibilities for generalizing about the nature of group interdependence do provide bases for ethical principles relative to it.

For example, to the extent that groups interdepend, they need to consider each others' nature and welfare when deciding what to do. The more one group depends upon another, the more it owes to itself the effort to concern itself with the welfare of the group upon which it depends. Whenever a group, like a dog, "bites the hand that feeds it," it places itself in jeopardy and acts wrongly because it endangers its own interests. The principle of reciprocity tends to work between groups, through the thinking of its responsible members. Hence, awareness of both common needs and of respective duties between groups, and ability and willingness to fulfill group duties, are required if group interdependence is to persist. Wherever values are at stake, each of two interdependent groups has duties, obligations or oughts relative to the other. When these duties are neglected, both groups may suffer. A specific problem common to all group interdependencies has to do with keeping the responsible members of both groups aware of the shared interests and of differential duties and needs, and sensitive to fluctuations in the ways in which the carrying out of duties needs to be reciprocated. Thus problems of justice and grace, rights and duties, etc., occur between groups as well as between individuals. The purpose of Part II of this volume is to examine problems involved in what is good for groups and what group members ought to choose and decide to do in order to attain such good.

Two kinds of relations between groups should be noted, namely, those between groups that are relatively coordinate or equal, such as two families, two cities, or two nations, and those between groups which have hierarchial relations, such as a family and a city, a city and a state, or a state and a nation. The former will be named "peer" groups, meaning that they are on a par with each other. The latter will be named "superior" and "inferior," or higher and lower, to indicate that the lower is a part of the higher and that the higher is a whole of which the lower is a part. Although some of the problems and ethical principles involved in these two kinds of relations are the same, some are different also. We will treat peer groups first.

Interdependence of Peer Groups. Many kinds of peer groups exist. They exist, doubtless, at every level, except at the top or world level, where there cannot be two truly world governments, and at the bottom, where a group of two companions can have no sub-groups. Two families, two villages, two cities, two states, two nations, two international alliances all illustrate relatively coordinate and coequal peer groups. Although, as we shall show in discussing hierarchically related groups, interdependence exists between them also, there is a sense in which the above-mentioned peer groups seem relatively independent of each other. In contrast, more clearly dependent peer groups exist within other groups. For example, within an incorporated city, various departments, such as the police, street maintenance, and tax collection departments, are coordinate in the sense that they all exist to provide needed services for the city group. Within a nation, legislative, administrative and judicial branches may exist coordinately, or corporations, such as mining, manufacturing, transporting, distributing, retailing, and banking, may exist coordinately. The kinds of interdependence differ somewhat when the peer groups are more dependent upon than independent of higher-level groups. Let us consider both kinds.

a. Two nations, in the present age of nationalism, tend to regard themselves as quite independent of each other. Their entry into any alliance seems wholly a matter of decision and consent by independent entities. Yet even the most isolated nations, now that jet plane speeds have made every portion of our globe accessible in a few hours, are dependent upon other nations in order to remain unmolested. When H-bomb owning countries can deliver total destruction anywhere in the world in a short time, people of every nation depend for their existence, quietude and welfare upon the willingness of H-bomb nations, at least, to refrain from disturbing them. Controversies about the morality of permitting atomic fall-out debris to drift over helpless countries has dramatized this kind of dependence. Likewise, to the extent that H-bomb possessing countries retain conscientious concern about the welfare of other peoples, they are forced to refrain even from experiments which may produce deleterious effects.

Other now-dramatic developments include population explosion, rapid growth in industrial production differentials between developed and developing nations, increasing imbalances in payments between nations for import-export inequalities, airline speed for the spread of contagious diseases, book copyright pirating, and difficulties in defense against international crime syndicates when they are protected in some countries. For a long time, our social scientists have been telling us about "the realities of economic interdependence. A famine or a boycott in India, a revolution in China, a depression in the United States affects the economic welfare of the whole civilized world." (R.M. MacIver, Society: Its Structure and Changes, p. 204. Ray Long and Richard Smith, Inc., N.Y., 1931, 1933.) Failure or refusal by any one nation to control conditions within or between nations relative to any one of the above problems may have a crucial bearing upon conditions in others. For example, public decisions regarding taxing or subsidizing the production of cotton in western Texas may make a difference in whether an Egyptian fellahin lives or dies due to the marketability of his cotton in the world market. The dependence of some individuals in one part of the world upon the behavior of individuals in other parts is much more intricate and much more delicate than is commonly believed. In an age of extreme nationalism, individuals depend upon the insight and willingness which their national leaders have in cooperating with leaders of other nations in dealing with joint problems. Solutions cannot be expected to be easy, because any action relative to one problem has consequences for other kinds of problems and the people affected by them. The intricacies of interdependence among even relatively independent nations stagger our imagination. Among our most troublesome moral problems are those involving attainment of sufficient insight so that we can act to solve some problems without creating still more other problems.

b. As examples of two peer groups coequally dependent upon a larger group of which they are integral parts, we select the legislative and administrative branches of the government of the United States, ignoring the judicial branch as a third such peer group. Each of these two specialized groups consists of persons who are officers. Each group has its nature and functions determined by the purposes it serves within the nation as formally, and actually, constituted. Each group is complex within itself: the legislative branch has two houses, the Senate and the House of Representatives, each of which organizes itself, with committees, chairmen, consultants, and varieties of staff members. The administrative branch divides itself into numerous departments, each headed by a secretary who has his own staff of specialists, functionaries, consultants, and clerical help. Except for the formalized overlapping, in which the administrative Vice President is also the President of the Senate, the two branches function as relatively independent bodies. Each has its own work to do. It is not a function of the legislature to administer and it is not a function of the administration to legislate. Yet the fact that they were both created to serve the interests of the nation makes their nature and functions such that they are constantly interinvolved.

The powers of administration are limited or enabled by legislative provisions; the financial support of legislative staff salaries and building maintenance comes from the administration. Problems faced by the administration in dealing with practical situations reveal needs for legislation not yet enacted and generate proposals by administrators for legislation which can be enacted only by the legislators. Sometimes the legislative and sometimes the administrative branch takes the initiative in seeking to improve affairs. But neither can be very effective for long without gaining the consent and cooperation of the other.   If the legislature enacts a law which the administration cannot enforce, the legislature is responsible for creating problems for the administration. If the administration refuses to implement legislation, the legislature is helpless. If the legislature refuses to enact the legislation enabling the administration to remedy a practical evil, the administration is helpless. When the administration oversteps the boundaries of either its legal rights or its duties, then the legislature may be compelled to enact further specific legislation to curb or enable administrative action. The welfare of each branch, both as an organization and the persons who work in it, depends upon the adequacy of both its own efforts and that of the other branch in maintaining the welfare of the nation.

The moral problems peculiar to the interrelations of legislative and administrative branches of our government include the need for constant sensitivity to shifts of the locus of responsibility for initiating and for supplementing services which each should provide for the other in their joint support of the national group.   Service to the interests of the national or superior group remain primary duties of coordinate subgroups, whereas the duties of each of two relatively independent nations remain focused primarily upon the interests of these groups themselves. Hence, there are fundamental differences in the primary loci of duties of relatively independent as compared with relatively dependent kinds of peer groups. In some ways the moral problems of dependent peer groups are more complicated than those of independent peer groups, for each must operate within conditions over which it has only subordinate control.   Yet, on the other hand, when some of the responsibility for dealing with the problems of a nation is borne by another group, one group has less responsibility than if it had to bear all the responsibility for the nation.

Interdependence of Hierarchically-Related Groups. Groups interdepend hierarchically. That is, higher or larger groups depend upon lower or smaller constituent groups. For example, communities depend for their existence and nature upon the families which constitute them. States depend upon the communities, rural and urban, which compose them. Our nation depends upon the fifty states of which it consists.   A federation of nations depends upon its nations.   But also, lower or constituent groups depend upon higher or more inclusive groups.   A family living in isolation may have less chance for survival than one living in community with others and sharing a division of labor, including joint protection. Communities depend upon their states for providing inter-community regulation, smoothing interrelations and preventing friction. Our states depend upon our national government for interstate disciplines and for protection against other nations, and for coping with problems within the nation too big for communities and states to manage. The magnitude of national military budgets is a measure of how much we now need a world government that will assure peace and do so at a lower cost.

That higher and lower groups depend upon each other should be quite obvious. But the multiplicity and complexity of ways in which they interdepend may not be so obvious. We mention two kinds of ways.

a. Doubtless there are some general kinds of ways in which hierarchial groups interdepend that are common to all of them. Sometimes the existence, but always the nature, of each is affected by the others. The kinds and amount of support, service, opposition, conflict, and either rigidity or initiation of change which each provides for the others, influence their natures. To the extent that the analogy between groups and individuals holds, these ways of interdependence are such that they involve relations contributing to typical moral problems. Since each group is a locus of value, typical value problems recur. Problems such as those dealt with in Chapters X-XII, pertaining to freedom, sovereignty, ownership, and justice, for example, are involved. These will be illustrated by considering justice. A higher group may be just or unjust in the distribution of its services (protection, support, utilization) to its various subgroups. E.g., a nation may distribute its welfare funds evenly or unevenly among its states. And a higher group may be reciprocally just or unjust in the ways it takes taxes from and returns its services to a single state or to all of its states together. Such problems will be explored in the following chapters.

b. Special purpose groups tend to have their ways of interdepending with higher and lower groups that are peculiar to their purposes. Some such groups are clearly subordinate, as a judicial branch within a national government. But sometimes special purpose groups have their own complex hierarchies within them. A banking system incorporated in one state may have regional and state organizations for its numerous city banks, each of which city bank may have several branches. Such an institution may in some respects parallel political units in the number of its hierarchical levels, even entering into international banking alliances. The same tends to happen regarding manufacturing, distributing, retailing, professional, religious, recreational, insurance and communicational institutions. When we realize how complicated are the hierarchical relations within each such private institution, how these hierarchical systems, e.g., two banking systems, interdepend in competition with each other as peer groups, how they interdepend with the political units at each level of political hierarchy, we may well wonder how social life manages to exist and function with as little friction as it does. The problem of keeping in mind how principles of reciprocity function between not only peer groups and between two hierarchically related groups, but also between hierarchies of peer groups and peer relations between hierarchies of groups, is beyond the capacity of most of us. Yet one can have no clear grasp of the full nature of ethics and ethical principles until one comprehends how complicated have become the interrelations between social groups.

We need to keep in mind also that a fundamental part of the way in which groups interdepend is through each particular individual which they serve. Each individual is a complex, multi-leveled, multidimensional personality some of whose parts are interinvolved with the complex interdependencies of the hierarchical group systems which serve them. These intricacies of inter-group cooperation and conflicts at many levels function also as cooperation-conflict areas in each of many personalities. And the ways in which these intricacies so function fluctuate dynamically throughout each person's growth, development, maturation and decline. Hence, the moral issues involved in both peer and hierarchical group interdependencies exist also as personal moral problems to the extent that individuals identify themselves with these groups.

Differentials, and shifts, in the extents to which higher-level groups depend upon their lower-level constituents not only operate as shifts in personalities, but involve shifts in moral problems for persons as changes in the relative amounts of authority, responsibility and capacity of higher versus lower-level groups occur. When such changes happen, changes in the insights of both the individuals affected and the individuals serving as officers are needed. Relatively stable societies, including relatively stable hierarchical group interrelationships, diminish the moral efforts of individuals, except to the extent that stability tends to be accompanied by obsolescence of service. Some kinds of functions, such as prevention of war, seem best managed by higher-level groups; when so, individualistic or anarchical tendencies, or over-assertion by lower-level groups, become evils and need to be restrained. Other functions, such as provision of affection, esteem, and companionship, seem normally best served by lower-level groups; when so, undue restriction, regulation or interference by higher-level groups tends to become evil and needs to be diminished.

The search for easy solutions, such as either totalitarian control, decision and execution of human welfare programs, or anarchical laissez faire, must be discouraged. Every way of reducing moral problems or of easing their solution needs to be encouraged. But sometimes the seemingly hardest way, i.e., becoming aware of and grappling with complexities as they exist, turns out to be the easiest way in the long run.

Society as Itself Societal. Social ethics, in being concerned with the moral problems of groups as groups, immediately involves itself in ways in which each group is interrelated with other groups. When the representatives of a group, such as a nation, seek to secure or pursue the best interests of that nation, they must consider not only how to prevent some individuals from taking undue advantage of the nation, and how to conduct national affairs internally in such a way as to be best for the nation in the long run, but also how to serve national interests through interactions with other nations as peer groups, international alliances and world government, if any, as superior groups, and both its constituent states or provinces, its legislative, judicial and administrative branches, and its private and semi-public corporations serving its special interests, as inferior groups. These multi-pronged needs make the task of dealing with them responsibly quite unenviable. But their existence needs to be recognized constantly. And the nature of society, as consisting of groups, is, in a dialectically significant sense, also societal. That is, not only is a group an association of individuals but a group also associates with other groups, and whatever problems arise from the ways in which groups associate with each other become problems in social ethics.

Chapter XX

SOCIAL POLICY

Self-Interest. How should a group act in order to produce what is best for itself in the long run? Questions of social policy have to do with the interests, values, or welfare of groups. Each group naturally is self-interested, or takes an interest in promoting whatever is good for it and in eliminating whatever is bad for it. If a course of action seems most likely to lead to best results for the group, it may be spoken of as a wise policy. Basic to questions of social policy are problems of discovering and deciding upon what is best for a group. To the extent that all groups are alike, we should be able to discover some principles for determining social policy which are alike for all. But also each kind of group has its own peculiar nature and problems, and hence peculiar kinds of interests and values, and kinds of action needed to attain and preserve them.

As we have seen in the previous chapter, all groups, except those at the extreme top or bottom of a social hierarchy, have at least three kinds of relationships, or interdependencies, inherent in their natures. First, groups are composed of subordinate constituents. These are either individual persons or groups which are composed either of persons or of other groups composed of persons, etc. So, the task of caring for the interests of such persons directly or through caring for the interests of subordinate groups is a kind of interest common to most groups. Secondly, groups normally function as members of larger groups. To the extent that the welfare of a group interdepends with that of a larger group, this group needs to consider the welfare of that larger group in determining its own social policy. Thirdly, most groups have peer groups, some of which may be relatively independent of them and some of which may be intimately interrelated with them through mutual integration in some hierarchy. Concern for the welfare of peer groups is thus involved in a group's social policy. Hence, most groups have at least three kinds of interests in common. So there are at least three kinds of social policy that every group should have, unless a group happens to be the highest in a hierarchy and so can have no peers or superior group-relations.

But these three kinds of relations, which partly constitute a group's nature, do not constitute the whole of its nature. Each group possesses also a kind of particularity or uniqueness in terms of which its self-interest and basic policy should be formulated. A group's policy should not be expected to be exactly like that of other groups except in the ways in which it is exactly like those groups. To the extent that a group is different from other groups, its policy should be expected to be different also. Where likenesses exist, one group may profit from studying the policies adopted by other groups. When groups differ, slavish, uncritical patterning of policy by one group after the policy of another group is likely to lead to misfortune. But no matter how complex the interrelations and interests of a group, a wise social policy should be designed to take care of those interests.

Conflict of Interests. Groups, like individuals, meet, sometimes constantly, the problem of discovering what are their true interests. Groups, too, interdepend with others, whether individuals or groups, which are in conflict with each other. Consequently, conflicts arise in groups much as personality conflicts arise in individuals. Let us consider these relative to the three kinds of relations summarized above.

A group may suffer from conflicts between its constituents. A mother, interested in what is best for her family, including her son and daughter, finds that if her son goes to college her daughter cannot go to college. She is interested in both, and in their feeling that she is fair to both. What is the best family policy? A nation, interested in the welfare of all its people, must choose between financing a huge dam for power and irrigation in some Western states and a badly-needed interurban rapid-transit system in some Eastern states. What is the best national policy? Despite the apparent unsolvability of the two foregoing problems, they seem simple when compared with those involving active antagonisms. When one child has deliberately destroyed another's cherished knick-knack and the other vows to "get even," how can a mother, interested in what is best, and fair, for both, and in preventing family harmony from degenerating into deepening conflict, decide what to do? When one nation has attacked and conquered some territory of a weaker nation, how can a world government act to readjust affairs, especially when it itself depends heavily for its own strength upon the stronger nation?

A group may suffer from conflicts with its superior group. Even when it depends upon its superior group and its superior group depends upon it, both having mutual needs and wants which can best be served by continuing interdependence, the superior group has other interests which, at times, it favors. The superior group may be too much concerned about its own major problems and neglect its services to the inferior group. For example, a family may depend upon its community for protective services, for food supply, utilities and even employment, and its community may depend upon it both as a source of taxes and a source of service, as when the spouse is a teacher. The community government may raise taxes even when a family happens to be in dire circumstances, and a teacher may have to remain at work when illness in his family would be served best by his being at home. Hence a family can be harmed as well as helped by its community. Likewise, a border state in a nation depends for its existence and welfare upon the protective army of its nation; yet, the nation may decide to fight at a time when this state is particularly vulnerable to devastation (as when harvests are ripe). The nation may decide that its best interests should be pursued even at the risk of great loss to the particular state. Then, such a state will suffer much from action by its nation. Furthermore, a superior group may favor one sub-group at the expense of others. For example, two needy, tax-paying families, both needing employment of one member as a teacher, find that only one can be employed. Or a state may discover that the nation is taxing it to support flood control facilities in other states, while its own flood dangers go unattended. Conflicts of interest between a group and its superior group occur normally, just as conflicts between an individual and his group naturally exist.

A group often suffers from conflicts with its peer groups. Families may compete with each other for jobs, property, esteem. Members of a family may collectively join in lying about stealing from or even killing other families; and thereby establish for themselves life-long enemies. Vendettas illustrate extreme cases. Nations likewise compete with each other for property, resources, markets and esteem. Tariffs, blockades, sorties, alliances, and war all illustrate techniques whereby nations seek to gain economic advantage. Although some genuine conflicts of interest exist, there are also ways of maximizing or minimizing those conflicts which are not genuine. That is, sometimes cooperation would improve the welfare of both of two non-cooperating nations. In such situations, any conflict which prevents cooperation is a needless additional conflict. Now, although the ethics of necessary and of needless conflict differ in some respects, the minimizing of suffering should be sought in both cases. This is true of two branches of a government as well as of two independent nations. Do moral principles of interaction between two peer groups exist which are analogous to those pertaining to interactions between two persons?

Evaluation of Interests. Each group faces the problem of discovering what is actually best for it. Having so many kinds of interests, it must decide both which are essential to it and which are most important to it.

Just as an individual must struggle with the question, "What am I?" so each group needs to obtain some working conception about its own nature. What is its purpose? Why does it exist? What are its functions? How far does it extend? Groups often formalize their conceptions in constitutions, charters, contracts, or rules for incorporation. Private companies typically become "Ltd." or limited in their nature, functions and responsibilities. Some marriage contracts specify "until death do us part." Democratic nations require constitutions. School districts determine their boundaries and quality and quantity of educational services oftentimes in charters. Some companies operate under a "license."

Sometimes a group establishes a very fixed and unchanging conception of itself. Constitutions may be unamendable. Divorce may be illegal. Other groups conceive themselves in terms of prospects for variability. A family may build a two-bedroom home but design it so that additional bedrooms can be added if more children arrive, or in such a way that a portion of the house can be rented, when children leave home. The United States Constitution was designed so that additional states could join as population expanded into new territories. A banking company may plan, in its initial charter, to add branches in the same city, or even in other states. Ethical problems of group incorporation include those of deciding how fixedly or how flexibly a group should conceive its nature and purpose.

Whereas groups with too rigid institutions suffer difficulties in making adjustments to unforeseen novelties, dynamic groups suffer discomforts of growing too much or too little, of becoming too large or too small, of evolving too complexly or remaining too simple. Among a family's oughts are: not to have too many children, and not to have too few. Such an issue cannot be settled in isolation from all other interests of the family; nor should it be decided merely on the basis of world statistics about family sizes. Clark Kerr, former president of the mammoth, sprawling University of California, asked the question recently in Harper's Magazine, "The Multiversity. Are Its Several Souls Worth Saving?" The "uni" in "university" has become such a vast "multi" with so many competing interests, that it can hardly retain more than a budgetary and formal control type of integrity. The "impersonality" which students experience in contacting its different offices results naturally from the growing independence and self-interest of each office relative to performing its limited functions. A nation or a corporation, like a family or a university, can grow too large for its own best interests as well as for the interests of those whom it serves. It may also become too small.

Hence, the ethics of groups self-interest involves oughts and ought-nots regarding growing or shrinking too much. A group not only ought to seek what is best for itself, but it ought also to conceive itself, and try to extend or to limit itself, in such a way as to remain within some optimum range of its opportunities for expanding or contracting.

Types of Interest. Since the purpose of groups is to serve the needs and desires of their individual members, all such individual interests may be expected to become the interests of some groups.

Especially in primary groups, such as families, children's play groups, and small self-sufficient communities, where relations between members are very intimate and personal, all, or most, of each person's interests may be expressed and served. Hence, the classification of interests used to organize Chapter V can serve as a basis for surveying the kinds of interests of primary groups also. While security is a fundamental concern, or presupposition, of all groups, desire for recognition or esteem and for companionship or love also occupy central places in primary groups. Groups of individuals, like individuals themselves, tend to be concerned about their esteem. When a neighborhood or a school contains many children, there is a tendency for them to form cliques, each of which regards itself as superior in some way. At certain ages, when consciousness of sex differences becomes socially significant, members of boys' groups and of girls' groups dare not risk their esteem by associating much with members of the opposite sex. Members of intimate groups also enjoy fun together, and often satisfy their recreational interests through group activities.

However, in larger, more impersonal groups, such as cities, states and nations, where intimacy often becomes impossible, companionship and recreation interests tend to disappear as group concerns, whereas security and esteem become predominant. In other specialized groups, such as associations for purposes of manufacturing, transporting or retailing, the types of interests become highly restricted. However, both nations and corporations which find that they prosper more when all the interests of their group members are satisfied, may give specific attention to efforts that will assure individual welfare in all areas. National parks, public welfare, medical, and mental health programs exemplify ways in which our nation takes an interest in recreation and companionship needs of citizens. Corporations often support or provide community services aimed at assuring sufficient recreational and family happiness. But we shall focus our attention upon security and esteem while discussing groups.

National holidays and festivals can be cited as examples of national interest in recreation; but originally these were more often motivated by concern about national pride, whereas the recreational aspects, appealing more to children, have come to predominate as dangers to security or esteem have declined. The importance of national pride to a nation may be observed in how often nations have gone to war over insults.

Systematic survey of types of interests of groups must be omitted here. Each of the social sciences has its own area of group interests to explore and explain. Sociology, anthropology, economics, political science, social psychology, and jurisprudence, for example, represent main fields of scientific inquiry. In each, the scientist has the task of trying to understand the nature and needs of many kinds of groups. In the process, he reveals what is good or bad in the way of promoting security or esteem, from which implications for moral behavior follow. No study of social ethics can be complete without considerable investigation into the current conclusions of all the social sciences.

The Principle of Reciprocity. In addition to multiplicities of specific principles of interaction by different kinds of groups under varying physical, geographical, biological, and psychological conditions, there is one principle basic to social ethics that parallels a principle foundational to individual ethics. This is the principle of reciprocity. Groups tend to treat each other as they are treated.

Although no entity which we can call a "group mind" exists, groups function through the thinking and feelings of their representative members, whether elected or hereditary officials or ordinary citizens whose voices express popular sentiment through press, radio, television or other effective media. When concerned about group interests, representative individuals experience hope and fear, enthusiasm and disappointment, pride and humiliation, greed and anger. When these individuals believe that their group stands to benefit from collaboration with, or gifts to or reprisals, to, other groups, they behave according to personal psychological principles. Patriots naturally despise other nations when despised by them. Statesmen applaud the generosity of other nations who have helped save their nation from starvation or military defeat. The principle of reciprocity operates. But does it function with as much sensitivity and assurance between groups as between individuals? As an ethical scientist, one should not hastily infer that, since the principle operates between individuals, it therefore also operates between groups. Recollections of one's own behavior as a group leader may be needed as evidence illustrating group behavior. A study of history, to say nothing of observing national policy as expressed through statements in current news, should be used in testing hypotheses about reciprocity as a normal principle of the behavior of groups.

The principle of reciprocity operates not merely relative to peer groups, but also relative to inferior groups (and individuals) and to superior groups, as observations will reveal. When a group finds that one particular member takes an especially great interest in its welfare and devotes oneself more fully to attending to its interests, this group is likely to reward that member with both increased responsibilities and the authority and honor which normally accompany bearing such responsibilities. When a state finds that the federal government takes an interest in providing it with highways and schools which it cannot itself afford, it tends to approve sharing further limited power of control relative to performance of these functions. We shall exemplify operation of the principle of reciprocity relative to nations, e.g., peer groups; but will neglect concern about its operation in hierarchical relations.

Let us review the ten principles (See Chapter V) relative to ways in which desires for national security and esteem may be pursued with profit.

1. Esteem of groups by groups is social, and security, at least of the kinds we shall consider here, is social. A group rates as high or low with respect to whatever ideas individuals happen to use for rating purposes. It may be idealized as ancient and venerable, as powerful, as wealthy, as having a high quality of some sort, as being wise, tolerant, just, or gracious. In any case, groups are esteemed, or disesteemed. Their esteem is social, whether they are rated by their members, by peer groups, or by superior groups. A group remains secure, socially, to the extent that it is not jeopardized by other groups.

2. In order to gain or retain esteem and security, a group must be or do what is required in order to warrant esteem and support or freedom from interference. Hence, representatives of each group need to be aware of how its esteem and security can be achieved and maintained, and to try to promote actions by the group that will bring abut the desired results. The value of an officer to a group may itself be judged by how effectively the officer is able to promote such security and esteem.

3. Members of groups which are admired tend to desire to have their group rated even more highly. Members of prosperous or powerful groups tend to desire to have their groups become more prosperous and more powerful. So they naturally seek to have their groups do what is required to improve these conditions.

4. Desire for greater recognition tends to increase beyond what can be achieved. A patriot's enthusiasm may induce him to wax eloquent and shift his praise from "great" to "greatest." Desire for greater security may lead to struggles for more wealth or power than are actually needed by, or best for, a group.

5. Excessive desire for esteem and security tends to beget circumstances which are detrimental to a group. When a patriot's over-extended eulogy of one's nation is heard by citizens of other nations, they find themselves belittled thereby. They become insulted. They resent such insult. Hence patriotism, which is essential for national support by its citizens, endangers a country whenever its excesses constitute insults to citizens of other countries who automatically feel need for protecting their own reputations. When a nation acquires more power than is needed for defense against actual enemies, it becomes feared as an aggressor. Creating such fears is a way of making enemies and of endangering one's own security and welfare. Hence, excessive desire for esteem or security tends to cause conditions which place these basic group values in jeopardy.

"Nations, like men, are their own worst enemies. The menacing might of human selfishness in every country is mankind's chief danger." (U.S. Secretary of War, Harry Woodring, quoted in Time, January, 1940.) "We face the paradox that the state is, nationally, the great instrument of social security, but internationally, the greatest menace to that security. This situation, growing ever more aggravated as the range and intensity of social and economic interdependence increases, has led to various expedients and programs aiming at the establishment of international security." (R.M. McIver, op. cit., p. 203.) Announcement of the U.S. Air Force's powerful intercontinental stratospheric missile system described secret placement of widely dispersed permanent launching sites, each given a specific target and aimed electronically in advance. When war comes, all that is needed is to press the firing button. This system, calculated to provide security for our nation, also stimulates fear in all other nations that may become possible targets. Individually and collectively they too feel insecure as a consequence of our way of achieving security; and they feel forced to take counter measures which, when materialized, may become even greater threats to our security than existed previously. The psychology of hydrogen-bomb production race clearly illustrates how the principle of reciprocity operates to produce escalation of dangers as a consequence of excessive desire for greater security.

6. The principle of reciprocity works between groups as well as between individuals. Negatively, fear produces fear. positively, trust tends to create trust. But since so many additional factors enter into the ways in which interactions occur between groups, many doubt whether efforts to reduce fear and produce trust can prove worthwhile. First of all, fear of other nations continues to be an important means of retaining interest and loyalty of each nation's citizens. The value that these fears have for a national group should be less than the dangers which such fears have in provoking enmity in other countries. Short-sighted, selfish, jingoistic nationalists often choose to promote fears when they can see short-run advantages for themselves or their nation. Some specialized groups within a nation, which stand to profit from military preparations, may deliberately provoke fears, not only in one but in several countries. (See Merchants of Death by H.C. Engelbrecht and F.C. Hanighen, Dodd & Mead, New York, 1934.) But historical studies reveal that, in the long run, both fears and trust leave their enduring effects upon the course of history. The fact that many accidents, happenstances and personal idiosyncracies enter into crucial events and decisions does complicate the situation. But general principles of reciprocity do not cease functioning just because they are forced to operate in more complicated ways.

7. Groups, like individuals, have power to initiate action which reaps rewards through operation of the principle of reciprocity. Negatively, the effects of aggression, of threats, and of name-calling are known to all. But positive action may seem more difficult to initiate. The magnitude of wisdom required to promote trust in the face of multitudes of fears remains missing from too many people to warrant the expectation that every person elected to a position of leadership can promote it. The multifarious political pressures upon national statesmen from both national and foreign, and from both individual and private corporation, sources, even when their own personal and family needs become insignificant, are so great that some persons of ability, perspicacity and wisdom must be expected to suffer lapses in their power to sustain an attitude of trust toward other nations which is needed in order to maintain lasting peace. As a nation, we could, and should, establish a Department of Peace having as much authority and power in promoting our national interests as our Department of War (now named "Department of Defense").

Expressions of willingness to disarm whenever effective guarantees of collective security can be achieved seem to be a proper part of national policy. Although willingness to inspect and be inspected may seem

minimal conditions for establishing confidence regarding the intentions of
competing nations, surely now the situation is one where the need for a
world federal government is evident to all. Expressions of willingness to
share power, to be controlled as well as to control, in matters of
international security seem minimal evidence of intention to trust. The
United Nations today, created by terms of a truce and intended as a
temporary means of staying war rather than as a truly democratic world
government, remains in a precarious situation. Its modification or
replacement by a more effective world government continues to be a
primary need of our time. A nation cannot begin to create the kind of
trust needed to maintain peace until it earnestly assents to shouldering its
share of the burdens of effective world government. If our nation is still
a leader among nations today, it has a duty to itself to take the lead in
designing and promoting fair and effective world government. The
initiative should be ours, if we believe that our wisdom matches our
might.

8. Genuineness of intentions is required if we are to benefit in the
long run from positive attempts to establish international trust. Sincerity
as well as insincerity reflect themselves through the principle of
reciprocity. The natural prevalence of suspicions among politicians within
a nation, and the tremendous power which fearful rumor-mongering has
in creating tensions, produce conditions in which anything less than
genuine commitments will lead quickly to exposure of insincerity,
hypocrisy and deceit. Deception will be met with more cunning deception
by our enemies, according to the principle of reciprocity; and once
committed to deception, we must develop even more subtle and intricate
forms of deception, we naturally believe. But eventually "truth will out."
And the cost of establishing trust, after revealing a history of relying on
deceit, is much greater, and will take much longer, than efforts to create
trust initially. Public recognition of the fact that our national self-interest
interdepends with the self-interests of other nations is prerequisite to
establishing international trust. History repeats a lesson which too much
of mankind seems unable or unwilling to learn; the quest for security
through "preparedness" of the sort that perpetuates fear in our fellow-
nations is self-defeating in the long run. Genuineness of intentions to
seek world peace can exist only when it becomes obvious that we
genuinely understand the extent to which our own national self-interest
actually depends upon establishment of feelings of security and trust in
other nations.

9. Never perfect in its operation, the principle of reciprocity evidently works even more imperfectly in more highly complex group inter-relations. The imperfections are so great that venturers and those seeking quick results often believe that they can ignore the principle and somehow escape its results. On national scales, too often sons and grandsons suffer the punishment resulting from the "sins" of fathers and forefathers. But the principle does not cease operation just because its effects are delayed. When group leaders disregard consequences for future generations, their character as disregardful of others becomes obvious to their associates and leads to distrust, with more immediate effects in another dimension of social relationships. The rewards of both labor and trust of fathers also enrich sons and grandsons; and contemporary American prosperity is due in part to the trust that our forefathers had in each other and their willingness to fight and die in the Revolutionary and Civil Wars for national independence, unity, and democratic government. Our current world leadership in military affairs is due in part to the willingness of our predecessors to share the burden of European wars against German Imperialism and Nazism and Fascism. The ways in which the United Nations Organization participated in promoting contributions of many kinds from many nations made success possible in the short Gulf War freeing Kuwait from Iraqi aggression. The principle of reciprocity works in devious ways. But one must be blind if he is unable to see that when it works the rewards are sometimes enormously good as well as enormously bad.

When I was a youth, observing the moral and psychological struggles of our nation during and after World War I, the question of German war reparations appeared often in the headlines. We pursued the policy that, since Germany started the war, Germany was guilty and should be made to pay for all the damages which were caused by the war. But the Kaiser had died and his government had disappeared. Among the surviving German people were many who opposed the Kaiser's decision to fight and who resisted war efforts. These people did not initiate the war, but were forced to serve in it unwillingly at considerable personal sacrifice. By the treaty imposed on the German people as part of the terms of surrender, they were regarded, as people, collectively responsible for paying damages caused by the Kaiser's war. Individual Germans were, in effect, judged to be guilty of the crime of starting the war, even when they themselves opposed it. The question, "Is every citizen of a nation guilty when some of its members provoke war?" has deep moral implications. The answer is not easy, because there is a sense in which all members of a group are collectively responsible for what their group does and another sense in which not all are responsible. And both subtleties, indefinitenesses, and shifts in the distribution of and limitation upon individual responsibility for group action have bearings upon ways in which the principle of reciprocity works. The amounts demanded in war reparations were in fact unrealistic, for they were greater than the German people could pay. Their industrial resources had been largely destroyed. We learned again that, in war, everybody loses, and that unrealistic treaty demands, no matter how seemingly justified morally, create their own conditions which can produce evil results according to the principle of reciprocity. Surely we have now learned, even if the angry militarists of still-developing countries have not, that devastation and conditions unfair to the people in defeated countries have a way of reacting to our disadvantage. Many historians believe that lack of foresight by those who drew up the treaty was partly responsible for the demoralizing conditions which produced fertile soil for the beginning of World War II. And World War III, we believe, can be prevented only if the gap between developing and over-developed countries can be narrowed in ways that maintain the self-esteem of all.

Perhaps I should not overstress the problem of difficulties inherent in the imperfect working of the principle of reciprocity. But any naive faith that it works in ways or in degrees in which it does not can prove exceedingly detrimental. Antipathies between nations, for example, become deeply entrenched. Throughout centuries, sometimes, the literature, language, holidays, statues of heroes, names of streets, and educational curricula have fixed in the minds of all citizens of one country some fear, hatred and despising of certain other countries. These enduringly create recurrent negative consequences. A citizen who cautions restraint risks being damned as unpatriotic. Yet only by deliberately refraining from perpetuating insults can we expect to reap the benefits of peace and prosperity in the larger arena of world politics, economics and social interdependencies. For the most part, we fail to decorate the heroes who sacrifice themselves in the interests of that kind of restraint which is required if world peace is to be achieve. Reciprocity exists very imperfectly. But it would be equally naive to believe that, because it works so imperfectly, it does not work at all. Ignoring, as well as ignorance of, the principle in ways which it does work also has consequences, according to the principle itself.

10. To the extent that the principle does work, a nation, and every group, has opportunities for taking the initiative in seeking to achieve

positive as well as negative results. A nation owes to itself the effort needed to understand both general and specific ways in which the principle works, to keep in mind the kinds of actual conditions which commonly conduce to negative reactions, and to initiate studiously attempts designed to motivate positive reactions. These should be normal functions of presidents, departments of state and the foreign diplomatic staff; but they exist as responsibilities of journalists, authors, educators, performing artists, business people, and tourists as well. Prudent use of the principle of reciprocity in ways in which it does work surely constitutes a part of what each group most wants to do. Wisely self-interested groups will often take the initiative in promoting their own welfare through the use of this principle.

Problems in Deciding Public Policy. Since the affairs of groups, such as a nation, require so much insight, maturity, self-sacrifice, devotion, and patience on the part of leaders, the issue arises of whether to allow persons who are temperamentally more selfish, ignorant, immature, impatient, or venturesome to become responsible officers. Just as a person is faced with the problem of keeping in mind his own long-range best interests, so that he will not risk losing his fundamental goods in some violent tantrum or lustful binge, so a nation needs to consider as an obligation to itself the trusting of only reliable personalities with offices of great importance. How best to deal with this problem differs somewhat with varying forms of government. Hereditary monarchies usually selected the eldest son because presumed most mature, but passed over the eldest if he proved weak, ill, demented, or fickle. Democratic electors seek the best person, though popularity and vote-getting ability may have little relation to ability to govern wisely. Political party systems rest on a theory of party responsibility as sounder than individual control. Although these traits have always been needed, competence, expertness, maturity, fitness, excellence, and whole-hearted devotion become even more important in group leaders as social interdependencies become more intricate.

That is, a most basic ought of any group is to assure itself that the persons who act for it in deciding what its oughts are have great moral insight, integrity, breadth of vision, prudence and loyalty. For when either deficiency in insight and ability or selfishness become ensconced in public office, evil consequences may be suffered by all, i.e., by group members, by peer groups, and inferior and superior groups. When, through the principle of reciprocity, evil influences multiply algebraicly, suffering becomes immensely greater. A basic self-interest of each group is to acquire as officers persons whose individual self-interest is closely identified with the interests of the group. But the persons must themselves be mature and prudent, or the group too will suffer.

In our time, when complicated interrelations require multiplicities of experts at many levels in each branch and division of government, responsibility for decision as well as for action has become widely distributed. The postman as well as the local postmaster, and the Postmaster General as well as the President, all have some responsible decisions to make, even though they also all have decisions made for them by other members of the political hierarchy. The illusion cherished by so many underlings that the boss has unlimited dictatorial power needs to be dispelled. In a revealing article, "How the President Makes a Decision" (Saturday Review, July 27, 1963, pp. 12-15, 49, and August 3, 1963, pp. 8-12, 46-47) Theodore C. Sorensen points out that "a president's authority is not as great as his responsibility." For example, "no President is free to go as far or as fast as his advisers, his politics, and his perspective may direct him. His decisions -- and their advice -- are set within at least five ever-present limitations. He is free to choose only (1) within the limits of permissibility; (2) within the limits of available resources; (3) within the limits of available time; (4) within the limits of previous commitments; and (5) within the limits of available information." "A decision in foreign affairs almost always depends on its acceptance by other nations." "A decision in domestic affairs...may depend on its being accepted...by the Congress...and may also depend upon its acceptance within the Executive branch itself...." "It must also be workable. It must be enforceable." Just to know how complicated one's limitations as an officer are, and to keep within them, involves not only considerable understanding but also tremendous moral willingness. Not until we develop the unreserved willingness idealized by Confucius and the spontaneous readiness to act as we ought actualized in Zen can we expect to have our training, insight and intelligence to bear their fullest fruits. The importance of embodying many virtues in our public servants cannot be too strongly stressed. There are no more crucial problems in social ethics than how to achieve wisdom in public decisions, especially when the decision-making functions, and the responsibility which goes with them, have become so widely distributed in persons of different capacities, perspectives, training and relative maturity.

"There Ought to Be a Law". Social problems may be dealt with as particular problems or as cases illustrating a general kind of problem, or as both. That is, sometimes decisions are made about particular difficulties without appealing to precedent and without intending to establish a precedent. To the extent that problems are unique, such intent may be always present. But since many kinds of social problems recur, both appeal to precedent and awareness that later solutions may point to a present solution as precedent, aggravate the moral issue of what general significance particular solutions may have. To the extent that the principle of reciprocity implies some concern for fairness or justice relative to whatever ways recurrent situations are alike, statements of generalizations about what ought to be done can serve as guides for solving future problems of the same sort. Whenever groups must deal with recurrent types of problems, a feeling arises that "there ought to be a law." Codes for conduct, i.e., rules for deciding how to make decisions and carry out actions, are necessary for group welfare.

Although the word "law" has a variety of meanings, ranging from naming any observed regularity, through mores which are opinion-enforced, to explicitly enacted legislation with enforced penalization for violation, we will limit, for convenience, our usage of this word here to laws enacted by legislatures, especially our national Congress. Whenever the best interests of a group are served by formulating a code of conduct which is uniform for all cases of a given kind, then that group ought to have such a law. That is, whether or not a group should have a law is itself an ethical matter. Ethics includes concern for obedience to law; but, even more basically, ethics includes consideration of whether to have any laws at all and, if so, what laws. Part of the problem facing every legislature, when considering enactment of a law, is whether the evil consequences of enactment will be greater than the benefits. That the best interests of the group should be served is obvious. But whenever a law is enacted, certain consequences follow that complicate our lives and cost us, both as individuals and through groups, in many ways. Few, if any, laws are self-enforcing. Consequently, problems of law enforcement arise anew with each additional law.

By definition, a "crime" is a violation of a law. No laws, no crimes. Every time we enact a new law that is violated, we create thereby a new variety of criminal. The actual evils which the law is designed to prevent may exist as evils whether a law exists which legislates the evil action as a crime or not. The purpose of law is to reduce evil and to increase good. But when violation of a law is not only not intentional and the actor intended to do what is good, being branded as a criminal produces not merely bad feelings but also some doubt about, possibly disrespect for, the worthiness of this law. When violation is unintentional, law enforcement officers have a problem of trying to decide whether a claim that violation was unintentional is true. Enough liars can be found so that otherwise lenient officers feel forced to adopt a policy of not trusting the statements of violators unless additional circumstantial evidence supports their claim. Liberties taken by some officers in being lenient often beget laws for law-enforcement, including "no exceptions." Thus enactment of laws causes evils as well as provides goods.

Evils include: difficulties in dissemination of knowledge of the law to all who may be concerned including many who will in fact never become concerned, keeping knowledge in mind by all, employing officers to observe or inspect public behavior in order to apprehend violators, discovery of violators, arrest of violators, judgment of penalties, collection of penalties ("punishment," whether incarceration, fine, restricted liberty, or repayment, has its own host of problems and costs), and efforts to inhibit recurrence not only in each violator but also in others who are not yet violators. Each of these functions has its varieties of detail, special additional problems, and costs in money, time, effort, and health and happiness. Thus, when all these things are considered, "there ought not to be a law" which is not necessary or from which more evils than benefits flow. Plenty of evidence exists to support the theory that "that government governs best which governs least." Yet, of course, this is only part of the story. Another part is that the more benefits that individuals can derive from collective action, the more they ought to utilize their opportunities for gaining as much as they can through group self-control. Neither of these parts constitutes the whole story, as some theorists advocate. Really, that government governs best which governs best, to put the matter redundantly. That is, when we can achieve more benefits through government, then we should have more government, and more law; when we can attain more benefits apart from government, then we should have less government, and less law. The issue becomes neither that "there ought to be a law" or that "there ought not to be a law," but whether and to what extent having a law will benefit us more than not having a law. This issue will be explored further in Chapter XXX, "Social Intelligence."

Chapter XXI

SOCIAL VALUES

"Now for the matter of social policy. The ultimate problem is what sort of social organization is best for man to live under." (Stephen C. Pepper. Ethics, p. 331, Appleton-Century-Crofts, New York, 1960.) We may debate whether people are "under" social organization or "within it," or have such organization "within persons," but surely we will all agree that social ethics is concerned with what is good or better or best for persons.

In exploring the nature of social value, or social values, we need to reconsider what is meant by "value." Do social values exist in groups, or in persons? Are groups good for persons, or persons good for groups? Recalling the fundamental distinction between instrumental and intrinsic values developed in Chapter VI, we can restate these questions: Are groups ends-in-themselves? Do groups have intrinsic value? Or do intrinsic values exist only in persons? Groups do have instrumental value. They are good or bad for persons. Persons also have instrumental value for groups. Persons are good or bad for groups. And groups may be good or bad for other groups.

Do Groups Have Intrinsic Value? Let us consider first the controversial question: Are groups ends-in-themselves? (See "The State as an Organism, as a Person, and as an End in Itself," by H.J. McCloskey, The Philosophical Review, Vol. LXXII, July, 1963, pp. 306-326.) We choose not to enter here into discussion of world views regarding whether all being, or beings, or only some beings, have intrinsic value. We need assume only that at least some do, that human beings do, and inquire further whether or not some groups do. First of all, it appears that the kinds of intrinsic good surveyed in Chapter VI, pleasant and unpleasant feeling, satisfaction and frustration of desire, enthusiasm and apathy, contentment and anxiety, exist in conscious human beings, and that groups, as organizations of human beings, have no additional consciousnesses, and no additional experiences of values, outside of persons. Whatever intrinsic values may be attributed to groups have their existence in persons as additional dimensions of their own intrinsic values. But that such additional dimensions do exist, and do exist as a consequence of the existence, nature and functioning of groups, may be asserted with confidence. Hence, groups too have intrinsic-value aspects due to the ways in which they function in human experiences. Persons and groups interdepend; and it is because groups depend not only upon persons but upon their intrinsic value experiences, and because the intrinsic value experiences of persons sometimes depend directly upon the existence and functioning of some groups, that attribution of intrinsic value to groups is sometimes functionally justified.

That is, we may define a group functionally or behavioristically, not merely relative to substance, but also relative to intrinsic value. Just as, in Chapter XVIII, we indicated that a group may be regarded as substantial to the extent that and in the ways that it remains through change, so here we suggest that a group may be regarded as good in itself to the extent and in the ways that it functions as if the locus of intrinsic good. It may do this in at least two ways.

One is primarily attributive. That is, we often attribute intrinsic good to some highly-valued groups. Just as in art, when we experience beauty or ugliness, which are experiences of intrinsic values, we attribute the beauty to an art object, a painting, for example, so in society, when we become overwhelmed with feelings of loyalty to, amazement at, or fear of, a group, we tend to attribute our feelings of intrinsic value, whether good or bad, to the group as an object. In this sense, we empathetically project our feelings upon or into or within a group as we conceive it, and act with respect to it in terms of these feelings. A group thus functions as if it exists as an intrinsic value through our own attitudes and behavior relative to it. And, just as in art, we often naively regard not only the art object but also its beauty as independent of us, so relative to groups, we often naively regard a group, and the intrinsic value we attribute to it, as existing independently of us. Both of these attitudes are mistaken, strictly speaking; for both the existence of beauty attributed to paintings and the existence of intrinsic value attributed to groups have their being in human experiences. Yet they serve as functionally useful working hypotheses with which we naively operate to great advantage much of the time. When our naive beliefs about the intrinsic value of a group leads us to enslave ourselves to that group in ways which are detrimental to our personal well being, we suffer from our mistakes, and need to correct our ideas.

The other is primarily identitive. That is, when we identify ourselves with a group, and thus identify that group with ourselves, we tend to regard our own intrinsic value and the supposed intrinsic value of the group as identical. Again, this is a functional identification; but now we feel that we are part of the group and that the group is embodied in us, whereas, in the previous way, the group is regarded as an object which may appear to have an independent existence. These two ways overlap, and intertwine and interdepend in our existence; so the distinction made here often remains unclear. But that we act as if some groups have intrinsic value seems quite clear.

If one should object to employing a functional definition of groups, we need to recall that we proposed a functional definition of an individual also, in Chapters II and III. And, although intrinsic goods such as pleasure, satisfaction, enthusiasm and contentment are intuitable and immediately obvious, their presence in, or attachment to, an enduring self involves certain hypothetical beliefs, or working hypotheses, about the nature of self. If we keep in mind that both individuals and groups are properly conceived in terms of functional definitions, then the analogy between groups and individuals, including group values and individual values, is less loose than otherwise.

But when we consider the moral consequences of carrying our naive attribution of intrinsic value too far, as well as carrying our critical rejection of all intrinsic value to groups too far, we realize that another host of difficulties complicates our moral situation. To the extent that attribution of intrinsic value to a group is justified, we are immoral, or act wrongly, in failing to accept and act accordingly. To the extent that such attribution is not justified, we are immoral, or act wrongly, in so attributing and acting. The line demarcating such extents too often is unclear, and may, in addition, be fluctuating. Hence, any attempt to formulate codes of social ethics is fraught with multiplicities of uncertainties. Yet, at the same time, to fail to recognize the actual functioning of groups as if having intrinsic values is to be blind to certain kinds of value-attitudes actually existing in human experience. Once the functional existence of intrinsic-value aspects of groups as experienced is recognized, it appears immoral, i.e., not to one's own best interests, to fail to try to keep it in mind. Surely it would be immoral of me, in my attempt to understand and teach ethics, not to try to make clear the extent to which people can and do attribute intrinsic values to some groups.

To illustrate organic interdependence of individual and social values, let us recall how completely a young child identifies itself with its mother, or with its siblings, especially when they are being jointly attacked or terrorized. This feeling of identity of self with an intimate family group tends to be extended, in tribal societies, to a whole clan or tribe. Some individuals regard their being selected for sacrifice as the highest honor which can be bestowed upon them by their group. And, in times of war, or other national emergency, a loyal citizen's identification of his own welfare, not merely instrumentally, but intrinsically, with that of his nation may lead him to believe that sacrifice of himself may be instrumental to the maintenance of a group intrinsic value he regards as superior to his own. People make such attributive judgments about groups to which they are loyal just as they may to some cosmic principle, usually deified, that appears to them as an over-arching principle of ultimate reality and value. But in both cases, feelings of identification and judgments of value-attribution may be carried too far. One who becomes a craven servant of a state or a god may be destroying other values and mistakenly diminish, or even deny, that he himself has any intrinsic value. Each child, as it grows and matures, should achieve larger measures of independence and recognize itself as a locus of substantiality and intrinsic value. But this growth likewise may be carried too far; for some individuals seem to believe that they alone are intrinsically good and that neither groups nor other individuals have any intrinsic value. Tendencies toward extreme independence, whether of individuals or groups, become destructive of the actual interdependence existing, variably, in all individual-group relationships.

Ways In Which Groups Have Instrumental Values. Details of the ways in which groups have instrumental value will not be explored here. But since much confusion exists in popular thinking about values, and since the preceding discussion has been limited to ways in which individuals attribute intrinsic value to groups, some mention of the importance, perhaps even greater importance, which the instrumental values of groups have should be made. The instrumental values of groups also interdepend with individuals, because groups consist of individuals, directly or indirectly, because groups depend upon the individuals who serve as officers or other representatives in order to function instrumentally, and because groups which serve as the locus of projected ends-in-themselves experiences depend for their functioning as if intrinsic values upon the individuals who so project. Hence, both the intrinsic and the instrumental values which groups have, borrow or derive their ways of functioning as values from their dependence upon, or interdependence with, persons.

What are some of the ways in which groups serve individuals instrumentally? Since almost everything that one does is done in some relation to groups, a review of the conditions of the existence, nature, welfare and esteem in persons would be needed to survey all of them. Primary groups serve not only as a source and means for protection, companionship, esteem and recreation on intimate bases but also provide foundations for the development of ability to live in, and be served by, secondary groups. Secondary, or more impersonal groups, supplement primary group services by extending the range of association and the degree of specialization available to individuals. Ranges of association, which include wider ranges of protection, travel, citizenship, etc., become progressively widened through community, city, state, regional, national, continental and world group organizations. Each serves individuals in its own way, both by preventing war over larger territories and making possible the provision of services that can exist only if organization of such areas exists, such as a postal system or an air travel system. Richness, complexity and cheapness of products resulting from specialization and division of labor, in mining, manufacturing, distributing, wholesaling, and retailing kinds of business, for example, result from group organization. The services of groups may be classified according to their political, economic, educational, religious and recreational functions. Each social science studies some aspects of group behavior and shows how individuals are served thereby. Each of these services constitutes an instrumental value to those individuals.

Roles of Values in Social Policy. Groups are good because they are good for persons. They contribute to the existence of both intrinsic and instrumental values. Social policy, and social ethics, is concerned with how to maximize good and minimize evil. Two aspects of social policy will be explored here. These pertain primarily to quantity and to quality.

1. Quantity of goods may be thought of in two ways: How many people exist to enjoy values? How many values does each person enjoy?

A. How many people should exist? Mankind, and sometimes each person, confronts no more basic question than this. It is faced in two ways: if too many people exist, how many and which ones should be eliminated and how should they be eliminated? If too few exist, how many should be sought, and in what ways? The question may appear at each of many group levels, and, indeed, by every group. When two people marry, they face the question: How many children shall we have? A family group may become too large or too small. A city, a state, a nation, even the world, may become too populous or too sparsely populated. Current questions about population explosion disturb many people. Formerly, certain nations, such as Canada and Australia, believed they suffered from having too few citizens. Canada, for example, invested money, as a nation, not only to attract immigrants but also to subsidize births, especially in rural families. Do any general moral principles for dealing with these questions exist?

If each person is an intrinsic good, then, other things being equal, the greater the number of persons who exist, the greater the intrinsic good that exists in the family, in the community, in the nation, in the world. If, quantitatively, each group incorporates more intrinsic good when it includes more members, then, other things being equal, it ought to increase its membership. Each family ought to grow as large as it can. Each nation should have as many citizens as it can. Mankind should seek to increase the population of the world as much as it can. From this point of view, the current population explosion means that mankind is doing what it most ought to do: increase the amount of intrinsic value in the universe. The universe increases in intrinsic value each time another person is born, and decreases every time a person dies.

Fears and complaints about too many people in the world grow from the fact that certain kinds of resources needed for life appear to be limited in supply. When these are exhausted, people will die. When minimal resources are limited, then if more people are born, others must die. When this is the case, an increase in present population which contributes to a depletion of later population does not increase the total amount of intrinsic good in the world, i.e., considering future as well as present goods. Furthermore, when people are forced to live at minimal standards, the misery experienced may be greater than their happiness. When such is the case, more intrinsic evil than intrinsic good exists. Hence, not merely existence, but happy existence, is the proper goal of social policy. Now when people remain sparsely settled, and lonely, more people are needed. But when people crowd each other annoyingly, fewer people are needed. So mankind's basic aim should be, not what is the maximum population which the earth's resources can support, but what is the optimum population, where factors of quality, relatively little misery accompanying relatively great happiness, and prospects for future population and happiness have been taken into consideration. Consumption now of irreplaceable resources may be justified only if prospects exist for discovering or inventing substitutes.

b. How much should each person enjoy life? Here the issue is a double one: how to increase one's share of resources or instrumental values and how to increase one's enjoyment of whatever one receives. That is, how high a standard of living should be regarded normal or optimum? And, what efforts should be made to induce in persons an attitude of yea-saying enjoyment of whatever they may have? The general principle, do what is best, implies that, other things being equal, the greatest possible happiness of each person ought to be sought.

2. Quality of goods is a much more difficult problem to deal with. Once we have decided upon what constitutes high quality, then, of course, social policy involves the principle that, other things being equal, one should seek the highest quality of goods for the group members. This issue of how to distribute such goods, when they cannot be distributed equally, continues to be disturbing. Is it better to have a few persons enjoying an extremely high standard of living and quality of enjoyment, while others remain at a much lower standard, or to have all persons enjoying as high a standard as possible, without any highest peaks? The issue of whether to prefer aristocratic or democratic ideals plagues many groups. If higher degrees of excellence can be obtained when only a few are favored, what shall a group decide?

Hence, issues of social policy involve not merely whether there should be more or fewer people in a group, or in the world, or higher quality living for few or many, but how to decide between preferring the existence of another person or a higher standard of living for those already alive. A particular family may face this question thus: "Shall we have another baby or all take a trip to Europe?" A nation may confront the problem: Shall we increase agricultural production so we can support more people or shall we increase industrial production and university education so we can provide a higher standard of living for fewer people? These problems are not easily resolvable. Even if they could be isolated from the complexes of other problems in which they are embedded, they would be hard to settle. How to balance quantity of pleasure with quality of pleasure troubles those called upon to make decisions for groups even more, perhaps, than those who make such decisions for themselves. Disagreements as to what constitutes high quality remain, at least during the present stage of development in human civilization, so that decisions favoring quantity may be made with greater feelings of assurance than those favoring quality. The principles for choosing, cited in Chapter VIII, hold for deciding group policy also.

Moral Ideals as "Social Values". The term "social values" also has narrower meanings than the universal scope we have intended here: any value of any group. Three such other meanings will be mentioned: 1. Popular standards of etiquette. 2. Sympathetically shared feelings. 3. Great ideals.

1. Popular discussions about morality by young people often center about everyday deportment problems, especially as these relate to friends, parents, teachers, and casual acquaintances. When some girls cut their hair short and others do not, or when some parents allow dates until twelve at night when others insist on their coming in by ten, or when some youths admit keeping overpay while others insist on returning it, the standards of conduct implied may be called "social values." They include not merely customs and mores, but also fashions and fads. This use of the term "social values" prevails usually without awareness of the possibility of the intricate analyses we have presented. Disputes easily arise about whether these values are subjective or objective, but that both variably interdepend and that clarity requires differentiation of means from ends usually remains hidden. Social values, in this sense, commonly receive discussion in Sunday School and elementary sociology classes; and beliefs about them often have been statistically generalized about through questionnaires. Consideration of social values, in this sense, is indeed a part of social ethics. They serve as excellent starting points for investigation. But when people accept them as social facts, which they are, without penetrating into the fundamentals of ethical theory, the confusions inherent in them tend to leave those who indulge in superficial discussions of them worse confounded.

2. The very act of sharing feelings constitutes a social value. What "constitutes values social," says DeWitt H. Parker, is "our awareness of the desires and satisfactions of other persons and their awareness of ours; not how we behave in relation to each other, but our knowledge of the feelings that accompany and determine behavior. All of our feelings are either known to others or, when they are not known, the very fact of their being unknown affects their character. Each person is a mirror to the others, and whatever is not reflected in it is warped or deflected. The unknown becomes the hidden, the secret. Hence our very privacy and solitude are paradoxically social.... Hence it is not that we both drink tea, or even that we do so side by side that makes tea-drinking social, but that each knows what the other feels when he is drinking." (The Philosophy of Value, pp. 16-17.) Such sympathetically shared feelings remain foundational to the existence of some groups, and groups continue to be strong or weak partly in proportion to the depth of sympathy and the numbers of kinds of feelings which group members share. Although such sharing of feelings, or "social values" in this sense, occurs more commonly or more obviously in primary groups, the morale of citizens of communities, states or nations also depends upon them.

3. The term "social values" may also be applied to great ideals, of persons, of nations, of civilizations, or of mankind. Whenever a person or a group broods over a persisting difficulty, shortcoming or evil, there emerges some idea of what things would be like if the troublesome condition were removed. Sometimes these ideas remain vague and nebulous. Sometimes they become formulated in literature. Sometimes they come to be stated in the dogmas of religious or political sects. Sometimes they seem so clear that they appear obvious to all persons in all civilizations in some form or other. Having ideals, i.e., ideas of goods yet to be attained, does not guarantee that they can be realized. Yet the formulation of ideals and continuing attention to them constitutes a kind of direction, directive or purpose. Ideals as ideas of goods that ought to be achieved come to be felt as obligations. They have power to mold our consciences. They exist in us as habits of wanting. They serve as goals toward which we strive. They persist as end-values, i.e., as apparently objective intrinsic goods, which motivate us to actualize them. When thus reified, these ideals may seem more powerful than we are. When thus stabilized, these ideals may appear to be more permanent than we are. When regarded as high intrinsic goods, these ideas may function as if they are more important than we are. Some philosophies, notably those influenced by our Platonic traditions, regard some ideals as eternal, whereas mortal persons live merely temporarily. When persons allow themselves to become enslaved by their own ideals, they are unintelligent. (See Chapter XXX.) But to fail to have ideals is to be something less than human; and to fail to utilize ideals that can help us to work toward and enjoy greater goods is to be foolish, short-sighted and, indeed, immoral. Having ideals, and living by high ideals, about what is best for oneself and for one's group in the long run, is part of what one most wants to do.

We cannot here study in detail the nature of ideals or the amazing variety of ideals cherished by people in different circumstances. But mention of some of the great ideals doubtless common to all persons should be worthwhile. Surely all idealize a life filled with happiness, even though ideas of what constitutes happiness differ greatly. Most will believe that considerable amounts of health, wealth and security are needed and wanted and should be obtained by all, enemies perhaps excepted. How health, wealth and security are conceived will vary from group to group and era to era; and the language, images, presuppositions and explanations given, even held to be necessary, as supports of such conceptions, differ both in general and in detail. Yet, no matter how fashioned, ideals of these sorts seem common to all mankind. Usually, when the difficulties of life have eased somewhat, ideals of recreation, of advanced education, and of enriched varieties of association normally also appear. When a lack is great, the ideal of eliminating the lack is extremely praised and urgently pursued. But when the lack has lessened, or especially when ideals have been pursued too far so that they have begotten additional evils, then ideals of moderation in the pursuit of ideals emerges usually.

These great ideals are moral in the sense that they function as oughts or obligations. A great ideal, by its very nature, is something which people ought to choose to realize. Hence they are moral ideals. They function also as standards for achievement. Each ideal goal serves as a standard whereby to measure achievement. Each accepted standard for achievement serves as an ideal goal. Thus, in a fundamental sense, ideals are standards and standards are ideals. The great ideals function as great social goods. Just as popular standards for etiquette constitute social goods in local communities, so the great ideals constitute social goods for mankind.

Among the difficulties encountered in considering ideals is the perpetual problem of having ideals that are high enough so that they have not yet been realized, i.e., so they will motivate us toward achievement, but not so high that we can never hope to realize them. When we lose hope that our ideals can be actualized, these ideals lose their motivating power. Then neither do we serve them nor do they serve us. When we lose all ideals, we cease to be forward-looking. We need ideals.

Chapter XXII

SOCIAL IMPROVEMENT

That groups can change, for better or worse (issues that we raised about individuals in Chapter VII), appears so obvious that discussion seems unnecessary. But whether groups can improve, and improve themselves, may be worth exploring.

How Can Groups Improve? The ways in which groups can improve are as various as the natures of the many different kinds of groups. We arbitrarily select three interrelated ways for consideration.

1. To the extent that groups depend upon, or interdepend with, individuals, the improvement of groups depends upon, or interdepends with, relevant improvement in individuals. Hence, increased awareness of the facts about such interdependence may itself be a necessary condition for some kinds of social improvement.

Here again different philosophies persist. Some say the only way to improve a group is by improving the individuals within it. Some say the only way to improve the individuals is to improve their social environment. But others say that failure to attack the problem of improvement from either of the two foregoing ways is to be negligent, so long as possibilities for such double attack exist. According to this latter view, groups can be improved, and hence should be improved, by a three-pronged approach: by improving individuals as individuals, which will enable them to function better as group members; by improving individuals as members of groups, even of many levels of groups, through increased sensitivity and conscientiousness regarding their group-membership roles and natures; by improving groups as groups, including the interrelations between groups. We focus upon the latter in the present chapter.

2. To the extent that groups exist as groups, how can they be improved? That is, in addition to, and involved in, problems of improving groups by improving individual members and the quality of their interdependence with groups, problems exist regarding the nature of groups as such. Each group, when its members become aware of it as such, tends to face the problem of whether or not it is as good as it can, or should be. Are there some kinds of problems common to all groups as groups? Are there some principles that apply to all groups as groups relative to whether or not they can improve? Granted that some groups exist without problems of their nature and improvement ever coming to consciousness in any one of their members, but when awareness of a

group does emerge and concern for its nature and welfare does occur, then does it automatically encounter certain typical problems and become involved in certain general principles?

Full answer to such question would require intensive sociological studies which must remain beyond the scope of the present work. But suggestions as to what research is likely to reveal seem desirable. When values are involved in social life, problems of how to increase goods and decrease evils naturally appear. Then problems of deciding who shall be responsible for actions needed to improve them arise. Then problems of deciding who shall be responsible for the actions needed to maintain or augment these goods, and of delegating authority enabling representatives to act effectively in carrying out such responsibilities arise. Since groups differ so greatly in their natures, from momentary, casual groups to centuries-old institutionalized groups, the particular ways in which these decisions are made and authority is delegated vary widely. In some, a mere nod of assent to a person in a favored position is sufficient (as when, in public, people are faced with the question of who shall pass through a door first); in others, expensive training, travel and meticulously-conducted councils or congresses are needed to modify even minutiae of rigid establishments. Yet problems of group welfare and of delegating authority are common to all of them.

Flowing naturally from these problems are others which have to do with the location and quality of responsible personnel and the need for establishing precedent and rules or laws.

Personnel problems may seem simpler when a group is small. Sometimes leadership automatically falls upon one who is most able or most active. Sometimes even small groups function within fixed moral systems which designate, for example, who shall be "head of the house." Sometimes division of labor occurs naturally on bases of age, sex, size, strength, or previous success. When groups become large, and conflicting interests develop, more intricate and cumbersome methods of determining who shall serve as responsible agents for a group develop. Large groups with complex needs tend to evolve division of labor relative to decisions and action and, even, of evaluation of judgment of whether officials have born their responsibilities properly.

The locus of responsibility may remain relatively fixed for some groups. Hereditary monarchy illustrates such fixity. The locus may be limited to one or more years of tenure, as when the President of the United States is elected for four years, and, through reelectable, is prohibited from serving for more than eight years. The locus may be tenuous, depending upon obtaining a vote of confidence which can be called for at any time. Surely stability is needed and, other things being equal, the more stable a group's official personnel the better. Yet also, circumstances change, both those constituting problems for group solution and the abilities of personnel. Each group tends to face problems of reallocating responsibilities, both as new problems arise and old ones disappear and as older officers decline in efficiency and newer ones seek more for authority.

Other problems common to all personnel situations have to do with the confidence that members have in officers, how far they can be trusted, how intelligent, devoted, conscientious and efficient they continue to be. In the face of doubts, reasonable or otherwise, officers too become plagued with doubts and often need morale support. Each group tends to need officers who can maintain morale in the face of criticisms by members. Furthermore, some problems occur which remain the common responsibility of all members and cannot be delegated to officers. Sometimes groups require too much from their officials, and may need official effort to call attention to the need for not delegating common tasks to particular representatives.

The need for establishing precedent and formulating rules for group conduct seems common to all except temporary, casual groups. These rules may continue to be merely implicit in the way persons conduct themselves relative to each other, or they may be formally enacted through ponderous legislative procedures. But problems pertaining to having either too few nor too many rules and laws seem perpetually characteristic of groups as groups. Since some problems occur only once, decision and action regarding them should not be burdened with formulation of laws. Yet also, when problems recur and the work of deciding again and again becomes onerous, resort to rules seems wise and efficient, when they become possible. But the need for sensitivity to rule revisions as circumstances become altered seems to remain a constant problem of groups as groups.

3. Recognition of ways in which groups inherently interdepend brings with it awareness of problems which may need to be dealt with in order to improve the quality of that interdependence and, consequently, the lives of group members. How can groups improve relative to their interdependence with other groups? Are there any general principles applying to all interdependencies that may be relied upon in deciding to try to bring about improvements?

Again, analogies between individual and social ethics are suggestive. Since interdependence involves both some independence and some dependence of each group, concern about both of these aspects of interdependence is needed.

Insofar as each group is a kind of entity which deserves to endure, suitable regard for its proper perpetuation is needed. Each group has a somewhat substantial nature which has been developed to function in certain ways. So long as its nature and functionings are good, respect for these is an additional good. The integrity of each such group should be maintained. "Improvement," as this term is employed in the present chapter, broadly includes reduction of dangers and preservation from undesirable decline or destruction, as well as increase in the goods which a group causes, the esteem in which it is held, or the enjoyment which people experience when aware of it. Each of two or more interdependent groups may be improved, even as interdependent, partly by giving attention and effort to the preservation or improvement of each also in ways in which it is independent. For the quality of interdependence itself depends in part upon the quality of each group as independent. To the extent that interdependent groups depend upon each of these groups having some degree of independence, improvement in such interdependence tends to depend upon independence.

But also, to the extent that groups also depend for their independence upon their interdependence, improvement in such independence depends upon such interdependence. Hence, the quality of service which one group provides for another may be quite vital to its own nature, existence and well-being.

Thus part of the way in which groups can improve is by giving attention to improving this quality. Typical problems inherent in interdependencies have to do with the overlapping of functions as well as with division of labor. When destructive conflict between interdependent groups occurs, reduction of such conflicts is one way to improvement. But when cooperation begets complacency, of the sort which leads to lethargy and indifference to vitality of service, then stimulation of competition may be the best means to improvement. Some overlapping of functions may be needed, some may be harmless, and some may be wasteful or destructive. Social improvement aims to eliminate the latter. Sometimes the needs of group members are served better when fewer rather than more groups exists. (E.g., the value to a community of having four relatively equal services of the same kind performed by four incorporated groups on all four corners of two cross streets, whether four gasoline stations, four supermarkets, or four churches, seems dubious to many.)

Hence, groups can improve most by becoming and remaining more constantly aware of the problems involved in balancing the intricate complexes of interests which group members have in the excellence of the service that can be performed adequately only through many interdependent groups. Problems of "the one and the many" continue to plague those interested in social improvement. Sometimes each new function seems to call for a new group to perform that function. And sometimes the very profuseness of groups, each performing a valuable function in itself, constitutes an evil because lack of smooth functioning relative to their ways of being interdependent is missing. That is, sometimes groups need to subdivide as more functions are performed, and sometimes separate groups need to be united so their functions can be more efficiently coordinated. Conscientious attention to shifts between these two "sometimes"may be necessary for optimum social improvement. The foregoing generalizations appear to hold regardless of whether the interdependencies exist between peer groups, between hierarchically-related groups, or, for that matter, between several hierarchically-related levels of peer groups.

How To Improve Groups. The foregoing discussion should serve as evidence that no simple solution is available for the improvement of all groups.

Those who dismiss the complexities of social problems by asserting that, if you merely improve the individual members all social problems will solve themselves, bury their heads in social sands. Both rationalistic utopians, who believe that when all persons become perfectly rational, each will do exactly what reason demands of him and hence all social problems will disappear, romanticistic Christians ("If your heart keeps right....") who believe that when "love casteth out fear" all social problems will cease, and quiescent Buddhists, who believe that when all discipline their wills into willingness to accept whatever they get as just what they want, tell only part of the story. Each has hit upon an essential. Social utopia can come to stay only when reason, love and willingness prevail; but none of these alone, nor even all together, are sufficient. On the other hand, those who offer facile solutions by claiming that if you merely improve group conditions, the social environment, enough, then all problems, individual and social, will subside, permit themselves to be blinded by clouds of social dust. Both those who advocate an "economic interpretation of history" (e.g., Marxists), those who support a political solution to social problems (whether Democrats, Fascists or Syndicalists), and those who try to demonstrate that culture, whether language, literature, religion, mores, or educational system, etc., are sufficient, stop short of presenting the whole truth. Each focuses upon one essential. Social utopia will arrive only if and when both economic, political and other cultural conditions conductive to efficient solution to problems come to prevail. But no one of these conditions alone, nor even all of them together, are sufficient. For, since both individuals depend upon groups and groups depend upon individuals, utopia can be hoped for only if we work at both the individual and the group ends of the individual-group polarity. So long as individuals and their groups remain interdependent, realistic faith that we are achieving substantial measures of social improvement will require adequate efforts both by individuals and by groups and in all of the ways which are essential to the healthy continuance of such interdependence.

Part of what is needed for social improvement is increased awareness of the existence, nature and needs of groups. Too often older members at home in a group presume that the nature and values of a group to which they have become habituated should be obvious to newer members. But, unfortunately, newer members experience the nature of groups too often in terms of restrictions regarded as necessary without becoming fully aware of the values which such restrictions serve. Hence, more deliberate efforts to enlighten new members by effective methods of induction may be needed. Neither citizenship courses for immigrants nor education for citizenship in our public schools can be effective unless each person acquires a genuine sense of the value of such citizenship through feeling that one has an actual stake in the national community and its welfare. On the one hand, a person can hardly comprehend the full significance of social life in America without considerable intellectual understanding of the contents of the social sciences: sociology, economics, political science, and ethics. On the other hand, surely one will remain unimpressed even by vast intellectual knowledge so long as one has no actual position of security and respect or no hope of attaining such. Megalopolis unfortunately includes many lonely, antagonistic, hopeless persons with high academic attainments, as well as many ignorant poor. A sense of belonging, of "identity," is essential to the welfare of both individuals and their groups; and the quality of interdependence cannot be improved greatly without improvement in both the awareness of and acceptance of a group by individual members as well as awareness of and acceptance of individuals by their groups.

Such feelings of having a stake in the community, of belonging, and of being accepted tend to have certain natural accompaniments. Whenever a person or a community accepts something as its own, interest in the nature and welfare of that thing follows. When the value at stake is enduring, especially if it is regarded as life-long, then one becomes committed to understanding it, appreciating it, preserving it, and, if possible, improving it. Such commitment is essential to life, to social life, and to social improvement. The quality of social life depends upon the quality of the commitment with which members and groups serve each other. One way to greater social improvement is through attainment of more enlightened and more devoted commitment. One way to more enlightened and devoted commitment by members is through providing awareness of and hope for greater social improvement. Group morale consists in the presence in members of willing commitment to group values.

True commitment results in putting forth whatever effort is needed to avoid danger, to maintain security, or to accomplish an improvement. Entailed herein is both trust and distrust. Whatever or whoever jeopardizes a group's values automatically becomes distrusted. Yet also, since some group values can be attained only through specialization and division of labor, trust of each person to whom responsibilities are allotted is required. Hence considerable degrees of mutual trust are involved in every social commitment. So long as room remains for some distrust, each alert member must also remain concerned about improving the quality of the performance, hence of both the commitment and the skill, of any dubious delegate. Tension occurs naturally in groups so long as doubt remains. Yet, since distrust itself tends to cause untrustworthiness and trust itself is conductive to trustworthiness, groups perforce must trust even some of those whose trustworthiness remains partly in doubt. This problem is perennial with youth whose skill, experience and judgment is still immature; but maturity can come only through exercise and experience, and this is possible only if youth is first trusted. Except for those groups which can employ or admit only persons with established records of competence, most groups find it necessary to commit themselves to considerable trust of persons who have not yet proved themselves. The importance of the home, school and church become magnified as we recognize how significant these agencies are in performing such a function as trusting those who are not fully trustworthy.

Delinquency counselors, parole officers and mental hospitals perform similar functions, but their job is more difficult because distrustful behavior patterns that have become hardened and publicly-recognized both give the distrusted person a status as a delinquent and further detach him from hopes and skills needed for establishing, both in himself and in others, the kind and degree of trust required for a sufficient sense of belonging which enjoys justified attitudes of mutual trustworthiness entailing mutual commitment to shared values.

Hence tolerance of some kinds and degrees appears to be an inherent need of group life. Social welfare often depends precariously upon the need for tolerance of distrusted members who show promise of becoming trustworthy. Hence, social improvement often depends upon the morale building abilities of groups to transform untrustworthy into trustworthy members. Where trust depends upon actual abilities, whether productive, preservative or merely associative, social improvement depends upon the improvement of such abilities. Hence, often nothing is more important to a group than its educational functions; and when this is so, nothing seems more important than its educational institutions and officers. Social education aims to improve both the trustworthiness and the trustingness of group members; the latter tends to increase as the former increases, though sometimes attitudes of distrust are perpetuated quite unwarrantedly.

Chapter XXIII

SOCIAL OBLIGATION

The term "social obligation" may be more familiar to many readers in its narrow sense of repaying a courtesy, such as inviting to dinner persons who have invited them to dinner. In Chapter VIII, the term "social obligation" was used to refer to any and every aspect of each individual's self-obligation that involved one's duties to others as parts of duties to oneself. Here we intend to use the term "social obligation" to refer to the obligations of groups. Three aspects or levels of group nature, values, and hence, obligations, have been distinguished: a group has obligations to its members both as members and as individuals; a group has obligations to itself as a group; a group has obligations to other groups with which it interdepends, both peer groups and hierarchically-related groups. "Social obligation," then, is something very complex.

What is "Obligation"? Nothing is closer to the core of ethics than the question "What is oughtness, duty or obligation?" We have already explored this topic at length in Chapters V-IX relative to individuals. Obligation presupposes the existence of intrinsic values which are at stake in some course of action that may be altered by decision. Generally speaking, whenever two or more alternatives occur relative to choosing between goods, oughtness consists in the power that a greater good has over a lesser good in compelling our choice. It is the believed greater good, and ultimately the believed greater intrinsic good, which is the basis for oughtness or obligation. This definition of obligation holds for social as well as for individual obligations, since all genuine social obligations are extensions of individual obligations. Hence, the social obligations of any group consist in trying to do what is believed to be best for the group. Since groups tend to be complexly interdependent, both with their members and with other groups, what is best for each group tends to involve weighing and choosing between many different kinds of values. The greater the number, kinds, and importance of values that a group has at stake, the more social obligations it has. Social obligation, as obligation which a group has, consists in choosing the greater rather than the lesser goods for itself as a complexly interdependent being.

A foundation has already been laid, in Chapters XX-XXII, for discussing social obligation. Like individuals, groups have typical fundamental interests, including those in security and esteem, and typical conflicts of interests, which cause and require choices, evaluations, and decisions. Like individuals, groups not only regard themselves as having values and function accordingly but also have problems of discovering and maintaining ideas about what are their ultimate values. Like individuals, groups face problems of eliminating or reducing evils. Like individuals, groups can improve and may be confronted with multiplicities of ways and means for improvement. Hence, social obligation involves groups having many interests and goods, knowing that, and what, are its goods and evils, having ways for improving or preventing deterioration of such goods, and having choices to make among them. Social obligation also involves groups in acting as agents, choosing freely, being self-governing, owning, being just, conscientious, and intelligent, as will be seen in Chapters XXIV-XXX.

A Group's Obligations to Its Members. A group's obligations to its members are of two main sorts: to its members as members and to its members as individuals. For example, decisions about what is best for a college class, whether made by the instructor, by student vote or both, involve the problem of treating all of its members fairly as members. Fairness usually requires giving all students approximately equal assignments and allowing each about the same amount of time for discussion in class. However, each member is also an individual with other interests that compete more or less with his interests in being a member of the class. When the parent of one member has been critically injured, a class may owe it to itself to give such member special privileges regarding examination make-up or delay in reporting; for if persons cannot be permitted exceptions for emergencies, they are less likely to become group members and the very existence of the group is threatened by adopting a policy in which rigid enforcement of principles, needed for fairness to persons as members, becomes destructive of equal or greater values of those persons as individuals. Hence, the problem of discovering and formulating those principles that seem involved in understanding a group's obligations to its members is fraught with need for keeping clearly in mind these two kinds of obligations.

1. *A Group's Obligations to Its Members As Individuals.* Since, with rare exceptions, each individual has more values at stake than those inherent in his membership in any group, a group does not serve its members well unless it takes such other values into consideration when making decisions regarding their welfare. The relative importance to each individual of his membership in a particular group is a limiting factor in determining how much his membership in that group permits exploiting him for purposes of such membership. Since such relative importance

often varies greatly with different individuals in a single group, each group is obligated to make due allowance for such variations. As a minimum, each group is obligated to restrict itself to those demands upon its members as individuals which are required as minimums for membership. As an ideal maximum, each group should, as much as possible, seek to promote the organic unity of rich, multi-leveled pluralities of interests of each member as an individual. Some groups, such as those in which individuals are single-item customers, members of a temporary audience, a book club, or a strictly honorary society, naturally have minimal obligations. Other groups, such as families, neighborhood communities, general educational institutions, states and nations, tend to have maximum obligations. Some groups have distinctly different kinds of obligations to different kinds of members; for a corporation, whether public or private, has a greater range of obligations to its long-time employees than either its temporary help or its occasional customers; and a corporation, public or private, may have more obligations to the citizens or steady customers it serves than to transients or occasional customers. Yet, complex and variable though they are, a group's obligations to its members as individuals are basic to all its other obligations.

2. *A Group's Obligation to Its Members As Members.* These may vary, as indicated in the preceding paragraph, whenever there are different kinds of memberships, and when the services which members perform for the group, or the services which the group performs for its members, differ significantly. In so far as conditions of membership and services remain the same, a group's obligations to its members remain the same; and to the extent that kinds of membership and amounts and qualities of service, whether of group to member or of member to group, differ, a group's obligations to its members vary.

In many formally incorporated groups, some of the group's obligations to its members are strictly defined. It is customary in England, for example, to indicate as part of the title of organization, "Limited," or "Ltd.," in order to make clear that obligations of the group have been legally limited. The group's charter or license indicates precise details. Since not all obligations which are likely to occur can be known in advance, some of these must be left to common sense, gentlemanly agreement, appeal to common law, or to be settled in courts.

However, in more inclusive groups, such as family, municipal or national groups with general-welfare philosophies, the ranges of obligations may tend to be unlimited, except by resources. Nations, for example, differ regarding how extensively they can provide for "human rights," "human freedoms," and "civil liberties." Some obligations are primarily negative, i.e., provide protection of rights. Others are primarily positive, i.e., provide services, such as education, medicine, employment, retirement insurance, etc. Some socialists idealize "cradle-to-the-grave" support for all citizens.

We cannot here explore the multitudes of conditions which exist in groups, but we may generalize that, whether limited or unlimited, and whether stable or changing, a group tends to have obligations to its members, i.e., as conditions of membership. That the obligations which a group has to its members interdepend with the obligations which a member has to his group, and, consequently, may shift also with the extent to which the member fulfills his obligations, is also obvious. Problems connected with a group's obligations to its members will occupy much of our attention in the later section dealing with principles for choosing for a group.

A Group's Obligations to Itself As a Group. We distinguish, for convenience, between a group's obligations to itself (1) as a group with interests in addition to those of its members and those involving other groups and (2) as an organic unity inclusive of its interests in its members and in other groups.

1. *A Group's Obligations to Itself As a Group with Interests in Addition to Those of Its Members and Those Involving Other Groups.* Each group, and especially an organized group with enduring needs, is naturally self-interested in the sense that it has its own purposes, functions, nature and continuing existence to consider. It has obligations to assure its survival, growth, where desirable, and fulfillment of its purposes. It owes itself such efforts as are needed to attain, preserve, create or otherwise optimize its own values and minimize its evils. It may have obligations to itself regarding its esteem as well as its security. A nation, for example, which existed before its present citizens were born is expected to have obligations not merely regarding the reputations of its traditional heroes and the prosperity of its future citizens, but also regarding its own integrity, endurance, and historical significance. A private business corporation may be judged to have an interest in its own perpetuity even beyond the lives of its current stockholders, officers, employees, and customers. A state university may have an interest in maintaining a spirit, a tradition, and a reputation of its own, in addition to the interests which the citizens of its state, its students, its faculty, administration and staff,

its community neighbors, and its alumni have in it. Whoever is concerned about the welfare of a group as a group will neglect some of its obligations if he fails to recognize those which it has to itself as a continuing organization.

2. *A Group's Obligations to Itself As An Organic Unity Inclusive of Its interests in Its Members and Other Groups.* Although we have differentiated a group from its members and its interests in other groups, the actual interdependence between a group and its members and other groups is so fundamental to its nature that its interests in them are integral to its interests in itself as a group. To the extent that this is so, pursuit of its interest in them constitutes a part of its obligations to itself as a group. Here the problem of doing justice to each of its many such interests becomes a central problem. Just as an individual with a multiplicity of interests in developing a "well-rounded personality," so a group with a multiplicity of interests often has obligations to equalize and reintegrate these many interests in maintaining itself as a wholesome group. Sometimes its primary obligations consist in enabling its members to pursue their own ends as individuals. At other times its primary obligations may shift to providing support for a superior group upon which it partly depends for its existence or income. Hence, at times the most important obligations of a group consist in maintaining flexibility regarding the shifting loci of its other obligations, and in reducing conflicts among its various interests while distributing its limited resources among them in the most suitable proportions. The more we recognize the nature of a group as an organic unity, the more important does this kind of self-interest and obligation appear.

A Group's Obligation to Other Groups. Recalling our distinction between peer groups and hierarchically-related groups, we distinguish between two other kinds of social obligation.

1. *A Group's Obligation to Its Peer Groups.* To the extent that a group interacts, whether directly through its executive officers or indirectly through its members, subgroups, or their effects, with its peer groups, it tends to have obligations regarding them. Whether cooperating in serving the same individuals or in serving the same superior group, or whether competing for such services or conflicting over limited resources, a group may find that the principle of reciprocity tends to operate. To the extent that it does, a group may have obligations to itself to promote its own interests through initiating action. Positively, a group may owe itself the duty of assuring its good will to its peer groups so that assurance of their

good will toward it may be warranted. Negatively, when a group is attacked by a peer group, it may owe itself the duty of responding defensively. On the other hand, where the need for assurance of good will is not worth the effort to promote good will, it may be that no such obligation exists. And, where responding defensively to a minor attack will tend to escalate and aggravate conflict, a group may have an obligation to itself to refrain from returning insult or injury to the attacking group.

2. *A Group's Obligations to Its Hierarchically-Related Groups.* Not only does a group have obligations relative to how far the principle of reciprocity tends to work between a group and its subgroups and superior groups, if any, but additionally it has obligations to itself through its relations of partial identity, its joint functioning, and its interdependent nature and existence, with such groups to the extent that they exist. Some groups are more dependent upon their subgroups than upon their superior groups, and, hence, may have obligations to themselves to serve their subgroups more than their superior groups. With other groups, the situation is reversed. And a single group may find its obligations vacillating so that first its duties are greater to its subgroups and later are greater to its superior group, or vice versa. The problems of deciding between allotting its services to subgroups and a superior group, when it cannot do both, may be among the most excruciating which a group must face.

Principles for Choosing for a Group. An adequate survey of principles for deciding ethical questions faced by persons acting as members of a group should somehow take into account all of the foregoing kinds of obligations. In the following, we shall attempt to formulate a set of principles for choosing for a group. First, we shall state a most general principle, i.e., one which is applicable to any and every group. Secondly, distinguishing between intrinsic and instrumental values, we shall seek to discover principles pertaining primarily to intrinsic values, and finally, to propose some principles pertaining primarily to instrumental values. Also, in the second portion, we shall differentiate the problems for groups with fixed membership from those with variable membership, and propose principles.

In what follows, we shall presuppose the principles for choosing already stated in Chapter VIII. These should be reviewed before reading further here. The present treatment is intended as supplementary, and should be entitled, "More Principles for Choosing." The focus here is limited strictly to choosing for a group, even though a group is conceived as such that it may have all of the levels of kinds of obligations listed above. We shall have to stress again, that each principle is stated as something universal only if, or to the extent that, "all other things are equal."

Always Choose the Greatest Good for the Group. This is the most general, and most obvious, principle relative to choosing for any group when all other things are equal (including equally irrelevant). It involves, more specifically, choosing good in preference to evil, the better of two or more goods, the lesser of two or more evils, and the better in preference to the worse. It presupposes understanding what constitutes the group and in what the good, and greatest good, for it consists. It is presupposed by all of the following principles.

Principles Pertaining to Intrinsic Values. We presuppose here that the reader knows what we mean by "intrinsic value." Its nature and kinds were discussed at length in Chapters VI and XXI. One does not need to accept our particular analysis of the nature and kinds of intrinsic value in order to accept the following principles, for they are stated in such a way that "intrinsic value"may be regarded as a formal or logical variable ("x") which may be filled with any "logical value" ("a"), i.e., intrinsic value as conceived in any other way, provided that it is regarded as residing in individuals and groups in the ways previously proposed.

Here, as in stating all scientific generalizations as universal principles, we have in mind ideal conditions that may or may not ever exist in actual life. So far as I know, we do not now have any way to measure accurately the end-in-itself quality of experiences, either in the same person at different times or of different persons at the same or different times. Nevertheless, we can reasonably infer that people are partly alike and partly different regarding their enjoyments, under similar circumstances, and these enjoyments do constitute an ultimate basis for decisions. We can recall that, on some days, we enjoy ourselves most of the time, and that on other days, we feel miserable most of the time. We recall that our experiences in some groups are much more enjoyable than in other groups. We observe that some people enjoy themselves in groups much more than others do. We observe that some seem to enjoy themselves with or without instrumental assistance, or to have more of their resources for enjoyment within themselves; whereas others appear to be much more dependent upon instruments for their feelings of enjoyment, and to depend more upon sources outside themselves. All of these, for example, are factors to consider in judging regarding the existence of "the greatest intrinsic good" in a group.

The present section is divided into two parts, the first dealing with intrinsic goods in persons as group members and the second with intrinsic goods imputed by persons to groups as entities.

1. *Principles Presupposing that Intrinsic Values Exist in Persons As Members of a Group.* First (a) let us consider circumstances where the group is regarded as a fixed entity so far as its number of members is concerned and then (b) circumstances where the group is considered as variable so far as the number of its members is concerned.

a. *Group Number Fixed.* Again, the problems, and principles, differ depending upon whether the intrinsic value per member is considered (1) invariable (fixed, incomparable) or (2) variable.

(1) *Intrinsic Value Per Member Invariable.* The term "invariable" here refers to situations in which the intrinsic value is regarded as remaining unchanged, equal, or alike, to the extent that the principle applies. We intend to include here those circumstances in which intrinsic values are incomparable. In whatever sense intrinsic values are incomparable, they may be regarded as equally incomparable, or as comparable only in the sense of being equal.   No problems occur for decision and no principles for choosing exist when no change in the number of group members having unchanging intrinsic value is possible, other things being equal. Problems, and principles, pertaining to efforts needed to maintain the status quo may exist, but these have to do with instrumental values, and will be dealt with later. We can say of such a group that it is good; and we can compare it with other groups which have more or fewer members and can say that it is worse or better in the sense that it contains less or more intrinsic good; but as long as there is nothing that can be done about improving, or preventing the degeneration of, such intrinsic good, no moral problem can exist relating to it and no principles for choosing are relevant.

(2) *Intrinsic Value Per Member Variable.* If, on the other hand, the intrinsic value of one or more of the group members can be changed, for better or for worse, then moral problems can occur and principles for choosing can be formulated. Assuming that when we use the terms "more" and "less" we can speak in terms of equivalent units, we can formulate the following principles.

(a) A group is better when the intrinsic good of its members is increased. This is true whether the increase is in one member, or any other member, or members. That is, a group becomes better when one member obtains one more unit of intrinsic good. A group is better when one member obtains many more units of intrinsic good even though no other members do so. A group is better when all members obtain many more units of intrinsic good. The foregoing principle specifies nothing regarding the distribution of such values among group members. In a group of ten members, the group as a group increases in good exactly as much when one of the members increases his good as a member by ten units while the others do not increase as when each of the ten members increases by one unit, other things being equal. Now if there is some qualitative problem involved relative to such distribution, then things are not equal and some additional principle must be invoked. Distinction between a law of diminishing returns from added increments of instrumental goods and added increments of presumed equivalent units of intrinsic good must be kept clear if our present principle is to be understood. If an additional unit of intrinsic good was not in fact so enjoyed, then it would not be a full additional unit, under our present premises.

The point we are making is that the "intrinsic good calculus" (i.e., the hedonistic calculus expanded to include enthusiasms, satisfactions, contentments and organic enjoyments) can be applied properly to the intrinsic good of a group as well as to an individual or to the universe. We can state a principle for choosing as a code item as follows: *Other things being equal, when choosing for a group and being faced with a choice between two alternatives, one of which consists in increasing and the other in not increasing, the intrinsic good of members of the group, one ought always to choose the former.* As a subprinciple to this, one may say that: Other things being equal, when choosing for a group and being faced with a choice between two alternatives, one of which consists in improving only one member of the group and the other consists in improving no members of the group, one ought to choose the former. (If someone should remark that increase in one without increasing the others is likely to produce envy, which is experienced as an intrinsic evil, then the conditions we have specified do not prevail and the principle does not apply because not all other things are equal.)

(b) A corresponding negative principle can be asserted likewise. A group is worse when the intrinsic value of its members is decreased (or when the intrinsic evil of its members is increased). Hence, we can state the foregoing principle for choosing as a code item: *Other things being equal, when choosing for a group and being faced with a choice between two alternatives, one of which consists in decreasing and the other in not decreasing the intrinsic good of members of the group, one ought always to choose the latter.*

(3) Other distinguishable possibilities, e.g., where the intrinsic good of some members of the group is regarded as invariable and of some other members as variable, or where the intrinsic good of members is sometimes variable and sometimes invariable, or, perhaps more significantly, where the intrinsic good of members is variable in some aspects and invariable in other aspects, must not detain us here.

b. *Group Number Variable.* Principles differ when the intrinsic good of every member is considered as (1) invariable or (2) variable.

(1) *Intrinsic Value Per Member Invariable.* To the extent that the intrinsic good of each person can be considered as equal to that of every other person among the members of a group, the following principles seem obvious. Other things being equal: (a) The group is better when another member is added (e.g., as when a child is born to a family). (b) The group is worse when one member is subtracted (e.g., as in death). (c) The greater the number of persons added, the greater the intrinsic goodness of the group. (d) The larger the number of persons subtracted, the less the intrinsic goodness of the group. Such principles appear to underlie the urge to procreate, the drive for increased membership in groups, and the expansion of tribes, cities, states and nations. They may have been in the mind of the Biblical writer who said: "Be ye therefore fruitful, multiply, and replenish the earth." They appear implied in the Christian, Islamic and Shin Buddhistic ideals of heaven, which will be better when more souls, each having intrinsic value, are there.

We can formulate these principles as code items as follows:

(a) *Other things being equal, when choosing for a group and being faced with the problem of choosing between two alternatives, one of which consists in adding another member, whose intrinsic good is regarded as equal to that of each of the other members, and the other of which consists in not adding another member, who's intrinsic good is regarded as equal to that of each of the other members, always choose the former.*

(b) *Other things being equal, when choosing for a group and being faced with the problem of choosing between two alternatives, one of which consists in subtracting a member, whose intrinsic good is regarded as equal to that of each of the other members, and the other of which consists in not subtracting a member, who's intrinsic good is regarded as equal to each of the other members, always choose the latter.*

(c) *Other things being equal, when choosing for a group and being faced with the problem of choosing between two alternatives, one of which consists in adding a larger number of members, each of whose intrinsic good is regarded as equal to that of each of the present membership, and the other of which consists in adding a smaller number of such members, one ought always to choose the former.*

(d) *Other things being equal, when choosing for a group and being faced with the problem of choosing between two alternatives, one of which consists in subtracting a larger number of members, each of whose intrinsic good is regarded as equal to that of each of the other members, and the other of which consists in subtracting a smaller number of such members, one ought always to choose the latter.*

(2) *Intrinsic Value Per Member Variable.* To the extent that the intrinsic good of persons as members of a group can be considered variable, the following principles seem obvious. Other things being equal: (a) The group is better when a person with more intrinsic good is added than when a person with less intrinsic good is added. (b) The group is better when a person with less intrinsic good is subtracted than when a person with more intrinsic good is subtracted. (c) The group is better when several persons are added if more of them have more intrinsic good than the average for the group than if more of them have less intrinsic good than the average for the group. (d) A group is better, when several persons are being subtracted, if more of those being subtracted have less good than the average for the group than if more of those being subtracted have more intrinsic good than the average for the group.

These principles may be formulated as code items as follows:

(a) *Other things being equal, when choosing for a group and being faced with the problem of choosing between two alternatives, one of which consists in adding a person with more intrinsic good and the other of which consists in adding a person with less intrinsic good, one ought always to choose the former.*

(b) *Other things being equal, when choosing for a group and being faced with the problem of choosing between two alternatives, one of which consists in subtracting a person with more intrinsic good and the other of which consists in subtracting a person with less intrinsic good, one ought always to choose the latter.*

(c) *Other things being equal, when choosing for a group and being faced with the problem of choosing between two alternatives, one of which consists in adding several more person, the average intrinsic good of which is greater than that of the present membership and the other of which consists in adding the same number of persons the average intrinsic good of which is less than that of the present membership, one ought always to choose the former.*

(d) *Other things being equal, when choosing for a group and being faced with the problem of choosing between two alternatives, one of which consists in subtracting several persons the average intrinsic good of which is less than the average for the remaining members of the group and the other consists in subtracting the same number of persons the average intrinsic good of which is greater than the average for the remaining members of the group, one ought always to choose the former.*

(3) Possibilities for formulating principles regarding situations where choice must be made between those aspects of a group in which the intrinsic good of a member is considered invariable and those in which his intrinsic good is considered variable, for example, need to be recognized but they will not be explored here.

c. And possibilities for formulating principles regarding situations where choices must be made between increasing the intrinsic value of a group by increasing the intrinsic value of its present members and increasing its value by adding members the intrinsic value of each of which is presumed to be equal to that of each of the present membership, etc., should be recognized, even though not here explored.

2. *Principles Presupposing That Intrinsic Values May Be Imputed to a Group as an Entity.* Recalling how a group may be regarded as functioning as a substantial entity (see Chapters XVII and XVIII), and how persons tend to impute value to it as an entity (see Chapter XXI), we will now explore some ways in which people sometimes do judge groups and some principles for choosing relative to such ways. Whether the group, one's nation, for example, is conceived primarily as an object, i.e., something spread geographically with headquarters in a capitol city, with national monuments and shrines, political, military and cultural heroes, and a national flag and anthem, or primarily as a superior spiritual power with which one's own self is identified and within which, as citizen, one lives and moves and has his being, occasions arise in which one is called upon to make moral judgments regarding it. When war threatens, for example, one may judge that his nation ought to attack or

that it ought to seek peace, depending on how the judger conceives what is best in the way of behavior for his group. If such moral judgments make any claim to truth, must they not presuppose certain principles for making decisions?

Here again we can distinguish two aspects of a group, namely, (a) its enduring, fixed or unvarying aspects and (b) its flexible, changing, or varying aspects.

a. To the extent that it is regarded as invariable, oughts are likely to pertain primarily to greater appreciation of its supposed intrinsic good. E.g., perhaps one who has been ignoring the greatness of his nation ought to take time to recognize it; the custom of celebrating national holidays is designed partly for this purpose. Today, the importance of professional groups is increasing, and doubtless some day a suitable world government will exist to claim our loyalties. To the extent that a group as a fixed entity is judged to have unchanging intrinsic good, each member, to the extent that he is aware of that intrinsic good as in some fundamental sense his own, owes himself the duty to experience due appreciation of it.

Hence, we may formulate as a code item: *Other things being equal, when choosing for a group and being faced with a choice between two alternatives, one of which consists in having group members recognize and appreciate its intrinsic good as an extension of their own intrinsic good, and the other which consists in not having such recognition and appreciation, one ought always to choose the former.* Such a code implies nothing about whether and when occasions for such choosing may arise; doubtless many groups exist which are not regarded as having much if any intrinsic good, and the excessive fuss which advertising agencies make about some groups may even be judged detrimental to sound social evaluation. Principles exist also relative to the wrongness of over-evaluation as well as under-evaluation of worthy groups, and of mis-evaluation of unworthy groups.

b. To the extent that a group is regarded as an entity that is flexible and which may fluctuate relative to the esteem in which it is held, anyone responsible for choosing concerning the maintenance or improvement of its imputed intrinsic good may be faced with certain typical problems. First of all, other things being equal, it seems that the intrinsic good of the group, like the intrinsic good of anything else, should be preserved. We may formulate the following as an obvious code item: *Other things being equal, when choosing for a group and being faced with a choice between two alternatives, one of which consists in permitting the supposed intrinsic good of the group to deteriorate and the other of which consists in maintaining it, one ought always to choose the latter.* Likewise: *Other things being equal, when choosing for a group and being faced with a choice between two alternatives, one of which consists in merely maintaining the supposed intrinsic good of a group and the other which consists in improving it, one ought always to choose the latter.*

3. Principles may be formulated relative to decisions involving comparisons of the intrinsic good of a group interpreted in terms of the intrinsic goods of its members with the intrinsic good imputed to the group as an entity. Such comparisons are complicated by the act that sometimes the intrinsic good imputed to the group is regarded as objective and owned by persons as an external possession and sometimes the intrinsic value imputed to the group is experienced as partly subjective through the members feeling personally identified with the group.

Principles Pertaining to Instrumental Values. Many readers will find themselves in more familiar territory in discussing instrumental value, for, somehow, people seem much more preoccupied with means to ends than with the ends themselves. This is true of both groups and individuals; we appear to be more interested in what they are good for than in what their ultimate goodness consists. However, here again we are plagued with problems of actuality and potentiality, and of "real" versus "conditional" potential instrumental values. (See pp. 55, 58, 131, 132.) Fortunately, many of the problems, and related principles, have been studied in great detail in the science of economics. Efforts will be make here to limit consideration to the most general problems and principles relative to choosing for a group.

First of all, a fundamental distinction needs to be made between (1) values of groups to individuals and (2) values of individuals to groups. Then, of course, we can also discover (3) principles pertaining to the mutual instrumentality of individuals and groups. The significance of this three-fold distinction may be strikingly illustrated by citing three historically well-known statements exemplifying principles of each type respectively: (1) "The greatest good for the greatest number." (2) "He who does not work shall not eat." (3) "From each according to his ability and to each according to his need." The following considerations should help to provide the readers with a basis for reevaluating each of these statements.

1. *Principles Pertaining to Instrumental Values of Groups to Individuals.* The multiplicity of kinds of groups, and of kinds of goods and evils that groups have for individuals, is so great that universal generalizations are

difficult to be sure about. Each kind of group tends to have its own kind of value. Distinguishing between two general kinds of groups may help to provide a broad perspective. Sometimes a person joins a group voluntarily; for example, first you do not belong and then you belong. When you join a group, you usually do so for a purpose, and the utilitarian or instrumental good of the group to you is usually somewhat evident. But also you are born into some groups so that you are an insider from the beginning; to the extent that you feel yourself identified with your native group, it may be regarded as constituting a part of your own being and as having an intrinsic good in which you share. Then, for you, although the goodness of your group for you may be evident, distinction between the felt intrinsic good in which you share and the instrumental goods of the group for you may not be clear.

The situation is complicated further by the fact that sometimes a member develops antagonisms toward his native groups, and even when he does not depart he still regards group pressures as evil, instrumentally at least. And some who voluntarily join groups, whether a profession, a corporation, a new country, a religious organization or a marriage, come to identify themselves, almost wholly in some cases, so that their new groups are more significant to them than their native groups. Furthermore, the instrumental value which any group may have for any member may fluctuate both frequently and violently. In seeking to generalize about the values of groups for individuals, we must take myriads of variables into account. In what follows, we shall try to state principles that may apply to all groups, though it should be obvious that they can apply in only a very limited manner to some highly specialized groups. However, highly specialized groups usually depend for their existence and nature upon their services also to other more general groups, and these dependencies usually can be observed if looked for.

So far as voluntarily-joined groups are concerned, the individual becomes a member because the individual believes that the group will provide some good which cannot be attained otherwise or which the individual cannot provide so well. A person's expectations are not always fulfilled, but the person's motives should be clear. Voluntary groups exist because they are intended to serve the needs of individual members. One may generalize about whether an individual should join a group. If joining the group is expected to result in more instrumental good than instrumental evil, then a person ought to join; if membership in one group promises to result in greater instrumental good than membership in another group, then a person ought to join the former. But our problem concerns existing groups and what principles may be used in making choices for a group. In general, we can say that the better a group fulfills its purposes, the better it is. Now the primary purposes of each voluntary group are to provide the instrumental values which it is specifically designed to provide. Native groups have a wider range of purposes, but all of them may be looked upon as instrumental or utilitarian. For even to the extent that a group serves as a basis for feelings of shared intrinsic values, such service may be regarded as an instrumental value.

Some choices have to do with service by the group to a particular member and some with service to many or all members. Principles may be stated relative to both of these conditions. (a) Other things being equal, a group ought always produce a greater rather than a lesser good for each member. Or, better, other things being equal, a group ought always to produce the greatest good it can for each member. (b) Other things being equal, a group ought always to provide as much good (or as many goods) as it can for as many members as it can. Traditionally, following the British Empiricists, this has been called "the greatest good for the greatest number." These principles may be formulated as code items: (a) *Other things being equal, when choosing for a group and being faced with the problem of choosing between two alternatives, one of which consists in the greatest good, and the other in less than the greatest good, which the group can produce for an individual member, one ought always to choose the former.* (b) *Other things being equal, when choosing for a group and being faced with the problem of choosing between two alternatives, one of which consists in the greatest good for the greatest number and the other in less than the greatest good for the greatest number, one ought always to choose the former.* Ambiguities or uncertainties regarding what constitutes "the greatest good" and "the greatest number" are so great that this latter principle, especially, seems more like the statement of a problem than a coded solution. To the extent that "the greatest good" is conceived as something that can be stretched, implicit in the foregoing is the principle which may be coded as: *Other things being equal, when choosing for a group and being faced with the problem of choosing between two alternatives, one of which consists in producing the greatest good for a smaller number and the other for a greater number, one ought always to choose the latter.*

We cannot here review what constitutes the values which groups have for individuals. Specialized groups perform specialized services. Native or general groups are expected to provide security and freedom, including security of life, limb, reputation, and property, and freedom from enemies, want and injustice. The history of the growth in the number of kinds of security and of "the freedoms" which nations, for example, have been able to provide for their citizens is amazing. What constitutes "the greatest good" that is possible under different historical circumstances has varied greatly. Ideals of what constitutes a proposed minimum of social goods for individuals have changed from "the Bill of Rights," through the U.S. Constitution, the United Nations Charter, to "cradle to the grave" proposals of some socialists. These changes, or inequalities, of circumstances must be taken into account before the "other things being equal" clause has meaning as a condition for the code item.

2. *Principles Pertaining to Instrumental Values of Individuals to Groups.* Groups cannot exist without members; and the nature, vitality, endurance and services of groups to individuals depend upon the services of individuals to groups. The problem being considered here is not so much that of an individual asking oneself how much shall I serve my group as how much shall I, in acting for a group, judge what the group ought to require, or expect, or assess, from each of its members. Some specialized voluntary groups specify certain requirements as conditions of membership. But general, especially native, groups are plagued with variations in what can be expected of different members as well as in kinds of services which may be needed by them. Infants, the aged, the ill, the able-bodied, etc., all have different abilities. Are there any minimal values which a group can expect of its members?

The problem is easy when payment of a membership fee or signing a statement of affirmation is all that is required. But when a person is inducted into life-long citizenship in a nation without one's prior consent, problems exist regarding how much value one has, except potentially, for his group. A national state usually protects its infants and children before they are old enough to ask for protection; when a certain age is reached, an initiation ceremony often occurs at which the individual may pledge his loyalty to the group in return for its loyalty to him. Excepting those who are helpless, a group tends to expect a certain minimum of service to it by its members. An attitude of loyalty to the group is usually regarded as a minimum, though stable and prosperous societies can often afford the luxury of permitting certain degrees of disloyalty among some citizens, even as they can afford to support infants, indigents, playboys, and even criminals. But those who endanger group existence or welfare may expect to be imprisoned, exiled or put to death. With so many variables affecting individual circumstances, the most that many groups expect is a willingness to put forth the effort to do the best one knows how to do when called upon. In large groups, certain standards must be adopted in order to assure group welfare. Laws are enacted to specify a citizen's duties, as well as rights, when unwritten mores prove insufficient. Minimal service of members usually involves a willingness to abide by the law of the group, though problems continue regarding the extent to which minorities that have opposed passage of laws unfavorable to them are expected to comply. Laws regarding payments of taxes, military service, registration of contracts, and payment of fines for law violations are among the most obvious requirements of a citizen.

As a most general principle regarding the instrumental values of members to their groups, it should be obvious that, other things being equal, a member should do the best he can for his group. This principle can be formulated as a most general code item: *Other things being equal, when choosing for a group and being faced with the problem of choosing between two alternatives, one of which consists in recommending to a member that he do the best that he can for his group and the other in recommending that he do less than the best he can for his group, one ought always to choose the former.* A corollary of this principle pertains to how one member should treat another member of a group. Although it should be obvious also that members often differ in the ways in which they should be treated (as we shall see further below), to the extent that a member is in good standing and has a particular status as a member, one member ought to treat him, relative to that status, in the best way that he can, other things being equal. The principle involved here has been expressed many times relative to family life, including that idealization of family life in which God is depicted as a father wanting his children to love, care for, and behave justly toward one another. Parents want their children to behave in a brotherly manner toward each other, not merely as individuals but also as members of their family group. This principle, formulated as a code item, is: *Other things being equal, when choosing for a group and being faced with the problem of choosing between two alternatives, one of which consists in recommending that one member do the best he can for another member of the group and the other of which consists in recommending that he do less than the best for the other, one ought always to choose the former.*

Of special importance, when considering the instrumental values of members to groups, are those members who become leaders or officers, regardless of whether they are elected, appointed, self-asserted, or otherwise acquire positions of more than usual responsibility. For convenience, we shall limit our references to officers. Officers have additional instrumental values to their groups, and consequently additional duties inherent in the nature of their services. Some such goods, services or duties are specified explicitly in formulated statements, either in a voluntary contract or through public legislation. But others are more indefinite, for some officers, a president, for example often is expected to meet and deal with all unanticipated problems no matter what they turn out to be. That is, some officers have the responsibility for assuming responsibility for dealing with group values even though the group has not formally delegated responsibilities relative to them. Even though groups often become especially concerned about defining and enforcing the appropriate behavior of officers in providing services, any additional general code item regarding officers seems redundant. In general, other things being equal, officers also should do the best that they can for their group; since they are often in positions to do more good, or more harm, to their groups than ordinary members, these other things which make their positions unequal are already, in effect, accounted for.

3. *Principles Pertaining to the Interrelations of the Values of Members and Their Groups for Each Other.* A group is better, in the sense that more instrumental goods exist within it, when both the group does the best it can for members and its members do the best they can for it, than when either the group fails to do the best it can for its members or when the members fail to do the best they can for it. The more fully persons become aware of the enrichment of instrumental values which derives from improving the mutual services of groups and their members to each other, the more interested they tend to become in the organic interdependencies that may be strengthened or weakened somewhat at will. Not only can we formulate (a) most general principles, incorporating the principles already cited, regarding the values of mutual instrumental values of groups and their members, stated above, but also (b) some principles relating to differentials involving the principle of reciprocity.

a. Our first principle may be stated as a code item thus: *Other things being equal, when choosing for a group and being faced with the problem of choosing between alternatives, one of which consists in both the group doing the best it can for its members and its members doing the best they can for it, another of which consists in the group doing the best it can for its members without their doing the best they can for it, and another of which consists in the members doing the best they can for the group without the group doing its best for them, one ought always to choose the former.* Corollaries may be stated regarding choosing relative to interrelations between a group and one member, and between a group in which members do and a group in which members do not do what is best for each other.

Other principles may be stated relative to intentions. Even when other things are equal, people do not always intend to do what is best for their group and their group, through its representative officers, does not always intend to do what is best for them. When such cases exist, other principles may be stated relative to intentions. Consider the following as a code item: *Other things being equal, when choosing for a group and being faced with the problems of choosing between alternatives, one of which consists in both a group intending to do what is best for its members and its members intending to do what is best for it, another of which consists in a group intending to do hat is best for its members without its members intending to do what is good for it, and another of which consists in the members of a group intending to do what is best for it without the group reciprocating by intending to do what is good for them, one ought always to choose the former.* Corollaries may be stated here also relative to interrelations between a group's intentions and one member's intentions, and between a group in which members do and a group in which members do not intend to do what is best for each other. The "other things being equal" relating to such principles and code items are involved with the difficulties inherent in the nature of intentions. (See Self As Agent, pp. 146-153.)

b. More interesting, perhaps, are those situations clearly involving operation of the principle of reciprocity. That is, when either a group or its members initiate improvement of, i.e., doing more good for, the other, and when the other responds reciprocally, then more good exists than when the other does not so respond. That is, the presence of the tendency to reciprocate is itself an instrumental value (which, of course, may operate negatively as well as positively). Hence, the code item: *Other things being equal, when choosing for a group and being faced with the problem of choosing between alternatives, one of which consists in a group doing more good for its members and its members reciprocating by doing more good for it, and another of which consists in a group doing more good for its members without its members reciprocating by doing more good for it, and another of which consists in its members doing more good for it without it reciprocating by doing more good for them, one ought always to choose the former.* Corollaries may be stated relative to reciprocating tendencies between a group and a single member, and to reciprocating tendencies between members of a group as a factor in reciprocating tendencies between a group and its members.

The foregoing principle and code item may be restated relative to intentions: *Other things being equal, when choosing for a group and being faced with the problem of choosing between alternatives, one of which consists in a group intending to do more good for its members with its members reciprocating by intending to do more good for it, and another of which consists in a group intending to do more good for its members without its members reciprocating by intending to do more good for it, and other of which consists in the members of a group intending to do more good for he group without the group reciprocating by intending to do more good for it, one ought always to choose the former.* Corollaries may be formulated here also.

Can principles be formulated regarding reciprocal relations between a group and individual members when differentials exist regarding services? That is, when one member serves (i.e., does good for) a group more than other members do, should the group reciprocally serve that member more than it serves the other members? This principle may be observed in operation where persons are paid for their services on a piece-work basis, for example, or on a per-hour or per-month work basis; those who produce more units or those who work longer hours are paid more proportionately. An increased rate of pay for overtime work is based on the principle that work after regular hours is worth more to the group than work during regular hours only. Consider the following code item: *Other things being equal, when choosing for a group and being faced with the problem of choosing between two alternatives, one of which consists in a member serving (i.e., doing good for) a group more than other members do and the group reciprocates by serving that member more than it does other members, and the other of which consists in a member serving a group more than other members do without the group so reciprocating, one ought always to choose the former.* Among the variables included in "other things being equal" may be such conditions as a person just wanting to serve the group without additional recompense, as a person regarding it an honor, hence a service to him, when his group permits him to serve the group in outstanding ways, as when many members compete for opportunity to serve, as when one is requested, against his will, to perform some task alone, and as when the service conforms to the group's consensus of what is good for it versus when the member alone decides what is good for the group.

Conversely, when a group, for whatever reason, selects and serves one member better than other members, ought that member reciprocate by serving the group better? Persons quite often, even quite naturally, respond to being selected by increased attention, interest and service. Sometimes reciprocation is required, as, for example, in a graduated income tax where, presumably, the national group has somehow favored individual citizens with opportunities for acquiring disproportionately greater incomes. The intricacies of factors involved in attempting to promote justice proportionately relative to income tax legislation and actual assessment are well known. Yet, despite the multiplicities of variables, a most general code item is formulatable. *Other things being equal, when choosing for a group and being faced with the problem of choosing between two alternatives, one of which consists in a group serving one member more than it does other members with the members reciprocating by serving the group more than other members do, and the other of which consists in a group serving one member more than it does others without the member reciprocating proportionately, one ought always to choose the former.*

The reader may have observed that we have not yet considered the principle stated as "from each according to his ability and to each according to his need." We have limited our efforts here to stating most general principles, and, although principles may be formulated relative to a group requesting service from each member in accordance with one's abilities, relative to a group serving its members in accordance with their needs, and a group both requesting services according to abilities and giving services according to needs, such principles do not seem so self-evident or as universally applicable as those we have been considering. Although it does seem true that in some groups, other things being equal, a group should expect services from its members according to their abilities, it is also true that other groups do not require the use of the abilities of all their members. We might be able to determine under what conditions in a group such a principle would hold, but the problem of determining these conditions appears to be more a problem in sociology or economics than in general ethics.

Although space has not permitted exploration of still another area of problems often involved in choosing for a group, namely, those pertaining to interrelations between groups, surely enough principles have been formulated to make evident that a science of ethics is possible. If ethics is concerned with what is good and how to get it, or what is best and what one ought to do, or choose to do, in order to attain it, then surely, no science is more important to persons and groups than the science of ethics. Is not formulation of a more adequate set of principles for choosing a part of what a person wants most?

Summary of Principles for Choosing for a Group. Other things being equal:

A. *Principles applying to both intrinsic and instrumental values:* Always choose the greatest good for the group.

B. *Principles pertaining primarily to intrinsic values:*

1. *Principles presupposing that intrinsic values exist in persons as members of a group:*

   a. Group number fixed:

      (1) Intrinsic value per member invariable. No principles stated.

      (2) Intrinsic value per member variable:

         (a) Choose increasing intrinsic value in preference to not increasing intrinsic value of group members.

         (b) Choose not decreasing intrinsic value to decreasing intrinsic value of group members.

   b. Group number variable:

      (1) Intrinsic value per member invariable:

         (a) Choose adding another member in preference to not adding another member whose intrinsic value is regarded as equal to each of the other members of   the group.

         (b) Choose not subtracting a member in preference to not subtracting a member whose intrinsic value is regarded as equal to each of the other members of   the group.

         (c) Choose adding a larger number in preference to adding a smaller number of new members each of whose intrinsic value is regarded as equal to each of   the present members.

         (d) Choose subtracting a smaller number in preference to subtracting a larger number of members from a group when the intrinsic value of each is regarded as equal to other members of the group.

(2) Intrinsic value per member variable:

(a) Choose adding a person with more intrinsic value in preference to a person with less intrinsic value when deciding which of two persons to add to a group.

(b) Choose subtracting a person with less intrinsic value in preference to a person with more intrinsic value when deciding which of two persons to subtract from a group.

(c) Choose adding several persons whose average intrinsic value is greater than that of the present membership in preference to adding the same number of persons whose average intrinsic value is less than that of the present membership.

(d) Choose subtracting several persons whose average intrinsic value is less than that of other present members in preference to subtracting the same number of persons whose average intrinsic value is greater than that of the other present members.

2. *Principles presupposing that intrinsic value may be imputed to a group as an entity:*

a. Group as an entity considered unvarying:
Choose having group members appreciate it in preference to not appreciating it.

b. Group as an entity considered variable:

(1) Choose maintenance of group intrinsic good in preference to permitting it to deteriorate.

(2) Choose improvement of group intrinsic good in preference to merely maintaining it.

C. *Principles pertaining primarily to instrumental values:*

1. *Principles pertaining to instrumental values of groups to individuals:*

a. Choose greatest good in preference to less than the greatest good for an individual member.

b. Choose greatest good for greatest number in preference to less than the greatest number of members of the group.

2. *Principles pertaining to instrumental values of individuals to groups:*

a. Choose recommending that a member do the best he can for his group in preference to less than the best.

b. Choose recommending that one member do the best he can for
    another member of the group in preference to less than the
    best.

3. *Principles pertaining to the interrelations of the values of members
    and their groups:*
    a. Choose both the group doing the best it can for its members
        and its members doing the best they can for it in preference to
        either one of these alternatives alone.
    b. Choose both a group intending to do what is best for its
        members and its members intending to do what is best for it in
        preference to either one of these alternatives alone.
    c. Choose both a group doing more good for its members and its
        members reciprocating by doing more good for it in preference
        to either one of these alternatives without reciprocation.
    d. Choose both a group intending to do more good for its
        members and its members reciprocating by intending to do
        more good for it in preference to either one of these
        alternatives without reciprocating intentions.
    e. Choose a group reciprocally serving a member more than other
        members when that member has served it more than other
        members in preference to a group which does not reciprocate.
    f. Choose a member reciprocally serving his group more than
        other members do when his group serves him more than other
        members in preference to a member not so reciprocating.

Chapter XXIV

SOCIAL ACTION

Social Agency and Social Action. "Social action," as this term is used here, consists in the actions or activities of groups. Anything which acts is an actor or agent; so when a group acts in any way we can call it an agent or an agency. Some groups are independent or sovereign agencies, e.g., such as national governments, because the source of authority for their action is entirely within themselves; some are dependent agencies which have their power or authority delegated to them by other groups, as when a private company is licensed to do business as an "insurance agency," "advertising agency," or "realty sales agency," or when a function of government is delegated to some specialized agency, such as a "social welfare agency" or a court or police department which may further delegate its authority through deputies.

1. *How Do Groups Act?* Groups act through their individual members functioning as members of the group. The ways in which groups act vary in complexity and kinds of organization. Occasionally a group acts spontaneously, without organization, when all of its members happen to respond in the same manner to some catastrophe, for example. But most actions of groups result from processes of decision-making organizationally established. Every large group must have leading members of some sort, either formally elected, appointed through some established system of delegating responsibility, self-asserted, or selected by accident from having attention focused upon them in particular circumstances. We will not review here the history of forms of government, from hereditary monarchies, through dictatorial oligarchies, to various forms of democracy. Some groups await need for action before making a decision about how to act. Other groups establish elaborate mechanisms of legislation, administration, and adjudication for passing and enforcing laws regarding actions of both members of groups, officers, and the group itself (as when the U.S. Constitution limits the powers of the Federal Government).

Groups act toward, or interact with, their members as individuals, their members as members, their members as officers, other peer groups, and, when present, subgroups and superior groups. Sometimes they act directly, as when a legislative assembly votes to have its sergeant-at-arms expel disorderly persons. Sometimes they act indirectly, as when a federal government loans money to a private banking agency to lower the interest rates to stimulate home building so that parents can more adequately house their children. Or a national leader may insult the leaders of another nation so that it will retaliate with military gestures which in turn will generate fear of enemies which tends to reduce the relative importance of conflicts within the national group. But no social action exists apart from persons, who either participate in decision making or in carrying out the action, whether willingly or unwillingly.

2. *Origins of Social Action.* Social agency originates, first of all, in the same way that groups themselves originate. Groups come into being for the purpose of acting, or of extending the power of acting by its individual members through collective organization. Native groups originate in the biological conditions of mother-child relationships, for example, and in their joint interests in protection from enemies and in division of labor in obtaining food and other needs.

Historically, persons functioned in groups before they discovered the existence of groups. They discovered the nature of group agency in just the same way that they discovered their own agency. They found themselves acting in a group, a familial or tribal group. A child, often afraid even without being attacked, sympathetically recoils when an enemy approaches the mother who is suckling the child recoils. Common interests are almost instinctively aroused originally. Not only do individuals often discover their own individuality, their own being, nature, substantiality and interests first by becoming aware of the attitudes which others take toward them, as G.H. Mead has shown (See Chapter VI), but also groups, through their members, often discover their group existence, nature, substantiality and interests by becoming aware of the attitudes which people in other groups take toward them. A group often discovers its agency, or some of its kinds of agency, as a consequence of its reagency, its reaction to the actions of other groups upon it.

Secondly, the social agency involved in particular acts, or in specific kinds of acts, originates in the same way in which particular or specific purposes arise. Some tendency toward social action occurs relative to every kind of social interest. Interests in survival, in production of goods, in increasing the power, cohesion, and welfare of a group, each generates its own kinds of group action. In a complex national society we can observe such specific kinds of agency as those needed in manufacturing, transporting, distributing, selling, managing, banking, loaning, insuring, legislating, policing, educating, and recreating. The need for each specific kind of social action originates with the emergence of each kind of social interest.

Although sometimes awareness of group needs occurs uniformly in members, as when devastating drought or floods or advancing enemies are obvious to everyone, oftentimes in bureaucratically organized groups, group problems and interests arise when someone complains. That is, particular individuals feel a difficulty first and then call it to the attention of the group through its officers. Sometimes special-interest subgroups organize to promote group awareness of a problem, and they may even succeed in deceiving the group as to what its own genuine interests are. Groups, like individuals, sometimes act on misinformation.

Social Intentions. Problems about the nature of intention, which plagues us in considering the nature of a self as agent, recur again, except that now we have the additional problems of considering the varying degrees of intention of different members of a group and how much consensus is required before we can say that the group intends. Only persons can intend, and we can say that a group intends only when it functions as an extension of the persons who are its members. Although, in a sense, we can judge the intentions of some groups by the way they actually behave or function, groups themselves often must face the problem of deciding what is required before they can regard themselves as having clear intentions. Some small groups may reach a "Quaker consensus" by discussion until unanimity is apparent. Some groups have a leading officer, such as the "head of the household," the "executive secretary," or "commanding officer," who is commissioned to make decisions regarding group intentions. Larger formally organized groups often have legislative sessions, either for all members or for elected representative delegates, where decisions about group intentions are reached.

The history of struggles to determine how much agreement is needed before a group decides it can intend is long and devious. Sometimes unanimous consent is required, sometimes only a simple majority, sometimes a two-thirds majority, and sometimes a three-fourths majority is specified. Usually more serious issues require a larger majority. Problems occur relative to whether a quorum, or a sufficiently large number of members to be considered fairly representative of the group, is present, whether the group has deliberated sufficiently long or with enough evidence, and whether the delegates are fairly chosen, may all confront groups concerned about clarifying their intentions. Sometimes decisions about trivial matters may be settled properly by only a few; for example, at some faculty meetings, where regular business must be transacted but only a few members attend because of lack of interest, the presiding officer is sometimes empowered to declare a quorum present anyway.

The problem of changing interests and shifting intentions of a group must be faced also. Sometimes legislation is enacted to be in force for a limited period after which reconsideration is required. Sometimes laws become obsolete without being repealed. Law enforcement officers often face the problem of judging whether the group's intentions remain as written or whether they have changed even without laws being revised or eliminated. Groups have problems of conflicting intentions, not merely as disagreements among members but also as contradictory laws enacted at different times. Courts are established, not merely to try civil and criminal cases, but also to pass upon questions of consistency between different laws. Courts which declare legislation unconstitutional in effect assert that the intentions stated by a legislature are in conflict with the more basic intentions stated in the Constitution.

Although group activity consists in anything that a group does, only some of such activity may be intended in the sense that the group has deliberated about it and reached a decision in advance about what to do. Of a group we can say what we did about individuals. Its actions may be partly rather than wholly intended. A group becomes an intending agency only to the extent that its activities have entered the awareness of its effective members and result from a decision reached by them. Although, as we shall see, a group may regard itself as responsible for results of its actions which were unintended, there is a sense in which a group is responsible only for its intended actions. We can judge a group, as well as an individual, as blameworthy, or praiseworthy, or as having acted wrongly or rightly. But we can do this only if we recognize the sense in which a group can have intentions.

Social Responsibility. Do groups have responsibilities? Yes. But not all groups have the same responsibilities, and some groups have many more responsibilities than others. In exploring social responsibility, and irresponsibility, let us consider the following questions: (1) What are some ways in which groups may be judged responsible? (2) For what are groups responsible? (3) To whom are groups responsible? (4) Who, in groups, are responsible for group responsibility?

1. *Ways in which groups are responsible.* In discussing the nature of responsibility in individual selves, we distinguished five different meanings

of "responsibility." All five are relevant for understanding the nature of group responsibility.

a. A group is responsible for any effect which it causes intentionally. Presupposed here is the existence of a group as an agent, i.e., a free agent in which acts originate, and as an intending agent. When the president of a nation, for example, intending to defend the nation's honor, responds to criticism from one foreign action with defensive remarks, if such remarks unwittingly offend those in still other nations, he was responsible for causing those offenses, even though he did not intend to cause them when he intended his defensive remarks. We blame him for acting for the group even without his being sufficiently aware of all of the consequences of his well-intended actions. To the extent that he is empowered to act for the group, the group itself is thereby involved in the responsibility for such action.

b. A group is responsible in the sense that it recognizes itself as an intending and causative agent, not unwittingly but wittingly. When a group consciously accepts its own agency as an ability to act, and to respond, not merely to the acts of other groups or persons, but in the sense that it recognizes the effects of its actions as its own, it is said to be responsible. If, on the other hand, a group refuses to recognize itself as an agent, then it may be said to be irresponsible. A group may recognize itself as an agent in some cases in which cases it is responsible, but refuses to recognize itself as an agent in other cases, in which cases it is irresponsible.

c. A group may recognize itself as the cause of ill effects but be unwilling to make amends. When a nation at war intends to damage another country but is unwilling to make reparations even for damages to non-combatant or to neutral countries, it may be said to be irresponsible in this sense. When the father of a family is willing to repay for damages which his son caused to his neighbor's window even when his family must forego some good, that family group may be said to be responsible, in this sense.

d. A group may be willing to pay reparations for damages it has caused, but be unable in the sense that it lacks the capacity, such as the money or goods needed. A nation may admit its debts, but have no resources with which to pay them.

e. Finally, a group may participate in some larger group, as a nation participates in a federation of nations, and have duties assigned to it as a member nation. It is then judged responsible for fulfilling such duties. Or duties may be claimed by a subgroup, and rightly so when organizational agreements allocate responsibility for actions of certain kinds. For example, a member nation may call upon the federation for protection against another member which is attacking it.

2. *For what are groups responsible?* Groups are responsible for intrinsic value. (See Chapter VI.) The answer, in general, is the same as for individuals Groups not only depend upon, but exist for the sake of, their members as persons in whom intrinsic goods exist. More specifically, a group is responsible, ultimately, for the intrinsic goods of its members, either generally, as with native groups, or specifically, as with special-purpose groups. Each secondary group has as its purpose to function as an extension of the interests of individuals who are its members. As such, it is instrumental, just as is an arm, the stomach, or the brain of an individual, to achievement, maintenance or improvement of the intrinsic goods of its members. To the extent that a group is regarded as itself an intrinsic good, either through a person's enjoyment of feelings of identity with the group or through a person's experiencing enjoyment when appreciating the intrinsic value that he projects into it as an idealized object, it itself serves, instrumentally, as a felt locus of intrinsic good. If there were no such enjoyed goods, there would be no responsibility, either individual or social.

3. *To whom are groups responsible?* Obviously, groups are responsible to themselves, or, rather, to their members as persons. But since not only each person is complex, but also each group is a complex of complex persons, it is not always easy to find the ultimate location of the persons, and that in persons, to which a group is responsible. Since we have already distinguished three levels of existence and goods of a group for individuals, we can state the range of loci of its responsibilities in terms of them. That is, a group is responsible, first, to its members both as individuals and as members, secondly, to itself as an ongoing entity, and, thirdly, to other groups, or to both their members and to the interests which its own members have in the members of other groups, whether they be peer groups, subgroups or superior groups.

Thus, the nature and locus of social responsibility is an extremely complex kind of thing, both with regard to what a group is responsible for and to whom a group is responsible. The problem is of sufficient magnitude that it needs a whole volume just to begin to explore the general outlines of the nature and kinds of responsibilities which different groups have. As people become increasingly interdependent, problems of social responsibility become more pressing, and adequate understanding of, and bearing beneficially, the many responsibilities which are crucial to megalopolitan and global existence become increasingly important. As Peter F. Drucker puts it, "Social responsibility...is the specific problem of 'virtue' in this post-modern society." (Landmarks of Tomorrow, p. 106.)

4. *Who is responsible for group responsibility?* Are all members of a group equally responsible? In native groups, surely infants, the ill, the illiterate, the infirm, are not all equally responsible? In large and highly organized groups, some members become officers with delegated powers and responsibilities for bearing group responsibilities. That is, some persons become more responsible than others, at least for certain kinds of decision and action for the group. The need for division of labor in groups begets a need for division of responsibilities. It may be that some responsibilities can and others cannot be delegated by members to other members. Those, such as maintaining personal attitudes of loyalty, appreciation, voting or assenting to policies, may be unrelinquishable. Just as there may be "inalienable rights," so likewise there may be inalienable duties of persons as members of groups which they cannot delegate. But, increasingly the growth of intricacies of social interdependencies requires the services of specialists who cannot perform their duties without their having delegated to them both sufficient power and responsibility to fulfill them.

Thus the problem of leadership in groups becomes increasingly important. Except in small groups, leadership is no longer something simple, as when one person arises and inspires the members of the group to follow some obvious social action, such as working together to build a bridge or to march in protest against some injustice. In a highly urbanized, technological society, leadership becomes distributed in intricate multiplicities of ways. Persons who become specialists thereby acquire, by virtue of their appointments to responsible positions, the specialized responsibilities inherent in the natures of their offices. Persons may be automobile mechanics, theoretical physicists, social case workers, tax assessors, state budget comptrollers, airplane pilots, statistical analysts, kindergarten teachers, armed forces commanders, bank examiners, newspaper reporters, or university reading assistants. Persons have responsibilities not merely to their employing officers and colleagues but also to many other persons, most directly to their immediate clients, but indirectly to still others who are affected by the welfare of their clients. In a cultural milieu where common standards of personal responsibility are well known and generally accepted and where the duties involved in the functions of an office are relatively simple and clearly defined, the problems faced by a person trying to locate one's responsibility do not appear very great. But in times of cultural transition, when older standards have become ineffective and general consensus has not yet been reached about newer standards, and when new subdivisions of labor and responsibility growing out of the demands of increased specialization create new and uncharted areas of responsibility with more complexly extending interdependencies, the problem of locating a person's responsibility is much greater. Yet, the more complex our interdependencies, the more important becomes the need to have responsibilities carried out adequately and efficiently. Since even the most conscientious officer may at times blunder unwittingly, at tremendous social cost, permission of carelessness in understanding and fulfilling crucial responsibilities may be inviting disaster.

Although the study of the history of social responsibility should help prevent repeating past mistakes, and a study of the kinds of responsibility needed in different kinds of groups in both developed and developing nations should broaden one's insight, a shift in ideals that has occurred in the United States in recent decades is worth noting. About the time of World War I, many people believed that each had some responsibilities regarding the status of things in general, in his company, in his community, in the nation, and in the world. But after World War II, the effects of expanding scientific, technological and industrial developments made comprehension of these responsibilities so difficult that many people came to believe they did not have responsibilities for making decisions about things which were too complicated for them to understand. Hence, it has become a common belief that the average citizen does not in fact have so many responsibilities as previously because they can be understood and dealt with only by people with specialized training, often of a very advanced sort. Hence, there has been a shift in the locus of responsibility from the citizen to the specialist. While this has been happening, has there been a loss or a gain in the efficient bearing of social responsibilities? (See "Are the New Conservatives Irresponsible?" The Midwest Quarterly, Vol. VIII, No. 2, Winter, 1966, pp. 105-121, and "Who Are the New Conservatives?" the Journal of Thought, Vol. 1, No. 3, July, 1966, pp. 8-15.) Although we have virtually eliminated the tyrannies of monarchs, dictators, and "capitalists," are more people suffering from dictatorship by specialists? Now that specialists are becoming increasingly responsible for group responsibility, the moral aspects of the training of specialists is becoming a more crucial factor in social welfare. What has been our response regarding the moral training of specialists? The picture is far from clear. As life becomes more complicated, we may expect more varieties of moral schizophrenia. Some persons are able to see that all personal and social activities have ethical aspects, whereas some reserve the term "ethical" for only some areas of life. Some with "loose morals" in marital matters, for example, may be strict self-disciplinarians on the job, though it is also true that people having conscientious temperaments tend to be more reliable than those habitually embodying careless attitudes. In many specialties, a novice cannot succeed in becoming a professional unless one acquires, through some sort of internship, the moral qualities, as well as the technical skills, needed to accomplish the specialized purposes. In fact, moral and mechanical skills interdepend in successful practice. Hence, the growth of specialization involves a new morality, or rather a whole complex of new moralities, which do not replace, but supplement the older ones; for people do continue to associate with each other as persons, and as citizens, as well as in their roles as specialists. Each specialist is, in a sense, a leader, or a decider, of social issues; hence the locus of social agency has become distributed widely among specialists. Many still conceive "social action" in terms of mob violence or propaganda campaigns; but basically social action consists in all that groups do, or refrain from doing, of a voluntary or intended sort, and the locus of social responsibility is, today, wide-spread among persons elected or appointed to specialized offices in which the specialist is primarily responsible for some of the crucial decisions and actions upon which the welfare of many groups depend. (See my The Specialist: His Philosophy, His Disease, His Cure, MacMillan of India, New Delhi, 1977.)

Chapter XXV

SOCIAL FREEDOM

What is "Social Freedom"? Freedom, we have said (See Chapter X), is ability to do what you want to do. Social freedom, as this term is used here, is the ability of a group to do what it wants to do. We have already explained in what senses a group can want, and act as an intending and choosing agency, by functioning substantially as an organized extension of the wants of its members. (See Chapters XVII, XX, XXIII, XXIV.) Thus group freedom presupposes individual freedom, for if there were no free individuals there could be no free groups existing as extension of those individual freedoms. Now freedom is never absolute, except in those individuals, and groups, which momentarily happen to get just what they want or, sometimes more enduringly, want just what they happen to get. And problems connected with unfreedom within an individual due to conflicts among one's own interests may function also as conflicts within one's groups; hence when conflicts of interest occur between members of a group, the problems of unfreedom of individuals in a group become magnified. Additionally, a group's freedom is sometimes opposed to an individual member's freedom, as well as vice versa, and by the freedom of other groups. In what follows, we shall first explore some of the complexities involved in the nature of freedom and unfreedom in groups and then examine some kinds and problems of political freedom.

Complexities of Its Nature. Before exploring freedom and unfreedom of a group from the viewpoint of the group itself, let us consider some kinds of freedom and unfreedom of group participation from the viewpoint of individuals. Although if interests of the various kinds outlined below never come to consciousness in an individual and the individual is then neither free nor unfree but indifferent relative to them, all are kinds which can become interests of individuals and which increasingly do so as persons mature in megalopolitan living.

1. First of all, the freedom of an individual to become a member of the groups one wants to belong to is a basic kind of individual freedom related to groups. This problem does not arise, of course, relative to groups into which one is born, for one finds oneself already a member without first wanting to become one. But when one discovers oneself to be not a member of an existing group which one would like to join, then one's inability to join is a kind of unfreedom. When one travels in a foreign country and is regarded as a foreigner, one feels unfree to participate fully in the affairs of the country. When one seeks to attend

school, but cannot because one lacks tuition money, one is not free to become a student. When one wants to play golf at a country club and cannot because one is not a member, one is unfree to play there. Also, one is unfree to join non-existing groups, as well as existing groups from which he is excluded. If one desires to attend school, but there is no school in one's neighborhood, one is unfree to join it as a group. If there is no golf club in one's community, one is unfree to become a member. Furthermore, one may be unfree to remain a member of an existing group, for either the group may cease to exist, as when a club dissolves, or one may come to the end of permitted membership, as when one graduates from high school, or one may be excluded from membership, as when one fails to pay required dues or violates other rules incumbent upon members. In all of these ways, an individual may be free or unfree to become and remain a member of a group.

2. Next is the freedom of an individual to not become or to not remain a member of a group. Freedom from groups is as much a kind of freedom, for people who want not to belong to a group, as freedom to join groups, for people who want to belong to a group. First, regarding native groups, if a person wants to leave home, leave the clan, or leave the country and is not permitted to do so, that person is unfree. Secondly, regarding voluntary groups, if one contracts, upon joining, not to leave unless certain conditions are fulfilled, then a person who wants to leave before they are fulfilled is unfree to do so. Where school attendance is required until a certain age, one is not free to become a dropout. Where marriage groups are formed contractually without possibility of divorce, one is not free to leave the group if one should happen to want to. Hence, so often people speak of the "bonds of matrimony."

3. The freedom of individuals to remain individuals while also being members of a group is an important kind of freedom relative to groups. Even though your membership in a group is an integral part of you, there is much more to you than this one part. Whenever a group demands more of your time, effort, money or attention than you want to give to it, that group makes you that much unfree. This may be true even of the groups to which you most want to belong. That is, you may find that membership in a group which provides you with what you most want, such as income, health, security, esteem, friendship and recreation, may keep you so busy that you have too little time "for yourself."

4. The freedom of individuals to do what they want to do as members of a group may seem to be the most obvious kind of freedom of

individuals in relation to their groups. If you want to attend school, marry, or be employed by a corporation and are free to do so, you may still be unfree in the sense that you fail to get as much out of your school group, your marriage group, or your corporation group as you want. Such unfreedom may have its source in your own ability to put as much into your group activity as you need to in order to obtain what you want, in the ability of other members of the group to provide conditions which are needed for them to obtain what they want, or in the ability of the group as a group, as an entity with limited resources and obligations to other groups, to provide such conditions. These problems represent our fourth kind of group freedom and unfreedom from the viewpoint of individuals.

Turning to problems of the nature of freedom from the viewpoint of the group itself, we can distinguish four varieties of freedom and unfreedom, namely, (1) those involved in the relations of a group to its members, (2) those due to conflicts between the various interests of the group itself, (3) those resulting from its relations to other groups, and (4) those due to its relations to its physical environment and, indeed, the rest of the whole universe.

1.a. A group itself may be free or unfree to have more members. Some marriages are childless, and, in most marriages, financial possibilities limit the number of children regardless of how many may be desired. Some schools, some villages, some corporations, some countries would like to have more members of their groups but remain unfree to do so. If there are no more persons who can join, the group is not free to have more members when it desires them.

b. A group itself may be free or unfree to have fewer members. "Two's company, three's a crowd." Some Hindu families cannot get rid of their older daughters by marriage because they lack sufficient dowry to attract prospective husbands. Some countries have become overpopulated but are unfree to restrict births. Some communities have criminals, or others with degrading characters, whom they would like to eliminate, but cannot. Freedom from members which it does not want is one kind of freedom for groups.

c. A group itself may be free or unfree to have its members as individuals devote themselves more to their other interests than to the interests of the group while they are participating in the group. A woman listening to a lecture who is knitting at the same time is obviously dividing her interests while in the group. A student sometimes, when discussing a class topic, may distract class attention by boasting about irrelevant achievements; when such is undesirable, a group can be freed from it only by elimination. All these are ways in which a group may be unfree relative to its members as individuals.

d. Even where the interests of members do not conflict with their other interests as individuals, a group may be free or unfree to have its members cooperate as much as it would like. Whether such cooperation is positive, as in performing services, or negative, as in demanding services, a group is unfree when it wants more services from its members than it obtains or when it wants fewer demands made upon it by its members than it receives. When parents want more help from their children than they receive, they are in this sense unfree; and when children require more attention, food or money than the parents want to give them, the parents are unfree also in this sense. When a city, through its government, wants citizens to vote for higher taxes so it can perform all of the services it needs to, it becomes unfree when they refuse; and when a city wants citizens to refrain from tossing trash on streets more than they do, it is unfree in this sense. Hence, there are at last four ways in which a group may be free or unfree relative to its members.

2. A group may be free or unfree relative to conflicts between its own interests. Groups, like individuals, tend to want more than they can obtain. When such happens, then a group continues to be unfree in this way so long as it cannot reduce its wants or so long as it cannot obtain what it wants. Some such unfreedoms appear clearly as conflicts of interest, as when a family must decide between having another child or taking a trip around the world, as when a college must choose between raising tuition and losing faculty members because of low salaries, and as when a nation must debate whether to surrender a profitable colony or fight a costly war. Almost all of the problems of deciding matters of social policy (See Chapter XX) involve groups in social freedom or unfreedom; when they can solve the problems which confront them as they choose, they are free, or able to do what they want to do, and if they cannot, they are not thus free.

3. A group may be free or unfree in its relations with other groups. When other groups prevent it from doing what it wants to do, it is unfree. When other groups enable it to do what it wants to do, it is free. Not only is it true that you are freer when you become able to join a group to which you want to belong, but also a group becomes freer when it is enabled to join a superior group to which it wants to belong. If the tiny mid-European country of Liechtenstein wanted to become member of the United Nations but was prohibited from doing so because of its size, it would be unfree to do so. Likewise, if a superior group, like the

United Nations, wanted Communist China to join but it refused, the United Nations would be unfree in this way. When two peer groups compete for the same benefits, when two families want to buy the same house, or when two colleges compete for the same professor or sports star, or when two corporations bid on the same contract, the one which succeeds is free, the other is unfree. When two peer groups want something which they can have only by cooperating, e.g., as when two families cooperate in building a duplex, or two colleges share a specialized professor part time, or two corporations pool their resources in order to win a bid, their willingness to cooperate with each other as groups in order to obtain what each wants is part of what makes them free in such cases.

4. A group may be free or unfree relative to conditions in its physical environment. A club is free to have its planned outdoor picnic and ball game only if the weather permits. A nation is free to feed its population, only if drought or floods do not destroy its crops. Mankind is free to perpetuate itself into the distant future only if planetary, solar and galactic conditions remain sufficiently stable for it to do so.

Social freedom, then, is complex. It is complex not only because there are so many different aspects of a group's nature but also because each of these generates wants which may or may not be satisfiable.

Political Liberty. Turning from social freedom generally, i.e., from generalizations about kinds of freedoms that may apply to all groups, to political freedom specifically, we mention a distinction, often overlooked, between freedom and sovereignty, the subject of the following chapter. In popular usage, political freedom and political sovereignty not only are often linked together but also even are thought of as synonyms. But if we distinguish between political freedom as the ability of a group to attain whatever control it wants and sovereignty as the ability of a group to control itself, then the two are synonymous only when a group is as sovereign as it wants to be. The non-synonymity of political freedom and sovereignty may be observed by distinguishing summarily between three general types of philosophy.

The first, which favors plurality and external relatedness generally, idealizes sovereignty in terms of independence. A group is politically free and sovereign when its control of itself is complete and it is completely independent of control by all other groups. This view presupposes that every group wants to be completely self-controlled and completely uncontrolled by any other group.

The second, which favors unity, totality and internal relatedness generally, idealizes sovereignty in terms of a group controlling itself, as a part of a larger whole, only as much as is needed to play its role in that whole. True sovereignty belongs only to the whole or totality, whether to the state, as in Fascism, or to God, as in theocracy; subordinate groups, such as families, communities and corporations, are completely dependent for their being and nature upon the totality. Since the welfare of the particular group is viewed as completely dependent upon the totality, and exercise of self-control by such a group in a way which would be detrimental to that whole is detrimental to itself. Hence, this view presupposes that every group, except the highest, wants to be controlled by that highest group as much as the highest group wants to control it. When it is so controlled, then it is politically free because it is controlled as much as it wants to be.

The third, which favors seeing groups as organic unity-plurality complexes, idealizes sovereignty in terms of interdependence. Since it observes groups as being partly independent of and partly dependent upon each other, whether peer or hierarchically-related groups, it does not interpret sovereignty as a matter of all or none, but of how much of which kinds are best for a group. If any group wants more sovereignty than it has, it is unfree; but also if it wants less sovereignty than it has, it is unfree. Sovereignty, as power of self-control, involves correlative responsibilities or, more often, more responsibilities than resources, which a group may wish to avoid. The goal of social control is optimum control; when it is better for a group to be served and controlled by higher or lower groups than to be self-controlled, then it ought to want that amount of self-control and control by other groups which is best for it.

Hence, we reserve discussion of political philosophies for the following chapter. The point being stressed here is that political liberty is conceived differently by different philosophical outlooks. According to the Organicist view, the stirring words of Patrick Henry, "Give me liberty or give me death," expressed a simplistic view which, though strikingly relevant to the American Revolution of his time, have become irrelevant in megalopolitan society, even though they may inspire citizens of still-developing countries. In megalopolis, political liberties are multidimensional, and those who suffer unfreedoms may do so multifariously, often feeling they must "die a thousand deaths" instead of just one.

Chapter XXVI

SOCIAL SOVEREIGNTY

Interpreting "sovereignty" as power of control, we have distinguished between "individual sovereignty," the power of an individual to control oneself, and "social sovereignty" or, preferably "political sovereignty," the power of a group to control itself. (See Chapter XI.) Just as an attempt to understand individual sovereignty was plagued with questions about both the nature of an individual self and the nature of self-control, so an attempt to understand political sovereignty is complicated by problems inherent in understanding the nature of a group "self" or "itself" and the nature of group self-control. Presupposed here is the treatment of the nature of a group in the foregoing chapters. (XVII ff.) We must restrict discussion of the multifarious forms and factors of social control to certain limited aspects of democracy. After (1) a quick review of some kinds of government and political philosophies, we shall focus attention here upon (2) the changing nature of democracy, and the problems of (3) levels of democracy and (4) democracy of levels.

Kinds of Government. The many ways in which groups have organized themselves into systems of collective self-control may be grouped for convenience into three: those in which a group governs itself by being controlled (1) by one of its members, (2) by some of its members, and (3) by all, or as many as possible, of its members. However, as society has become more complex, (4) additional types of systems perforce have appeared in which some kinds of control are delegated to one member, some kinds to several members, and some are reserved for all members. Although the following summary will be limited primarily to decision-making aspects of government, forms of government differ relative to whether the legislative, administrative and judicial functions are concentrated in the hands of one or a few or distributed among different people. In the smaller groups, concentration is more practical; in larger groups, a wider distribution is more necessary. Whether we like it or not, the increasing complexities of megalopolitan society today involve us in proliferations of divisions of responsibility for social control. In some areas, where the problems pertain to all members of a nation, for example, specialized branches of legislation, administration and adjudication may be needed; yet also in dealing with some particular problems, even a large group may find it necessary to delegate responsibility for both decision, action and even evaluation regarding details of social control affecting the whole group to particular individuals.

1. Forms of government having one ruler are called "monarchies." Varieties include those in which the one person has absolute authority, sometimes called absolute monarchies, autocracies or dictatorships, and those in which the one person has limited authority, often called limited monarchies or constitutional monarchies. Ways in which a member becomes a monarch are numerous; and systems sufficiently common to have received names are matriarchies, patriarchies, hereditary monarchies and revolutionary dictatorships. The moral aspects of monarchical systems are very complicated and one cannot dismiss them as inherently evil. In some cases, they may be the only, or only practical, options, even as today the U.S. Government emergency powers of a dictatorial sort are delegated to the President. Some argue that a benevolent despotism is better than perpetual bickering and violent clashes by selfish factions or than riotous devastation by undisciplined ignorant masses.

2. Government by some, whether a few or several, also occurs in many forms. Control by some may be hereditary, as in families and family-controlled kingdoms, acquired by force, as when several revolutionaries must pool their resources in order to win control, or by confederation of representatives from provinces in a non-democratic republic. When the rulers manage group affairs primarily for their own selfish ends, the system may be called an "oligarchy." When the governors rationalize their superiority in evaluative terms, they may be spoken of as an "aristocracy." However, aristocracy, as government by the best people, leaves open the question of who are the best people. Those already in power usually are in a position to press claims for themselves. Some claim divine origin or divine authorization, as in the doctrine of the "divine right of kings." Some claim to be better because they have the wealth with which to purchase their positions of power. Some idealize wisdom and advocate that philosophers should be kings; but others prefer saints. Technocracy, idealizing scientific, mechanical and managerial know-how, advocated government by engineers. Nazi and Fascist schemes accepted as rulers those persons who most wholeheartedly embodied ideas of "thinking with the blood" of a super race or submitted most completely to serve the will of the state. The Marxist "Dictatorship of the Proletariat" included only persons loyal to the Communist Party.

Regardless of how one judges the merits of each particular system of this type, in general government by some, rather than either by one or by all, has certain typical advantages. On the one hand, a single autocrat cannot be expected to know all and keep everything in mind. No matter how good his intentions, some unfairness will occur due to ignorance of some of the factors involved in crucial situations. Irrational and violent ruthlessness has no check. Many minds, by having among them both more information and a restraining effect upon each other's excesses, tend to promote government stability, unless, of course, they start quarreling among themselves. On the other hand, except in small groups or on extremely broad issues, it is impossible for everyone to participate effectively in governmental decision-making, partly because of difficulties involved in having sufficiently widespread mechanisms for collecting, organizing and summarizing opinions. The notorious political illiteracy and irrationality of the masses is also an important factor. Although ignorance and irrationality can be as detrimental in some as in one or all, when some have been delegated power to decide for all others, they tend both to acquire a wider range of concern and vision and to accumulate expertise in decision-making. When a few must share responsibility and blame for failures and public censure, they tend to become somewhat more conscientious than either one of the many or the autocrat alone. As the problems of government increase in quantity and complexity, distribution of decision-making powers is becoming more necessary, and the prospects for rule by some, rather than by all or by one, are increasing. The problem of how to decide which system of distribution of powers, and which person to fill each office, will continue to plague mankind forever.

3. Government by all, or as many as possible, constantly recurs as an ideal in all humanitarian sentiments. In practice, children, the ill, the ignorant, the indifferent and the disloyal are customarily excluded. In small groups, where the interests of all are fairly clear and the abilities of participants are sufficiently adequate, democratic procedures usually seem most fair and effective. In large groups, especially those with millions of members, democratic procedures have to be modified by electing delegates to legislative bodies. Here problems of which system of representation is best, as well as attainment of able representatives and fairness in election methods, become important. The merits of systems based primarily upon geographical distribution versus population distribution versus social function, class, professional organization and other specialized interests need to be considered. Likewise, the willingness of people to participate in government, once the tasks of acquiring needed information and the trouble of reaching a decision and going to vote become onerous, is a factor in democratic systems. The undeniable merits of some democratic ideals and practices, which have lead humanitarians to eulogize it as the only solution, must now be

reconsidered in light not only of recent setbacks in experiments in newly-arrived nations but also of the evolution of both technological and political conditions in the United States. We will explore factors of this sort in the following section.

4. Although convenient for outlining types of government, the classification of such types into governments by one, by some and by all is extremely naive in light of the multiplicities of compromises and intricately varied adaptation adopted in actual practice. For, in complex groups such as the United States or an effective United Nations, some kinds of control functions are best centered in one presiding officer, some are best handled by a committee, and some are best dealt with through popular participation on the widest possible scale. With the multiplication of areas of group concern, each becoming increasingly complex, the above pattern tends to repeat itself within each area, such that some functions become the integrated responsibility of a single director who needs the support of a staff of experts, not merely in administration but in supplying information and assisting in decision-making, and who owes it to himself and his constituents both to inform them of his agency's issues and to obtain their response of at least partial assent and cooperative participation.

A study of the government of the United Stated provides and instructive example of kinds of compromise among forms of government, since even from its foundation it was conceived complexly, with a division of governing powers into three main branches. The ways in which the decision-making officials in these three branches achieve office illustrate some differences. In the administrative branch, the President and Vice-President are elected on a popular nation-wide basis after candidates have been selected by party conventions which themselves involve complicated manipulations of delegations from local precinct and state party conventions. The Legislative Branch consists of the two houses of Congress, the Senate, whose members traditionally represent their states as a whole, and the House of Representatives, whose members represent geographical districts presumably somewhat in proportion to quantities of population. In the Judicial Branch, the Judges are not elected but appointed by the President with the approval of the Senate. Within the Legislative Branch, problems of various kinds are allotted to standing committees which exercise considerable discretion regarding legislation; these function through subcommittees which, in practice, often become the primary locus of crucial decisions. Since responsible officers in the various branches of the administration, headed by Cabinet Officer, which cabinet itself often functions as an Administrative Committee, have primary access to both information about needs and experience, in practice their recommendations often necessarily play a major role in formulating the decisions of legislators. The growth of new agencies which have become necessary as the federal government has been called upon to perform new functions for citizens has resulted in a rapid multiplication of new forms of control, some through cooperation with private agencies, some through exercising supervisory services regarding standards desired by the public, and some to assure new rights and privileges such as those relating to social security, education, health and employment insurance.

Ethical problems, some of which are peculiar to each of the three general forms of government, i.e., by one, by some, and by all, not only continue in our more complicated society, but problems relative to distribution of control powers among officers representing each of these three forms within our complexly interdependent system of control continue to assume greater importance. Since the attainment and maintenance of individual goods through social cooperation depends upon wise exercise of social sovereignty, constant and conscientious awareness of the ethical aspects of each kind of compromise between different forms of government continues to be needed.

What Is Democracy? Democracy, as a system of social self-control is commonly summarized as "government of the people, by the people and for the people." (See "Democracy Defined," School and Society, Vol. 66, No. 1704, August 23, 1947, pp. 135-138.) In general outlines, it is clearly distinct from monarch and oligarchy. Yet, since in the history of its practice so many changes have occurred, it now appears that even greater differences exist within different schemes of democracy than between democracy and non-democratic forms of government. We cannot here give more than a brief sketch of a few typical stages in the development of democracy in the United States.

We still idealize the New England town councils in which each individual male could, and often did, arise to speak his views about issues before voting occurred. Each member of the community came face to face with his neighbors inside and outside the meeting house, and factors in the needs and peculiar circumstances of most members could be taken into consideration. This same situation continues to prevail in some committees in contemporary society; but the conditions in which almost all completely self-sufficient and self-governing communities can manage their affairs have gradually disappeared in the United States. Rapidity of transportation, in the nation and the world, have produced conditions which multiplied the interdependence of people in most communities with people in so many others that only a small fraction of any community's self-governing problems can be dealt with finally in isolation from the agencies of other governmental groups.

Establishment of the United States as a federal republic involved acceptance of a representative form of democracy, both through state legislatures and a national Congress. Citizens no longer dealt with their common problems directly, but elected representatives to carry out discussion of them and to make decisions about them. Shift from direct to indirect participation in governmental decisions made possible the expansion of a democratic type of government to serve a larger group, both in territory and population. But it involved a diminution of the fullness with which the individual member could participate in the process of self-government. Problems of fair representation, both regarding the selection of representatives and regarding the fulfillment of trust by the persons elected became paramount. When the process of initiating legislation favorable to the needs of a local community became so great that expensive campaigns, highly organized political party cooperation, and the sacrifice of some interests in order to obtain action on a few others, the effectiveness of the democratic system came in doubt. Although early Constitutional amendments resulted in great improvement, later difficulties have made the Constitution almost impossible to amend. Control of party organization by persons and private corporations making the largest contributions to party funds tends to exclude the average individual from having any power to influence national policy except through voting in national elections on candidates whom others have chosen for him or through organized lobby organizations whose high-priced officers presumably have specialized know-how in influencing the legislative processes in the Capitol city. Although both systems are democratic, there is a great qualitative difference between the way in which a citizen participated face to face in a town council of fifty members and the way in which a citizen participated through several stages of indirectness as one person among more than a hundred million voters for one or two or three sets of party officers who are then authorized to administer the affairs of the country for four years without further appreciable influence by the average voter.

A third major stage in the evolution of American democracy is still in process. It is a consequence of the multiplication of specializations involved in understanding and dealing with increasing complexities not merely in scientific, technological and industrial development but in the increasingly complicated interdependencies of persons and groups. In private business, an accompanying change has been called the "managerial revolution." (See James Burham, The Managerial Revolution, John Day Co., New York, 1941.) The capitalist tycoon who personally managed his financial-industrial empire has given way to massive holding companies in which most of the policy decisions are made by managerial experts who may, themselves, own little or no stock in any of the hierarchically-interrelated corporations. In government, the multiplication of specialized functions requires the training of multitudes of technical experts, functioning either as civil servants or as consultants, who are paid to make decisions relative to the technical aspects of public problems. Both legislators and top administrators have now become dependent upon the advice of technicians, and so much so that, in many cases, they are, in effect, committed beforehand to accepting the decisions of such experts. Although speciocracy, i.e., government by specialists, has not yet completely replaced democratic government, the process has already gone far enough for us to predict that it will continue much farther. We do not yet live in a post-democratic age. but, as Max Lerner warned long ago, "It's later than you think." (Max Lerner, It's Later Than You Think: The Need for Militant Democracy, The Viking Press, New York, 1938.)

When citizens no longer deal with most of their political problems directly as in a town council, nor even indirectly through elected representatives, but more and more indirectly through contractual employment of specialists, many new problems appear. The expense of obtaining decisions increases, for example. And with the multiplication of specialties, a major problem becomes that of to which of the many kinds of specialists shall the major responsibility for deciding be allocated. When jealous rivalries appear among specialists for such positions, additional vitiating factors enter, over many of which the average citizen has no control. Not only do the interests of public welfare often depend upon democratic participation by specialists, i.e., in which all who are actually needed will obtain a fair hearing, but also how to prevent some from attaining undue control of the situation. Tyranny by a specialist, or by an oligarchy of specialists, is just as dangerous as any other type; and the costs of trial and error learning how to live under speciocratic forms of government may be very great. Does growth of speciocratic practices fore-destine development of a more richly intricate form of democracy, or will democracy disappear by being crushed in the jurisdictional disputes among tyrannical technicians? (See my Computocracy, World Books, 1986.)

As a close-to-home example of increasing government by specialists, to some readers of this volume studying in multiversities where administrative staffs have become professionalized, the results of campus design by architects may be obvious. Although it is part of the task of the architect to take into consideration all needs, including those of student pedestrians and motorists, it becomes all too obvious, in many cases, that the architect's own interest in a particular aesthetic style and set of standards have taken precedence over the convenience of campus users. It is true that we cannot leave such a complicated matter as campus design to pedestrians and motorists, yet the relative lack of recourse by them to have some effective voice in control of architectural decisions constitutes such practice as being less democratic than it could be.

A curious consequence of the uneven development in so-called advanced and retarded nations is that the United States government is now engaged in exporting democracy, i.e. attempting to assist countries with dictatorships to develop elementary representative democracies, while at the same time technological advances have made such democratic practices largely obsolete within many parts of the United States government itself. Such unevenness in development seriously affects our prospects of achieving a workable democracy at the world level.

Levels of Democracy. Despite the growing difficulties involved in an individual exercising one's own sovereignty or power of self-control through the self-control mechanisms of the various groups of which one is a member, these are the ways open to one and it may be to one's own best interests to make as much use of them as one can. Obsolescence of democratic practices in highly technical aspects of government does not necessarily involve their elimination from all local phases of government. Individuals may still participate personally in community councils, party precinct meetings, professional societies, and club, union and corporation committees. Some of these are ultimate loci of decisions and particular individuals can exercise unusually large shares of group self-control.

In contemporary American society, each individual is a citizen in or a member of a complicated hierarchy of groups. The problem of democratic versus dictatorial procedures recurs at each level. To begin with, a family of five may or may not govern itself democratically, or, more likely, may find a division of decision-making labor necessary, such that the father is responsible for how much income can be spent consumptively and how much saved or invested, the mother is responsible for choice of foods and clothing, both parents share in decisions about major family expenditures, whereas all may participate in deciding vacation plans.

At the community level, in smaller villages, opportunity for direct participation remains, and group decisions affecting many areas, economic, educational, recreational, medical, cultural, religious, and interrelations with other communities and with state, national and international organizations may be energetically pursued. Initiative and responsibility of a local community group may, through influencing international cultural exchanges, have a tremendous impact on world affairs. Sometimes persons pursuing self-control through even a single-community organization, such as a parent-teacher association or a United Nations support society, extend the range of both cultural and practical interests of their community.

In larger urban centers, possibilities for extensive local community activities may be more limited because some of them are in fact more effectively cared for on a city-wide scale. Participation in urban, as in state, national and international politics, tends to require organization or groups for the specific purpose of influencing legislation. Some of these are temporary, pertaining to a single issue. Some are more permanent, taking the form either of a promotional or propaganda organization or of a political party. Once the main channels of control become organized through political parties, then individuals find it necessary to shift the locus of their efforts toward democratic practices within such party organizations. Curiously enough, the opportunities for active participation in local party precinct activities have no glamour in American society, and the failure of Americans to exploit their opportunities here raises serious doubts about the depth, quality and significance of the democratic spirit in American life.

Attention to personal interests in municipal, state and national welfare is usually sufficiently well exploited by party organizations so that citizens become aware of some issues and arguments relative to them. But a growing feeling of hopelessness on the part of many voters to influence outcomes has produced both dismay and widespread indifference to minuscule opportunities. Growth of public services at all such levels means that individuals have more at stake in good government at such levels. Consequently, concern for assurance about effective democratic procedures at each level tends to increase at the same time when increasing complexities militate against ease in pursuit of democratic processes. The point being made here is that, despite complications, ethical problems involved in improvement of the democratic qualities of each of these three levels of government are more obvious to most Americans than of some other levels. Democracy at these three levels is more talked about than at others, it appears.

Perhaps the greatest deficiency in democratic self-control today occurs through the lack of effective world government. The feeble gropings toward world government occurring under the League of Nations and the United Nations Organization have begun to provide some practical experience in international political organization. But the predominance of nationalism as the highest form of sovereignty today prevents rapid growth. If a third world war is needed to bring people to recognize the practical necessity of a world government, it will, doubtless, be one of mankind's greatest tragedies. Lack of will to participate in such a government may imply a lack of willingness to be democratic with respect to it. People may be willing to be democratic at some levels, e.g., community or national, without being willing to be democratic at others, e.g., family or world. The field of the ethics of world government, both whether it ought to be and how it ought to be, remains wide open for exploration. There is a long history of humanistic ideals about the oneness of mankind and the desirability of treating all men and women as brothers and sisters. But, except for those who advocate world dictatorship to bring about such unity, the problems of working out satisfactory systems of the division of sovereignty at different levels and of achieving suitable democratic mechanisms at a world level have still to be tackled with seriousness.

The purpose of the present section is to point out that democracy not only occurs in many forms, but is also something which operates at many levels. The exercise of political sovereignty by individuals through their groups involves them in many different levels of such sovereignty and democracy.

Democracy of Levels. To the extent that you participate in self-government through many different levels of groups, you are involved in the question of how equitably to distribute such self-control among such levels. That is, just as imbalance of influence within a group may be regarded by you as undemocratic, so an imbalance of exercise of sovereignty by you through participating in only some, or in some more than others, of the levels of government which are available to you may also be regarded, in a sense, as undemocratic. That is, if you exercise some of your sovereignty through family, community, state, national and world governmental groups, you may be said to exercise more sovereignty, and do so more democratically in this sense, than when you exercise sovereignty only through your family, or your community, or your national group, for example. The people in some community groups, for example, are very much concerned that as many members of their community endeavor to participate also in state, national and international groups, whereas the people in other communities are socially quite self-centered, even regarding persons who are interested in national affairs exclusively as traitors. Such self-centered groups actually restrict the sovereignty of their members to the extent that they discourage or prevent them from participating in higher levels of self-government.

Lack of democracy of levels can occur at lower or intermediary levels, as well as at the highest level of world government. Just as a person is prohibited from exercising sovereignty democratically at a world level through lack of existence of a democratic world government, so another may be prevented from participating in more immediate and intimate forms of self-government through lack of having a family and family life. The extended period of residence required before persons moving permanently into a new state can vote constitutes a limitation upon the sovereignty of people during that period. Persons who, perforce, must move often for occupational reasons become effectively disenfranchised by such restrictions, as do persons living in states without absentee-ballot arrangements. Growth of megalopolitan areas, such as those extending from "Boston to Norfolk, Virginia, in one disorganized sprawl, the super-metropolis that stretches from Milwaukee to South Bend, or the super-metropolis of Tokyo-Yokohama in Japan" (Peter F. Drucker, Delbert C. Miller, Robert A. Dahl. Power and Democracy in America, p. 13, Notre Dame Univ. Press, Notre Dame, 1961), without a level of government organized to deal with problems of megalopolitan magnitude, constitutes the appearance of a new level of need for sovereignty without the organization needed to exercise that sovereignty emerging. Individuals caught up in such anarchy lack one level of democracy which they now need.

Not until one fully understands and participates in many, if not all, levels of government, and does so democratically, i.e., with some suitable distribution of one's powers of self-control through all of them, can one be said to achieve being completely democratic. The point of the present section is to round out some of the complications involved in the notions of sovereignty and democracy. Not only is democracy something which is different in different contexts, which has evolved through many stages from town councils to federal bureaucracies plagued with democratizing squabbles among specialists, which exists, or not, at many levels, but also it characterizes the extent to which an individual, or even a group, participates in all of the many levels of government. The purpose of pointing out the complexities involved in democratic theory and practice is not to discourage participation but to challenge the reader to more vigorous aliveness to the richness of one's opportunities. While so many seem to have become jaded into boredom by overexposure to exciting variety and others seem hopelessly lost in confusion, an alert and enthusiastic citizen who is willing to take the trouble to master some of the intricacies involved will find an amazing and limitless richness of challenge. If, as we have indicated earlier, being ethical is what one most wants to be, then responding to the challenge of being ethical in the richly complex ways open to American citizens through their various levels of government may, indeed, be just what some will most want to do.

Chapter XXVII

SOCIAL OWNERSHIP

"Ownership" consists in having something as one's own. A person owns one's own self, one's own body, one's own clothes and property, and one's own groups. (See Chapter XII.) By "social ownership" we mean owning by groups. A group has its own members, and in this sense may be said to own them, as well as any property, reputation, and stable ways of functioning which can be characterized as its own. Thus, although all ownership is basically ownership by individuals who extend their ways of owning collectively through forming, owning and belonging to groups which then function as owners, there is a sense in which individuals and their groups mutually own each other. Whenever an individual accepts a group as one's own and that group accepts one as its own member, such double acceptance constitutes a kind of mutual ownership.

"Disownership" is also social whenever a group excludes a person from membership or when a group of groups excludes a group from membership. Systems of racial, sexual, religious or political segregation illustrate social disownership. When a college counselor advises a financially able student to join a fraternity and he refuses and when the fraternity also refuses to admit him, a case of mutual disownership exists.

Just as ownership by individuals is multi-dimensional, so also is ownership by groups. An organized group, such as a university, has its own students, its own faculty, its own administrative and other staff officers, its own alumni, and its own financial supporters. It also has its own physical properties, such as land, buildings, furniture, research, teaching and maintenance equipment. It also has a reputation, or perhaps several reputations pertaining to its various functions, such as teaching, research, sports, or student achievements. It has its own history, and its own hopes for the future. All these are examples of social ownership, broadly conceived. Each may be regarded as a different dimension of such ownership, and each of the dimensions tends to interdepend with all of the others. For in such a university, students speak of "our president," faculty members speak of "our team," and the custodial staff may speak of "our leading professor." Social ownership may be very complicated, for citizens of the state and of the nation also speak of this institution as "our university."

What is Wealth? What is owned is usually regarded as good, although it may also be evil, or, even, neutral in value. Wealth (or well-th) consists of what is good, and illth of what is evil. Economics, the science concerned chiefly with the production, distribution and consumption of goods and services, is basically a value science. The goods produced, distributed and consumed are part of the wealth of the group, such as a community, state or nation. Agreeable climate, native intelligence, enjoyable companionship, happy temperaments, and much health may constitute wealth even when not deliberately "produced, distributed and consumed." Limiting our discussion to goods of the kinds economists deal with, we should note a need for distinguishing at least four kinds of value or value-concepts in order to understand the nature of social ownership of values. We call these "intrinsic," "instrumental," and "economic" values and "price."

The nature of intrinsic and instrumental values has been discussed at length already. (See Chapters V and XX.) An intrinsic good is one enjoyed as an end-in-itself, needing nothing else to complete it. An instrumental good is the good of anything which is "good for" something else and ultimately for the production or maintenance of some intrinsic value. In economics, instrumental values are often spoken of as "utilities," i.e., things which are useful. All of the factors which are useful in bringing about the production, distribution and consumption of other goods are instrumental values. They are instrumental values actually to the extent that they result in enjoyments, i.e., intrinsic goods. But, since it is not possible to eliminate all waste, i.e., the production of some instruments which are never used or never fully utilized, it is customary to stretch the terms "instrumental values" or "utilities" to include instruments which have conditional potential instrumental value.

Turning to "economic value," we encounter the notion of exchangeability of goods. When two persons exchange things which have value to each other, the value of such things when exchanged may be called their "exchange value." Such exchange value is clearly social, involving at least two or more people in an exchange group, even if not members of some larger group which makes the exchange possible; whereas it is possible for some instrumental values to be merely personal and private. "Economic value," also social in nature, is said to involve not only utility, but also scarcity and exchangeability. Scarcity is required because, when any utility is present in such sufficient abundance that anyone can have it without obtaining it from others, there is no need to exchange something else for it. Out in open air, oxygen is essential to life, but as long as there is enough for everyone, no one needs to pay anyone else anything to obtain it. Things, or services, have economic value because they are desired by persons who have other things which they can exchange for them. That is, the economic value of things depends upon their supposed instrumental value which, more ultimately, depends upon some expected enjoyment of intrinsic good.

Whereas primitive peoples exchanged eggs for berries, sticks for hides, milk for rice, with the development of monetary systems, people exchanged eggs, rice, and milk for money and then exchanged money for berries, hides or sticks. Early money consisted often in some precious metal, such as gold or silver, which was itself something which had instrumental value because it could be melted and molded into jewelry, for example. But later paper money, based on a promise to pay, in gold or goods, was introduced, and its superior convenience continues to make it popular, as long as the government or private bank making the promises remain able and reliable. Today, monetary specialists still speak of gold coins as having "intrinsic" value when referring to the instrumental value of the gold itself which the paper in paper money does not have; such usage should not be confused with the intrinsic good experienced as enjoyment. "Price" is exchange value expressed in terms of money. Supposedly, the price should bear some genuine relationship to the expected actual instrumental value, but since so many factors enter into production, distribution, consumption and exchange, some of which fluctuate erratically, such relations are likely to be only approximate at best. Since our estimation of the value of some goods is influenced by the price-tag itself, sometimes a price influences the enjoyment actually experienced by the consumer. Thus, although price basically depends upon economic value, economic value upon instrumental value, and instrumental value upon intrinsic good, all four intricately interdepend because even artificially determined prices sometimes influence salability, use, and consequent enjoyment.

Ethics, in being concerned with what is good and what one ought to choose to do in order to obtain it, automatically encompasses concern about the goods and services with which economics deals, including economic values and prices. Questions such as the following are all ethical questions: "How much ought a group (family, corporation, state) produce?" "How much of our natural resources should be used at one time?" "How should goods be distributed?" "What price should be charged?" "How much profit should be permitted where group welfare is at stake?" "How should production, sales, or consumption be taxed in order to pay for the governmental control system needed to make possible the peace needed for production and a reliable monetary system?" "What is a fair wage?" "Should there be any limit upon what proportion of the total economic wealth or income may be owned by one person?" These general questions entail more specific ones constituting what is often called "business ethics." The intricacies involved in conducting business leave one aghast at the perpetual plethora of ethical problems involved. Some of those recently occupying public attention include truth in advertising, high-pressure salesmanship, and truth in packaging. The situation is complicated by the different conceptions of ethics practiced by different persons. (E.g.: "Dad, what is ethics?" "Son, when a customer mistakenly gives you ten dollars extra in change, ethics is should you tell your partner?")

Probably most of mankind's ethical problems have to do with ownership of economical wealth. Doubtless the majority of laws, at national, state and local levels, pertain to ownership of property. Stealing, and all other "crimes against property," are of this sort. The problems of group ownership include whether a group owns too much in comparison with its members as individuals, whether one group owns too much in comparison with other groups, and whether a group steals from another group, and whether one group consumes more than its share of resources and products. Since there are levels of ownership, i.e., by local, state, national and international groups, questions about whether it is better for a particular kind of good, such as ocean resources, to be owned primarily by the local, state, national or international group level appear to be coming increasingly important.

Individual Versus Group Ownership. Focusing attention upon a particular kind of problem, let us explore the persisting issue of whether it is better for wealth to be owned by individuals or by groups. In ethics, the way to settle such an issue is to try to discover which is better. If individual ownership is better than group ownership, then we ought to have individual ownership. If group ownership is better than individual ownership, then we ought to have group ownership. If it is better to have some things owned by individuals and other things owned by groups, then that is what we ought to have. Although each particular situation will have to be dealt with in terms of all of the many factors involved, some have attempted to formulate typical arguments for and against group ownership. In the present section, we refer to ownership by groups generally, without differentiating, as we do in the following section, between private and public groups or, where groups are incorporated, between private and public corporations.

Arguments for group ownership include the following: (1) When an individual owns something exclusively, then no others can share in owning it. But when several persons constituting a group owns something, they all share in owning it. When the supply of anything is extremely limited, such as a village well, a regional river, or a corporation holding exclusive patents on products needed by all persons, then more persons can benefit from group ownership than when one only is the owner, other things being equal. (2) When something is so complicated and expensive to own and operate that many must pool their resources if it is to exist at all, then group ownership is necessary. Newsweek reported: "The cost of research and development is now so high that no one nation the size of Britain or Germany can afford to tackle more than a handful of special fields. There is a shortage of funds and trained manpower. In a growing number of fields, only a joint European effort is possible -- aerospace, computers, electronics, nuclear power." (July 25, 1966, Vol. LXVII, No. 4, p. 36.) (3) Some things can be owned better by groups than by individuals: home by a family, streets and sewage disposal system by a city, highways and universities by states, mints and armies by nations, interstate telephone systems by corporations. Partnerships, co-ops, corporations, holding companies, and metrocorporations (See "The Metrocorporation" by Richard Eells in Contemporary Moral Issues, edited by H.K. Girvetz, pp. 173-176, Wadsworth Publishing Co., Belmont, 1910.) all exist because they seem to serve better than individually-owned enterprises.

Arguments against group ownership include: (1) Group ownership does not always entail equality of ownership, or even shared ownership, as claimed. For (a) some private, or even public, groups can be more viciously self-interested than some individually-owned enterprises in excluding outsiders from its benefits. (b) Although each member of a group may theoretically share equally with others, benefits which come from use, rather than from mere ownership, often are not evenly distributed. For example, public highways which are owned by all are of no use to a person who has no automobile, military bases which are owned by all may be regarded as evil rather than good by a pacifist, state universities are owned by all but of no use to those who cannot attend them, national parks are owned by all but may be too far away for those who cannot travel to them. (c) Inequality is illustrated further when publicly owned roads are used by some for driving only a few miles each year whereas others, such as transportation companies, use public properties for private gain through fleets of trucks. (2) Disagreements about policy complicate, sometimes cripple, corporations whereas an individual owner can go ahead on his own decision. Individuals operate companies more efficiently. "Too many cooks spoil the soup." (3) Individuals obtain more satisfaction from individual ownership, because they can feel more proud of themselves for personal achievement.

Of course, in some specific cases, it is much better for wealth to be owned by individuals than by their group, such as clothes, and in other situations it is much better for wealth to be owned by a group than by individuals, such as huge corporations or atomic bombs. The Organicist view is that "ownership is inclusive as well as exclusive. Some things are yours alone, but others, many others are ours. Both joint ownership and exclusive ownership are ownership.... Organicists welcome new levels of ownership when and if they increase the amount of ownership by individuals." (Philosophy: An Introduction, p. 405.) The problem of individual-versus-group ownership is not a question of which, exclusively, but of how much of each is best in particular situations.

Private Versus Public Ownership. The issues involved in public-versus-private ownership, where "private" includes both individual and private group ownership, are somewhat different from those entailed in individual-versus-group ownership, where "group" includes both private and public groups. Private ownership is sometimes spoken of as "capitalism," although "capitalism" also usually connotes an accumulation of "capital," i.e., goods or money which may be used for earning more goods or money, decisions made relatively free from government control, and acceptance of the profit motive. Public ownership is sometimes spoken of as "socialism," though when contrasted with capitalist, it refers mainly to public ownership of the means of production and distribution, i.e., economic goods, rather than to public buildings, such as a legislative hall or court house. The term "communism," like the terms "community," "communion" and "communication," means having or owning things in common. Since the advent of Marxism, the term "Communism" has come to refer to an extreme form of socialism advocated by Karl Marx which urged collective ownership of all means of production and distribution, except some personal and family instruments. We cannot here explore the many varieties of capitalism, socialism and communism, or their complicated histories and doctrines. None of the schemes proposed has existed in its pure form, and current trends indicate that so-called capitalistic nations are becoming more socialistic and so-called communistic nations are finding private ownership and profit incentives often more efficient.

Our purpose here is to summarize in a schematic way some typical arguments for and against public ownership.

Arguments for public group ownership include those previously mentioned for group ownership, private or public, because all public ownership is group ownership. When more people share in owning, there is greater equality in the distribution of wealth. Some things which are too expensive to be owned by individuals can be owned only by groups, and things which are too expensive to be owned by private groups can be owned only by public groups. Some things are better owned by groups, and some of these are better owned by public groups, especially those upon which group welfare greatly depends. Additional arguments include the following, all of which claim, like the preceding argument, that group welfare will be served better by public than by private ownership: (1) Public officials are more likely to take into consideration other values than mere profit, such as the health and retirement benefits of workers, services to customers, relations of the group with other groups. They are more likely to favor human rights as against private property rights. They are more likely to consider long range benefits of production policies, such as conserving natural resources for future years and future generations rather than squandering them at present and producing irreplaceable shortages. (2) Public officials are in a better position to plan wisely because they may also have control of other factors in the community, such as educational, police, political, import-export, environmental and financial stability conditions. They can promote a balance of different industries and eliminate wastes of competition through coordinating cooperative efforts. (3) Public ownership would eliminate the dangers of private monopolies which have people at their mercy, especially in the field of public utilities.

Arguments against public ownership include those previously mentioned against group ownership. Equality of ownership does not assure equality of use of benefits. Disagreements about pubic policy sometimes prevent decisions needed for efficient action. The more that public groups own the less persons can own individually and take pride in as individuals. Additional arguments include the following: (1) Misuse of public property, both by the public and by those to whose care it has been trusted, is notorious. "Everybody's business is nobody's business." The temptation to use public goods and funds for private purposes, when such will remain undetected, is too great for many persons to resist.

Hence graft and corruption and the exorbitant cost thereof follow naturally from public ownership. (2) Evils of bureaucracy are well known. Bureaucrats tend to become more interested in their own vested interests in their position than in their service to the public. The public suffers. (3) When property is publicly owned, it is no longer taxable, so a source of public income is eliminated. Regulation of private industry, or giving a franchise to a private corporation for a limited number of years, may both eliminate the evils of public ownership and retain it as a source of tax income.

Each of the foregoing arguments must be modified in specific application, since peculiar factors in particular contexts often make the arguments irrelevant. In addition to arguments for and against public ownership generally are those arguments for what John Dewey calls "social intelligence," i.e., using whatever amount of both public and private ownership proves itself to be best. "Organicist doctrine holds that what is best in the way of government ownership as well as in government control is a matter that has to be worked out experimentally, and is something that changes from time to time, but that the extremes of no government ownership and of complete government ownership are both alike undesirable and impractical.... The best kind of economy, both in theory and in practice, has not yet been fully worked out. Accepting the doctrine of 'an open future,' such that the future will be really somewhat different from the past, we should expect to continue to experiment with different forms of economy, adopting whichever seems best suited to particular times and places, yet keeping always open to and alert for newer possibilities, and newer necessities, as newer factors enter actually into functional determination of economic conditions." (Philosophy: An Introduction, p. 408. Also my The Philosophers World Model, Chapter 7, Greenwood Press, 1979.)

Chapter XXVIII

SOCIAL JUSTICE

The idea of social justice, which connotes the idea of equality in some fundamental sense, also involves the notion of rights. Most questions about justice or injustice which concern groups have to do with whether or not persons, as members of groups, or groups, are deprived of their rights. Rights, as claims upon others, including other groups, exist actually only if those others do their duties. If obtaining less than one has a right to, or deserves, is unjust, then receiving more than one deserves is called "grace." The present chapter, like Chapter XIII, pertains to rights and duties, and to justice and grace. That these exist for groups as well as for individuals, and that they rest ultimately upon intrinsic goods located in persons, is presupposed here.

Rights and Duties. Do groups have rights? Do groups have duties? Groups do have rights and duties because these exist as extensions of individual rights and duties. As such, they do exist. Just as the rights of one individual involve duties in other individuals, so the rights of one group involve the duties of other groups: peer groups, and subgroups and superior groups, if any. But also, individual-group relations entail rights and duties such that the rights of each member become duties of the group as a group to that member and the rights of a group as a group constitute some of the duties of its members to that group. Finally, there is a sense in which a group has rights and duties relative to itself as a group. Let us examine each of these kinds of rights and duties: (1) those of groups relative to its members, (2) those which a group has to itself as a group, and (3) those of groups in their relations to other groups -- peer groups, and (4) those of groups in relation to superior groups and subgroups, if any.

1. Considering first the interrelations between a group and its members, a group's rights constitute duties of its members to it, and a group's duties to its members constitute some of their rights. But let us examine a group's duties first, for then it may become clear why a group has rights, indeed must have rights, and what kinds of rights it must have.

a. A group has duties to its members because its members have certain rights relative to it. What these rights are differ from group to group, because each kind of group has its own particular purpose, or purposes, and nature, or functions which it performs for its members, and consequently its own peculiar duties and rights. Native groups, such as families, communities, states and nations, all tend to have a multiplicity of services to perform for their members. Multipurpose groups have many needs for performing these duties properly. Special-purpose groups, such as a grocery store, a vacuum cleaner repair agency, a garbage collection department, usually have fewer and more specific duties, and consequently fewer rights. The duties and rights of single-purpose organizations are relatively easy to define. Normally their constitution, franchise or license defines their limits. However, a group which has been licensed for a special purpose ordinarily exists within a larger community, so its members and officers do not become exempt from the duties and rights relative to such larger groups while functioning as members of the special-purpose group.

The duties of native groups are harder to define, partly because these have varied greatly during different periods in history and do today vary greatly with the comparative prosperity or poverty of groups. The growing concern for more and more group duties in Western civilization may be summarized by recalling successive efforts to secure what has come to be called a "Bill of Rights." The reader doubtless is already acquainted with the English Bill of Rights, the Bill of Rights (first ten amendments) in the Constitution of the United States, the French Declaration of the Rights of Man, and, more recently, the Universal Declaration of Human Rights adopted by the General Assembly of the United Nations, Dec. 10, 1948. Whereas rights to liberty and property were hardly possible in a feudal economy, and rights to work, to health or to education seemed unnecessary to the framers of our Constitution, today we not only include these but add rights to security in old age and to rest, recreation and adventure. Apparently we are not yet ready to assert individual rights to world citizenship or to freedom from international war.

The following statement of a bill of rights, prepared by the National Resources Planning Board, March 10, 1943, is selected as illustrative because of its relative brevity, simplicity and yet comprehensiveness.

1. The right to work, usefully and creatively, through the productive years.

2. The right to fair pay, adequate to command the necessities and amenities of life in exchange for work, ideas, thrift, and other socially valuable service.

3. The right to adequate food, clothing, shelter and medical care.

4. The right to security, with freedom from fear of old age, want, dependency, sickness, unemployment, and accident.

5. The right to live in a system of free enterprise, free from compulsory labor, irresponsible private power, arbitrary public authority, and unregulated monopolies.

6. The right to come and go, to speak or be silent, free from the spyings of secret political police.

7. The right to equality before the law, with equal access to justice in fact.

8. The right to education, for work, for citizenship, and for personal growth and happiness; and

9. The right to rest, recreation, and adventure, the opportunity to enjoy life and take part in an advancing civilization.

Too often a bill of rights is a statement of ideals which can be realized only imperfectly. But gradual enactment into law of these ideals, as a group becomes both more able and willing to actualize them, gives hope that all of them, and still other new ideals, will become part of the accepted heritage of all mankind.

b. The rights of individuals proposed in a bill of rights, such as the foregoing, can be assured only if the groups entrusted with providing them do, because they are enabled to do, their duties in enforcing them. If a group does not have rights correlative to its duties, i.e., the rights needed in order to do its duties, including the authority and power to carry them out, then it does not actually have those duties and its members do not really have those rights. "There are no costless rights." (W.E. Hocking, What Man Can Make of Man, p. 50, Harper & Brothers, New York, 1942.) When individual members of a group fail to provide the support needed by a group in order to perform its duties, they thereby forfeit the rights which they have as duties of the group to them.

2. What duties does a group have to itself as a group and what rights does it have relative to those duties? Does a group have a right to exist, to grow, to acquire members, to acquire property, to acquire a reputation, to perform functions, to be free and sovereign in certain ways? Does a group have a duty to itself to try to continue to exist, to fulfill its purposes, to achieve excellence in its own way? Given the existence of groups as extensions of individual interests, groups then actually function as if they were value agencies, and as such involve the intrinsic goods inherent in such functioning. In this sense, a group has a value basis, and has duties to itself as a group functioning as such, to preserve itself as a group so long as its value basis persists. It may be that, after a group has served its purpose, it ought to be abandoned, and that it has a duty to

discontinue its existence; if so, then it also has a right to discontinue its existence.

3. What rights and duties do groups have in relation to other groups, i.e., first to its peer groups? Again, rights and duties will differ with the kind of group, including whether or not two groups are coordinate subgroups in a larger group. Two families, two cities, two nations, two corporations, two religions, two universities may all have some differences in their relations with their peer groups which constitute differences relative to rights and duties. The degree of independence has consequences, since, generally speaking, the greater the independence of two groups from each other the fewer duties, and rights, they tend to have relative to each other. The more interdependent two groups become, the greater the number of factors with respect to which rights and duties may occur. When two groups are partners in a larger group, they acquire duties to respect each other's membership in that larger group.

If we ask, "Are there any rights and duties common to all groups?" we may not find an answer. For some groups are even created for the purpose of eliminating other groups, as when an army is organized to destroy both an opposing army and the nation which supports it. However, since each group has its basis in the rights of persons, insofar as each group officer has a duty to respect the rights of other persons, including those expressing themselves through opposing groups, he, and his group, have duties to respect groups as extensions of persons. To the extent that the principle of reciprocity works, and works between groups, and works between two particular groups, then each of those two groups has a duty to recognize the rights of the other group if it expects to have its own rights recognized by the group.

4. Hierarchically-related groups have additional problems about rights and duties. Again, differences occur relative to the dependence of higher groups upon lower groups and of lower groups upon higher groups and, further, upon greater or lesser degrees of mutual dependence. When several regional philosophical societies decide to federate, then the new federal group is quite dependent upon the regional societies. Normally, the regional societies collect dues from their members and agree to pay a percentage to the federal group for its budget. Such a federal group is, at first, completely dependent upon the regional groups, and tends to continue to be more dependent upon them than they are upon it. It derives its existence, nature, purpose, and financial support from them; hence, it derives its rights from them, and it has duties toward them. However, although they are the source of its rights and duties in a way in

which it is not the source of their rights and duties, their collective decision to establish it to serve them mutually involves them in certain duties to support it. Each regional group continues to have a right to participate as a member of the federation only as long as it continues to do its duties in supporting the federation. Hence, even where a higher-level group depends completely upon the lower-level groups for its existence, and its rights and duties, the lower-level groups also have certain duties as well as rights relative to the higher-level group which depends upon them.

When a corporation operating branches in several states decides to incorporate a new branch agency in another state, that agency functions as a subordinate group which depends completely for its origin, and original nature and rights and duties, upon the corporation as a superior group. The branch depends upon the corporation more than the corporation depends upon the branch. Does such a dependent branch therefore have more duties than rights, and the corporation more rights than duties? Or does the decision of the corporation to establish the branch involve the corporation in duties as well as rights? Perhaps it has more duties than rights, for if the branch should fail, the corporation has a duty to absorb the cost of such failure. Even where a lower-level group depends completely upon a higher-level group for its existence, and rights and duties, the higher-level group also has certain duties as well as rights relative to the lower-level group which depends upon it.

Does the height of a hierarchy affect rights and duties? That is, when a family is related to a world government through its community, state and national organizations, such that it depends for its operation, and for some of its rights and duties, upon the ways in which rights and duties exist and function between all of the higher levels of groups, do difficulties in maintaining rights and doing duties at any of the higher levels thereby jeopardize the rights of such a family? As group relations become more complicated, failure of any one person or group to do its duties may thereby actually destroy some rights of many other groups and persons. To the extent that this is so, the importance of groups doing their duties is greater as societies become more complex.

Justice, Injustice and Grace. Distinguishing between "self as just" and "society as just," or between "individual justice" and "social justice," as these terms are used here, "social justice" pertains to groups. Here we ask, "Are groups just or unjust?" Social justice, too, involves several dimensions: justice between a group and its members, between peer groups, and between hierarchically-related groups. It involves, also, the question about whether a group is just or unjust to itself, as when we say a group fails to do justice to all of its interests or, especially, when it fails to do justice to one particular need. Social injustice, whether retributive or distributive, exists when what a group receives, or gives, is less than what is deserved, and social grace exists when what a group receives, or gives, is more than what is deserved. Hence, social justice, injustice and grace all presuppose that groups can deserve.

How can a group deserve anything? Strictly speaking, only persons, or at least living beings, deserve. But groups, existing and functioning as extensions of persons, tend to acquire a life of their own, not one that is independent of persons but one which is more than that of any one of its members and even, in a sense, more than that of all of them collected together merely as individuals. Officers of a group naturally become concerned about the group's welfare and behavior and about whether or not it deserves anything. Deserving may be defined in terms of obligation. If a person or group ought to respect the rights of another person or group, then such another person or group deserves to have its rights respected. A group deserves to exist, to remain in existence, to have rights, and to receive benefits, basically, because its rights and its deserts have their basis in those of individual members. Yet also, once existing and functioning in relation to other groups, a group may so act toward other groups in such a way that it does its duty relative to their rights and thereby earns a debt and thus deserves to have its own rights respected by other groups. If one nation, for example, which could easily cause trouble for another nation, deliberately refrains from doing so because it respects the desires of the other nation to remain at peace, it thereby may be said to earn a right, if it did not already have one, to remain free from trouble when such could easily be caused by the other nation. By acting, or refraining from acting, deliberately, one nation may regard itself as deserving to receive the same consideration from the other nation. If the other nation does not refrain from meddling, then the first has been unjustly treated. If one nation has troubled another, and then the other refrains from troubling the one, when it could do so easily, the first nation may be said to have been treated graciously by the first nation.

Let us glance at each of the four dimensions or levels of social justice.

1. A group may be just, unjust, or gracious in its relations with its own member, both distributively and retributively. How can a group be just to its members? It is one and they are many. If justice involves equality,

how can there be equality between one group and its many members? We have already explored many of the complexities involved in ways in which persons are unequal. All of these inequalities continue to effect persons as they function as members of a group and complicate the problems which a group faces in trying to be just to its members. If the members of a group are unequal in any way, how can a group treat them justly where justice entails equality? One suggestion comes from an analysis of the word "equality," which not only includes the word "quality," but is related to the word "equate" which constitutes a part of the word "adequate." "Ad-equate," meaning "equal to," not in the numerical sense of an eye for an eye, retributively, or of infants and adults doing the same amount of labor and paying the same amount of taxes, distributively, but in the sense of being fitted or suited or sufficient to the particular circumstances. That is, a half bottle of warm milk may be adequate for an infant while its parents require a well-balanced meal of meat, vegetables, fruit, drink and dessert for adequacy. A group can be just, distributively, when it supplies food adequately, even though different members consume quite different kinds and quantities. It can be just, retributively, for example, when it requires a father to earn all of the money, a mother to care for the household, and an infant merely to coo and refrain from crying.

A nation is faced with the problem of trying to be just to all of its citizens. Adequate treatment of persons who are and persons who are not criminals is different. Adequate treatment of persons who are wealthy and persons who are poor is different. Adequate treatment of persons who are well and persons who are ill is different. It is not possible to equalize all conditions in all ways. But, as sociologists have pointed out convincingly, a nation which has sufficient resources is unjust to its citizens as long as it fails to provide certain levels of educational opportunities which will enable them to develop capacities for fuller participation in group activities. As John W. Gardner, U.S. Secretary of Health, Education and Welfare, has said: "The traditional democratic invitation to each individual to achieve the best that is in him requires that we provide each youngster with the particular kind of education which will benefit him. This is the only sense in which equality of opportunity can mean anything. The good society is not one that ignores individual differences, but one that deals with them wisely and humanely." (Quoted in The Christian Science Monitor, Vol. 57, Sept. 13, 1965, p. 11.) Distributive justice involves adequacy; a nation which is able to provide educational opportunities for all of its citizens but fails to do so is thereby unjust. Of course, when a nation provides them with more such opportunities than they need, or can make use of, it becomes gracious. Citizens may deserve equal or adequate opportunities in the sense that a group owes it to itself to provide them if it can in order to maximize the goods constituting itself as a group. When its providence becomes more than adequate, in the sense being discussed, it is gracious.

2. A group's being just or gracious to its members is one way of being just or gracious to itself. A group as a group has its nature and purposes determined by its many functions, and these include not only its relations to its members but also its relations to other groups. Where values are at stake in each of such relations, a group fails to do justice to itself, i.e., to all of its own goods, when it neglects to be adequate in each of them.

3. Turning to problems of justice and grace involving relations between peer groups, we focus again upon the principle of reciprocity. For, although the principle operates also between a group and its members, between a group and its subgroups and a group and its superior groups, if any, I suspect that the ratio of relative importance of retributive as compared with distributive justice is greater more often in relations between peer groups, especially between highly interdependent peer groups.

Although families may seek to be fair distributively to neighboring families, communities to be fair distributively to neighboring communities, states to be fair distributively to neighboring states, and nations to be fair to other nations, problems of justice and grace more often pertain to retribution, whether positive or negative, between such peer groups. A family tends to be more concerned about returning dinner invitations to families who have invited it already than in being sure that it has invited all the families in the neighborhood to dinner. A community usually becomes more excited about beating its chief rival community in sports than in defeating all nearby communities. A state is more likely to be agitated about unfairness to it by a bordering state which has deliberately lowered its wedding or divorce fees or its gasoline or sales taxes, for example, in order to compete for business than it is to have reciprocal equality with all states whose fees and taxes have been set, even if differently, for reasons inherent in the peculiarities of their own cultures and economies. A nation seems more inclined to adjust its tariff rates in ways which discriminate against other nations which discriminate against it than to try to be equally restrictive to imports from all nations.

4. The problem of justice and grace in relations between hierarchically-related groups are complicated by the ways, and degrees,

in which such groups interdepend. When one group is very much dependent upon another group, then it is to its own self-interest to promote the welfare of the group upon which it is so dependent. In such a situation, what appears as magnificent grace may be an expression of great self-interest.

Chapter XXIX

SOCIAL CONSCIENCE

"By 'public conscience' I mean the judgment made by members of a community concerning those social relations by which they wish to encourage their institutions and those which they wish to discourage....The ultimate appeal is to what I have called the public conscience." (Herbert W. Schneider, Three Dimensions of Pubic Morality, pp. 51, 52, Indiana University Press, Bloomington, 1956.) Schneider's assertion exemplifies what we mean by "social conscience," i.e., the conscience of any group, whether family, nation, college or corporation. The conscience of a group is not something separate from the consciences of its members, for it is a part of the conscience of each member who functions as a member of the group and concerns himself with the interests and obligations of the group. To the extent that a group has interests, and rights and duties relative to them, which may at times be different from those of some of its members, the conscience of a group may also be distinguished from those of such members. As long as a group behaves as a functioning entity with interests and obligations of its own, we are warranted in speaking of that group as having a conscience.

Although the term "social conscience" is more often employed in discussing problems of crucial or of currently newsworthy importance than when thinking about maintaining group goods about which little question is being raised, its general meaning covers the whole range of feelings of obligation relative to all value-decisions of each group and of all kinds of groups. A group's conscience is most obvious when the group is greatly disturbed about a debt or duty which it cannot repay when nonpayment involves serious threat to its existence and future welfare. A family facing bankruptcy often experiences pangs of conscience. A community which has recently refused to appropriate available money for flood or traffic control tends to be terribly agitated by news that several helpless victims have perished because the dangerous conditions were not removed. "New York government is grappling with its conscience." (Godfrey Sperling Jr., "New Yorkers Weigh Stiffer Ethics Law," Christian Science Monitor, Feb. 20, 1964, p. 4.) Issues of suspected graft where public officials use their influence in private-public financial transactions stir the consciences of the citizens of a state especially when serious graft is uncovered and failure of legislation to provide adequate safeguards for the future remains obvious. A nation's conscience may be bothered about its failure to assure civil rights for all of its citizens, about its failure to support a needed ally especially when its failure is taken as exemplifying its policy toward other needed allies, and about its failure to support a world government, such as the League of Nations, whose foundering results in another world war which turns out to be very costly in money, lives and friends.

No matter how conscience originated (See Chapter XIV), it has to do with goods and with choices between them, and thus with obligations. We can say that conscience, including social conscience, "tells" us what to do because conscience consists in our feeling of obligation, and obligation, or oughtness, consists in the power we feel when a greater good seems to command our choosing it rather than a lesser good. As a member of a group, a conscientious person concerns oneself with helping the group to do what is best for itself. If a person is naive, believing that supporting one's group means opposing other groups, one may conscientiously promote antagonism. But when a person realizes that a group's goods are multidimensional, one tends to become interested in all of its dimensions and then conscientiousness involves one's attempting to become sensitive to the fine points needed to discriminate between the various value dimensions. One's interest in social justice leads one to try to understand the complexities of group dynamics and the need for continuing effort to promote justice both at many levels and between levels of the group's interests. Social conscience is necessarily multidimensional when it is adequate to megalopolitan living.

Chapter XXX

SOCIAL INTELLIGENCE

What Is Social Intelligence? John Dewey not only interprets intelligence as a "social asset" but also regards it as social in its origin. "Henry George, speaking of ships that ply the ocean with a velocity of five or six hundred miles a day, remarked, 'There is nothing whatever to show that the men who today build and navigate and use such ships are one whit superior in any physical or mental quality to their ancestors, whose best vessel was a coracle of wicker and hide. The enormous improvement which these ships show is not an improvement in human nature; it is an improvement of society. It is due to a wider and fuller union of individual efforts in accomplishment of common ends.'" (Liberalism and Social Action, pp. 67-68, G.P. Putnam's Sons, New York, 1935.) While agreeing with Dewey about "the actual social character of intelligence as it actually develops and makes its way" (ibid., pp. 68-69), without thereby minimizing the biological character of intelligence, we extend the notion of intelligence to groups. Groups, too, are more or less intelligent, depending upon whether their members survive happily. Intelligent individuals make good use of their groups while intelligent groups make good use of their members for the benefit of their members. Groups behave or function more or less efficiently in attaining their goals. Groups too adapt themselves to changing situations, including that kind of change which initiates and perpetuates stability.

A group becomes unintelligent when it fails to adjust itself so as to serve its members in their attempts to realize the purposes of their own lives. Cultural lag, corresponding to habits in individuals which they cannot break, consists in a group's persisting in following old behavior patterns which no longer serve the needs of its members as adequately as they once did. That social intelligence exists, few today doubt. But how to cure groups of their unintelligence, i.e., both of permitting unwise or irresponsible persons to function as executive officers, of eliminating evils caused by mores, laws and institutions which have ceased to remain efficient, and of neglecting to plan with foresight new and better institutions, continues to be a plaguing problem. If social intelligence is the ability of groups to solve their group problems, including, or even especially, their moral problems, then nothing is closer to the core of ethics than the concern of a group for maintaining, or improving, its intelligence.

Factors in Social Intelligence. An analysis of the factors in social intelligence continues to be a function of social scientists. Some sociologists have distinguished five kinds of factors "conditioning the play of intelligence in groups: . . . (1) communication; (2) the quantity and quality of new ideas available; (3) the group attitude; (4) the total situation, i.e., the time available, the number of problems pressing for solution, etc., and (5) organization." (Charles H. Cooley, R.C. Angell, L.J. Carr, Introductory Sociology, p. 381.)

Easy communication among members of a group is needed, both for discovering the needs of individuals and the inadequacies of the group in providing for them and for exploring and testing new ideas suggested for solving problems. The need for new ideas, both greater quantities and a higher quality, grows as groups become larger and their problems become more complex and multifarious. But the prevalence of fertile minds and the encouragement of new varieties of expertness depend upon an attitude of willingness in a group to profit by them. Such an attitude involves a willingness to tolerate not merely freedom of thought and expression but to do so even to the extent of supporting some deviants, radicals and rebels. Tolerance of the "expression of extreme views is essential to the efficiency of intelligent readjustment: (A) They may be right.. . . (B) They contribute to the complete picture of the actual situation. . . . (C) Extremists often become less extreme when forced to examine their own ideas. . . . (D) Radical groups force the discussion of principles and thus serve to educate all concerned." (Ibid., pp. 382-384.) Censorship is a common form of intolerance.

"The total situation, i.e., . . .the number of problems pressing for solution" at one time also affects the intelligence with which a group can respond. When a crisis approaches because the group is faced with too many problems to grapple with intelligently or when a problem becomes too intense to deal with democratically, "the narrower the circle" (ibid., pp. 394, 395) of those making final decisions, and upon those whose intelligence the wisdom or folly of such decisions depends. Finally, organization, of ideas as well as actions, determines group intelligence. Organization is so fundamental to groups that we often speak of a group as "an organization." Really, a group, especially, a large or complicated group, involves many different kinds of behavior structures, each of which may be regarded as an organization. Behavior patterns of group members are structured by ideas about how one ought to act in order to accomplish certain desired ends. When these are based on too few experiences, they may soon become inadequate. Since such behavior patterns, commonly called "codes," were established long ago, and were based upon conditions that now have largely ceased to exist or upon the insights ("revelations") of seers whose perspective was limited, they may have become obsolete. For a group to operate on a code which is obsolete is to behave unintelligently. To the extent that newer conditions and new problems arise, intelligence requires discovery or invention of new solutions and consequently new codes for behaving. Cultural lag is inherent in the nature of social organization. The more intelligent the group the more it minimizes the deleterious effects of such lag. Organized efforts for self-criticism and improving foresight are needed, and such efforts have come to be called "social planning."

Cultural Lag. One of the best brief descriptions of the nature and naturalness of cultural lag appears in Chapter XXV of Introductory Sociology by Charles H. Cooley, R. C. Angell and L. J. Carr, which we have just quoted. We summarize its "cycle of institutional development," including the following typical phases of growth, each of which influences group members in ways that are worth noting. These phases may be designated as (1) incipient organization, (2) efficiency, (3) formalism, (4) disorganization, and either (5) disintegration or (6) reorganization.

1. When people in groups find common problems affecting their welfare, they naturally try to do something about them. Whether by trial and error or by invention of some leader, a solution, consisting in ways of behaving in order to deal with the problem, which works becomes established in the sense that when the problem arises again members of the group respond in the same way, and, since they are interested in their children's welfare also, teach them to behave in that way. The period during which such a tentative solution is found and tried out may be called the phase of "incipient organization." Here participants tend to remain somewhat uncertain about their new forms of behavior, though organizations may sometimes be initiated with great rejoicing and enthusiasm because a solution has been found, or in a coolly calculated manner, as when establishing a business, or as unconscious growths such as folkways.

2. Established behavior patterns, called "institutions," are efficient when they serve the needs of members in just the way they want to be served; consequently such members feel at ease when participating in them. As long as such feelings persist, they fuse with other feelings of being benefitted and of reciprocal loyalty to the group for maintaining this

pattern. The behavior patterns are accepted by the individuals as natural parts of their personalities and of their groups, so no external pressure is needed to enforce conformity.

3. However, when children learn to conform without comprehending why, their affirmation tends to be pervaded with uncertainty. If they are not taught what problem needs and achieves solution through such behavior patterns, they do not understand why they should conform. If the problem itself has disappeared but leaders continue to teach and force conformity which has ceased to be useful, the institution has reached the stage of formalism. Formalism is characterized by a demand for conformity to a behavior pattern from which no benefits are derived. People seem to conform to the law for its own sake rather than for their own sake. Behavior becomes mechanical and lifeless. People more often feel forced to follow the letter of the law when its beneficial spirit is missing. Law enforcers cannot permit deviation when all they have to work with is the law itself, in contrast to the previous stage when enforcement was unnecessary because the purpose of the institution was clear from the benefits derived. At this stage, what was good has become an evil. When ethical behavior is identified with the established mores, with the form of the institution which has become lifeless, members become antagonistic to such ethical behavior because it appears as more evil than good. Growth of institutional formalism is detrimental to ethics, and the longer formalism remains the more "ethics" comes to seem identified with a useless, of not an evil, status quo.

4. When institutions become formalistic, increasing numbers of members resist participation and finally refuse to participate. During this period of disorganization, some do and some do not conform. Now, those who conform regard those who do not as immoral, while those who do not, consider those who do as foolish. Members mistrust each other, and they have no common ground for settling their differences. Moral disorder prevails. During such a period, delinquency and crime tends to increase.

5. When disorganization continues, the institution gradually disintegrates. That is, it loses all of its vitality and collapses. New members cannot be induced to participate, and the old diehards become impotent as group members. Thus, it ceases to be an effective influence in group behavior.

6. When the need which the institution originally served continues, disintegration of the old institution does not solve the problem. For example, a need for regularizing relations between the sexes exists in any

society, and the failure and disintegration of one system does not thereby eliminate all need for system. With the disappearance of the old forms, people again become faced with the problem in its naked appearance. The need itself reoccupies attention when the inhibiting forms have been removed. New suggestions occur, and new attempts are made to solve the problem with a different institutional pattern. "A period of disorganization creates a great need, and furnishes a fruitful soil, for constructive leadership. In order to reorganize institutions successfully and bring them back to the stage we have termed efficiency, there must arise persons with vision and forcefulness to formulate and build a new order." (Ibid., p. 414.) If new and better forms are found, then they too tend to become efficient, and as time goes on, to pass again through the stages of formalism, disorganization, and eventual disintegration.

The foregoing sketch of the cycle of institutional development should not leave the impression that the stages are fixed and unvarying. Some institutions remain efficient for a long time and become reorganized quickly. Others attain efficiency only briefly, if at all, and remain formalistic for centuries. Some institutions complete the cycle rapidly, while others structure the minds and associations of civilizations throughout their history. Even if an institution should skip some stage in the cycle, still it appears that a tendency exists in all institutions to go through such stages just because, as in all kinds of problem-solving, our needs change and when our solutions do not change correspondingly, they become obsolete and need to be discarded; when habits are hard to change, obsolescence is prolonged and change, when it does come, is likely to be more violent and revolutionary.

Historians, anthropologists and sociologists point out that such changes are quite natural, and evidence can be cited from all societies and in all historical periods. But, whereas often either single institutions, or institutions in single areas of life whether economic, political, religious, marital, educational, or recreational, tend to undergo disorganization at one time. Our own age is one when many, if not all, of our basic institutions are undergoing revolutionary changes at the same time. If disorganization of one institution is critical, then disorganization of many institutions at once is crisis compounded. Whereas regard for group mores suffers when only one institution becomes disorganized, concern for being ethical almost disappears when many institutions disintegrate at once. The need of groups for getting what is good and of having beneficial agreed-upon behavior patterns becomes even more crucial as more of the previously-relied-upon institutions disappear. When the members of a group can no longer trust each other's behavior, the group itself disintegrates.

Social intelligence exists only when a group survives and prospers. Social disorganization signifies that the group has ceased to be intelligent. The group has needs for which it has no adequate solution. Groups are intelligent in proportion to the percentage of time their institutions remain in stages of efficiency. When groups maintain formalistic ethical codes, they are unintelligent. Having an intelligent group is part of what each individual member most wants, surely. So a most important ethical concern, of each member and of each group, is to try to maintain its ethical codes in a stage of efficiency. Since, in most cases, this cannot occur without deliberate attention and effort, intelligent groups should feel obligated to devote some of their efforts to social planning.

Social Planning. The purpose of social planning, whether for the solution of immediate problems or for determining policy aimed at long-run benefits, has as its ultimate goal the optimization of the intrinsic goods of a group's members. Immediate problems, which naturally vary with the type of group, usually center about improving some instrumentality or shifting responsibility among persons as officers as a result of a particular crisis. Long-range planning may be more able to take into account the more basic and long-lasting goods of the group. Social planning, in seeking to prevent or eliminate some evil or to achieve some good, includes especially problems of reducing or eliminating inefficiency in existing institutions or of inventing new and more efficient institutions. All such planning, which pertains to how people shall behave in order to reduce evils or improve goods, is ethical planning, or planning how members ought to choose and to behave in order to attain these goals. Those who are involved in planning about planning are, thus, concerned with the ethics of how to be more ethical.

Today, when entangled in increasing complexities in both megalopolitan and global living, we confront a need for a highly complicated ethics. As we become increasingly dependent upon specialists, we are involved in needs for increasingly specialized planning and, thus, for increasingly specialized ethics. To the extent that specialization fits our needs, we adapt our behavior patterns accordingly, and our specialized institutions, or at least many of the new ones, seem to be in a stage of efficiency. Youngsters, even when impatient to drive an automobile, seem quite willing to submit to driver training programs and to mastering and embodying in themselves the ethical principles

needed for safe driving. Since general principles of morality are inherent
in specific varieties of morality, youths who accept the principles needed
for driver training thereby become involved in accepting some general
moral principles. Such training may be even more complicated and
detailed in pilot training, especially for pilots of commercial airplanes.
Gradual transfer of effective teaching of ethical principles from traditional
Sunday Schools still emphasizing the Mosaic Ten Commandments to
multiplicities of specialties gives some the impression that we are
becoming less ethical. But the rapid growth of specialties, each having
inherent in it the need for doing what one ought to do in order to obtain
the benefits desired from the specialized behavior, involves complicated
increases in ways of behaving ethically. Lag appears most obvious in the
interrelations between different specialists, for to the extent that each acts
as if he were autonomous when in fact he is complexly interdependent,
the lack of institutionalized behavior patterns in this area constitutes a
genuine inadequacy.

To realize how far the ethics of social planning has advanced, we
observe the emergence of specialists in the field of understanding details
of the nature of planning for social change. Authors of a recent volume
describe their purpose as follows. Their problem is "the application of
systematic and appropriate knowledge to human affairs for the purpose
of creating intelligent action and change. Thus, this is a book that focuses
on planned change; a conscious, deliberate, and collaborative effort to
improve the operations of a system, whether it be a self-system, social
system, or cultural system, through the utilization of scientific knowledge."
(W.G. Bennis, K.D. Benne, and R. Chin, The Planning of Change, p. 3,
Holt Reinhart and Winston, New York, 1958.) The authors of another
volume say: "The subject of this book is planned change -- that is, change
which derives from a purposeful decision to effect improvements in a
personality system or a social system and which is achieved with the help
of professional guidance. In the following pages we have undertaken a
comparative study of the principles and techniques which furnish the basis
of the work in the various types of professional helpers concerned with
change....The fact that we consider the idea of planned change an
important one probably has much to do with our location in Western
culture, or, to be more specific, in American culture. Taking initiative to
exert control over one's fate or to influence the fate of others is not a
mode of thinking common to all societies." (Ronald Lippit, Jeanne
Watson, and Bruce Westley, The Dynamics of Planned Change, p. vii,
Harcourt Brace, New York, 1958.) These books deal with such topics as

"The Phases of Planned Change," "Initiating Planned Change," "The Scientific and Professional Training of Change Agents," and "Three Pivotal Functions of Planned Change: Training, Consulting, and Research." Few people are yet aware of the existence of the American Society of Planning Officials and of how significant they have become in molding the ethical policies by which we will increasingly guide our lives.

That dangers doubtless lurk in the new behavior patterns being proposed by our corps of social planers, while they are still in the state of incipient organization, should be obvious to all. Apart from the confusions arising from divided allegiance to ancient codes encrusted with cultural lag and the need for trying out new codes which remain in an experimental stage, other difficulties, such as the growth of tyranny among specialists upon whom we depend so completely for some services, are becoming magnified. Many who rejoice that we are now free from the tyranny of kings do not yet realize how much we already suffer from a new kind of tyranny, the tyranny of the specialist. That speciocracy, i.e., government by specialists, has already arrived, many are aware; but that we still need some form of "generocracy," i.e., government by generalists, is a problem not sufficiently dealt with. The present prospect is that social planning pertaining to general welfare will be handled by a new branch of social planners, those who are specialists in generalities. Such, historically, as been the role of philosophers.

In conclusion, simple societies require only simple systems of ethics, but complexly interdependent societies need many interdependent complex systems of ethics. As social change becomes increasingly dynamic, the need for attention to the ethics of planning for social change become a more pressing aspect of social intelligence.

Chapter XXXI

SOCIETY AS ORGANIC

Gathering together the main ideas of the foregoing thirteen chapters, we try here to summarize the nature and purpose of social ethics. The purposes of Part II have been (1) to show how social ethics is a natural extension of individual ethics, (2) to explore the nature of groups, (3) to see how groups deal with typical ethical problems, and (4) to observe how interdependence, characterizing the nature of individuals, becomes more complicated and intricate as groups and group functions multiply.

Personality and Society. Although throughout Part II attention is focused primarily upon groups, concern to show how social ethics is a natural, even necessary, extension of individual ethics has remained obvious. As was pointed out repeatedly in Part I, the full nature of personality, of personal problems, and of personal ethics cannot be understood until it becomes clear how a person's interests in one's groups serve to enlarge and enrich one's personality and how the ethical problems of one's group function as additional and more complicated aspects of one's own ethical nature. Hence each chapter, although devoted to exploring some phase of social ethics, functions also as an expanded examination of a similar phase of individual ethics.

For example, the policies of your groups do, or should, serve your own interests in such a way that their security makes you more secure and their improved reputation enhances your own self-esteem. A group has instrumental values for you whenever it promotes your welfare, and it may appear as having intrinsic good either as an object enriching your experiences of adoration or as an amplification of your own intrinsic good through your feeling identified with it. You may enjoy a measure of self-improvement through participating in your group's improvements. A group's obligations often function as additions to each member's other obligations. When you identify yourself with your group, then when it acts as an agent, you experience its action as an enlargement of your own agency. You can feel freer when your groups are able to do what they want to do and what you want them to do. Your kinds and ranges of sovereignty and of ownership may be augmented through those of your groups. Your rights become multiplied through sharing in those of your groups, as are your opportunities for participating, as receiver and giver, in justice and grace. Your conscience becomes enlarged and more complicated through concern about your group's duties, and your own intelligence may be magnified through participating in the benefits of your group's achievements, survival powers and adaptabilities.

The other side of the coin must be equally reckoned with. For you depend upon your groups often more than your groups depend upon you, and you serve the interests of your groups as well as they serve yours. You may become insecure when you deviate from the group's pattern as well as when your group is endangered. You may be humiliated not only when you deviate from your group's pattern but also when your group is dishonored. You must serve as an instrumental good for your group if you are to continue as a member, and your own intrinsic value may be neglected and even diminished as a result of group action. The conflicts and other evils embodied in your groups exist as complications of your own personality conflicts. Your groups may contribute to, or even necessitate, your own deterioration, as evidenced by slum conditions and cultural conflict situations. Your groups' obligations may be onerous and their effects on your obligations may increase your burden to the point of unbearability. Your may be compelled to act in ways that you prefer not to act as a consequence of being caught up in the actions of your groups, as when a citizen is drafted for military service. You may become unfreer both when your group fails to do what it wants to do and when it compels you to do what you do not want to do. Your own sovereignty may be limited by that of your groups, and your ownership may be reduced by taxes, confiscation, or prohibitions against acquisition. Your rights may be nullified, both by persons within your groups, by your groups' decisions and actions and by other groups which maltreat your groups. Your duties become multiplied through sharing in those of your groups, as are your chances for being treated unjustly. You may suffer from the pangs of conscience due to your groups' unfulfilled duties, and your own unintelligence may be caused in part by the formalisms and other failures of your groups.

Surely the chapters of Part II have illustrated many ways in which individual ethics is incomplete until your extended interests in his groups have been accounted for. Persons are, by nature, social animals, and social ethics is an extension of individual ethics.

Ethical Aspects of Groups. Each group has a nature and interests of its own, and although continuously depending upon the stability or instability of its members, has a kind or degree of independence in the sense that its own nature and interests coincide completely with those of no one of its members nor even with all of them together, for conflicts between its members constitute aspects of its own nature. To the extent that a group behaves as an entity, certain aspects of its nature appear to function somewhat analogously to those of individuals, and to the extent that intrinsic values appear to be at stake in the decisions made by, or for, the group, such a group may be said to be behaving ethically or even, to be an ethical being. Failure of interpreters to keep in mind that such partially independent ethical behavior is only a matter of degree will lead to their imaginatively creating a completely independent ogre which tends to disregard or thwart the interests of the members upon which it continuously and intimately depends. If the fundamental need for depicting a group's nature, interests and ethical behavior as aspectival, rather than as a completely independent substance, is overlooked, the viewpoint expressed in this volume will have been misunderstood. The degree of independence of a group from its members is comparatively so small and the degree of dependence is so large that it is better not to speak of independence at all if the aspectival character of this independence cannot be kept in mind.

Just as individuals depend upon other individuals for parts of their nature and welfare, so groups depend upon other groups for parts of their nature and welfare. And just as individuals depend also upon subordinate parts, whether organs of their bodies, cells, atoms or subatomic particles, so groups depend upon subgroups, if any, upon individuals as members, and upon the subordinate parts of individuals; and as individuals depend in some ways upon their groups, so each group, except the highest group, depends in some ways upon the behavior of superior groups. This hierarchical character of group interdependencies involves many groups in several levels of ethical behavior. That is, each group has basic interest in the welfare of its members, and ought to take into account the welfare of its members not merely as members but also as individuals having other interests. Each group has an interest in its own welfare as a group, or as a functional entity with its own prospects for continuation and prosperity. Each group has an interest in its subgroups, if any, and in its relation to its peer groups, of various sorts and degrees of interrelatedness, and to its superior groups, if any. Each of these levels of interest needs to be kept in mind as we explore each of the several other aspects of a group's ethical nature. For a fundamental part of the nature of each group is its action as a complex unity which retains a measure of integrity to the extent that no one of these levels of interest dominates over the others so completely that they suffer as a consequence. A group's policies, goods, improvements, obligations, agency, freedom, sovereignty, ownership, justice, conscience and intelligence all involve all of the levels in its hierarchical nature. Social ethics, as a study, remains inadequate so long as any of these aspects and levels is neglected.

Social policy as pursuit of groupal self-interest, thus, is best conceived as multi-complex or multidimensional. Group health and integrity continue to be endangered by conflicts of interests among its members and between its levels of obligation. Problems entailed in a group's evaluation of its own interests, much like those facing each individual with personality conflicts, present it with some of its most crucial ethical decisions. Each group needs to keep in mind both its central purposes and its peripheral tasks and opportunities, and to weigh the merits of proposals for action in terms of their comparative benefits relative to both types of interest. Oftentimes a group finds itself amid changing circumstances and faces the problem of modifying, evolving and redefining its nature and purposes somewhat. Evaluation of the reliability of the principle of reciprocity relative to prospective investments in services at each of its levels of interests continues to plague many group officials. Those groups which have been able to institutionalize their relations and codify ways of behaving at each level tend to reduce the number of decisions which must be remade recurrently. If they can avoid cultural lag, with consequent formalism and disorganization, and satisfy each level of interest adequately, they are fortunate in having established patterns of reciprocal behavior which optimize mutual benefits.

Social values and evils constitute bases for social ethics. Popularly, confusion of intrinsic with instrumental values, of economic values with prices, of mores with principles, of ideals with actualities, and each of these with the others, tends to result in uncertainty about, fear of, and antagonism toward, ethics. Those who resentfully interpret oughts, duties and obligations as external impositions upon persons by their groups naturally despise multiplication of groups as multiplication of evils. Anarchistic sentiments beget dreams of utopias completely without ethics, so conceived. But such childish notions stem from failure of members to achieve full participation in their groups' goods and to share in responsibility for both understanding issues and in making decisions, as well as from failure to achieve clear analysis of the kinds of value aspects functioning as constituent components of group value situations. That groups have instrumental value, and instrumental evil, for individuals, few can doubt, though one needs to grow into responsible positions in many kinds and levels of groups in order to appreciate fully the variety, quantity

386 Why Be Moral?

and quality of such goods available to individuals. That groups also function as if having intrinsic good is obvious to those whose feelings of security depend upon not only feeling identified with the group and its welfare but also feel as if the group itself embodies great intrinsic good. Such persons also tend to project their feelings of good through ideas or icons symbolizing such good. Awareness of evil or of any lack of good naturally generates ideals of what the group would like if the evil were banished and the good perfected. Such ideals then function as conditional oughts, as standards to be striven for, or goals to be sought. Some such ideals arise spontaneously in members as difficulties occur; some become embedded in traditions, whether national, sectarian or familial, and may be typified in the struggles of mythical, legendary or actual heroes. People who cannot trace the goods projected into their ideals back to the intrinsic goods present in immediate experiences tend to become enslaved by them. Enlightenment about social goods is itself one of the greatest of social goods.

Social improvement and social degeneration are both possible and actual. Groups, even whole civilizations, begin and end, arise and decline, improve and degenerate. Social ethics is concerned with the improvement of groups and prevention of evils. Elimination of conflicts and promotion of cooperation as well as exploiting of natural resources for group welfare play central roles. Not least among the ways of improving groups is to first improve understanding of ways to improve groups. Since social ethics has to do with how to improve groups, a study of social ethics tends to become an important step in social improvement. Then knowledge of the many ways in which improvements may be initiated should aid and direct members to act accordingly.

Social obligation, as the obligations which groups have for choosing the greater over the lesser goods, or lesser over the greater evils, is multileveled. When only a single choice is presented to a group at one time, the problem is fairly simple. But when a group has obligations not only to its members, to itself as a group, and to peer groups and to hierarchically related groups but also to maintaining a healthy dynamic balance among these different obligations, its sense of obligation must remain very complex. Although, when narrowly conceived, a group's obligations to itself may be thought of as in opposition to those of its members and to those of other groups with which it competes, broadly conceived, a group's obligations to itself not only include its obligations to its members and to other groups but also to sustain efficient organic unity among these various obligations. Principles for choosing for a group interdepend with those for choosing by each individual, with additional complications when groups may grow or decrease by adding or losing members having intrinsic as well as instrumental goods which may be variable as well as, in some respects, incomparable.

Social action, which involves a group acting as an agent, is ethical whenever it is intended. A group can have no intentions apart from those of its members, even though not all of its members share in affirming each decision to act reached by its effective leaders. Conflicting intentions among members of a group sometimes prevent a group from deciding and acting, just as an individual may have a multiplicity of interests each of which one desires, and conditionally intends, to realize, but which prevent one from acting because one cannot make up one's mind which of one's conflicting interests to sacrifice. Groups are responsible, in several ways, for fulfilling their obligations which, ultimately, are obligations to achieve the greatest amount of intrinsic value for their members and which, intermediately, are obligations to employ the means available to them most efficiently. As groups become more complicated, many varieties of specialists develop and each becomes responsible for making some of the decisions for the group.

Social freedom is the ability of a group to do what it wants to do. Such freedom interdepends with the freedoms of its members and with the freedoms of other groups with which it is related. A group may be free or unfree to have more members, or fewer members, or more devoted members, or less demanding members. A group may be free or unfree to achieve its wants because it desires what cannot be had or has more wants than can be fulfilled because they conflict with each other. A group may be free or unfree to cooperate with or compete with peer groups, to join superior groups, or to enjoy the support of subgroups. If a group desires more independence than it can have, or more dependence than it can have, it is unfree. If it wants more improvements, more powerful agency, more sovereignty or ownership rights or even intelligence that it can have, it is unfree. Social freedom, too, is partly a matter of fitting a group's wants to its opportunities and capacities as well as a matter of succeeding in improving both its capacities and its opportunities.

Social sovereignty is the power of a group to control itself rather than being controlled by some other group. Some sovereign groups are controlled by one of their members, some by a few of their members, some by many, if not all, of their members. Nowadays, complex societies tend to have different functions controlled in different ways, such that some are controlled by a single person, e.g., a specialist or by a president, some by a few, e.g., a committee or a congress of delegates, and some by many, as in popular elections. Democracy, as a system of group self-control, has evolved many forms, and the town-council type of democracy, which gave way to representative democracy, is now rapidly being replaced by speciocracy, government by specialist, whether elected or appointed. When persons participate in many levels of groups, the problem of attaining and maintaining healthy democracy recurs at each level. When the control of activities pertaining to a person's interests at one level is endangered by the control system at another level, some of one's power of self-control is thereby in jeopardy. We use the term "democracy of levels" to designate a system by which individuals and groups control themselves in such a way that their interests exercised through different levels of groups tend to receive equally adequate treatment. The need for attaining a democratic world government, which would be both a highest level of democracy and an additional level to a democracy of levels, appears to many as one of the most important ethical problems facing mankind today.

Social ownership, i.e. a group having something as its own, is of many kinds. In addition to a group owning, and being owned by, its members, most of what a group owns is spoken of as wealth. Wealth consists of whatever is useful in serving the wants of the group or, more ultimately, the desires of its members. Price, economic value, instrumental value and intrinsic value all interdepend in may ways, for, on the one hand, price should, ideally, represent economic value which should be related to instrumental value which should rest upon intrinsic value, but, on the other hand, the appreciation which a person enjoys in consuming some goods is influenced by the price. Group ownership, whether by private or public groups, increases the amount owned by individuals when more individuals share in such ownership but decreases the amount owned by individuals to the extent that more individuals are excluded from such ownership. Likewise, public group ownership increases the amount owned by individuals through sharing in such ownership but decreases the amount of individual ownership in the sense that an individual owns his wealth exclusively. Arguments for and against group ownership, generally, and public ownership, specifically, continue. Doubtless some kinds of wealth and some types of enterprise are better owned publicly and others better owned privately, and the same wealth or enterprise may be better owned publicly under certain circumstances and better owned privately when circumstances change in certain ways, or vice versa. Some groups, doubtless, ought to keep an experimental attitude toward their system of ownership and change from one to the other if such a shift promises better results.

Social justice occurs when groups get what they deserve, distributively or retributively; social injustice exists when groups obtain less than they deserve; and grace prevails when groups receive more than they deserve. Groups have rights and duties, as extensions of individual rights and duties, which have their bases ultimately in intrinsic goods. Groups have duties to their members, to themselves as groups, and to other groups, because their members have rights, they themselves have rights, and other groups have rights. Rights and duties of groups involve correlativity and appropriate functioning of the principle of reciprocity.

Social conscience here refers to the conscience of a group, which is inseparable from that of its members. A group's conscience consists of its feelings of obligation. These may be directed toward its members, toward other groups, or toward harmonious and adequate fulfilling of its own desires. A group's conscience may lead it to act or refrain from acting, to seek more freedom of choice or more freedom from choice, to desire more or less sovereignty, more or less public ownership, more or fewer rights and more or fewer duties, to achieve greater justice, or to become more intelligent. Conscience both depends upon all other value aspects of a group's nature and all such aspects may depend for their achievement upon an effective conscience.

Social intelligence is the ability of a group to attain its ends, which, of course, includes aiding its members in achieving more of their own goals. A group's intelligence is conditioned by facility of communication among members and between groups, by the quantity and quality of new ideas available as hypotheses for solving the group's problems, by the attitude of willingness or unwillingness with which a group accepts a problem as its own, as solvable and as solvable by means of a particular proposed solution, by the total number of problems to which it can attend at one time, and by the rigidity or pliability of its system of organization. Too many groups suffer from cultural lag, which results in their institutions functioning inefficiently, and becoming formalistic and disorganized. An intelligent group is able to foresee growing obsolescence in its mores, laws and institutions and to revise them before the resulting evils become greater than the good which can be obtained from newer behavior patterns. Social intelligence thus involves ability and willingness on the part of a group to engage in social planning. Growth in complexity of social interdependencies has begotten a need for increased numbers of kinds of specialists in social planning. Whether or not such specialists are themselves intelligent and untyrannical will have great bearing upon how intelligent their groups can become.

Conclusion. Our survey of some of the ethical aspects of groups has shown them to be complexly interrelated with each other in ways which make them intricately interdependent. Social ethics, as a study of the concern which groups have for what is best for them and what all they ought to do in order to attain what is best, involves an understanding of these intricate interdependencies and an attempt to formulate general principles, holding for like situations, which may be utilized in deciding how to act in order to attain such best. Some aspects of social ethics remain relatively simple, as when much of the give and take in some contemporary families is like that in ancient families. But other aspects, involving intentional relations between two warring countries each having semi-private trading companies entangled in multi-leveled megalopolitan hierarchies as well as in both the peace and war states of each of the two multi-lingual countries, seem endlessly complex. Such complexity does not eliminate ethics; it merely makes it more complicated. That the solution of some practical ethical problems must be delegated to specialists seems obvious. Consequently, the ethics of training and managing such specialists constitutes an additional important problem in social ethics.

That social ethics interdepends with individual ethics surely must be clear by now. That both individual and social ethics may have still other dimensions, in whatever ways persons have rights and obligations relative to animals, for example, or the rest of the universe, will be dealt with in Part III. Inter-dependence between persons and groups is complicated further by their interrelations with the rest of the world.

PART III

SATISFACTION

Chapter XXXII

FINAL ETHICS

The Meaning of "Final". The word "final," from the Latin finis, like the word "finish," connotes end, termination, perfection. As presupposed throughout the foregoing chapters, each intrinsic good, whether a feeling of pleasure, enthusiasm, satisfaction, or contentment, is experienced as an end-in-itself. In this sense, all ethics is final ethics, for all ethics is concerned with what one ought to choose and to do in order to achieve such ends in themselves. However, tradition favors another meaning of "final," namely, the goal or end of life. That is, although each experienced intrinsic good is final in its own way, we have come to ask what is the meaning and value of life as a whole, and to seek to shape our answer in terms of some "supreme value" which is final in the sense that it is the end of life itself rather than the end experienced when satisfying a desire for a particular good such as an evening at the movies. The Latin words, summum bonum, "the highest good," are commonly used to designate the goal of life itself. Thomas Aquinas spoke of "man's last end," distinguishing our most ultimate values from minor or intermediate ultimates.

If there is a most ultimate value of life, then surely attainment of it is what a person most wants. And those aspects of ethical principles and ethical behavior which are directed toward achievement of such a value constitute what are here called "final ethics." If life has a most ultimate intrinsic good, then surely the attainment of it is one's greatest self-interest, is the pinnacle of self-improvement, is one's supreme obligation, is the primary message of one's distorted conscience, is the goal of one's intelligence.

However, even though there appears to be general agreement among people and among mature ethicists that life has a goal and that final ethics is the most important part of ethics, disagreements continue about whether such finality is one or many, whether it can be achieved within this life or only after death, whether it can be achieved only at the end of life or throughout life while it is being lived, and whether it consists merely in all the ordinary enjoyments or whether it is some special kind of intrinsic good. In the following chapters, we shall explore answers to these questions. In Chapter XXXIII, we shall inquire into the aesthetic or immediately experienced character of any supreme good. In Chapter XXXIV, we shall consider some implications of the aesthetic nature of the goal of life for conceptions of the nature of life and its goal, reviewing and evaluating some traditional views. In Chapter XXXV, we shall summarize our conclusions regarding the organic nature of final ethics, including its interdependence with the details of individual and social ethics. The problem remaining in the present chapter is to examine more fully the meaning of "final" as representing a person's concern for the purpose or goal of life as a whole. We do this by exploring two other terms which are intimately related with final ethics, namely, "satisfaction" and "success."

The Meaning of "Satisfaction." Part III has been entitled "Satisfaction." "Satisfaction," from the Latin satisfacere, meaning to make (facere) complete (satis), conveys the idea of fulfillment, of doing enough, of attaining sufficiently, of achieving completion. Satisfaction, in this sense, is making something complete. Final satisfaction, the ultimate goal of ethics, is to make life as complete as it can be in the sense of achieving its fullest, including its highest, intrinsic good. In this broad meaning, the term "satisfaction" connotes realization of the goal of life.

Since we are now using the word "satisfaction" in a second and more general sense than that used in Chapters VIff, clarification of the difference seems needed. In Chapter VI, we distinguished between feelings of pleasure, enthusiasm, satisfaction and contentment, each of which is experienced as an intrinsic good. There "satisfaction" meant the fulfillment of desire, i.e., of any desire, no matter how trivial or significant, where the feeling of satisfaction may be distinguished from feelings of pleasure, enthusiasm and contentment, if one tries. Here "satisfaction," i.e., "final satisfaction," means achievement of the goal of life, however conceived. The latter meaning may be thought of as an extension or expansion of the former, as it is by Voluntarists. But it may also be thought of as the goal of life as conceived by Hedonists, Romanticists, Anandists and Organicists. And it tends to have both aesthetic and cosmic ingredients, as we shall point out in the following two chapters. "Final satisfaction" connotes consummation of life as a whole, insofar as that is possible. It is thus inclusive of all of its intrinsic good and of all of the personal, social and cosmic instrumentalities pictured as needed to make possible and actual such life and its consummation.

The Meaning of "Success". "A person ought to try to succeed in life," we say. Or, "The goal of life is success." Part III has been difficult to entitle because so many different words are available, none of which quite captures all of the intended meaning. The term "success" is one of these words. It is another of those terms which is on everybody's lips, which everyone understands without stopping to define it. But, again, we refer here to "success in life," not just success in business or success in getting to dinner on time. We sometimes try to make this distinction clear by using such terms as "genuine success," "complete success," "ultimate success," "final success." What is meant is success in achieving the goal of life. Hence, the nature and purpose of ethics may be restated in this language: Ethics is concerned with what is good and how to get it, not just food and fun, money and marriage, excitement and security, but the good of life. The purpose of a study of ethics is to help one to understand how to succeed in life. Final ethics pertains to how to achieve complete success in life.

However, the term "success" also at times has a brass ring about it. It is used to refer to success in crime and war as well as in business conducted by foul means. Furthermore, it is not quite as popular around the world as in America, and, hopefully, this volume is intended for use by persons who are not limited merely to American tastes.

Success in life involves not merely getting what one wants but also wanting what one gets. It involves an aesthetic a well as a practical achievement. And since one's feelings of achievement are perceived in terms of certain ideals of success, it entails some conception of the nature of life in the universe, and thus is inseparable from one's conception of the cosmos. The following chapters may be interpreted as exploring questions about how to actualize full and final success in life.

Chapter XXXIII

SATISFACTION AS AESTHETIC

The present chapter on final ethics will be devoted to exploring the nature of aesthetic experience, how it relates to moral experience, the role it plays in religious experience, and ways in which moral and religious experience interdepend.

Aesthetic Experience and Moral Experience. "Experience is 'aesthetic' when it is enjoyed as complete in itself and 'moral' when it is felt as incomplete and as needing something more to complete it. Hence, 'aesthetic' and 'moral' are conceived as opposites.... This distinction between 'aesthetic' and 'moral' may be stated also in terms of intrinsic and instrumental values...an experience is itself an intrinsic value to the extent that it is experienced as complete in itself. Such an experience 'aesthetic.' An experience is itself an instrumental value to the extent that it experiences itself as a means to something more. Such an experience is 'moral.'" ("Aesthetic Experience and Moral Experience," The Journal of Philosophy, Vol. LV, Sept. 25, 1958, pp. 837-839.) "Instrumental value appears as leading on to something else, as having a goal beyond, as unfinished in the sense that it has a further contribution to make. Value is experienced as intrinsic, on the other hand, when its value is experienced as all there or when an interest in it is wholly satisfied in it or by it. In some ways, aesthetic intuition is the most perfect, most complete, most ultimate kind of intuition, for in it nothing more is needed." (A.J. Bahm, Types of Intuition, p. 8, University of New Mexico Press, Albuquerque, 1961.)

Ethics, in being concerned with what is good and how to attain it, is future-oriented. The good being sought is not yet found. The goal aimed at has not yet been achieved. The purpose intended has not yet been realized. The choice being decided pertains to what one ought to choose to be done but has not yet done. One's obligations consist in what one yet owes, and one's duties consist in what one still ought to do. Interest in self-improvement is ethical because one can become better than one is or because some evil can be removed which has not yet been eliminated. Conscience is ethical because it consists in one's concern for maintaining present welfare, or for attaining something better, in the future, whether immediate or remote. Ethical intelligence consists in the ability to attain what has not yet been attained. Ethics, thus, is greatly concerned about means to ends, and about what one ought to do in order to achieve those ends. The greater the future reward, or the farther distant it seems to be, or the harder one must work in order to attain it, the more conscientious one needs to be. And, conversely, the more conscientious a person appears to be, the greater, the more distant, or the more difficult to attain, the goal or value may be inferred to be. Whenever the goal is experienced as unattained and still in the future, it is experienced as moral. In this sense, most people are moral most of the time.

Aesthetics, which is concerned with aesthetic experience, regardless of whether such experience is characterized also by works of art, beautiful dreams, beatific visions, or yogic ananda, is present-oriented. That is "Aesthetic experience consists in intuition of intrinsic value." ("Comparative Aesthetics," The Journal of Aesthetics and Art Criticism, Vol. XXIV, Fall, 1965, p. 109.) The value experience is present, here and now. It is experienced as needing nothing more to complete it. It is not something being aimed at, but something being enjoyed. It is not something to be achieved, but something already actual. It is not something which one ought to do, but something which one is already doing, or being, or feeling. The aesthetic attitude is thus an appreciative attitude. It is focused upon the end-in-itself character of an experience rather than upon its means character. Its nature is constituted by being appreciative of what is present as the goal itself, rather than looking away from the present to some other goal. A painting may be judged beautiful, but this judgement occurs when one enjoys some aspect of the painting, or even its apparent whole, as an end-in-itself. Sometimes vivid colors, sometimes balanced forms, sometimes interesting themes, and sometimes a harmonious blend of all of these, organically unified, occupy the focus of attention. But it is the end-in-itself character of one's experience which constitutes them aesthetic. This is the reason why both the satisfaction accompanying a delicious meal and the feeling of contentment permeating the "Amen" terminating a prayer of profound appreciation are experienced as aesthetic.

Final ethics is concerned with achieving the goal of life as a whole. Final aesthetics, so to speak, is concerned with appreciating the goal of life as a whole. Final satisfaction should be, when it is attained, an aesthetic experience. It consists in experiencing life itself as an end-in-itself, as an intrinsic good. Just as final ethics pertains to looking forward to fulfilling the purpose of life, so final aesthetics pertains to presently enjoying life as fulfilling, or as having fulfilled, its purpose. Hence, the ethical and the aesthetic, though conceived in one sense as opposites, interdepend and supplement each other. So final ethics and final aesthetics sustain each other and exist because they depend upon each other.

Although, in distinguishing aesthetic from moral experience, we have sharpened their difference for purposes of clarity, many, if not most, experiences partake of both moral and aesthetic aspects. That is, although some experiences seem to be primarily moral, they may also retain an element of the aesthetic; for when a person is moral, and concerned about the future, one often enjoys being moral, and appreciates the fact that one has such a concern. And although some experiences seem to be primarily aesthetic, they may also contain some elements of the moral; for when one is preoccupied with appreciating a painting which one regards as very beautiful, one may also entertain suggestions about how it might be improved, how one's friend might enjoy it also, or how one would like to continue seeing it or return to see it again. Thus, the aesthetic and moral not only interdepend; they also intermingle in experiences. These facts, so often overlooked, have bearings upon the nature of religious experience, and have implications for the ethics of both religious beliefs and practices.

Aesthetic Experience and Religious Experience. "Religion consists in man's concern for his ultimate value, and how to attain it, preserve it, and enjoy it." (The World's Living Religions, p. 16. For further details, see all of Chapter 1.) So conceived, religion is both ethical and aesthetic in character. Religion is essentially ethical in the sense that it is forward-looking. Religion is essentially aesthetic in the sense that what it looks forward to in enjoyment of the goal of life as an end-in-itself. Religion, understood in this way, is inseparable from final ethics and final aesthetics. Final ethics and final aesthetics together, as we have described them, constitute a philosophy of religious experience.

Let us here examine the view that religious experience is, or aims to be aesthetic. What is the purpose or goal of religion? It is the same as the purpose or goal of life. Religion is one's concern for, i.e., both one's beliefs about and one's pursuit of, the goal of life. When achieved, the goal, to be enjoyed, must be appreciated as present. Before it is achieved, it must be conceived in some way or other, but that way always involves an aesthetic ingredient which, indeed, is the most important part of it. If being aesthetic consists in enjoying something as an end-in-itself, the goal of religious endeavor is depicted as some place, state or condition in which one is enjoying it as an end-in-itself. A study of the various religious ideals will reveal the universal presence, and importance, of aesthetic ingredients.

Consider, for example, various Christian views of what heaven is like. Those who derive their vision from Hebrew sources in the Old Testament depict it as a happy family, with a loving father, one's beloved spouse, and one's loved and loving children, brothers, and other relatives. Such happiness involves aesthetic experience. Some Christians, whose theological ideals have been influenced by the philosophy of Plato and Aristotle, whose theological ideals picture a person as an inherently imperfect image of a perfect being, conceive God, the Father, as man's "Last End." God alone is pure intrinsic good. "God alone is truly beautiful." When persons realize their true condition, they desire to "see God," to "look on his face," to attain a beatific vision. Heaven, the goal of life, is a state in which one is permitted to enjoy eternal bliss; that is, to have an unending aesthetic experience of God's pure intrinsic good, even though one does not deserve such a reward due to one's own imperfection ("sinfulness"). Still other Christians, finding all schemes for structuring an afterlife defective, conclude: "I have no idea what it will be like, but I do know that when I get there I'm going to enjoy it."

Consider, next, various Hindu ideals of nirvana. Typically conceived, nirvana is a quiescent state in which all of the miseries experienced in this world have disappeared. Since desire too often ends in frustration, it is regarded as our chief source of evil; hence in nirvana all desire has ceased. So also have ideas, forms, memories, and all distinctions; for these tend to arouse interest, desire, and suffering. But nirvana involves sat-chit-ananda, the being of blissful awareness. Ananda is enjoyment of pure intrinsic good. Nirvana is the state of such enjoyment. Advaita Vedanta conceives this state as resulting from elimination of selfhood, including self-awareness, when the "veil of ignorance" inhibiting atman from its awareness of its identity with Nirguna Brahman disappears. Sankhya-yoga regards the individual soul, purusha, when freed from all contact with the body and mind, prakriti, as existing in a state of eternal isolation, kaivalya, as pure blissless awareness. Here a paradox of religious ethics which we are about to discuss, i.e, the moral ending in the amoral, is carried even farther, i.e., the aesthetic purified of intrinsic good is regarded as even better than experience of pure intrinsic good.

Buddhist descriptions of nirvana vary, with the Theravadins as bhavanga, with the Madhyamikans as sunya, with Shin as living in the Pure Land, and with Zen as satori. Bhavanga is a flux of contentless and desireless awareness. Sunya, voidance of all distinctness, is experienced as "suchness," the voidance of distinctness between distinctness and indistinctness, which leaves intuition of whatever is presented as ultimate value. Living in the Pure Land is, like living in heaven, perpetually blissful awareness of the utter graciousness of Amida in rescuing all sentient beings from a life of tormenting desires. Satori, also "suchness," is alert, spontaneous appreciation of whatever is presented in experience as just what is wanted, without interest in planning for a better future. Jains, like Sankhya-Yogins, depict the aesthetic experience of eternally isolated souls as omniscient awareness of all detail in the universe, but without desire to use or improve anything.

The foregoing samples all illustrate the view that the goal of life, and of religion, is aesthetic. In explaining, for those who are not now enjoying such a goal, how to arrive there, each must give some account about what needs and ought to be done. Hence all religions also involve ethics and stress the importance of attention to ethical experience, i.e., to conscientiousness about doing what needs to be done in order to attain the goal. But most of them also involve a paradox, namely that the moral has its goal in the amoral. The ethical, which involves a sense of urgency for attaining an unattained goal, has as its goal an experience which is both goalless, in the sense that there is nothing to look forward to, and without a feeling of urgency. Religion is an urgent endeavor to eliminate urgency. Is one most religious when one has arrived in the goal, or has one then ceased to be religious? Is religion (from the Latin re-ligare, to bind back) a process of being brought back to an original quiescence conceived as the goal of life, or is it also a condition of being in the goal of life? Is religion only moral, or only aesthetic, or both moral and aesthetic? Many religions, in depicting the goal as aesthetic, i.e., and enjoying intuition of intrinsic goodness, idealize complete elimination of evil. Ethical experience, involving problems of choice between good and evil in shaping the future, involves evil; hence ethical experience and aesthetic experience are conceived as antithetical. The logic of such a view of the ethical and the aesthetic implies: "Let the end come quickly." That is, we should seek to escape from the ethical into the aesthetic as quickly, or as efficiently, as possible. Unfortunately, the way is often long and hard, and those who look for shortcuts may easily deceive themselves. However, the long way may also be the wrong way, for in many religions, the goal may be found along the way, even only in the way. How this is so may be seen from the following six illustrations.

1. Hofus, the stonecutter. An ancient story, which I read as a child, has been unforgettable. It was about Hofus (Hafiz, etc.), a stonecutter

who, wearying of his endless task, wished he might be a king, like the one passing by with servants, gorgeous clothing delicious food, and luxurious carriage. Suddenly, a voice spoke out, commanding him to be, and making him, a king. Hofus was happy, but not for long, As the sun beat down upon his company, they wilted and wearied and Hofus himself was miserable. Realizing that the sun was more powerful than he, he wished that he might be the sun. Again the voice spoke out, and Hofus became the sun. As the sun, he was proud of his power, which he shined forth fiercely. But as lakes dried up under the heat of his rays, evaporation produced clouds which hid the sun from the earth, thus demonstrating that a cloud is more powerful than the sun. Angered again, Hofus then wanted to be a cloud. Before he realized what he was doing, the voice spoke again, making Hofus a cloud,. As a cloud, he rained so hard that rivers overflowed and the land was washed away before its torrents, all except one great rock, which resisted all of Hofus' efforts to dislodge it. Wishing then to be that immovable rock, Hofus became the rock. His pride in his present strength was short-lived, for soon along came a man with a hammer and chisel who started chipping away at his side. Then realizing that the man was more powerful than he, Hofus wished he were that man. Then, becoming a stonecutter again, Hofus was happy. This truncated version of an old story illustrates how one can be happier being what one is than what one would be if one were anything else. One who enjoys one's present life as being as good as it can be has no need for wanting it to be different. (For a more recent story, see Russell H. Conwell, Acres of Diamonds.)

2. Jesus. Although the teachings of Jesus are too complex to reduce to simple statement, he did often put great emphasis upon appreciating the present, partly by trying to dissuade people from worrying about the future. "Care not for the morrow." (Matthew 6:34.) "The kingdom of heaven is at hand." (Matthew 10:7.) "Give us this day our daily bread." (Matthew 6:11.) His central thesis was that "perfect love casteth out fear" (1 John 4:18), and that the way to the goal of life, the heavenly kingdom, is to replace fear of others and fear of the future by a love which, when embodied in one, is like a rebirth of life and confidence. If one does not embody such love, then one must look forward to the day when one may attain it; one should be moral. But if one already embodies such love, one finds the kingdom of heaven already within one. God is love, and when we embody love we embody God and dwell enjoyably in heaven. Such an experience is aesthetic; and those who do not have it should seek it. "Seek and ye shall find." (Matthew 7:7.) What will you find?

Confidence and present enjoyment. "Consider the lilies of the field, how they grow; they toil not, neither do they spin; and yet I say unto you that even Solomon in all his glory was not arrayed like one of these. Wherefore if God so clothe the grass of the field, which today is, and tomorrow is cast into the oven, shall not he much more clothe you, O ye of little faith?" (Matthew 6:28-30.) "Therefore take no though of the morrow." (Matthew 6:34.) Although Christian orthodoxy, following Paul and the Patristics, placed heaven in a life after death, Jesus seems much more concerned about the heaven which is "at hand." For God "is not the God of the dead, but of the living." (Matthew 22:32.)

3. Gotama. Buddhism, more than any other religion except perhaps Taoism and Confucianism, emphasizes finding the goal in the way, which it calls "The Middle Way." Other worldly aspects have been retained from earlier Hinduism and added from Chinese folklore, but the central message of Gotama to all who are suffering is to stop wanting what you are not going to get. "Desire for what will not be attained ends in frustration; therefore, to avoid frustration, avoid desiring what will not be attained." (A.J. Bahm, Philosophy of the Buddha, p. 15.) One who seeks an unattainable goal of life not only will not find it but will have made oneself unhappy in the process. When persons believing in reincarnation quizzed him about a future life, he replied: If you want a next life and there is no next life, you will be frustrated. If you want a next life and there is a next life, you have no problem. If you want no next life and there is a next life, you will be frustrated. If you want no next life and there is no next life, you have no problem. The important thing, for happiness, is not whether there is or is not a next life but whether you are willing to accept it whichever way it comes. This willingness to accept things as they are, and are going to be, is the middle way. If you can find it, and stay in it, then ". . .to whatever place you go, you shall go in comfort; wherever you stand, you shall stand in comfort; wherever you sit, you shall sit in comfort; and wherever you make your bed, you shall lie down in comfort." (The Book of the Gradual Sayings, Vol. IV, p. 200. Tr. by E.M. Hare, Luzac and Co., London 1955.) Such a life is lived in nirvana; its appreciation of the present as intrinsic value, i.e., of what one gets as just what one wants; is to find the goal of life by living it.

4. Krishna. Regardless of whether the message of the Bhagavad Gita, sacred scripture of the Hindus, was formulated by the man, Krishna, or by the editor, Vyasa, its aim is clear. No matter which of paths (marga or yoga) one takes toward the goal, one not only cannot reach the goal but one cannot make much progress along the path unless one does so

with "disinterested interest" (nishkama yoga). Whether one endeavors to
work one's way by sweat and sacrifice (karma yoga), by loving devotion
to parents and to deities (bhakti yoga), through study of the scriptures
and philosophy (gñana yoga), or through bodily self-control, such as
breathing, postures, withdrawal of senses, and stilling the mind (hatha,
and raja yoga), the very zeal and anxiety of one's endeavors prevent one
from achievement. For the goal of life, nirvana, consists in blissful
enjoyment of quiescent, i.e., desireless, being. Paradoxically, one who
desires desirelessness cannot attain it unless one stops desiring. Hence
the karma yogin must work for results without interest in rewards. The
bhakti yogin must love selflessly without expecting to be loved. The
gñana yogin must learn that the knowledge he desires is a knowledge that
is not knowledge, but a desireless, i.e, objectless and subjectless,
awareness. The raja yogin must discipline himself so that he can fully
realize that he is no individual self, and concentrate so much that nothing
is left but pure concentration. Although the ideal goal is beyond this life,
its attainability can be expected only if one already partially attains it in
this life. Yogas are both moral and aesthetic. Yoga, as union with the
ultimate, is purely aesthetic. But yoga as a path is moral. One who
travels a path with complete disinterest has already arrived in ultimacy.
The practice of nishkama yoga aims to find the goal in the way. (See my
Union With The Ultimate [Patanjali's Yoga Sutras], 1961.)

5. Lao Tzu. The greatest book in Chinese philosophical history is the
Tao Teh King., attributed to Lao Tzu. Its naturalistic doctrine now called
"Taoism," advocates doing what comes naturally. "Whoever acts naturally
is nature itself acting." "All aiming is Nature's aiming, and is nature's way
of being itself." (A.J. Bahm, Tao Teh King by Lao Tzu, p. 77, 1958.)
"Whoever acts unnaturally comes to an unnatural finish." "The way to
success is this: having achieved your goal, be satisfied not to go further."
"To be in accord with nature is to be achieving the goal of life. But to
seek excitement is to invite calamity." "There is no greater evil than
desiring to change others. There is no greater misfortune than desiring
to change oneself. . . . Only he who is satisfied with whatever satisfactions
his own nature provides for him is truly satisfied." (Ibid. pp. 87-88.) He
is "as unconcerned as the rolling ocean, without a care to bother him."
(Ibid., pp. 90.) "Therefore the intelligent man accepts what is as it is."
(Ibid., p. 104.) The goal of life is to be found by living life each day
without trying to change it. To fail to appreciate such a way as the goal
is to miss the goal of life.

6. Confucius. Whereas Lao Tzu pictured natural living as rural, and urban life as so artificial that it should be avoided, Confucius was a Taoist who regarded living in families, including large families, as also natural. Although noted for emphasizing the principle of reciprocity as naturally necessary to family harmony, he also idealized chih, wisdom, which "consists in actual achievement of contentment and enjoyment of profound confidence." (Ibid., p. 114. See also my The World's Living Religions, p. 189.) Chih is spontaneous yea-saying to whatever the situation demands. The attitude of the spontaneous yea-sayer is one of appreciation. One's spontaneity is so instantaneous that one has no time to doubt. Hence the wise person's response is more aesthetic than moral. When one's spontaneity is habitually complete, one transcends morality. Zen, perhaps more obviously to many readers, idealizes such spontaneous yea-saying without being concerned to provide the elaborate set of reasons expounded by Confucius. Zen, a Taoized form of Buddhism, locates the goal of life in the present way perhaps more clearly than any other religion. (See my The World's Living Religions, pp. 206-221, especially pp. 209-210.)

The goal of religion, then, is aesthetic, regardless of whether it appears attainable only in some life after death or only along the way. Although, when distinguishing between aesthetics and religion, we say that aesthetics is not religion and religion is not aesthetics, still, the religious and the aesthetic, as aspects of experience, interdepend. For, if the aesthetic is intuition of intrinsic good and if the goal of religion is aesthetic, then the religious certainly depends upon, for it partly consists in, the aesthetic. And the aesthetic, which appears in parts of life, is more fully realized when it is experienced as intuitive appreciation of life itself as a whole, i.e., as religious. From an Organicist viewpoint, it seems appropriate to say that a religious experience is more religious when it is more aesthetic, and an aesthetic experience is more aesthetic when it is more religious. Not every aesthetic experience is religious (e.g., one had while viewing artistic advertising design), and not every religious experience is aesthetic (e.g., one had when conscience-stricken about moral shortcomings); but when, dialectically, each involves the other more fully, each becomes more fully itself. One who appreciates life itself as a whole, including all its other appreciations, is more appreciative, i.e, more aesthetic, than one who does not. One who appreciates life itself as a whole, including all its other appreciations, has more fully reached the goal of religion, and hence is more religious, than one who does not. "Final satisfaction" is aesthetic and religious at the same time.

Ethics and Religion. In relating aesthetic experience, as intuition of intrinsic good, with moral experience, as a sense of incompleteness imbued with the feeling that one ought to do something to fill the want, and in relating aesthetic experience, as any appreciated enjoyment, with religious experience, as appreciation of the intrinsic good of life, as a whole, we have already indicated some of the relations between ethical experience and religious experience. There is more to ethical experience than to religious experience, for ethical experience includes multitudes of trivial and intermediate oughts, whereas it is those oughts which pertain to the ultimate goal of life as a whole which constitute part of religion. Some of our ethical experiences are also religious experiences. But also, there is more to religious experience than to ethical experience, because religious experience includes some trans-ethical aesthetics appreciations, when, or to the extent that, one has arrived in and enjoys living in the goal. Some of our religious experiences are also ethical experiences, i.e., those in which we feel an obligation to seek to achieve the goal of life; but some religious experiences are amoral, or fully aesthetic. Religion is complicated in many ways, and we have yet to see, in the following chapter, how ideals of the nature of self and the universe are essential to it as well as the ethical and aesthetic aspects discussed here.

Consider further the relations between ethics and religion by examining the distinction between ethical religion and religious ethics. Religion is ethical whenever it is concerned about obligations. Being ethical is religious whenever it is concerned about the goal of life. We can observe that some religions are more ethical than others in the sense that their doctrines and practices stress attention to the ethical more than to the aesthetic. They are more attentive to ultimate oughts and their achievement, i.e., about bringing the moral to the amoral more quickly and fully, without dwelling upon how much we have already achieved. And we can observe that some ethics, some ethical codes for example, are more religious than others in the sense that they emphasize attention to the goal of life more than to occupational commercial, architectural or other technical oughts.

However, too often we overlook the aspectival character of religion and ethics and the additional values which can come from knowingly experiencing them together. For an experience (and a life) which is obviously both aesthetic and moral is more aesthetic than one which is merely aesthetic; for if life involves both aesthetic and moral aspects, then, when an experience is both, it is more complete, or more of a whole, or more wholesome, than when it lacks the moral, which lack itself may be experienced as a kind of incompleteness. And an experience (and a life) which is obviously both moral and aesthetic is more moral than one which is merely moral; for one who continues looking forward without experiencing some attainment tends to have doubts, which are not only experienced as unaesthetic, even as anti-aesthetic (i.e., as intrinsic evil rather than merely absence of intrinsic good), but also as immoral, or anti-moral, not merely in the sense that one may feel that one ought not to doubt but also in the sense that the justification felt for one's doubt constitutes a kind of ought-not regarding one's hope of final attainment. Morality is not self-sustaining; for if one feels one ought to seek a goal without any assurance that the goal is attainable, one soon looses the feeling of oughtness. Aesthetic amorality is not self-sustaining; for needs arise no matter how persistently we ignore them, and hunger, disease, misery or death stalk the unwary, except in climates and societies which succor monks who themselves willingly abandon all interest in moral life. Those who are merely moral, i.e., who are anxious without justified hope, live miserably. Those who are merely aesthetic, i.e., enjoy life without striving, become lazy and destitute. Both tend to become both anti-moralistic and anti-religious. "The grapes are sour to those who cannot reach them." Pessimism plagues both. Only by being both aesthetic and moral (i.e., religious), or at least somewhat aesthetic and somewhat moral, can one enjoy life at all.

We have not, in using the term "religious" in the foregoing, presumed any particular metaphysical scheme. Instead of beginning with theological presumptions, for example, and then deducting what they imply for aesthetic experience and ethical behavior, we have examined the ethical and the aesthetic first, and will try to draw some implications of our understanding of these for metaphysics, including theology. If the goal of life and of religion is to intuit the intrinsic goods of life, then every scheme for interpreting the nature of the universe must somehow account for how this is possible. Each of the world's religions has done this, even if in different ways. But those which somehow manage to be both realistic, in the sense that their views are true, and idealistic, in the sense that they seem to warrant hope for goods that have not yet been realized, tend to be better, i.e. both more moral and more aesthetic, than those which demand realism without hope or hope without warrant. Generally speaking, those religions which enable their followers to experience the intrinsic value of life here and now provide warrant for hope. But also those which promise no more than testable experience justifies enable their followers to hope with confidence.

Religion is partly a matter of beliefs, which we will explore in the next chapter, but also partly a matter of attitude. Religion, in part, is a matter of yea-saying, of saying "Yes" to life as it is, for nay-saying is itself unpleasant, or unaesthetic, and results in both anti-moral and anti-aesthetic experience. Now, of course one must say "No" to evil; but there are those who would also say "No" to good. Whoever wants the world to be different than it is and can become is, in effect, saying "No" to the good that is and will become. One thereby forfeits a part of one's heritage of good. One is unethical in the sense that one chooses to experience evil when one might otherwise be experiencing good. Yea-saying is a way of transforming the ethical into the aesthetic, and so may be a part of what one most wants to do. If being more religious means being both more moral and more aesthetic relative to the intrinsic good of life as a whole, then being more religious may be a most important part of what one most wants to be.

Chapter XXXIV

SATISFACTION AS COSMIC

Final ethics is concerned with satisfaction in the sense of making life complete. Such satisfaction is aesthetically complete when life itself as a whole is experienced as being an intrinsic good, or as being an end-in-itself. Such satisfaction is cosmically complete when life is experienced as having its fullest, i.e., widest deepest and most inclusive, extent in the universe. The purpose of the present chapter is to explore the problem of how little or how much a life is involved with the rest of the universe. This is an ethical problem because you will not know what you ought to do in order to achieve the goal of your life unless you understand the nature of your life and the universe in which it exists. If you have any choice in the matter, and surely most readers do have some such choice, you will seek to understand more about the nature of both yourself and the universe so that you may then improve yourself in whatever ways you can, both within yourself and in your relations to the rest of the universe. You will want to ascertain how far you extend into the cosmos, both space-wise and time-wise and to discover the levels, if any, of identification and differentiation of yourself with otherness. How you will choose among many options will vary with your culture, with your education, and with the amount of dissatisfaction you feel with the picture preferred by most of your fellows. Regardless of what intellectual scheme you follow, you will feel that your efforts to understand are inadequate until both your life as a whole and the universe as a whole are taken into account. Such an effort is religious in the sense that it is concerned both with the goal of your life as a whole and its place in the universe as a whole. And your endeavor is experienced as ethical to the extent that you are searching for some good that you do not yet have. Each person, at some time or other, doubtless faces the question of how much time and effort one ought to spend in thinking things through, or in working out a philosophy of life by one's own efforts. Some are so busy making a living, or enjoying sports, or caring for urgent miseries, that they do not have time for serious reflection. Some believe that others have already done the job adequately, or at least better than they can, so willingly accept instruction by others. Some feel that they are incapable of understanding the nature of ultimate reality, and some of these believe that it is beyond the wit of any person to do so. Appeal is made here to those who believe that persons can succeed or at least think that "it is better to have tried and failed than never to have tried at all". The history of people's efforts to understand, despite so many obvious mistakes, gives evidence of

progress in insight. Now, with so many previous philosophies from all of
the world's civilizations to draw upon, opportunities for achievement are
greater than ever before. Although the danger remains that the great
ideas in the great books may be also great delusions, enough criticism of
each is also available to enable cautious thinkers to evade many
traditional types of mistakes. Enough variety is also available to provide
bases for generalizations about which kinds of metaphysical hypotheses
are both most satisfactory and at the same time most in accord with the
facts. Some thinkers, enamored by the elegance of an intellectual scheme,
deduce their theories of value, beauty and morality from previously
decided upon metaphysical presuppositions. But the importance of
axiology, aesthetics and ethics in shaping a philosophy of life is so great
that it should not be left to a subordinate position. It is just as
reasonable to found a philosophy of life upon the aesthetic and the ethical
as upon the metaphysical, if one feels that one has to choose between
them. The Organicist view is that neither metaphysical, epistemological
or axiological (including aesthetic and ethical) theories are adequate until
each has taken full account of the others. The three are interdependent.
Neglect of the metaphysical in this volume is an inadequacy, and one that
cannot be ignored entirely in exploring religion as the field of final ethics.
But our attention here will be focused upon the problem: which
conceptions of the universe are preferable, i.e., aesthetically and ethically
preferable? This problem involves us in the question: Are there any
principles for choosing among alternative metaphysical interpretations?
Involved in this is the question: Are there any principles for choosing
among religions?

More Principles for Choosing. In attempting to think things through
about the nature of the universe and what kind of belief one ought to
hold, one may wonder whether there are any principles which will help
one to decide which of two or more alternative conceptions one ought to
prefer? Of course, one ought to prefer a view which is true, or truest;
and we shall discuss the aesthetic and moral reasons for such a preference
rather than merely epistemological reasons, as is usually done. First, let
us consider as proposals some principles which appear to follow
immediately from the problems discussed in the previous chapter.

1. *Other things being equal, when faced with the problem of choosing
between conceiving a universe in which the goal of life is experienced as
aesthetic (i.e., as intuiting life itself as having intrinsic good) and conceiving*

a universe in which no such goal is experienced, one ought always to choose the former.

2. *Other things being equal, when faced with the problem of choosing between conceiving a universe in which the goal of life involves enjoying a greater and one in which it involves enjoying a lesser amount (quantity, quality, intensity), of intrinsic good, one ought always to choose the former.*

3. *Other things being equal, when faced with the problem of choosing between conceiving a universe in which the goal of life requires less and one in which it requires more ethical endeavor, one ought always to choose the former.*

The foregoing principles seem to be intuitively obvious, and, if so, should continue to appear obvious when tested by practice. They seem obvious quite apart from dependence upon any particular type of metaphysical system, except of course one which does not exclude intrinsic value, its enjoyment, the existence of life, its goal, and moral endeavor. Before turning to implications of the foregoing for metaphysical aspects of religion as final ethics, let us examine some implications for epistemological aspects.

Epistemology is concerned with the nature of knowledge, truth and certainty and their opposites, ignorance, falsity, and doubt. Knowledge, truth and certainty are not, by definition, necessarily either intrinsic or instrumental goods. However, when one wants to know, wants to have true knowledge, wants to have certainty, then they do become instrumental goods and the experiences in which one enjoys believing that one has desired knowledge, desired truth, and desired certainty are experienced as intrinsic goods. Focusing attention upon truth, let us recall Aristotle's statement: "To say of what is that it is not, or of what is not that it is, is false, while to say of what is that it is and of what is not that it is not, is true." (The Works of Aristotle, Vol. VIII, Metaphysics, tr. by W.D. Ross, Second Edition, p. 1011b. See also, "The Generic Theory of Truth," The Personalist, Vol. XXXVIII, Autumn, 1947, pp. 370-375, and "The Organicist Theory of Truth," The Southwestern Journal of Philosophy, Vol. VI, Fall, 1975, pp. 197-201.) Except for pre-reflective and other unreflective experiences, the problem of truth is always present, implicitly if not explicitly, in experience. It is part of the nature of critical or reflective knowing to want to know the truth, or to have true rather than false knowledge. Once the problem of error has arisen, the appearance of error is experienced as evil, either, or both, as intrinsic evil and as instrumental evil. The annoyance felt while the appearance of error is present constitutes an experienced intrinsic evil. Hence, since, ethically, one seeks to avoid what is evil as well as to attain what is good, one owes it to oneself to try to eliminate such apparent error. Thus, in choosing among alternative views of the nature of the universe, part of what one most wants is a view which is true, or, if complete truth is regarded as impossible, then a view which seems truest.

4. *Other things being equal, when faced with the problem of choosing between two world views, (i.e., conceptions of the nature of life and the universe) one of which appears to be true and one of which appears to be false, one ought always to choose the former.*

5. *Other things being equal, when faced with the problem of choosing between two world views, one of which appears to be more true and one of which appears to be less true, one ought always to choose the former.*

The two foregoing principles have implications for methods of knowing, for if some ways of knowing are better than others in the sense that they are more likely to yield true, or truer, views, then, ethically, one ought to seek to use those methods.

6. *Other things being equal, when faced with the problem of choosing between employing a method which is more likely and a method which is less likely to result in a true view of life and the universe, one ought always to choose the former.*

This principle has implications for deciding upon particular methods, such as appeal to authority, tradition, public opinion, revelation, prejudice, wishful thinking, deductive, inductive, pragmatic, and scientific methods. We shall not explore these here. But surely it is clear that, if some ways of learning, knowing, and discovering the truth are better than others, then one ought, ethically, to be concerned about discovering and using the best way.

Interinvolved with the problem of truth is the problem of certainty or, as some prefer to think of it, the problem of eliminating doubt. "Doubt is an uneasy and dissatisfied state from which we struggle to free ourselves and to pass into the state of belief." (Charles S. Pierce, "The Fixation of Belief," Popular Science Monthly, Vol. 12, November, 1877, pp. 1-15.) Since the feeling of uncertainty is experienced as an evil, one ought to seek to remove it. That is, one ought to seek certainty as a part of one's quest for security. One who doubts thereby experiences at least one moral ought, namely, the feeling that one ought to remove one's doubt if possible. When such a doubt is removed and followed by a feeling of belief, such a feeling is experienced as aesthetic. When one has had doubts about the worthwhileness of one's life or about the prospects of achieving the goal of life and then arrives at a feeling of assurance that one's life is worthwhile or that one will achieve the goal, one experiences aesthetic enjoyment of a religious sort. Hence, feelings of assurance, of certainty, are preferable to feelings of doubt.

7. *Other things being equal, when faced with the problem of choosing between a conception of life and the universe of which one feels assured and one of which one feels unsure, one ought always to choose the former.*

Although the feeling of assurance is itself experienced as an aesthetic good, the presence of evidence of falsity or of dubiety constitutes a part of the "other things" which are not "equal." Hence, when it is true that the evidence for a belief is lacking or insufficient or that there is evidence against the belief, then one ought to doubt. When one continues to believe what one ought to doubt, one recognizes oneself as dishonest; and again suffers an unaesthetic experience. Hence, the assurance one seeks is not a false assurance but a genuine assurance. One may be able to feel assured to some extent only if one also maintains doubt to a certain extent, in the face of a given set of data.

Another principle has to do with adequacy. In trying to understand life and the universe, one seeks to understand fully, or as fully as possible, not merely some one part of a few parts, but the whole. That is, one can feel one is achieving final satisfaction only if one believes that one has achieved the most adequate view available to one. One's conception of adequacy itself is likely to include certain dimensions, such as length (of time), breadth (of inclusiveness, in space and complexity), and depth (of penetration). The more metaphysical issues that one becomes acquainted with, the more complicated, and perhaps more difficult to achieve, will one's notion of adequacy become. The more specialized branches of learning with which one becomes familiar, the more intricate will one's conception of his task become. For one who is aware of physics and astronomy, chemistry and biology, geology and economics, sociology and psychology, logic and philosophy of language, aesthetics and ethics, etc., will require some conception which incorporates all of them before one regards it as adequate. If this is so, then it seems natural to formulate a principle of adequacy as necessary for the kind of interpretation of experience felt needed by religion, or final ethics.

8. *Other things being equal, when faced with the problem of choosing between a more adequate and a less adequate conception of life and the universe, one ought always to choose the former.*

Regarding the goal of life, some picture it as beyond life rather than within life, some believe it to be forever unachievable and something only to be sought for, some view it as achievable only once rather than repeatable, and some think of it as temporally finite rather than everlasting. Is it possible to formulate, i.e., discover, principles for deciding between such alternatives? The following principles (9-16) are proposed tentatively for critical examination.

9. *Other things being equal, when faced with the problem of choosing between two world views, in one of which the goal of life is viewed as achievable and one in which it is not, one ought always to choose the former.* For if the goal is unachievable, then all moral endeavor to achieve such a goal is futile. If one proposes that one ought to be moral, even though the goal of life is unachievable, just so that one can stay alive, is one not implying that such staying alive is somehow inherently worthwhile and, hence, is the goal of life? If the issue of whether the goal of life can be achieved by all or by only some, then ought one not prefer the former? For example, if, when other things are equal, one is comparing a view in which some will achieve the goal of life, e.g., Heaven, and others will not achieve it, but will be condemned to Hell, as in orthodox Christianity, and a view in which all will achieve the goal of life, e.g., the Pure Land, as in Shin Buddhism, is not the latter better in the sense that more people will attain the goal? Although, from the viewpoint of one who knows one will reach the goal (e.g., a Calvinist who knows one is elect), the fate of those who will not may not interest one, if one also identifies oneself with the universe in such a way that one feels that his universe is better if more people achieve the goal than do not, one has an aesthetic reason for wanting all to reach the goal. Hence consider the following:

10. *Other things being equal, when faced with the problem of choosing between two world views, one in which all will achieve the goal and one in which only some will achieve the goal, one ought always to prefer the former.* This principle is an exemplification of a theory cited earlier, pertaining to the greatest good for the greatest number. Those who hold that one ought to seek the greatest good for the greatest number should, by implication, extend their idea of the greatest number to the greatest number of persons in the universe, if, perchance, they formulated it first relative to some particular group or groups. This raises a further problem relevant to the question of population explosion. If each person is or has intrinsic good and thus in some sense does achieve the goal in

life by enjoying whatever intrinsic good one is or has, then, other things being equal, would not a universe with more rather than fewer people be regarded as better? Hence, we propose the following principle:

11. *Other things being equal, when faced with the problem of choosing between two world views in which all achieve the goal of life, in one of which there are fewer persons and in one of which there are more persons, one ought always to choose the latter.* The reason why fears about population rightly cause some to advocate population restriction methods through birth control, for example, is that they believe that the food supply and other resources are limited and that unless some limitation is placed upon the size of the world's population, many of those who are born will suffer greatly, i.e., so that their lives will endure more intrinsic evil than enjoy intrinsic good. That is, limitations of resources constitute factors among the "other things" which are not equal.

12. *Other things being equal, when faced with the problem of choosing between two world views, in one of which the goal of life is viewed as enjoyed everlastingly and in one of which it is viewed as enjoyed for only a limited period of time, one ought always to choose the former.* This principle, if accepted, is not, in itself an argument for belief in everlasting life, for among the "other things" which are not equal there may be facts which imply that the belief is untrue. If so, then the principle previously stated regarding choosing a true rather than an untrue view may take precedence. On the other hand, where the evidence appears to be clearly ambiguous, then, as we shall see below in considering principles regarding obligations relative to wishful thinking, one may appear to be warranted in believing in an everlasting life, partly on the basis of this principle.

13. *Other things being equal, when faced with the problem of choosing between two world views in one of which the goal of life can be fully achieved only within life and in the other of which the goal of life can be fully achieved only beyond life, one ought always to choose the former.* For, given equality of achievement, and assuming that assurance of achievement is greater when it can be and is achieved within life than when it cannot be achieved within life, the assurance of such achievement as compared with doubt about achievement only in the future has preferable aesthetic qualities, which have already been mentioned as Principle 7, above. If the assurance were, somehow, exactly equal, then there would be no warrant for preference on this basis.

14. *Other things being equal, when faced with the problem of choosing between two world views both of which picture achievement of the goals for*

all persons but only while living on earth in a body, in one of which each person has only one life and in the other of which each person has more than one life, one ought always to choose the latter. For if one life in which the goal of life is actually achieved is good, two such lives are better, other things being equal. Furthermore:

15. *Other things being equal, when faced with the problem of choosing between two world views both of which picture achievement of the goal of life for all persons but only while living on earth in a body, in one of which each person has fewer such lives and in one of which each person has more such lives, one ought always to choose the latter.*

16. *Other things being equal, when faced with the problem of choosing between three world views, in one of which the goal of life is achieved, for all persons, only within life, in one of which the goal of life is achieved, for all persons, only beyond life, and in one of which the goal of life is achieved, for all persons, both within life and beyond life, one ought always to choose the latter.*

Turning next to the problem of wishful thinking, we face the issue of whether or not wishful thinking is ever justified relative to views about the nature of life and the universe. On the one hand, since thinking which is recognized as wishful involves an element of doubt which is unaesthetic, it should be avoided if possible. We have already stated, in Principles 4-8, that a true or truer, or more likely true, or more assured, or more adequate view is preferable to its opposite. On the other hand, as long as persons are not omniscient, room for doubt remains, and especially when we know that there is so much that we do not know, large areas of doubt are not only warranted but mandatory. Paradoxically, persons both want to remain "objective," that is, believe only what is warranted, which means remaining in doubt about what is not warranted, and want to enjoy the aesthetic experience of having all doubts removed, if possible. This latter want is sometimes called "faith." Now I do not propose here to resolve this paradox, regarding which it may be possible to formulate a principle, but only to explore possible principles relative to how far wishful thinking may be justified. For, although one may seek to be completely realistic in one's world view, one is likely to find areas in which realism is irrelevant or in which assurance about such realism remains unwarranted. To the extent that knowledge is impossible, the wildest wishing is possible. In this area, wishful thinking may be justified.

Insofar as wishful thinking is justified, one is still morally obligated in choosing regarding world views. That is, one ought always to choose what is best. This means that, where wishful thinking is justified, one ought always to wish for the best. We do not here suggest how one's conception of what is best will shape itself, or how many different such conceptions a person may have at different times. But, generally speaking, statement of a principle seems appropriate.

17. *Other things being equal, when wishful thinking is warranted, one ought always wish for the best. Or, other things being equal, when wishful thinking is justified and one is faced with the problem of choosing between two world views, in one of which what one wishes for is better than what one wishes for in the other, one ought always to choose the former.* This principle has implications for theology, for example. Without here considering areas in which theological speculations or conclusions are justified by realistic evidence, and limiting our consideration to those areas where wishful thinking is justified in theology, one ought to wish for a god, or gods, or a condition without gods, which appears to be better or, of course, the best. Now, if one can survey varieties of conceptions of the nature of god and find, relative to areas where wishful thinking is justified, that some conceptions of god are better than others, whether better for persons, or better for such a god, or better for both, then one is thereby obligated to prefer the better, or best, conception. The following statement is a redundant subvariety of the foregoing principle: Other things being equal, when wishful thinking is justified relative to various conceptions of the nature of god, or gods, or conditions without gods, one ought always to choose, i.e., to wish for, the best.

Although, surely, more principles can be stated regarding obligations for choosing among alternatives relative to world views, i.e., to religion and final ethics involving conceptions of the nature of life and the universe, enough have been stated to illustrate, in an introductory way, the kinds of obligations persons may have about the cosmic aspects of their experiences. Further such principles are implicit in the following treatment of levels of identification of self with other aspects of the universe.

Cosmic Levels and Religious Obligations. Although we have deliberately refrained from elaborating a specific metaphysical system here, and have aimed at pointing out its implications of ethics, as we understand it, for any metaphysical scheme, certain minimal presuppositions have been made. We are assuming that selves exist, that some knowledge of self, the universe, including other selves, is possible, that persons and the universe persist at least for some time, and that there appears to be levels of complexity in the organization of what exists. In Chapter II, "Self as Physical,' we proposed acceptance of the conclusions of contemporary sciences regarding the nature of existence as including subatomic particles, atoms, molecules, the earth, the solar system, galaxies, the Milky Way, and of cells, organs, bodies, persons, and groups as exemplifying different kinds or levels of existence. No final picture of the nature of self or the universe is needed in order to draw some conclusions about interrelations between a self and such levels as it does know. Doubtless the sciences, including metaphysics, will have a long history of development ahead of them, and it would be foolish to state conclusions about ethics which would in any way preclude such development. But it is possible to outline certain principles regarding ethical aspects of conceptions of the relations of each self to such levels as are known and, even, to others yet unknown insofar as they will, when known, be like those now known.

We have seen, in Chapters III and IV, how a person may vary in the extent to which one feels identified with one's body or parts of it, with one's mother, with one's family, with one's possessions, with one's community, etc. Part of the problem of evil, with which it is the business of ethics and religion to deal, has to do with fear of whatever is inimical to self. The more narrowly a person conceives oneself, the more there appears to be outside of one to endanger one. The more broadly one conceives oneself, the less there appears to be outside of one to cause one to fear. To the extent that this is so, and to the extent that a person owes oneself the duty of reducing unnecessary fear, one ought to conceive oneself more widely. That is, if, by conceiving oneself more widely, one thereby reduces fear, and thus evil, that is a part of what one ought to do, other things being equal. For example, when a person conceives oneself as a member of a race, or of a nation, rather than of mankind, one may have reason to fear people of all other races of all other nations. But if one considers oneself a member of mankind, then people of all races and all nations are also members of the group with which one feels identified. Not all of the aspects of the problem of evil are thereby solved, but some of them may be, namely those resulting from fear of members of outgroups. To the extent that expansion of conception of self to include other person, groups, living beings or the non-living universe, helps to free oneself from needless fear, one owes it to oneself to do so. To the extent that such an obligation has a bearing upon one's conception of the nature of self and of the universe, one ought to conceive oneself as widely as one can. If there are several levels of complexity with which one is acquainted, then a person may have a duty to consider, at least, with how many of them it is in one's interest to feel identified. One will, of course, be conditioned by what one believes to be the truth about the nature of oneself, the universe and levels. And one may need to fluctuate in one's conceptions, and feeling of identification, at different times. Some mothers, for example, are, of necessity, so completely occupied with family matters that they have little time or inclination to enjoy their membership in the human race. Since this is so, some persons deliberately set certain times for giving attention to their various obligations. Many religious sects establish specific days, such as Sunday for Christians, as desirable time for devoting attention to cosmic interests. Some add other days, or certain times of every day; Moslems, for example, pray five times each day. Meditative prayer includes awareness of identification of self with larger aspects of the universe; with yogins, for example, its aim is to eliminate the "veils of ignorance" which prevent one from awareness of complete identity with ultimate reality. When prayer is conceived in this way, it appears that a person has an obligation to pray, i.e., to become aware of one's larger goods. Such prayer need not be spoken and does not ask for anything; it is prayer of fuller self-realization. One who fails to achieve the fullest may, of course, express a wish for such achievement as a way of partial recognition of its possible existence and good. Persons who attach the word "prayer" to formalistic rituals, superstitious sacrifices, or petty begging, will want to use some other word. What is at stake is a person's final satisfaction, the goal of one's life conceived in terms of expansion to its cosmic fullness, or enjoyment of the whole of life by including in it as much as one can of the whole of his universe.

Although the foregoing discussion has, in effect, urged experimenting with conceiving one's self more broadly so that one has less to fear, it is also quite possible to experiment in conceiving one's self more narrowly for the same purpose Whereas Advaita Vedanta illustrates the foregoing experiment carried to a logical extreme, one may also study the Sankhya-Yoga scheme in which the genuine self is conceived as a pure awareness which has become entangled in the world. Yogic practices are then designed to eliminate such entanglement. When successful, a self destroys all self-awareness as well as awareness of anything else in the universe in order to enjoy kaivalya, perfectly isolated bliss. Organicism favors continuing experimentation with many different such views proposed by others until one finds a view which seems most suited to one's own preferences. But awareness of opportunities for such experimentation is recommended. Some will prefer not to venture far from their inherited views, and other will refuse to cease venturing. Both such types of persons may be seeking and achieving cosmic satisfaction, each in a different way.

The foregoing issue of whether to seek the goal of life through conceiving one's self, and one's self-interest, more inclusively or more exclusively may be illustrated relative to three topics; national governments versus world government, racial segregation versus intermarriage, sectarian religions versus world religion. Those who would conceive themselves more inclusively consequently ought to favor the emergence of world government, racial intermarriage, and world religion, assuming that the methods for bringing these about would be peaceful rather than destructive. However, those who, for whatever reason, are so afraid of extra entanglements that they idealize isolation and exclusiveness in attempting to allay their fears will tend toward opposing extremes. The issues become not one of national versus world government but of government versus no government, as with anarchists, not one of intermarriage versus racial segregation but of association versus disassociation, as with Lao Tzu's "Shun Society," and not one of organized religions versus a world religion but one of religious organizations versus private opinion and practice, as with solipsists or with A.N. Whitehead when he says: "Religion is what one does in his own solitariness."

Organicism sees human nature as multi-aspected, wanting both government and freedom from government, both association and self-sufficiency, both religious fellowship and aloofness. However, just as people are partly ambidextrous and partly right-handed or left-handed, so they tend in one of the above directions more than the other, in shaping their personalities and in depicting their life ideals. Those tending toward greater inclusiveness and believing that the ultimate goods of their lives can be achieved in terms of some expansive cosmic scheme will find their primary religious obligation simplified therein. Those disposed to withdrawal and seclusion generate religious ideals which obligate them to retirement, even if not estrangement. But just as a right-handed person wishes one were more ambidextrous, so there are times when those who prefer either a more expansive personality or a more purely private soul may wish to enjoy endoubled richness though pursuing both directions, sometimes successively but also, when possible, both at the same time. That is, one may find privacy in a church, individuality in marriage, and indifference to government even in legislative halls. In megalopolis, one has need of both kinds of ideals, for when one must associate, the need for expanding one's feeling of identity with many levels and kinds of groups, variably, becomes increasingly something presented to one as a part of the status of things in which one's goal of life is to be realized. But a person retains integrity also by realizing that there is something more to one than one's many facets, and that one owes oneself the duty of enjoying that something more which cannot be dissected into multiplicities of parts. Some people feel very lonely even in crowds. Some people feel very much a part of a swarming city, an expansive cosmos, an a developing civilization, while alone. Although people can live happily without being ambidextrous and without having both social and solitary tendencies, persons who do have both seem to live a fuller life, so to speak, than those who do not. Hence, in designing a goal for living, one may wish to adopt "bothism." If so, then the ideals inherent therein will imply obligations to seek both. Then, one will feel that one's religion requires one to be both broader and narrower, and often both at the same time in different ways.

Speaking in a theological language, we may say that one will then sometimes feel identified with God, sometimes opposed to God, and sometimes to feel alone as a god. Anyone who holds any of these views exclusively is likely to encounter typical troubles. But one who fails to enjoy all of these is somewhat lacking in religious dexterity. For those whose experiences with theistic religion have been unhappy, a non-theological language may be preferred. A nature-lover may then feel at one with Nature, yet at times feel opposed to Nature, and even regard oneself as a unique epitome of Nature. And, since both theism and atheism are cosmic options, a person whose outlook has remained exclusively either one or the other may also be regarded as less dexterous religiously than one who has understood, or concurrently does understand, how to appreciate the virtues of both.

Religion and Ethics. Religious beliefs about the goal of life, including conceptions about the aesthetic nature of that goal and about the cosmic setting which makes its achievement possible, generate the oughts which constitute final ethics. The two aspectival ingredients of such beliefs, aesthetic completeness and cosmic completeness, supplement each other, for one can feel one's achievement as aesthetically complete in terms of some conception of the cosmos only if one also feels that such a conception is itself as complete as it can be. To the extent that it cannot be as complete as one might wish, for one does not expect one's wish for omniscience to be fulfilled, Gotama's advice needs heeding: Avoid desiring to know more than you can know, not merely about daily affairs but about the nature of self and the universe. To desire more than one can know about the cosmos is to be frustrated, or to suffer unaesthetic experience and to fail to enjoy the goal of life. Hence, final ethics includes also an attitude of willingness to accept not only the universe as it is, but also one's ignorance for what it is; thereby one may transform aesthetic evil due to feeling that one's conception is inadequate into aesthetic good by assenting to the knowledge one has as completely all that is in store for one. Final ethics entails religious yea-saying to the goal. When life incudes ineradicable evil, one ought to say yes to it also, not as evil, but as ineradicable The spirit of final ethics may be summed up in a theistic prayer: "God grant me the serenity to accept the things I cannot change; the courage to change the things I can; and the wisdom to know the difference."

Summary of More Principles for Choosing. Other things being equal; when choosing between world views:

1. Choose one depicting experiencing the goal of life as aesthetic (i.e., as intuiting life as intrinsic good) in preference to one which does not.
2. Choose one depicting the goal as enjoying more in preference to less intrinsic value.
3. Choose one requiring less moral endeavor to reach the goal in preference to one requiring more.
4. Choose one which appears to be true in preference to one which appears to be false.
5. Choose one which appears to be more true in preference to one which appears to less true.
6. When choosing between methods for ascertaining a world view, choose one which appears more likely to result in a true view in preference to one which appears less likely to so result.
7. Choose one about which one feels assured in preference to one about which one does not.
8. Choose one which appears more adequate in preference to one which appears less adequate.
9. Choose one in which the goal of life appears achievable to one in which it does not.
10. Choose one in which all will achieve the goal in preference to one in which only some will do so.
11. When all will achieve the goal, then choose one in which there are more persons in preference to one in which there are fewer persons.

12. Choose one in which enjoyment of the goal is everlasting to one in which it is not.

13. Choose one in which the goal can be fully achieved only within life in preference to one in which it can be fully achieved only beyond life.

14. When all will achieve the goal only while living in a body on earth, choose one in which each person will have more such lives in preference to one in which each will have only one life.

15. When all will achieve the goal only while living in a body on earth, choose one in which each person will have more such lives in preference to one in which each will have fewer lives.

16. When all will achieve the goal, choose one in which the goal is achieved twice, once within life and once beyond life, in preference to one in which it is achieved only once.

17. When wishful thinking is warranted, choose one in which what one wishes for is better in preference to one in which what one wishes for is not better.

Chapter XXXV

SATISFACTION AS ORGANIC

This final chapter, summing up both Part III and the whole volume, first shows both how various aspects of aesthetic and cosmic satisfaction interdepend in final ethics and how various aspects of individual and social ethics interdepend with final ethics. Then it summarizes even more succinctly by presenting, so far as this volume is concerned, a final definition of ethics.

Satisfaction As Organic. Not only do the aesthetic and cosmic aspects of religious experience supplement each other in a general way, as was pointed out in concluding the previous chapter, but the polarities within each interdepend in great detail. We omit these details but review examples of ways in which they interdepend.

Consider first the aesthetic aspect. In discussing the aesthetic, as intuition of intrinsic value, we noted interdependence of intrinsic and instrumental values, and of the aesthetic as experiencing completeness and of the moral as experiencing incompleteness or a need for something more, and of ethics and religion. Here we should note additionally that such a discussion presupposed interdependence of ways in which a self is or has value (See Chapter VI), and in which a group may be regarded as being or having value (See Chapter XXI) with ways in which the cosmos, including selves and groups, may be or have value (See Chapter XXXIV). Belief that the goal of life to be found and experienced, whether narrowly or expansively, in the universe depends upon there being a self which is or has intrinsic goods which participate in and thus contribute to those intrinsic goods in terms of which the goal of life as a whole is experienced. All such intrinsic values, including those attributed to one's groups, may so participate. So long as one feels that one has not reached life's goal, one's various aesthetic experiences are infected with morality in a way which connotes a lack of fullness which can be achieved only in those experiences we have called "religious," i.e., in which one's life as a whole, including its interrelations with the rest of the universe as a whole, is enjoyed aesthetically. Thus each particular experience of intrinsic good in ordinary life tends to retain yearning for something more which only an experience intuiting the intrinsic good of life as a whole can terminate fully or finally.

In contrasting the aesthetic and the moral aspects of experience, we might have reviewed multiplicities of ethical polarities, some of which were discussed in Parts I and II. For example, self-improvement vs.

unimprovability (Chapter VII), self as agent or as patient, self as free or unfree, self as controlled by self or by others, self as owner and as owned, self as just or gracious, self as conscientious or without conscience, and self as intelligent or unintelligent. All illustrate moral polarities, as do social improvements, social unimprovability, etc.

Questions about the principle of reciprocity and its workability between individuals (Chapter V) and between groups (Chapter XX) may be extended to relations between a self and his universe. Awareness of polar relationships between self and the universe may take many forms. For example, some seem to believe: "the world owes me a living." Others feel they should earn their way or even leave the world a better place to live in when they die than it was when they were born. To the extent that one feels one has rights just because one has been born in a universe, one also tends to feel that, to the extent that the principle of reciprocity works, one has duties to the universe also. This tendency begets questions, ideas and often ideals about the universe itself being moral. Some who personify the universe as God interpret religious sacrifice as an act of reciprocating gifts, including the gift of life itself, or if wanting more, then of giving to God so that God will reciprocate beneficially. For such persons, additional questions about the moral nature of the universe, or of God, become significant; and they face the same set of questions, or polarities, all over again in another dimension: Is God improvable or unimprovable (perfect)? Is God agent or patient? Is God free or unfree? Is God sovereign or controlled by others? Is God owned or owner? Is God just or gracious? Is God conscientious or without conscience? Is God intelligent or unintelligent? Those who do not personify the cosmos may still face similar questions about the impersonal universe. All these are examples of moral polarities which were involved, even if not explained, in our assertion that the aesthetic and the moral interdepend.

Consider next cosmic aspects. We explored space-wise levels of expansion and contraction of self-conceptions, e.g., whether life is merely temporal or everlasting, existing in only one body or reincarnated in many. In order to be consistent, we should have explored interests in conceiving self as temporally contracted; some people believe they exist only at the present moment, not over a lifetime, thus withdrawing themselves time-wise even as some withdraw themselves spacewise to being only within their body or in some part of it. There is some aesthetic and religious merit in the view that a self may complete itself in a moment. One who has no care for the morrow, not even caring whether the care-not-for-the-morrow philosophy is true, experiences the goal of life as completely attained in that moment. With Omar Khayyam, one "Takes the cash and lets the credit go." Time-wise and space-wise conceptions of self have bearing upon the extents to which, and way in which, a self experiences both aspects of the moral-amoral polarity. One may, contractedly, enjoy an amoral moment aesthetically and thereby feel the fullness of life. One may, expansively, identify oneself with the universe, as in Advaita Vedanta and enjoy oneself as identical with cosmic amorality. On the other hand, not only is a purely aesthetic interpretation of life, whether contractedly or expandedly, inadequate because unrealistic, but there is a fundamental sense in which a life, and universe, conceived as both moral and aesthetic, are richer when these are conceived as merely either one or the other alone. The Organicist view is that a life which conceives itself and the universe and the interdependencies between them in terms of multidimensions of polarities is richer than one which does not. Then religious endeavor entails multidimensional moral efforts; but the fullness of life is conceived as including multiplicities, even multidimensions, of goods which organically interdepend in such a way that final satisfaction involves both moral and amoral aspects of the ways in which all other dimensions are experienced both as moral and amoral.

We cannot review here all of the metaphysical polarities that seem to be involved in the nature of existence. (See my Metaphysics: an Introduction, 1974, and my The Philosopher's World Model, Chapter 4, 1979.) But they too, according to the Organicist view, interdepend in constituting those cosmic aspects of experience which interdepend with the aesthetic aspects of experience to complete experience as religious. Organic enjoyment, religiously experienced, may involve not merely feelings of pleasantness, enthusiasm, satisfaction and contentment intermingled or fused but also enjoyment of experiencing interdependent mingling and fusion of multidimensions of polarities, both morally and amorally, through such feelings. Paradox, which we have not emphasized in this volume, pervades experience in subtle as well as in obvious ways, and to the extent that paradox, or multi-paradox, persists as something that cannot be eradicated from a final view of life in the universe, one's religious experience will remain too much moral and insufficiently aesthetic if one fails to say "Yes" to such paradox.

Final Definition of Ethics. This volume opened with a "beginning definition" of ethics: "Ethics is concerned with what is good and how to get it" or what one ought to do in order to obtain it. In Chapter I, this definition was elaborated to include conditional and categorical oughts, principles and codes, theory and practice, and individual and social aspects of goodness and oughtness. The nature of ethics was explored further through the remaining thirty-three chapters of the volume, indicating the roles of intention, free will, self-control, ownership, justice, conscience and intelligence, for example, in the ethical nature of a self, of a group, and of the universe. Our conclusion that ethics, in being concerned also with what is good in life as a whole, becomes identical with religions having both aesthetic and cosmic aspects, leaves open many questions about the nature of such whole. Let us mention only two of the kinds of problems involved in framing a final definition, one pertaining to ethical theory and one to ethical practice.

In any proposed final definition of ethical theory, we must not only try to be inclusive in the sense of incorporating individual, social and cosmic ethics, but also in the sense that there has been an historical development of ethical theories, in both Asian and Western civilizations, which has not yet come to its end. Our final definition of ethical theory surely must intend to be saying that there is more to ethical theory, past, present and future, than one does fully understand. So, unless mankind should terminate immediately in some cosmic catastrophe, our final definition of ethical theory should include provision for an open future.

In my proposed final definition of ethical practice, likewise, we must leave the future open for new kinds of ethical problems as well as newer mores and codes of ethical behavior. Ethics, as practice, includes the problems and responses of infants and children, the uncertainties and convictions of youth, of the perplexities of sexual attractions, newly married couples, and parents, and the adjustment problems of maturity, old age, and facing death, as well as those involved in employer-employee, government-citizen, teacher-pupil, and interracial and intercultural situations. Just as the types of ethical problems shift somewhat with stages in the life of each individual, and in the cultural, political and economic development of political groups, so an adequate conception of the nature of ethical practice must include not only these but recognize the probability that new problems and forms of practice will emerge as the average life-span of the population becomes longer and the structure and complexity of world-society becomes larger.

What, then, is ethics? It is every person's wondering about all the ways of enjoying and of attaining goods and avoiding evils. It consist in all of the ways that people use when they feel they ought to seek good and avoid evil. It consists in the advice one gives oneself and others, and which others give to one, either personally or through established mores and laws, and one's response in accepting or rejecting such advice. Rebellion and revolution are ethical just as attempts to maintain law and order are ethical. Cultural lag and cultural revision and creation are ethical. Ethics is life-wide and life-long, in the life of each individual and in the life of the human race. The ethical consists, as we have so often said, in what one most wants to do when one really understands one's own nature and its needs. Our final definition consists in saying that ethics consists in all of what one really most wants to do. The contribution of the present volume has been to aid in achievement of a broad as well as complicated conception of what is good, i.e., individual, social and cosmic, and of an open mind regarding how any variables may have to be taken into consideration before deciding, in any particular situation, what is right.

INDEX

Ability, 159-160, 165-168
Absence of restraint, 159-160, 172
Absolutism, 114-116, 236
Action, 328-336
Actual value, 59-61, 89, 129-131
Advaita Vedanta, 93, 169, 399, 418, 425
Adventure, 43-47, 55
Aesthetic experience, 339-404
Agency, 136-157, 171-173, 328-336
Ahimsa, 23
Ananda, 76, 439
Anandism, 76-78, 80-85, 105, 113
Anandistic paradox, 88
Angell, R.C., 375, 376
Anxiety, 77, 80, 81, 82
Apathy, 76, 82
Aquinas, Thomas, 69, 393
Aristotle, 69, 111, 169, 410
Augustine, 69, 111, 169
Authority, 156-157

Bad, 54-90, 91,, 99-100
Becquer, 75
Bentham, Jeremy, 64, 65, 96, 125
Bergson, Henri, 69, 75
Bernard, L.L., 30
Blake, 78
Boodin,John E., 245
Buddha, 70, 162, 399, 402
Burnham, James, 349

Calculus of pleasures, 64
Calvin, John, 111, 169, 413
Carr, L.J., 375, 376
Cassirer, Ernst, 33

Causal dependence, 123
Change, 91-94, 98-99, 235
Chateaubriand, 75
Chin, R., 380
Chinoy, Ely, 245
Choice, 9, 162
Christian, 339, 401-402, 413, 418
Chuang Tzu, 77
Codes, 4-5, 124-135
Companionship, 40-43, 35
Conditional oughts, 3-4, 130-132, 386
Conflicts of interests, 101-102, 266, 269-271
Confucius, 77, 282, 404
Conscience, 9, 25, 272-273, 396
Contentment, 76-78, 80-81, 82, 85, 86, 121
Conwell, Russell H., 401
Cooley, Charles H., 257, 375, 376
Creativity, 229
Crime, 383
Cultural lag, 374-379, 427
Cultural relativism, 115
Cultural riches, 27, 32-35
Culture, 32-35
Cycle of institutional development, 376-378

Dahl, Robert A., 353
Descartes, 169
Desire, 67-71, 82, 83-86, 167-168
Desire for adventure, 43-47, 55
Desire for companionship, 40-43, 55
Desire for esteem, 36-38, 55
Desire for love, 40-43, 55

Desire for recognition, 36-39, 55
Desire for security, 47-53, 55, 273, 275-281
Desirousness, 71-76, 78-86
Democracy, 347-350
Democracy of levels, 352-354
Determinism, 163-165, 176-179
Dewey, John, 69, 227, 374
Discontentment, 76-77
Distributive justice, 203-206
Drake, Durant, 11
Drucker, Peter F., 156, 334, 353
Duties, 9, 102, 200-203, 239, 251, 255, 363-371

Economics, 356-358
Education, 302
Eells, Richard, 359
Emergentism, 177-1183
Emerson, Ralph Waldo, 73, 91
Empathy, 86
Ends, 40, 56-59, 62-89, 91-100
Engelbrecht, H.C., 277
Enjoyment, 78-86, 122, 142-157
Enthusiasm, 71-76, 78-86, 104-105, 121
Epistemology, 410
Equality, 363
Esteem, 36-38, 275-281
Ethics, 3-13, 17-20, 425-427
Evil, 250, 255
Existentialism, 76

Farris, Ellsworth. 36
Fichte, 75
Final aesthetics, 396-407
Final ethics, 393-395, 425-427
Fitness, 165-168

Freedom, 159, 161-176, 185, 237, 250, 337-342
Freedom-determinism controversy, 165, 176-179
Freud, Sigmund, 69, 73, 217
Frustration, 67-71, 74-75

Gardner, John W., 369
George, Henry, 374
Girvetz, H.K., 359
Goethe, 75
Good, 54-90, 91, 94-100, 235
Gotama, The Buddha, 70, 77, 162, 399, 402, 420
Government, 343-354
Grace, 214-215, 239, 251, 367-371
Group conscience, 251-252
Group dependence, 256
Group duties, 251, 255, 261-262, 363-367
Group esteem, 273, 275-381
Group intelligence, 252, 374-381
Group interdependence, 260-268
Group interests, 260-261, 269-274
Group improvement, 250, 295-302
Group justice, 260, 363-371
Group loyalty, 257
Group morale, 257, 297, 301
Group obligations, 250, 255, 259, 303-327
Group organic unity, 307
Group oughts, 259, 262, 272-273
Group reciprocity, 262, 266, 274-281

Group rights, 251, 254
Group security, 273, 275-281
Group self-interest, 260-261,
    269-274, 281-282
Groups, 245-390
Groups as agents, 250
Groups as causes, 256
Groups as evil, 250, 255
Groups as free, 250
Groups as just, 251, 266
Groups as owners, 251, 256
Groups as selfish, 248-249
Groups as sovereign, 251
Groups as substantial, 256, 258,
    259, 260, 286, 298
Groups as values, 249-250, 254,
    285-294

Habits, 132
Hanighen, F.C., 277
Happiness, 290-291, 393
Hare, E.M., 403
Hawley, Amos H., 261
Hedonism, 62-67, 81, 82, 87,
    104, 113
Hedonistic paradox, 63, 73, 88
Heine, 75
Heisenberg, 164
Herder, 75
Hierarchy, 262, 265-268, 269,
    366-367, 399
Higher-level groups, 262, 263,
    265-268, 269, 308, 366-367,
    399
Hindu ideals, 399, 402-403
Hobbes, 66, 75
Hocking, W.E., 365
Holderlein, 75
Hugo, Victor, 75

Ideals, 7-8, 27-32, 291-294
Identity, indentification, 23-26,
    28-37, 286, 300, 386
Indeterminism, 163-165, 174
Individual sovereignty, 187-188
Institutions, 376-378
Instrumental value, 40, 56-88,
    89, 102, 117-119, 123-129,
    134-135, 142-143, 148, 210,
    238, 254-255, 288-290, 316-
    321, 325-326, 356-357, 385,
    423
Integrity of groups, 243
Intelligence, 100, 223, 225-231,
    252, 274-381, 393, 397
Intention, 136, 144-151, 183-
    185, 237, 330-331
Interdependence, 10, 19, 91,
    98-99, 109, 137, 142
Interests, 246-247, 269-274
Intrinsic value, 40, 56-85, 89,
    98-100, 102-109, 117-123,
    126-129, 134-135, 142-143,
    148, 153, 155, 157, 194, 225-
    227, 254-255, 285-293, 303,
    308-316, 356-357, 385, 423
Intrinsic value of a group, 309-
    316, 325-327, 385

Jain, 69, 93,162, 400
James, William, 67, 277
Jesus, 69, 235, 401
Justice, 194, 196-215, 251, 363-
    371

Kaivalya, 399
Keats, 76
Kerr, Clark, 272
Khayyam, Omar, 425
Kinds of government, 343-347

Krishna, 402
Kunkel, Fritz, 235, 258

Lao Tzu, 77, 112, 170, 403, 419
Laws, 383-384
Leibniz, 169
Lerner, Max, 349
Lessing, 76
Levels of democracy, 350-352
Liberty, 341-342
Lippit, Robert, 380
Loeb, Jacques, 111
Love, 40-43, 55
Loyalty, 257

MacIver, R.M., 263, 276
Madhyamika, 107, 399
Marx, Karl, 344, 360
McClosky, H.J., 245, 285
McDougal, William, 245
Mead, George Herbert, 30-32,
    33, 34, 137, 233, 329
Means, 56-62, 89, 101
Mill, John Stuart, 65, 256
Miller, Delbert C., 353
Moral, 11-13
Moral experience, 396-398
Moral ideals, 291-294
Morgn, C. Lloyd, 177, 178
Moslems, 418

Napoleon, 75
Nietzsche, 73, 75
Nirguna Brahman, 399
Novalis, 75

Objectification of values, 86-88
Obligation, 100-110, 250, 255,
    293-294, 303-327
Opportunity, 159-160, 165-169

Organic, 19, 78, 137
Organic agency, 142, 143
Organic enjoyment, 78-86, 95,
    105-110, 117-118, 122
Organic freedom, 173-176
Organic interdependence, 287-
    288
Organic interaction, 138
Organic suffering, 107-108
Organic unity, 96, 306-308
Organicism, 78-86, 105-108,
    113-114, 116-117, 122, 123,
    171, 173-179, 360, 362, 394,
    404, 409, 410, 418-419, 425
Organicistic paradox, 88
Oughts, oughtness, 3-5, 55-56,
    101-108, 116,-135, 259, 304
Ownership, 189-195, 251, 355-
    362

Pain, 62-67, 81-85
Parker, DeWitt H., 70, 218, 292
Patiency, 136, 137, 138
Peer groups, 262-265, 307
Peirce, Charles S., 411
Pepper, Stephen C., 285
Permanence, 91-93
Perry, Ralph Barton, 69
Personality, 30-32, 267, 382-383
Persons, 245-247
Planning, 376. 379-381
Plato, 169, 399
Pleasant feeling, 62-67, 78-83,
    85, 119-120
Political liberty, 341-342
Potential value, 58-62, 89, 129-
    131, 236
Practice, 5-8
Pragmatic method, 138, 227-
    228

Primary groups, 40, 273, 288-
    289, 292
Principle of reciprocity, 37-39,
    42-43, 46-47, 50-52, 214-215,
    234, 267, 274-281, 424
Principles, 4-5
Principles for choosing, 116-
    131, 134-135, 308-327, 409-
    416, 421-422
Private ownership, 360-362
Prudence, 226-227
Public ownership, 360-362

Quality of goods, 291, 300
Quantity of goods, 289-291

Raja Yoga, 105, 162
Rationalists, 111, 170
Reagency, 136
Reciprocity, 36-39, 41-43, 44-
    47, 48-52, 262, 266, 274-281,
    470-471
Recognition, 36-40
Relativism, 114-116, 236
Religion, 12, 230, 397-427
Religious experience, 398-407,
    423-425
Responsibility, 136, 137, 151-
    157, 185, 237-238, 331-336
Restraint, 161-163, 173
Retributive justice, 203-204,
    206-215

Rightness, 17
Rights, 9, 194, 196-203, 239,
    255, 363-371
Roberts, W.H., 41
Romanticism, 74-76, 78-86, 104,
    113, 142, 169
Romanticistic paradox, 73, 88

Ross, W.D., 69, 410
Rothschild, Richard, 167, 203
Rouseau, 75

Samkhya Yoga, 93, 107, 400,
    418
Sanayana, George, 86
Satisfaction, 17, 67-71, 77-78,
    78-86, 95-98, 107, 120, 394,
    396-427
Satisfaction as aesthetic, 396-
    407, 423-424
Satisfaction as cosmic, 408-422,
    424
Satisfaction as organic, 423-427
Schelling, 75
Schlegel, 75
Schleiermacher, 75
Schneider, Herbert W., 372
Schutz, Alfred, 258
Shelly, 76
Science(s), 3, 21-22, 24-26, 113
Secondary groups, 289
Security, 47-53, 273, 275-281
Self, 11, 15-242, 423-426
Self, sources of, 27-32
Self as agent, 136-157, 222, 232,
    237
Self as conscientious, 216-223,
    239-240
Self as cultural, 141
Self as free, 158-185, 337-339
Self as instrumental value, 59-
    62
Self as integral, 242
Self as intelligent, 225-236, 240
Self as intender, 150-152
Self as interdependent, 241
Self as intrinsic value, 62-86,
    95-100, 235, 285-288

Self as just, 196-215, 222, 239
Self as moral, 242
Self as organic, 232-242
Self as owner, 189-195. 238
Self as physical, 21-26, 140, 233
Self as social, 28-35, 108-109,
     140-141, 233-234
Self as sovereign, 186-188, 222-
     223, 288
Self as unknowable, 232
Self as value, 55-86, 95-100, 235
Self-conception, 29-35
Self-degeneration, 91, 98-99
Self-determinism, 165, 171, 174
Self-ideals, 28-32
Self-improvement, 91-100, 235-
     236
Self-interest, 36-53, 234-235,
     242, 269
Selfishness, 248-249
Self-obligation, 110-135
Self-permanence, 91
Self-realization, 17
Shin Buddhism,, 399, 413
Social action, 328-336, 386
Social agency, 328-336
Social conscience, 251, 372-373,
     389
Social ethics, 245 -253
Social freedom, 337-342, 386
Social improvement, 295-302,
     386
Social intelligence, 252, 374-
     381, 389
Social intentions, 330-331
Social justice, 251, 363-371, 389
Social obligation, 108-110, 303-
     327, 386
Social ownership, 355-362, 288
Social planning, 376, 379-381

Social policy, 269-284, 289-291
Social responsibility, 331-336
Social sovereignty, 251, 343-
     354, 386
Social values, 240-250, 285-294
Society as organic, 242, 283-390
Sorenson, Theodore C.,282
Svereignty, 186-188, 238, 251,
     343-354
Specialists, 335-336, 349-350,
     379-381, 390
Sperling, Godfrey, 372
Spinoza, 111, 169
Standards, 394
Steveneson, Robert Louis, 71
Submission, 168-171, 175
Success, 394-395

Taylor, A,E, 91
Temmer, Mark, 75
Theories of freedom, 161-176
Theravada Buddhism, 93, 399
Thomas, William I., 36, 243
Titus, H.H., 177

United Nations, 278, 346, 351,
     352, 346
Unpleasant feeling, 64-67
Utilitarianism, 66
Utilities, 356
Utopia, 300

Values, 54-90, 285-294
Value ideas, 249
Value judgements, 89-90
Voluntarism, 71-76, 81, 82, 88,
     104, 113, 120
Voluntaristic paradox, 82

Watson, Jeanne, 380

Wealth, 355-358
Westley, Bruce, 380
Whitehead, A.N., 419
Wisdom, 226
Wissler, Clark, 112
Woodring, Harry, 276

Yoga, 69, 402-403, 418

Zen, 77, 105, 121, 282, 339, 404
Zhanieki, Florian, 36